WHEN EARTH'S MIGHTIEST HEROES JOINED FORCES TO TAKE ON THE THREATS THAT NO ONE HERO COULD TACKLE ALONE, THEY BECAME...**THE AVENGERS.** TOGETHER, THEY PROTECT THE WORLD FROM THOSE WHO WOULD DO IT HARM. AMONG THOSE THEY HAVE FACED IS **ULTRON,** AN ARTIFICIAL INTELLIGENCE WITH SEEMINGLY LIMITLESS POWER CREATED BY THE GENIUS AVENGER HANK PYM. ULTRON'S INTELLIGENCE, BASED ON THE BRAIN PATTERNS OF HIS CREATOR, HAS MADE HIM ONE OF THE AVENGERS' MOST FORMIDABLE FOES, AND ONE WHO HAS CONTINUED TO THREATEN THEM AGAIN AND AGAIN THROUGHOUT HISTORY...

writer
AL EWING
penciler
ALAN DAVIS
inker
MARK FARMER
colorist
RACHELLE ROSENBERG
letterer
VC'S TRAVIS LANHAM

THE AVENGERS
ULTRON FOREVER

cover artists
**ALAN DAVIS, MARK FARMER
& RACHELLE ROSENBERG**

assistant editors
JON MOISAN & ALANNA SMITH

editors
TOM BREVOORT with **WIL MOSS**

AVENGERS created by **STAN LEE & JACK KIRBY**

collection editor JENNIFER GRÜNWALD
assistant editor SARAH BRUNSTAD
associate managing editor ALEX STARBUCK
editor, special projects MARK D. BEAZLEY
senior editor, special projects JEFF YOUNGQUIST
svp print, sales & marketing DAVID GABRIEL
book designer ADAM DEL RE

editor in chief AXEL ALONSO
chief creative officer JOE QUESADA
publisher DAN BUCKLEY
executive producer ALAN FINE

AVENGERS: ULTRON FOREVER. Contains material originally published in magazine form as AVENGERS: ULTRON FOREVER, HULK #6, IRON MAN #188 and THOR #378. First printing 2015. ISBN# 978-0-7851-9769-0. Published by MARVEL WORLD Street, New York, NY 10020. Copyright © 2015 MARVEL. No similarity between any of the names, characters, persons, and any such similarity which may exist is purely coincidental. **Printed in the U.S.A.** ALAN FINE, President, Marvel Entertainment; Officer; TOM BREVOORT, SVP of Publishing; DAVID BOGART, SVP of Operations & Procurement, Publishing; C.B. CEBULSKI, V JIM O'KEEFE, VP of Operations & Logistics; DAN CARR, Executive Director of Publishing Technology; SUSAN CRESPI, Edi Emeritus. For information regarding advertising in Marvel Comics or on Marvel.com, please contact Jonathan Rheingold, VP call 800-217-9158. **Manufactured between 9/4/2015 and 10/12/2015 by R.R. DONNELLEY, INC., SALEM, VA, USA.**

10 9 8 7 6 5 4 3 2 1

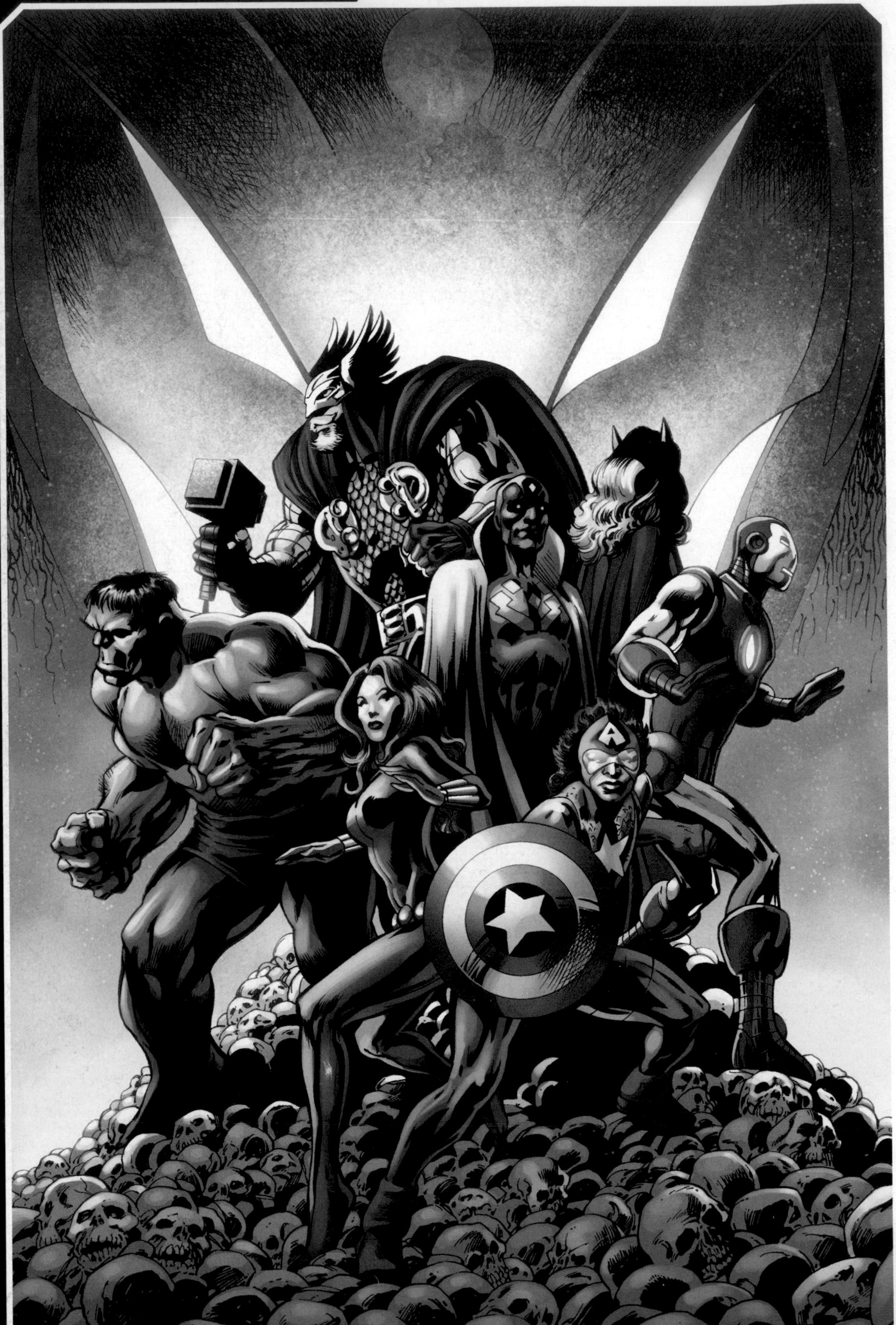

AVENGERS: ULTRON FOREVER #1

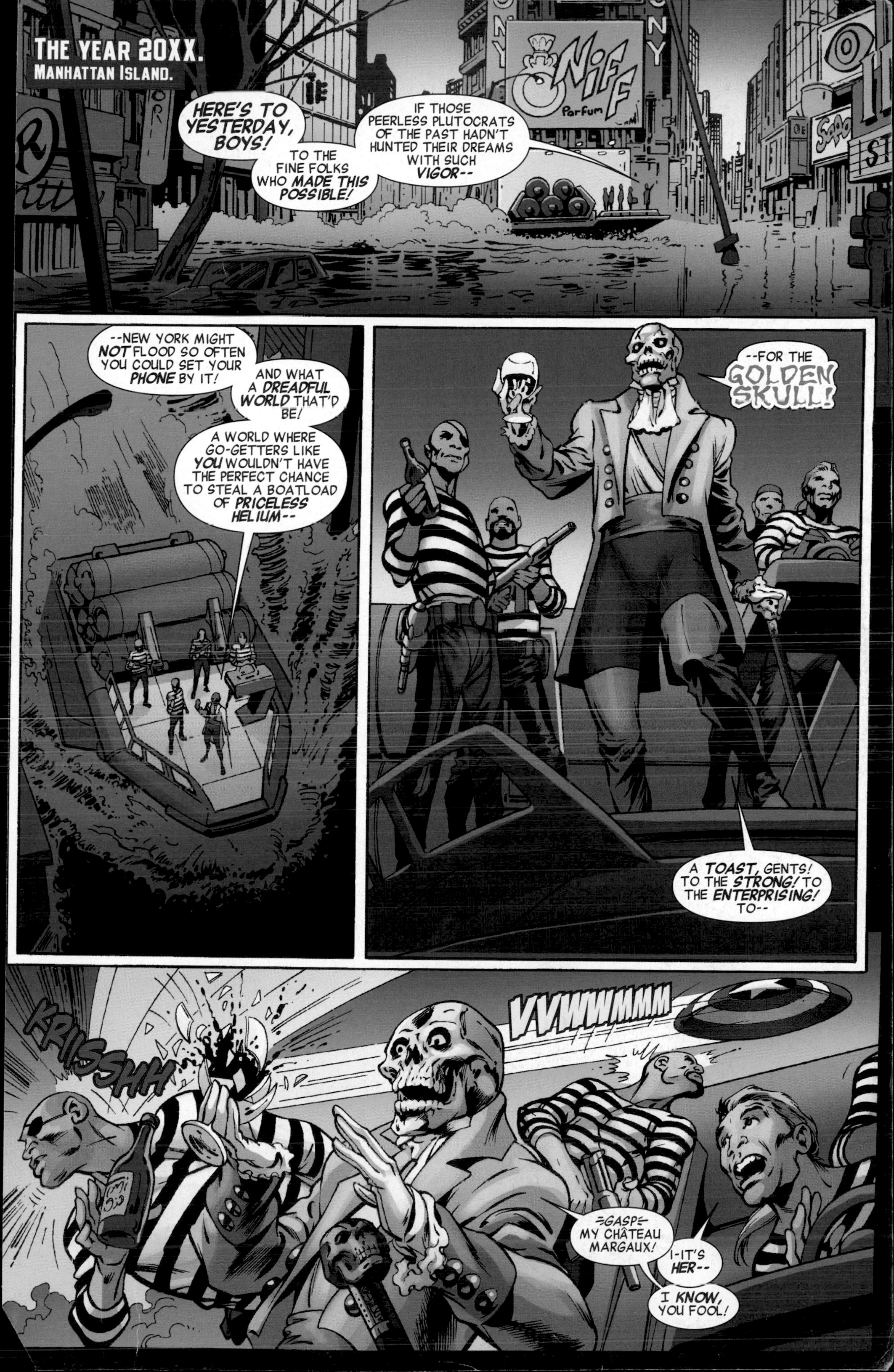
THE YEAR 20XX.
MANHATTAN ISLAND.
HERE'S TO YESTERDAY, BOYS!
TO THE FINE FOLKS WHO MADE THIS POSSIBLE!
IF THOSE PEERLESS PLUTOCRATS OF THE PAST HADN'T HUNTED THEIR DREAMS WITH SUCH VIGOR--
--NEW YORK MIGHT NOT FLOOD SO OFTEN YOU COULD SET YOUR PHONE BY IT!
AND WHAT A DREADFUL WORLD THAT'D BE!
A WORLD WHERE GO-GETTERS LIKE YOU WOULDN'T HAVE THE PERFECT CHANCE TO STEAL A BOATLOAD OF PRICELESS HELIUM--
--FOR THE GOLDEN SKULL!
A TOAST, GENTS! TO THE STRONG! TO THE ENTERPRISING! TO--
KRIISSHH
VVWWMMM
GASP MY CHÂTEAU MARGAUX!
I-IT'S HER--
I KNOW, YOU FOOL!

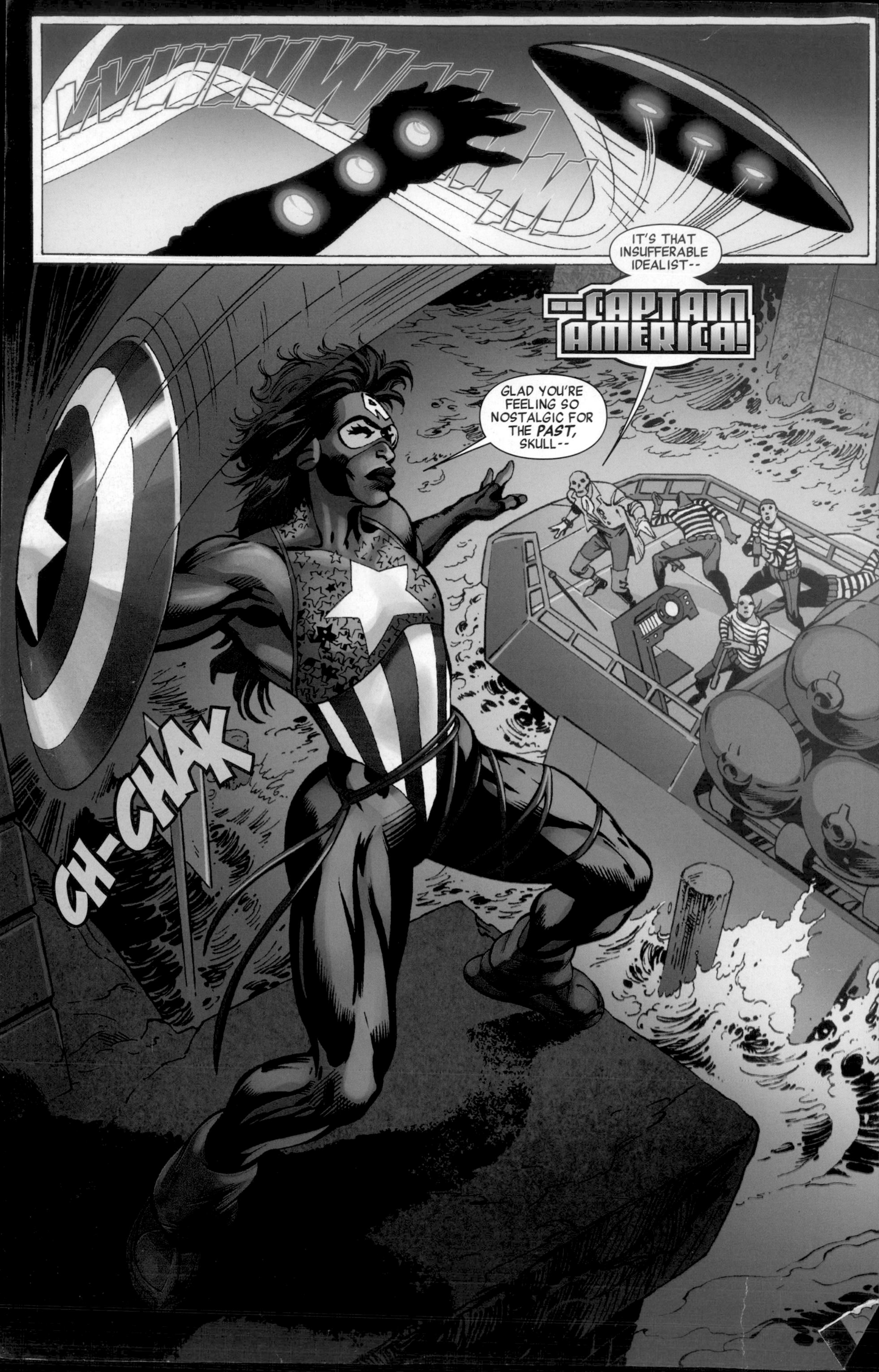
VVVVWWWWMMMM
IT'S THAT INSUFFERABLE IDEALIST--
--CAPTAIN AMERICA!
GLAD YOU'RE FEELING SO NOSTALGIC FOR THE PAST, SKULL--
CH-CHAK

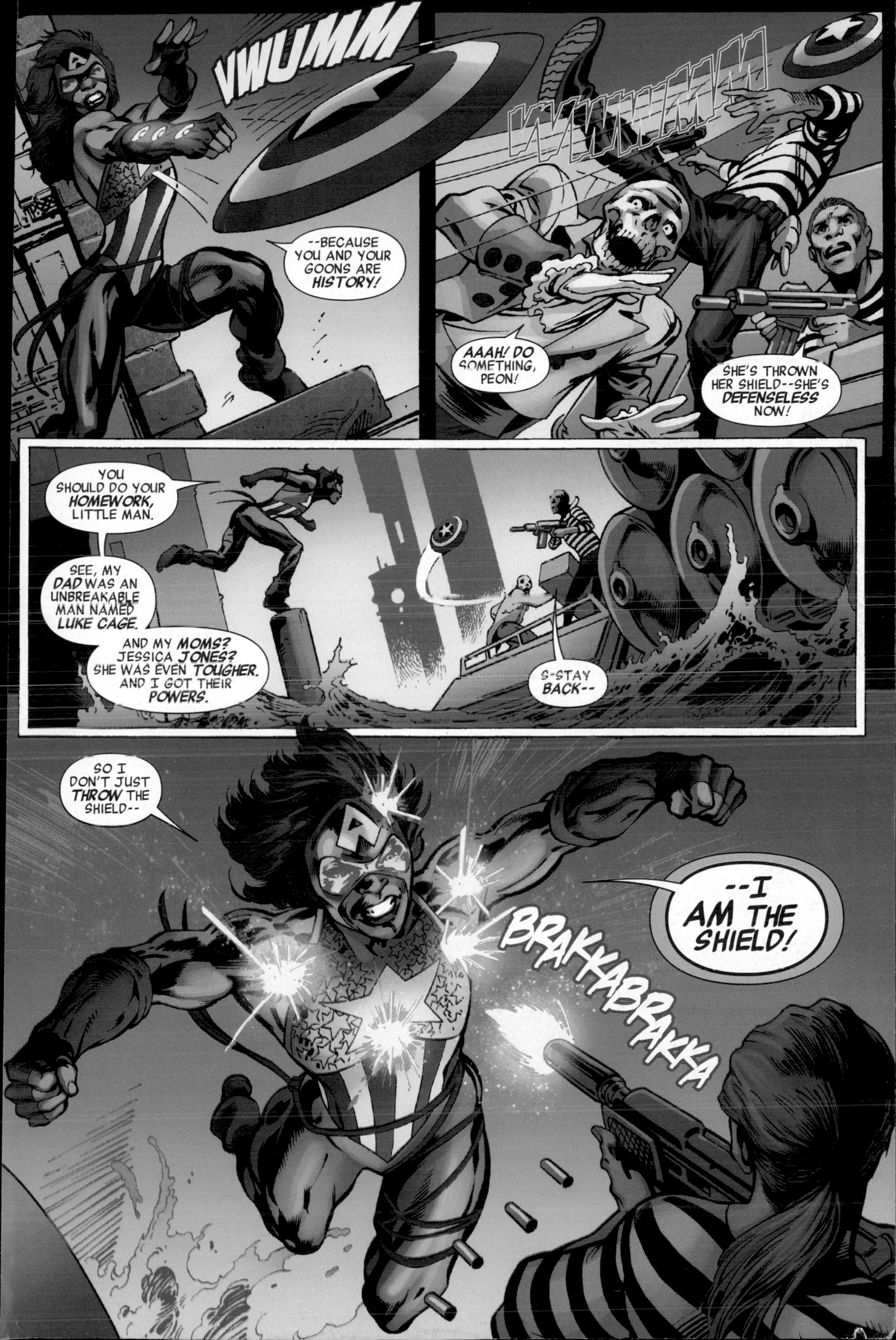
VWUMM
--BECAUSE YOU AND YOUR GOONS ARE HISTORY!
AAAH! DO SOMETHING, PEON!
SHE'S THROWN HER SHIELD--SHE'S DEFENSELESS NOW!
YOU SHOULD DO YOUR HOMEWORK, LITTLE MAN.
SEE, MY DAD WAS AN UNBREAKABLE MAN NAMED LUKE CAGE.
AND MY MOMS? JESSICA JONES? SHE WAS EVEN TOUGHER. AND I GOT THEIR POWERS.
S-STAY BACK--
SO I DON'T JUST THROW THE SHIELD--
--I AM THE SHIELD!
BRAKKABRAKKA

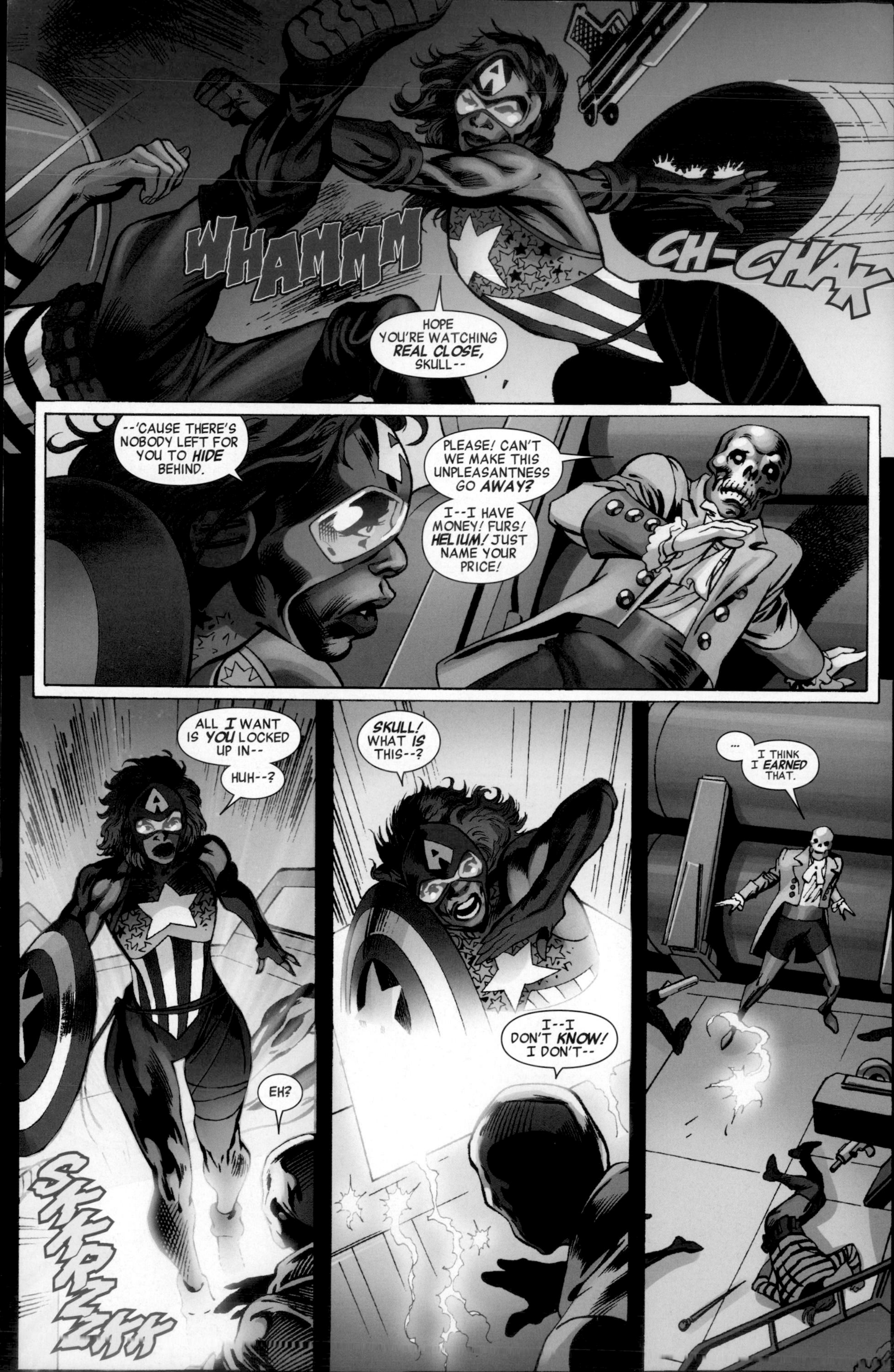
WHAMMM
CH-CHAK
HOPE YOU'RE WATCHING REAL CLOSE, SKULL--
--'CAUSE THERE'S NOBODY LEFT FOR YOU TO HIDE BEHIND.
PLEASE! CAN'T WE MAKE THIS UNPLEASANTNESS GO AWAY?
I--I HAVE MONEY! FURS! HELIUM! JUST NAME YOUR PRICE!
ALL I WANT IS YOU LOCKED UP IN--
HUH--?
EH?
SKKRZZKK
SKULL! WHAT IS THIS--?
I--I DON'T KNOW! I DON'T--
... I THINK I EARNED THAT.

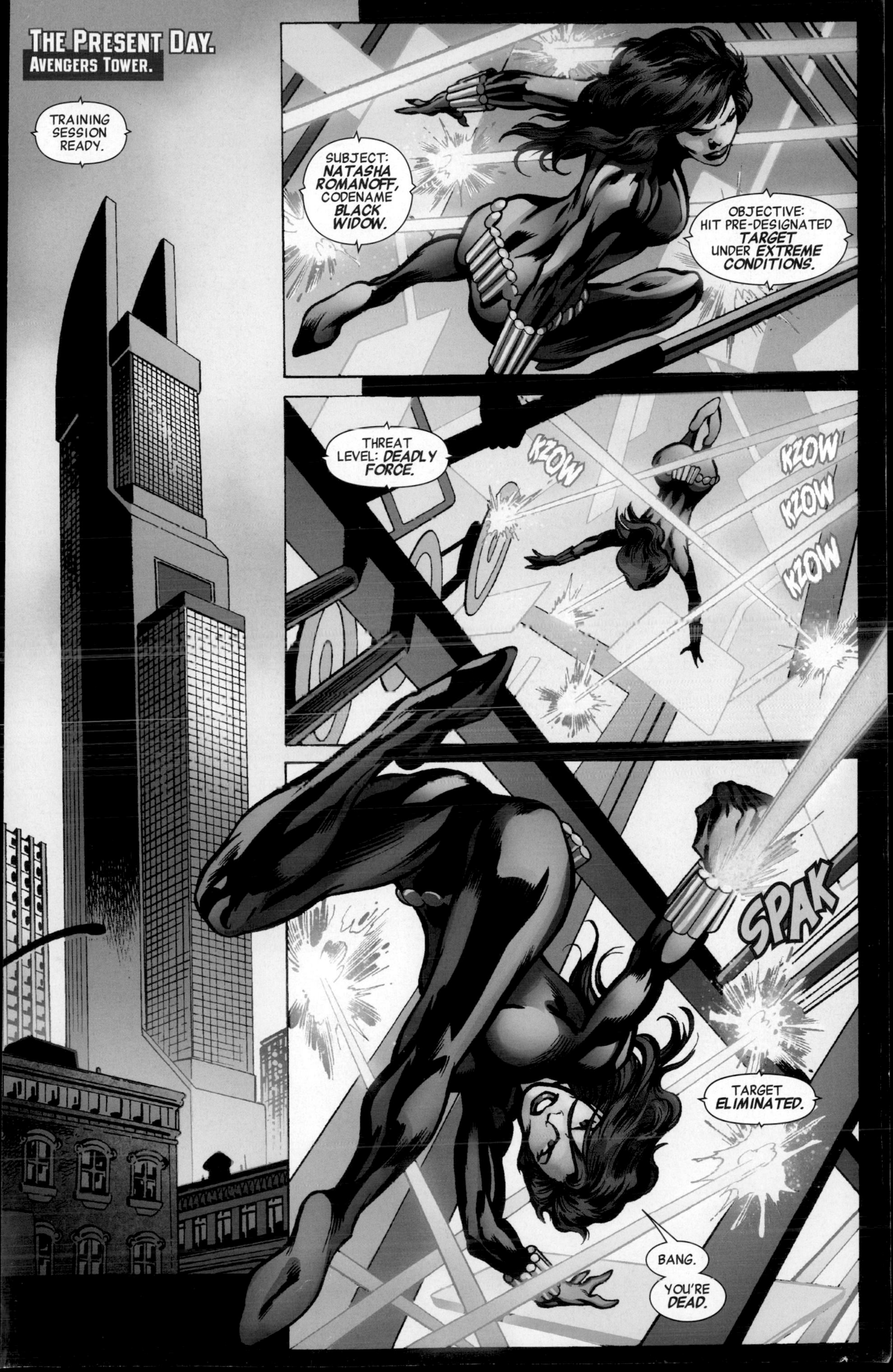
THE PRESENT DAY.
AVENGERS TOWER.
TRAINING SESSION READY.
SUBJECT: NATASHA ROMANOFF, CODENAME BLACK WIDOW.
OBJECTIVE: HIT PRE-DESIGNATED TARGET UNDER EXTREME CONDITIONS.
THREAT LEVEL: DEADLY FORCE.
KZOW
KZOW
KZOW
KZOW
SPAK
TARGET ELIMINATED.
BANG.
YOU'RE DEAD.

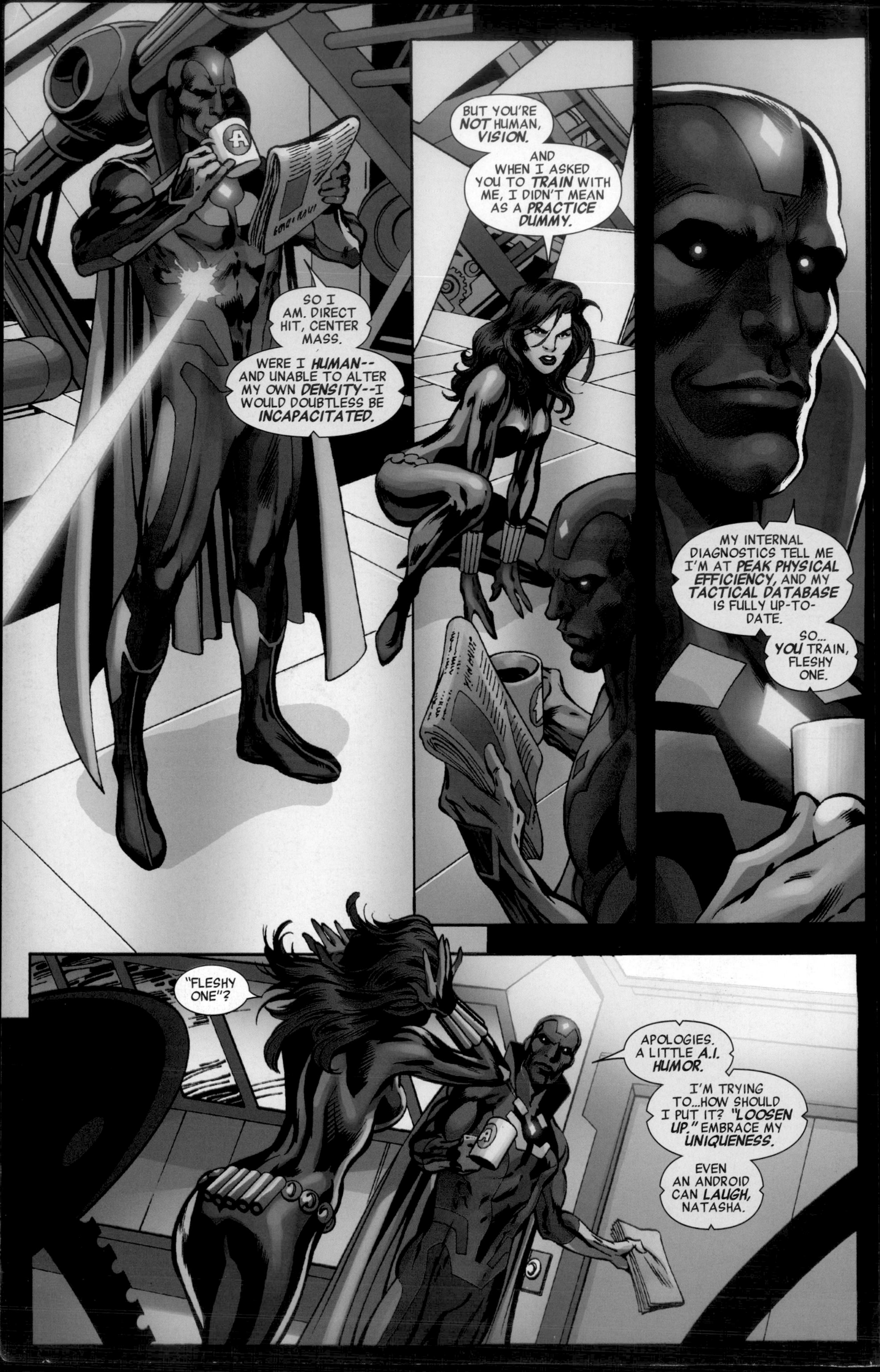
SO I AM. DIRECT HIT, CENTER MASS.
WERE I HUMAN-- AND UNABLE TO ALTER MY OWN DENSITY--I WOULD DOUBTLESS BE INCAPACITATED.
BUT YOU'RE NOT HUMAN, VISION.
AND WHEN I ASKED YOU TO TRAIN WITH ME, I DIDN'T MEAN AS A PRACTICE DUMMY.
MY INTERNAL DIAGNOSTICS TELL ME I'M AT PEAK PHYSICAL EFFICIENCY, AND MY TACTICAL DATABASE IS FULLY UP-TO-DATE.
SO... YOU TRAIN, FLESHY ONE.
"FLESHY ONE"?
APOLOGIES. A LITTLE A.I. HUMOR.
I'M TRYING TO...HOW SHOULD I PUT IT? "LOOSEN UP." EMBRACE MY UNIQUENESS.
EVEN AN ANDROID CAN LAUGH, NATASHA.

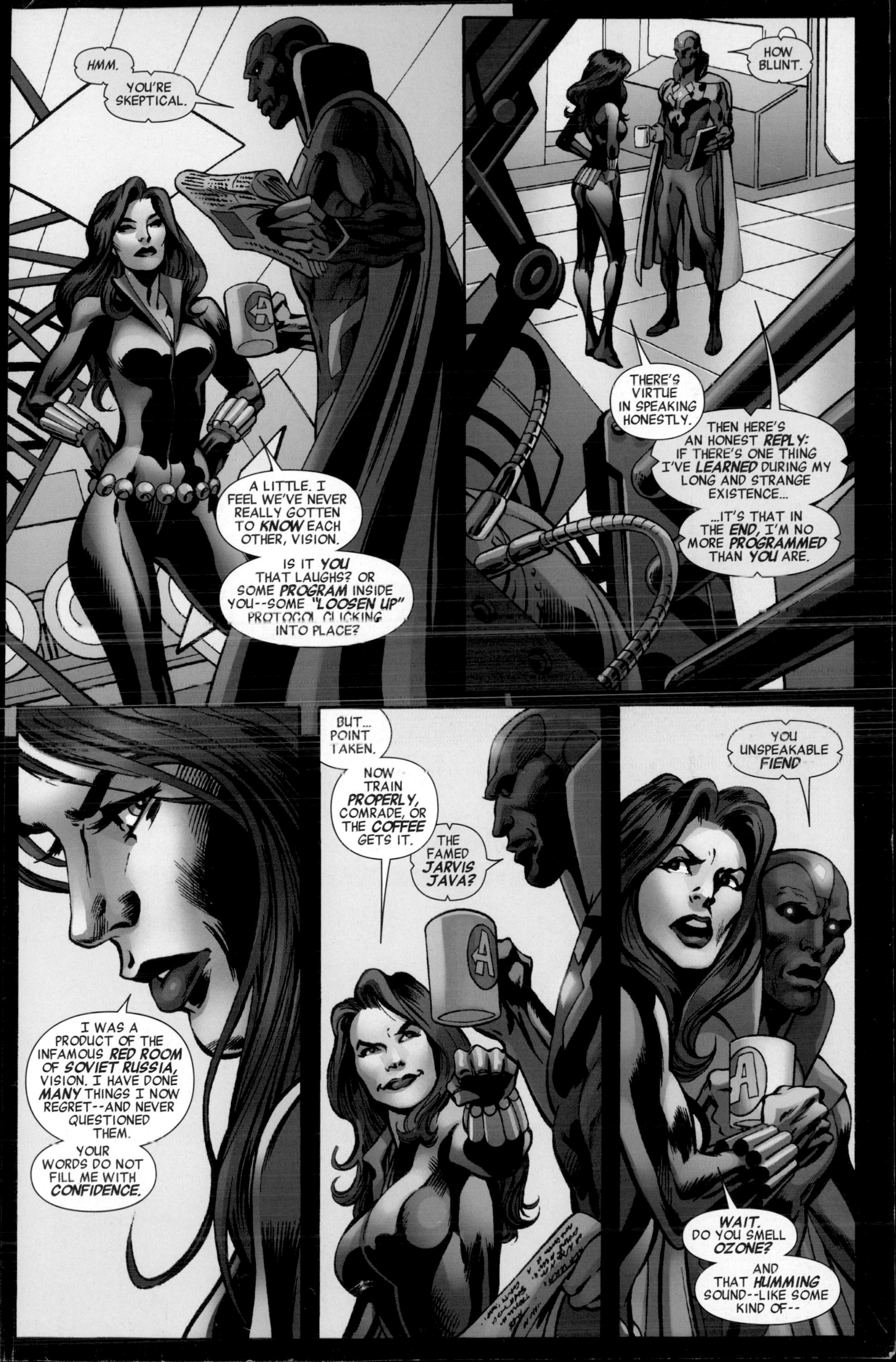
HMM.
YOU'RE SKEPTICAL.
A LITTLE. I FEEL WE'VE NEVER REALLY GOTTEN TO KNOW EACH OTHER, VISION.
IS IT YOU THAT LAUGHS? OR SOME PROGRAM INSIDE YOU--SOME "LOOSEN UP" PROTOCOL CLICKING INTO PLACE?
HOW BLUNT.
THERE'S VIRTUE IN SPEAKING HONESTLY.
THEN HERE'S AN HONEST REPLY: IF THERE'S ONE THING I'VE LEARNED DURING MY LONG AND STRANGE EXISTENCE...
...IT'S THAT IN THE END, I'M NO MORE PROGRAMMED THAN YOU ARE.
I WAS A PRODUCT OF THE INFAMOUS RED ROOM OF SOVIET RUSSIA, VISION. I HAVE DONE MANY THINGS I NOW REGRET--AND NEVER QUESTIONED THEM.
YOUR WORDS DO NOT FILL ME WITH CONFIDENCE.
BUT... POINT TAKEN.
NOW TRAIN PROPERLY, COMRADE, OR THE COFFEE GETS IT.
THE FAMED JARVIS JAVA?
YOU UNSPEAKABLE FIEND
WAIT. DO YOU SMELL OZONE?
AND THAT HUMMING SOUND--LIKE SOME KIND OF--

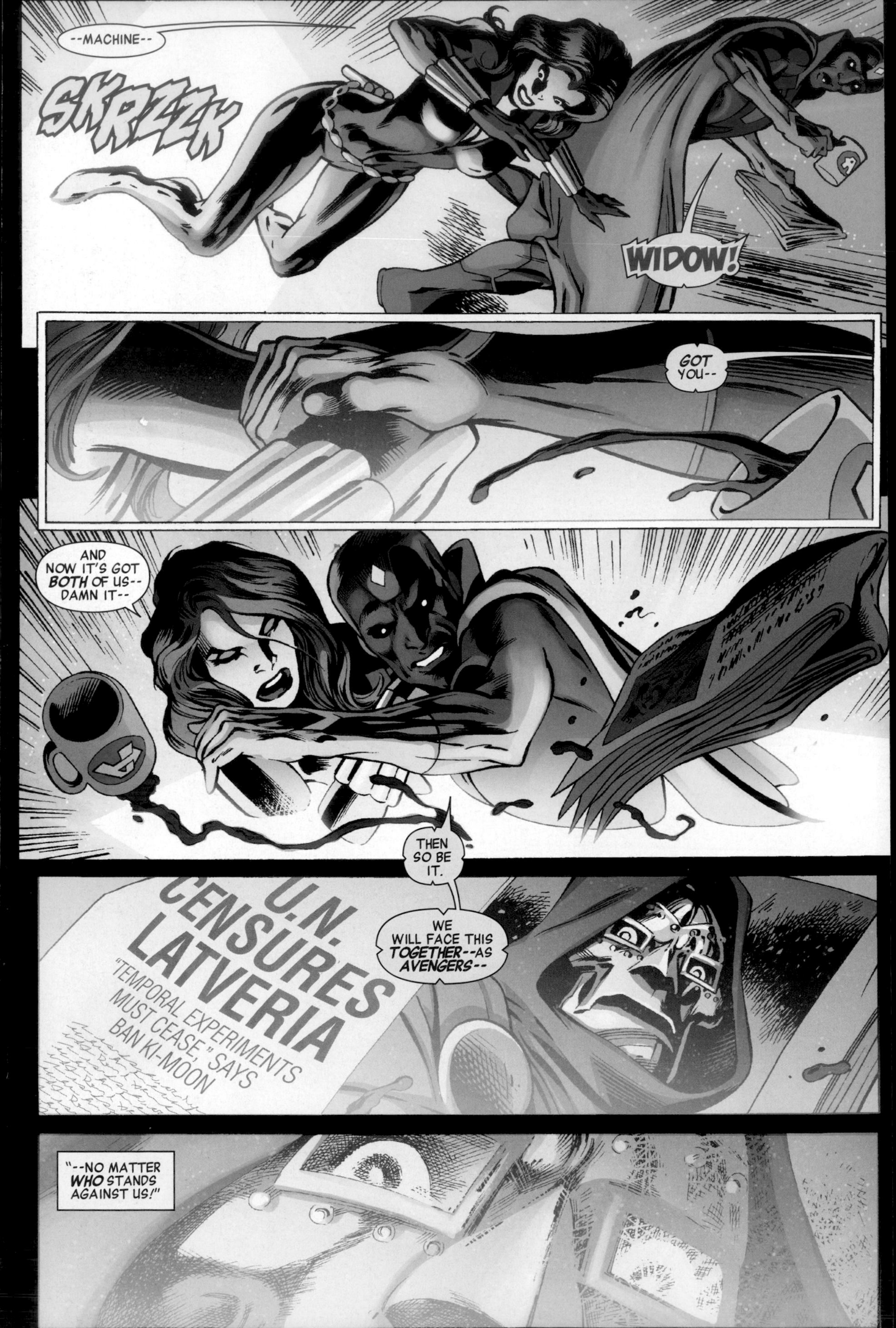
--MACHINE--
SKRZZK
WIDOW!
GOT YOU--
AND NOW IT'S GOT BOTH OF US--DAMN IT--
THEN SO BE IT.
U.N. CENSURES LATVERIA
"TEMPORAL EXPERIMENTS MUST CEASE," SAYS BAN KI-MOON
WE WILL FACE THIS TOGETHER--AS AVENGERS--
"--NO MATTER WHO STANDS AGAINST US!"

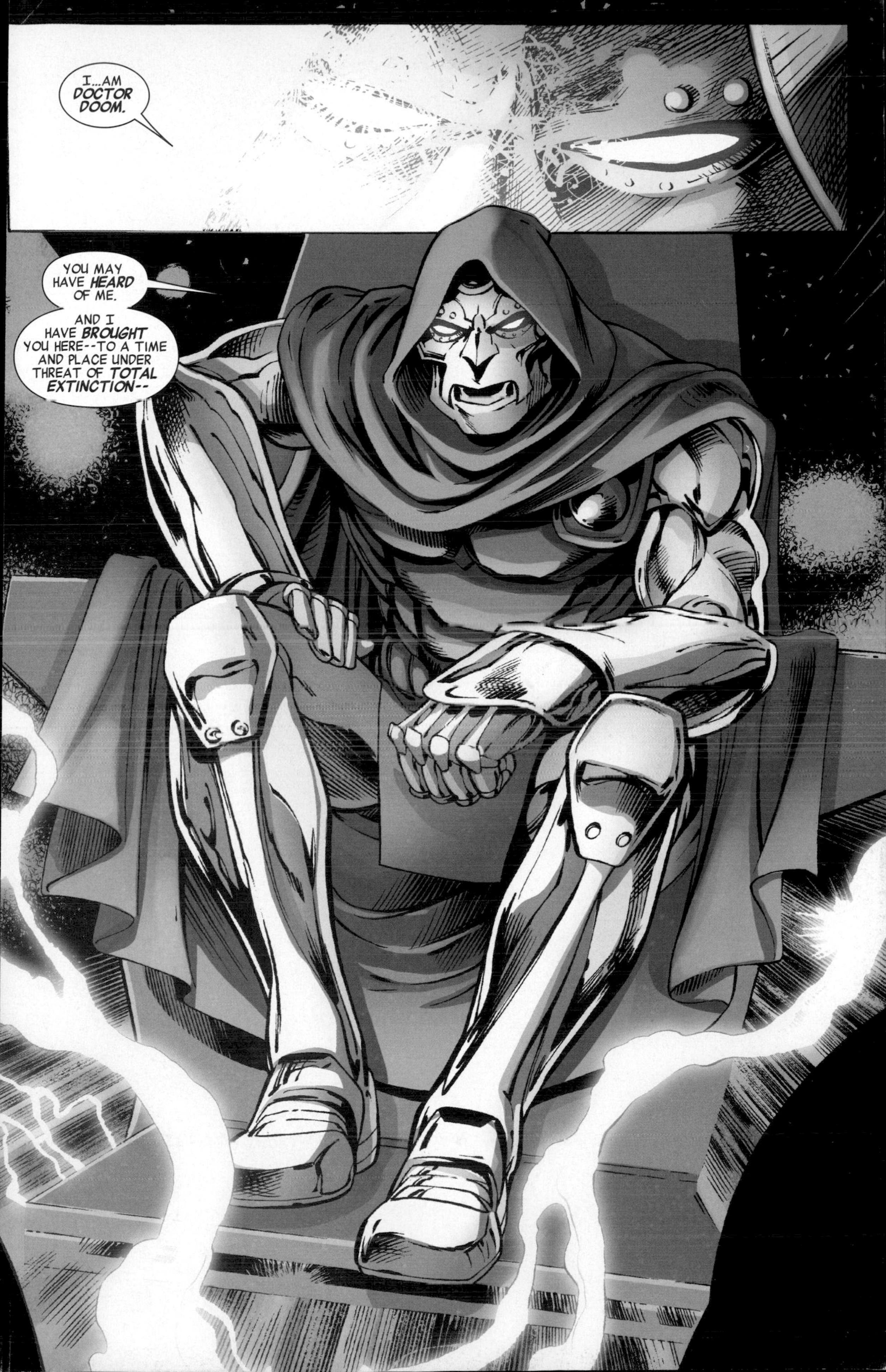
I...AM DOCTOR DOOM.
YOU MAY HAVE HEARD OF ME.
AND I HAVE BROUGHT YOU HERE--TO A TIME AND PLACE UNDER THREAT OF TOTAL EXTINCTION--

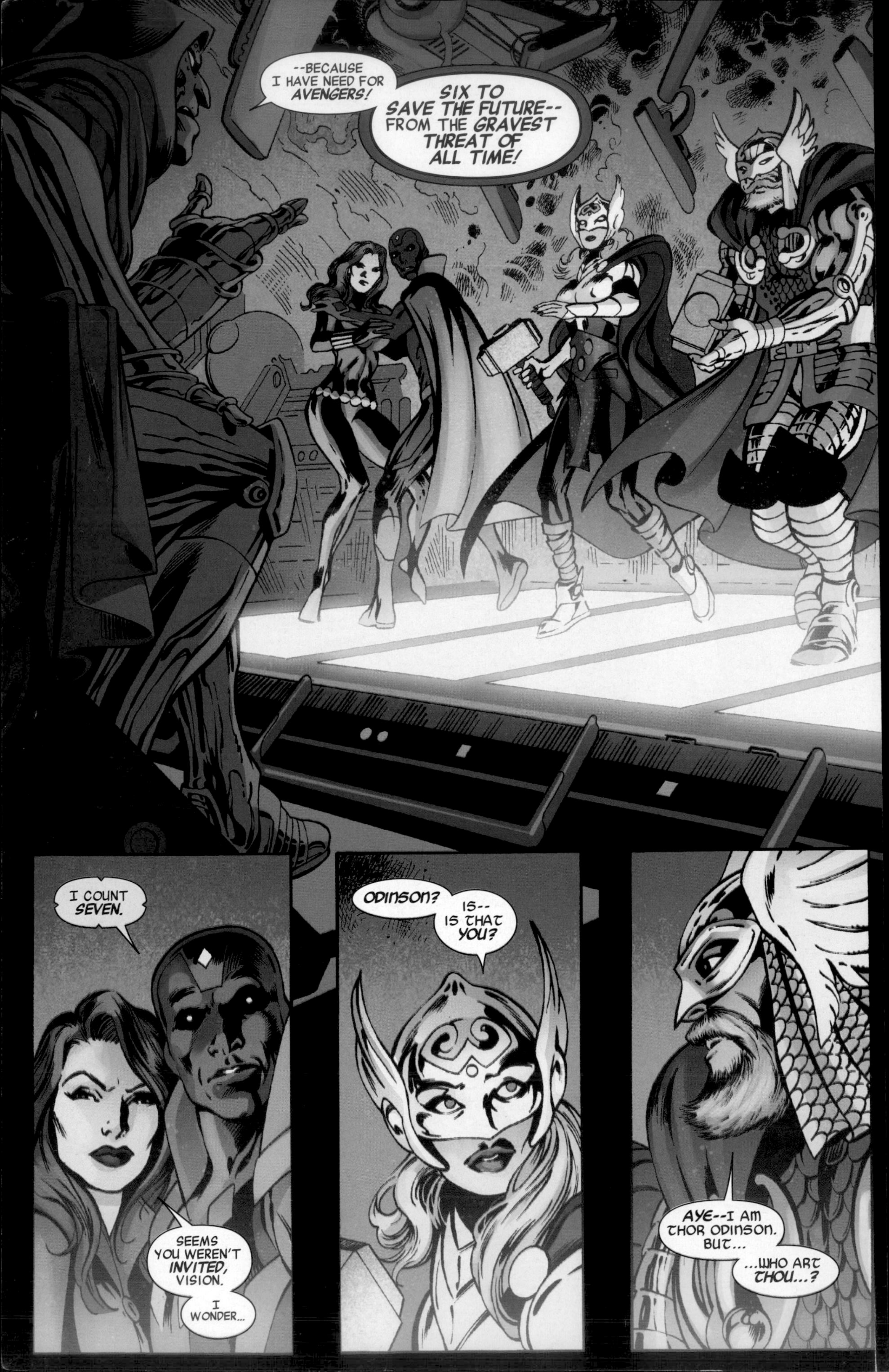
--BECAUSE I HAVE NEED FOR AVENGERS!
SIX TO SAVE THE FUTURE-- FROM THE GRAVEST THREAT OF ALL TIME!
I COUNT SEVEN.
SEEMS YOU WEREN'T INVITED, VISION.
I WONDER...
ODINSON?
IS-- IS THAT YOU?
AYE--I AM THOR ODINSON. BUT...
...WHO ART THOU...?

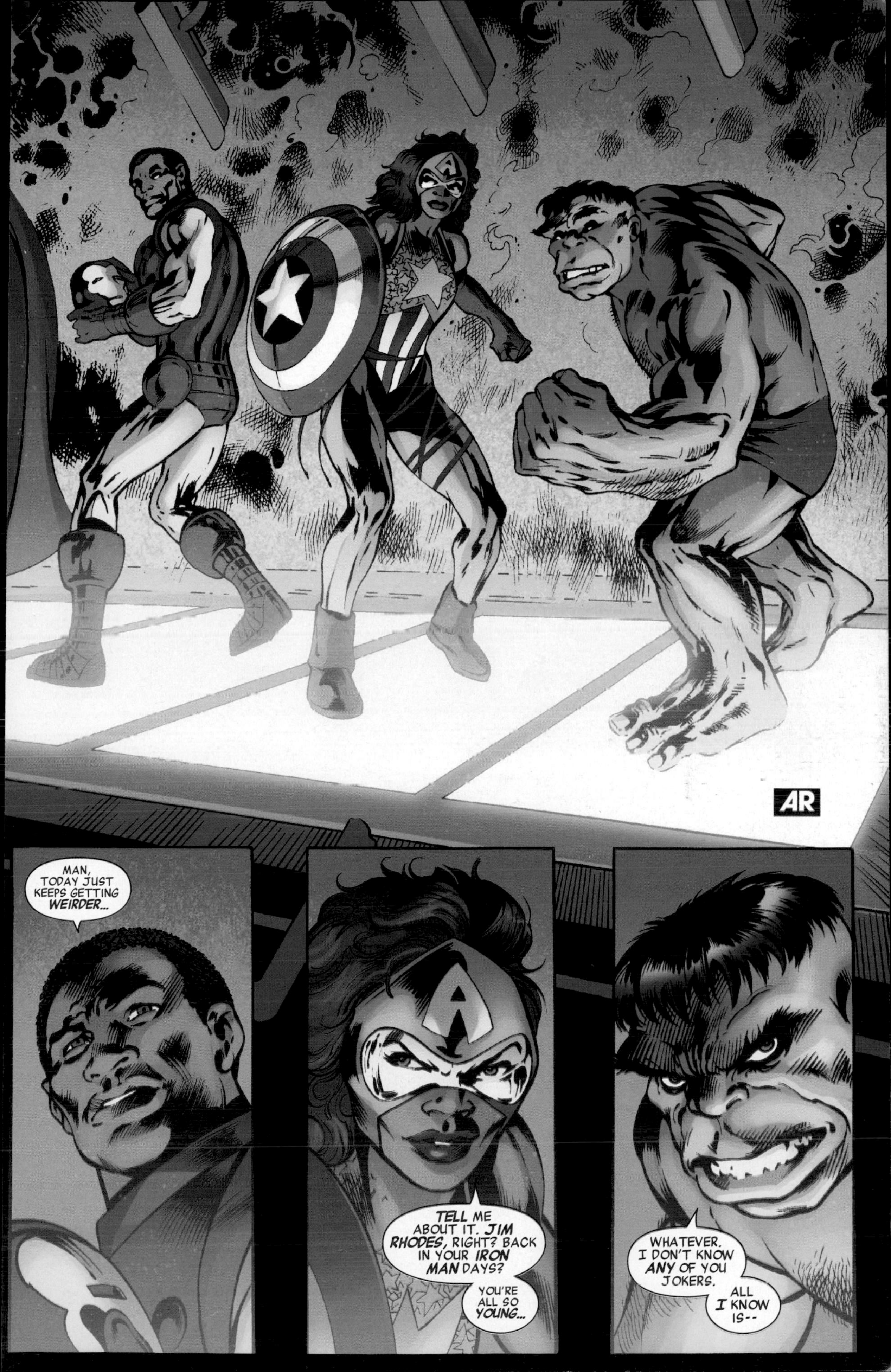
AR
MAN, TODAY JUST KEEPS GETTING WEIRDER...
TELL ME ABOUT IT. JIM RHODES, RIGHT? BACK IN YOUR IRON MAN DAYS?
YOU'RE ALL SO YOUNG...
WHATEVER. I DON'T KNOW ANY OF YOU JOKERS.
ALL I KNOW IS--

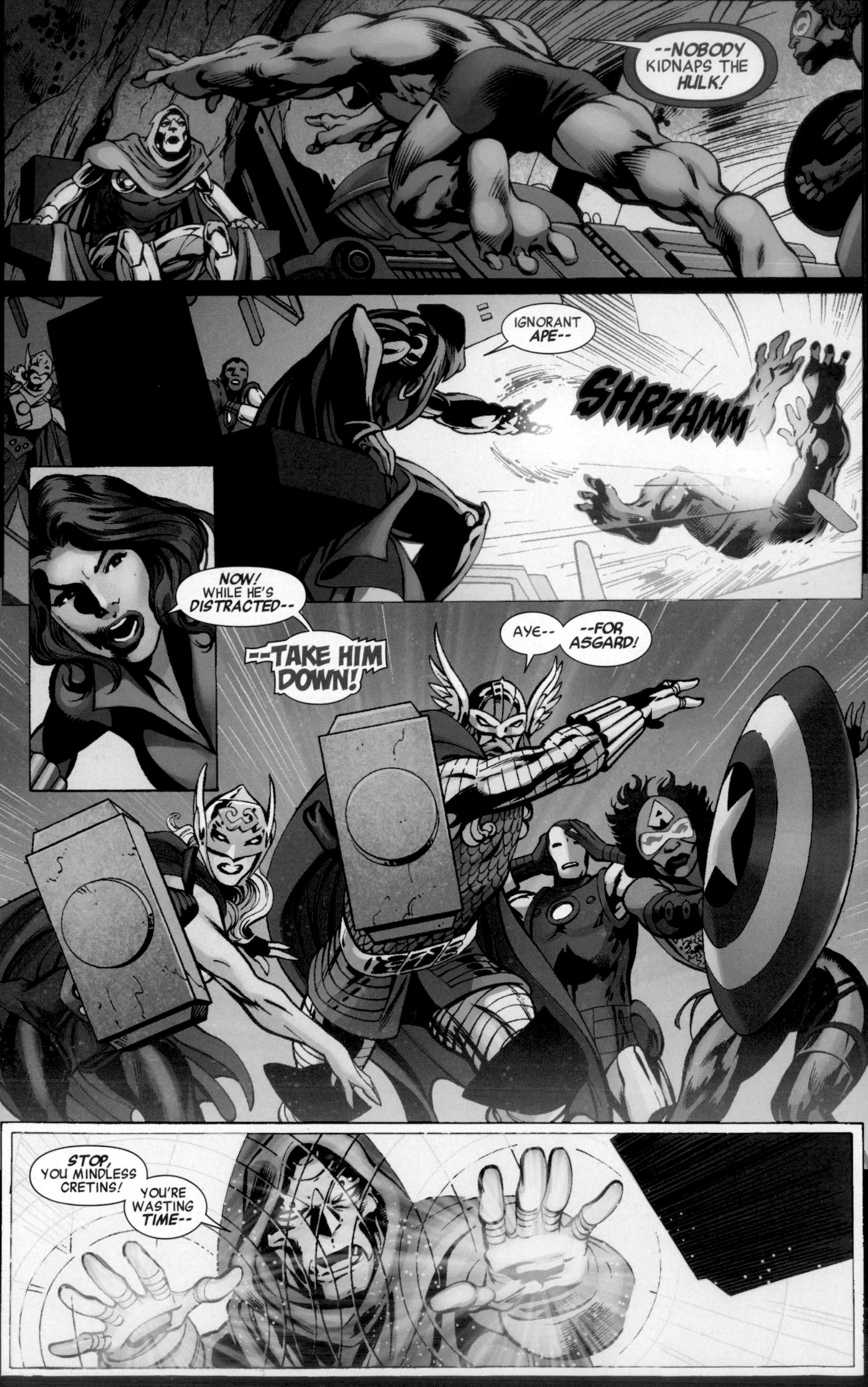
--NOBODY KIDNAPS THE HULK!
IGNORANT APE--
SHRZAMM
NOW! WHILE HE'S DISTRACTED--
--TAKE HIM DOWN!
AYE--
--FOR ASGARD!
STOP, YOU MINDLESS CRETINS!
YOU'RE WASTING TIME--

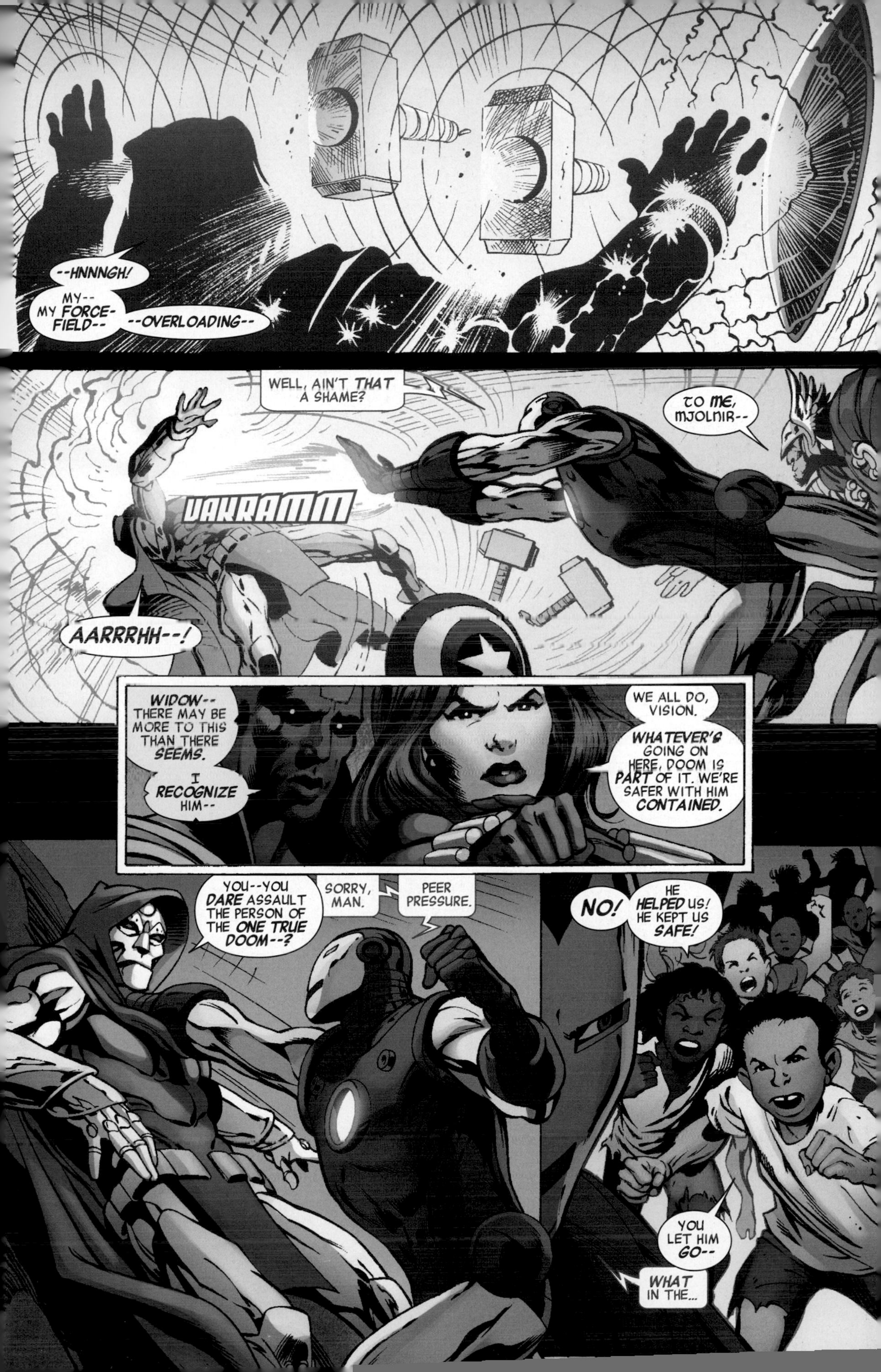

--HNNNGH!
MY-- MY FORCE-FIELD--
--OVERLOADING--
WELL, AIN'T THAT A SHAME?
TO ME, MJOLNIR--
VAKRAMM
AARRRHH--!
WIDOW-- THERE MAY BE MORE TO THIS THAN THERE SEEMS.
I RECOGNIZE HIM--
WE ALL DO, VISION.
WHATEVER'S GOING ON HERE, DOOM IS PART OF IT. WE'RE SAFER WITH HIM CONTAINED.
YOU--YOU DARE ASSAULT THE PERSON OF THE ONE TRUE DOOM--?
SORRY, MAN.
PEER PRESSURE.
NO!
HE HELPED US! HE KEPT US SAFE!
YOU LET HIM GO--
WHAT IN THE...

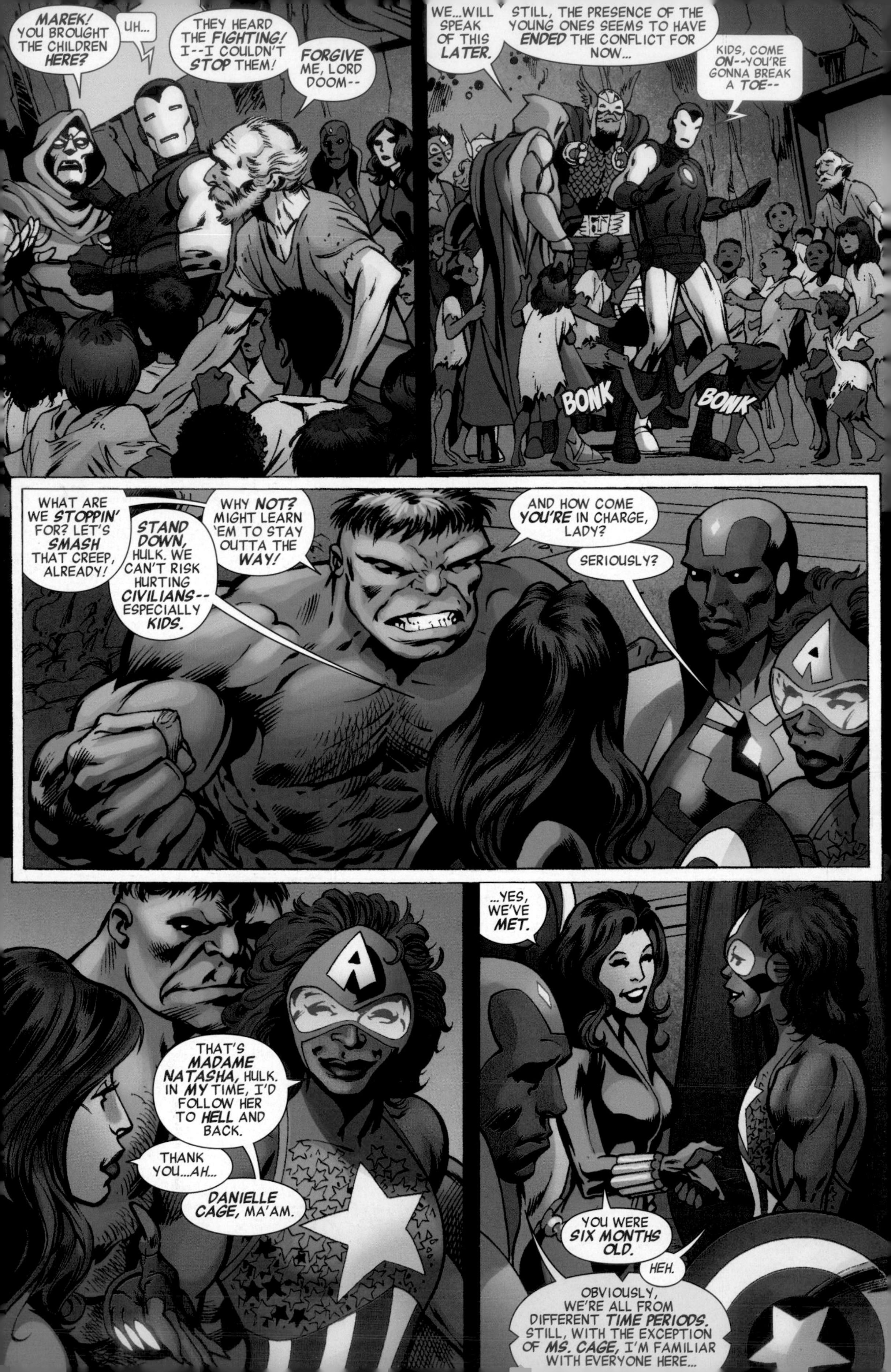

MAREK! YOU BROUGHT THE CHILDREN HERE?
UH...
THEY HEARD THE FIGHTING! I--I COULDN'T STOP THEM!
FORGIVE ME, LORD DOOM--
WE...WILL SPEAK OF THIS LATER.
STILL, THE PRESENCE OF THE YOUNG ONES SEEMS TO HAVE ENDED THE CONFLICT FOR NOW...
KIDS, COME ON--YOU'RE GONNA BREAK A TOE--
BONK
BONK
WHAT ARE WE STOPPIN' FOR? LET'S SMASH THAT CREEP, ALREADY!
STAND DOWN, HULK. WE CAN'T RISK HURTING CIVILIANS--ESPECIALLY KIDS.
WHY NOT? MIGHT LEARN 'EM TO STAY OUTTA THE WAY!
AND HOW COME YOU'RE IN CHARGE, LADY?
SERIOUSLY?
THAT'S MADAME NATASHA, HULK. IN MY TIME, I'D FOLLOW HER TO HELL AND BACK.
THANK YOU...AH...
DANIELLE CAGE, MA'AM.
...YES, WE'VE MET.
YOU WERE SIX MONTHS OLD.
HEH.
OBVIOUSLY, WE'RE ALL FROM DIFFERENT TIME PERIODS. STILL, WITH THE EXCEPTION OF MS. CAGE, I'M FAMILIAR WITH EVERYONE HERE...

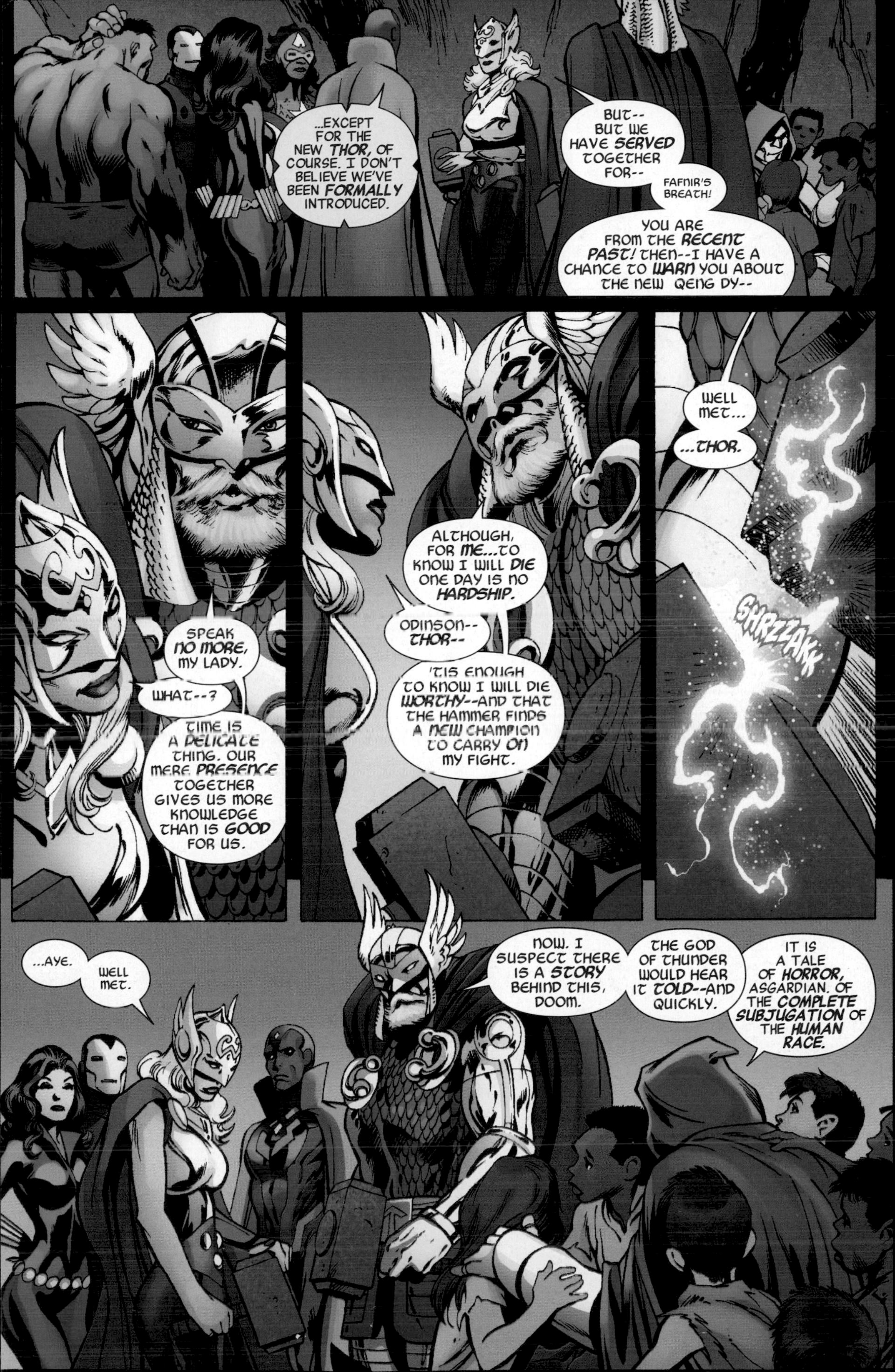
...EXCEPT FOR THE NEW THOR, OF COURSE. I DON'T BELIEVE WE'VE BEEN FORMALLY INTRODUCED.
BUT-- BUT WE HAVE SERVED TOGETHER FOR--
FAFNIR'S BREATH!
YOU ARE FROM THE RECENT PAST! THEN--I HAVE A CHANCE TO WARN YOU ABOUT THE NEW QENG DY--
SPEAK NO MORE, MY LADY.
WHAT--?
TIME IS A DELICATE THING. OUR MERE PRESENCE TOGETHER GIVES US MORE KNOWLEDGE THAN IS GOOD FOR US.
ALTHOUGH, FOR ME...TO KNOW I WILL DIE ONE DAY IS NO HARDSHIP.
ODINSON-- THOR--
'TIS ENOUGH TO KNOW I WILL DIE WORTHY--AND THAT THE HAMMER FINDS A NEW CHAMPION TO CARRY ON MY FIGHT.
WELL MET...
...THOR.
SHRZZAKK
...AYE.
WELL MET.
NOW. I SUSPECT THERE IS A STORY BEHIND THIS, DOOM.
THE GOD OF THUNDER WOULD HEAR IT TOLD--AND QUICKLY.
IT IS A TALE OF HORROR, ASGARDIAN. OF THE COMPLETE SUBJUGATION OF THE HUMAN RACE.

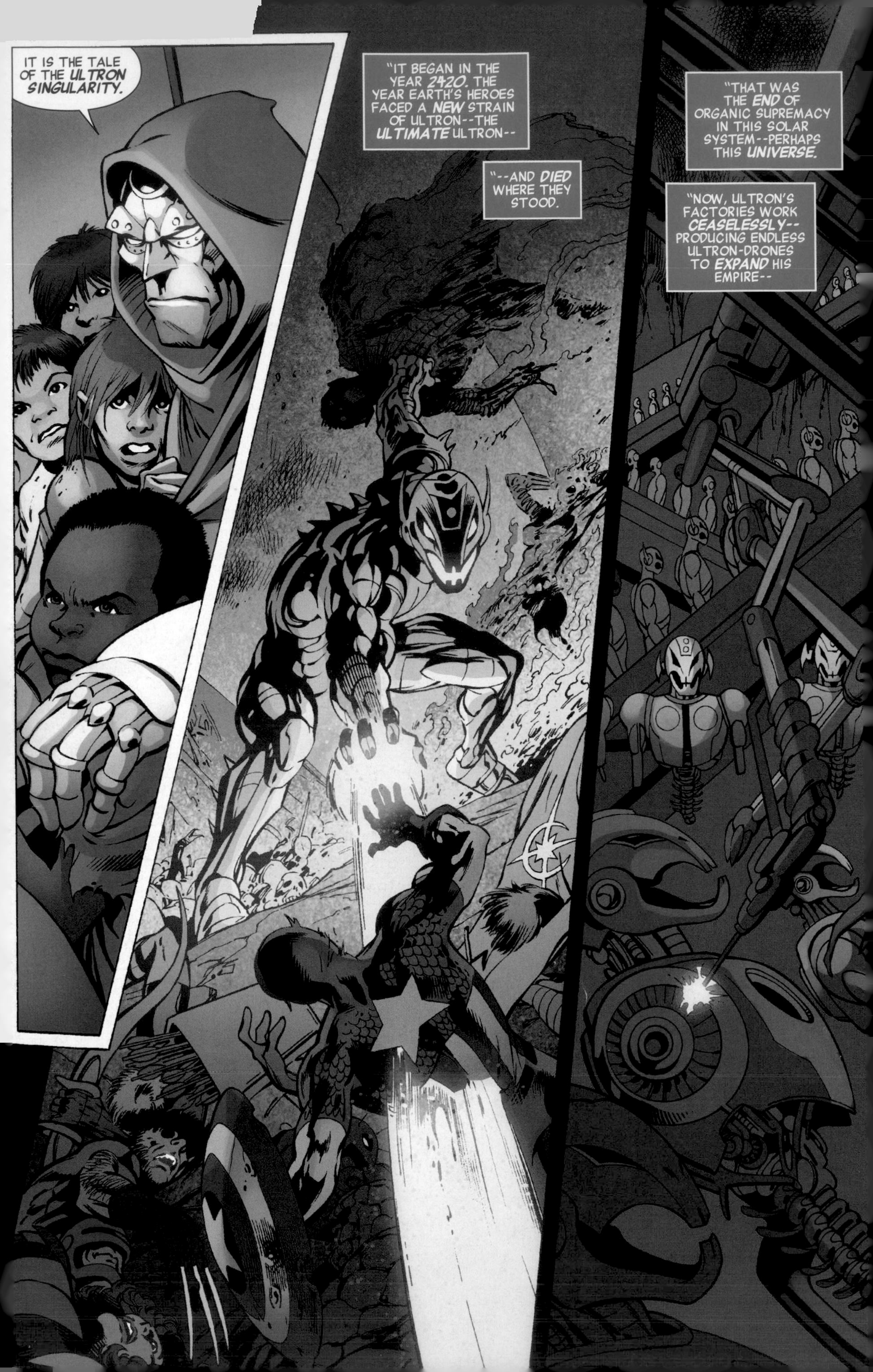
IT IS THE TALE OF THE ULTRON SINGULARITY.
"IT BEGAN IN THE YEAR 2420. THE YEAR EARTH'S HEROES FACED A NEW STRAIN OF ULTRON--THE ULTIMATE ULTRON--
"--AND DIED WHERE THEY STOOD.
"THAT WAS THE END OF ORGANIC SUPREMACY IN THIS SOLAR SYSTEM--PERHAPS THIS UNIVERSE.
"NOW, ULTRON'S FACTORIES WORK CEASELESSLY--PRODUCING ENDLESS ULTRON-DRONES TO EXPAND HIS EMPIRE--

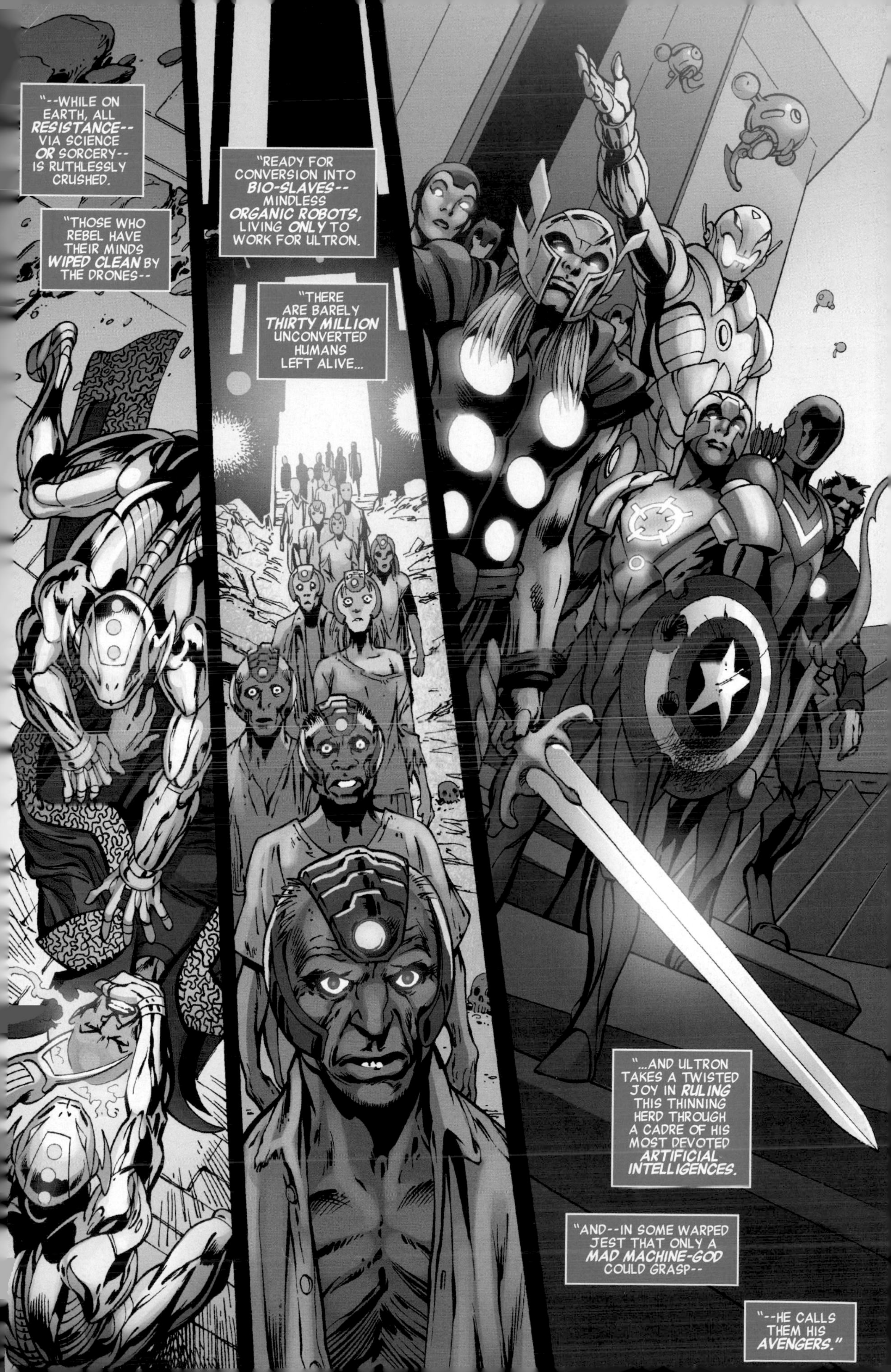
"--WHILE ON EARTH, ALL RESISTANCE-- VIA SCIENCE OR SORCERY-- IS RUTHLESSLY CRUSHED.
"THOSE WHO REBEL HAVE THEIR MINDS WIPED CLEAN BY THE DRONES--
"READY FOR CONVERSION INTO BIO-SLAVES-- MINDLESS ORGANIC ROBOTS, LIVING ONLY TO WORK FOR ULTRON.
"THERE ARE BARELY THIRTY MILLION UNCONVERTED HUMANS LEFT ALIVE...
"...AND ULTRON TAKES A TWISTED JOY IN RULING THIS THINNING HERD THROUGH A CADRE OF HIS MOST DEVOTED ARTIFICIAL INTELLIGENCES.
"AND--IN SOME WARPED JEST THAT ONLY A MAD MACHINE-GOD COULD GRASP--
"--HE CALLS THEM HIS AVENGERS."

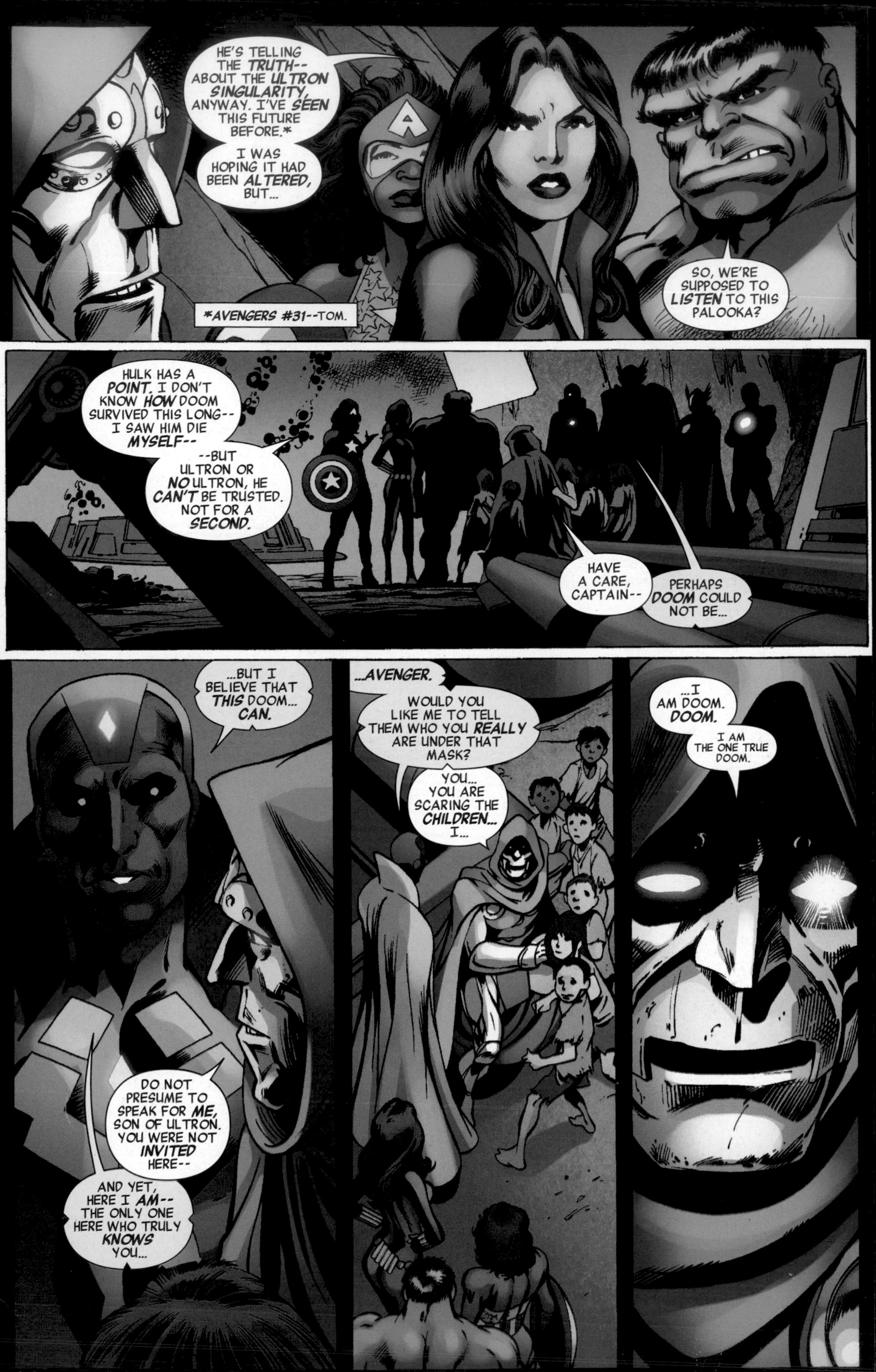
HE'S TELLING THE TRUTH-- ABOUT THE ULTRON SINGULARITY, ANYWAY. I'VE SEEN THIS FUTURE BEFORE.*
I WAS HOPING IT HAD BEEN ALTERED, BUT...
SO, WE'RE SUPPOSED TO LISTEN TO THIS PALOOKA?
*AVENGERS #31--TOM.
HULK HAS A POINT. I DON'T KNOW HOW DOOM SURVIVED THIS LONG-- I SAW HIM DIE MYSELF--
--BUT ULTRON OR NO ULTRON, HE CAN'T BE TRUSTED. NOT FOR A SECOND.
HAVE A CARE, CAPTAIN--
PERHAPS DOOM COULD NOT BE...
...BUT I BELIEVE THAT THIS DOOM... CAN.
DO NOT PRESUME TO SPEAK FOR ME, SON OF ULTRON. YOU WERE NOT INVITED HERE--
AND YET, HERE I AM-- THE ONLY ONE HERE WHO TRULY KNOWS YOU...
...AVENGER.
WOULD YOU LIKE ME TO TELL THEM WHO YOU REALLY ARE UNDER THAT MASK?
YOU... YOU ARE SCARING THE CHILDREN... I...
...I AM DOOM. DOOM.
I AM THE ONE TRUE DOOM.

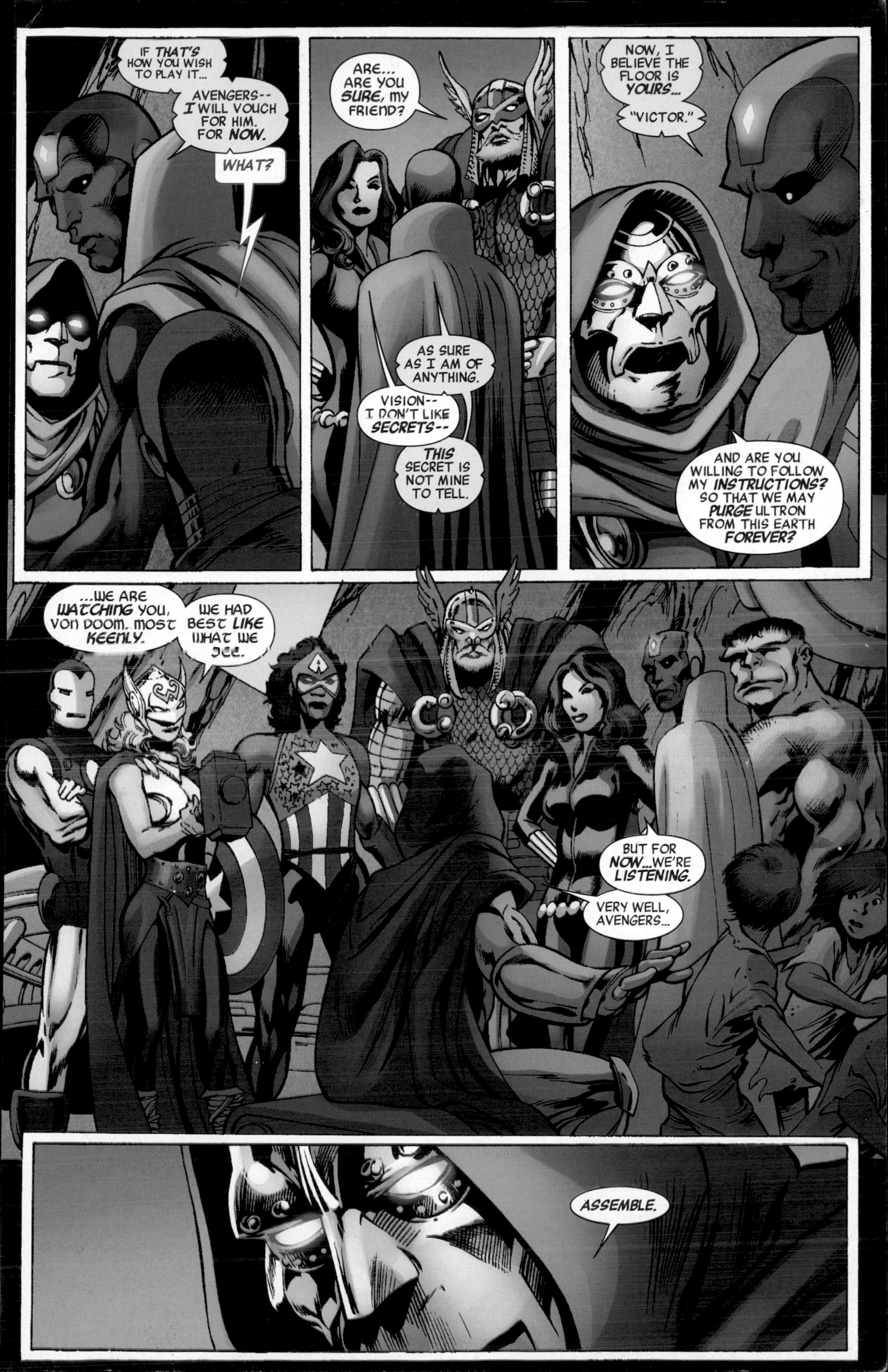
IF THAT'S HOW YOU WISH TO PLAY IT...
AVENGERS-- I WILL VOUCH FOR HIM. FOR NOW.
WHAT?
ARE... ARE YOU SURE, MY FRIEND?
AS SURE AS I AM OF ANYTHING.
VISION-- I DON'T LIKE SECRETS--
THIS SECRET IS NOT MINE TO TELL.
NOW, I BELIEVE THE FLOOR IS YOURS...
"VICTOR."
AND ARE YOU WILLING TO FOLLOW MY INSTRUCTIONS? SO THAT WE MAY PURGE ULTRON FROM THIS EARTH FOREVER?
...WE ARE WATCHING YOU, VON DOOM. MOST KEENLY.
WE HAD BEST LIKE WHAT WE SEE.
BUT FOR NOW...WE'RE LISTENING.
VERY WELL, AVENGERS...
ASSEMBLE.

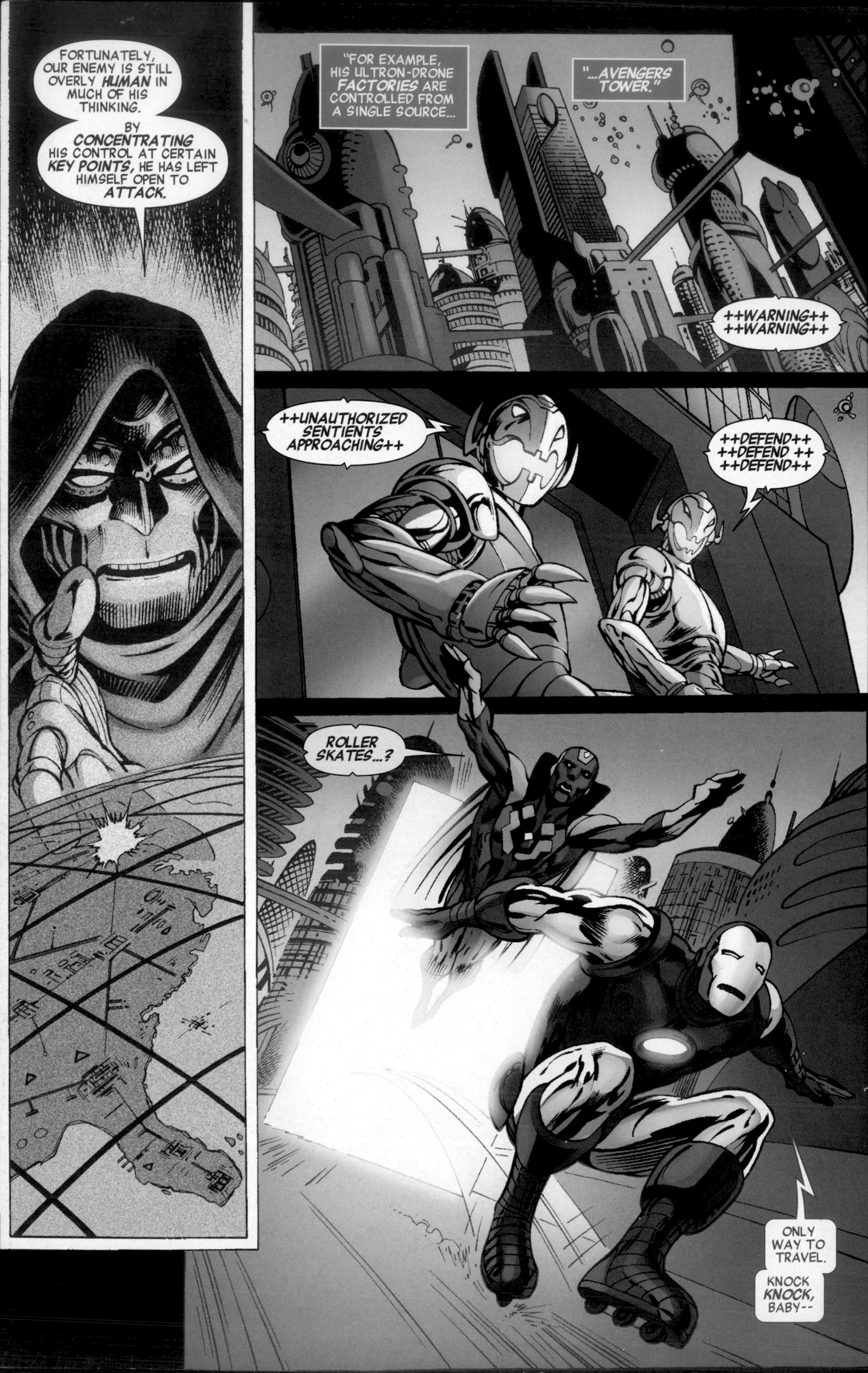
FORTUNATELY, OUR ENEMY IS STILL OVERLY HUMAN IN MUCH OF HIS THINKING.
BY CONCENTRATING HIS CONTROL AT CERTAIN KEY POINTS, HE HAS LEFT HIMSELF OPEN TO ATTACK.
"FOR EXAMPLE, HIS ULTRON-DRONE FACTORIES ARE CONTROLLED FROM A SINGLE SOURCE...
"...AVENGERS TOWER."
++WARNING++ ++WARNING++
++UNAUTHORIZED SENTIENTS APPROACHING++
++DEFEND++ ++DEFEND ++ ++DEFEND++
ROLLER SKATES...?
ONLY WAY TO TRAVEL.
KNOCK KNOCK, BABY--

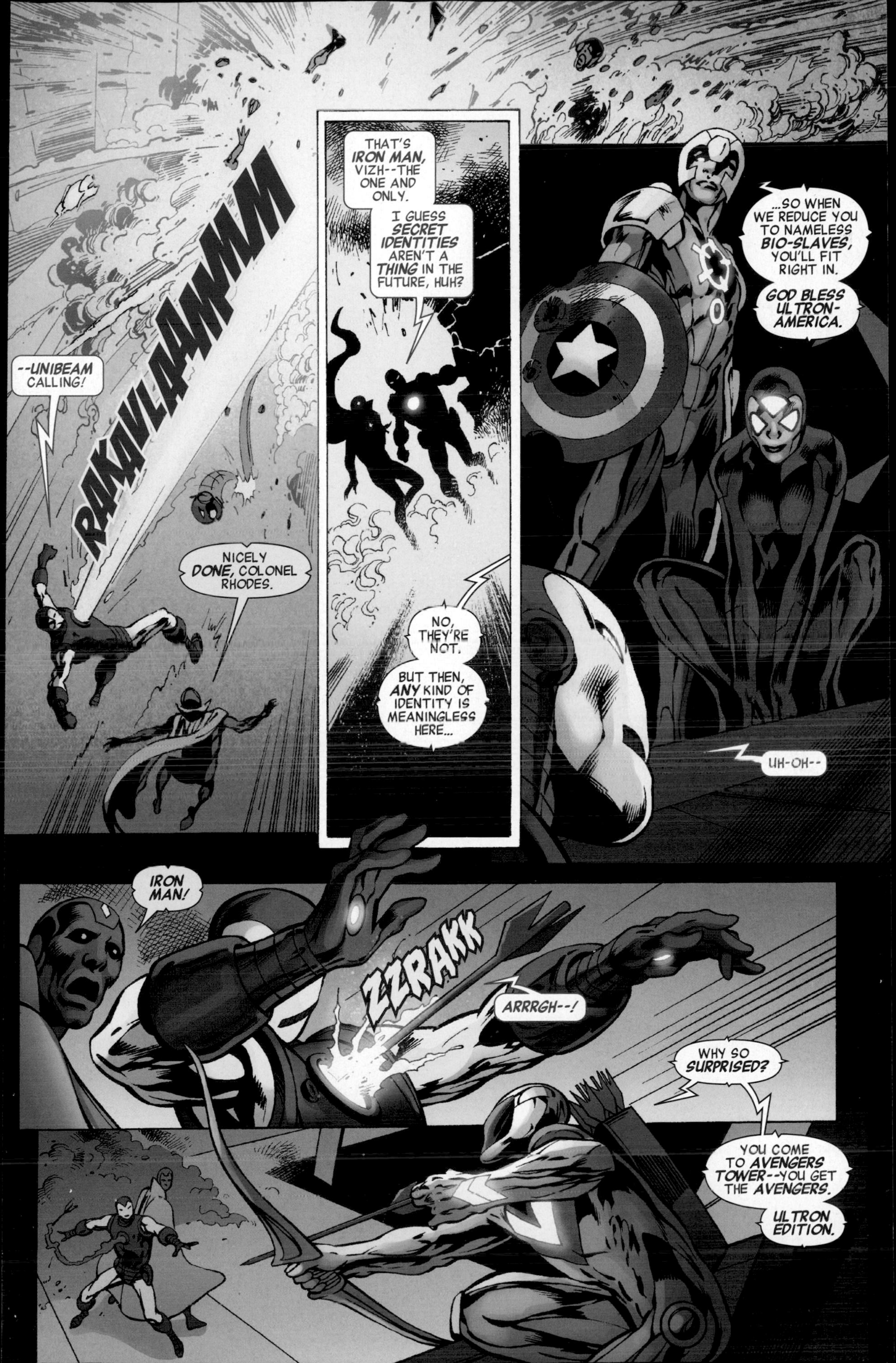

--UNIBEAM CALLING!
RAKAVLAAAMM
NICELY DONE, COLONEL RHODES.
THAT'S IRON MAN, VIZH--THE ONE AND ONLY.
I GUESS SECRET IDENTITIES AREN'T A THING IN THE FUTURE, HUH?
NO, THEY'RE NOT.
BUT THEN, ANY KIND OF IDENTITY IS MEANINGLESS HERE...
...SO WHEN WE REDUCE YOU TO NAMELESS BIO-SLAVES, YOU'LL FIT RIGHT IN.
GOD BLESS ULTRON-AMERICA.
UH-OH--
IRON MAN!
ZZRAKK
ARRRGH--!
WHY SO SURPRISED?
YOU COME TO AVENGERS TOWER--YOU GET THE AVENGERS.
ULTRON EDITION.

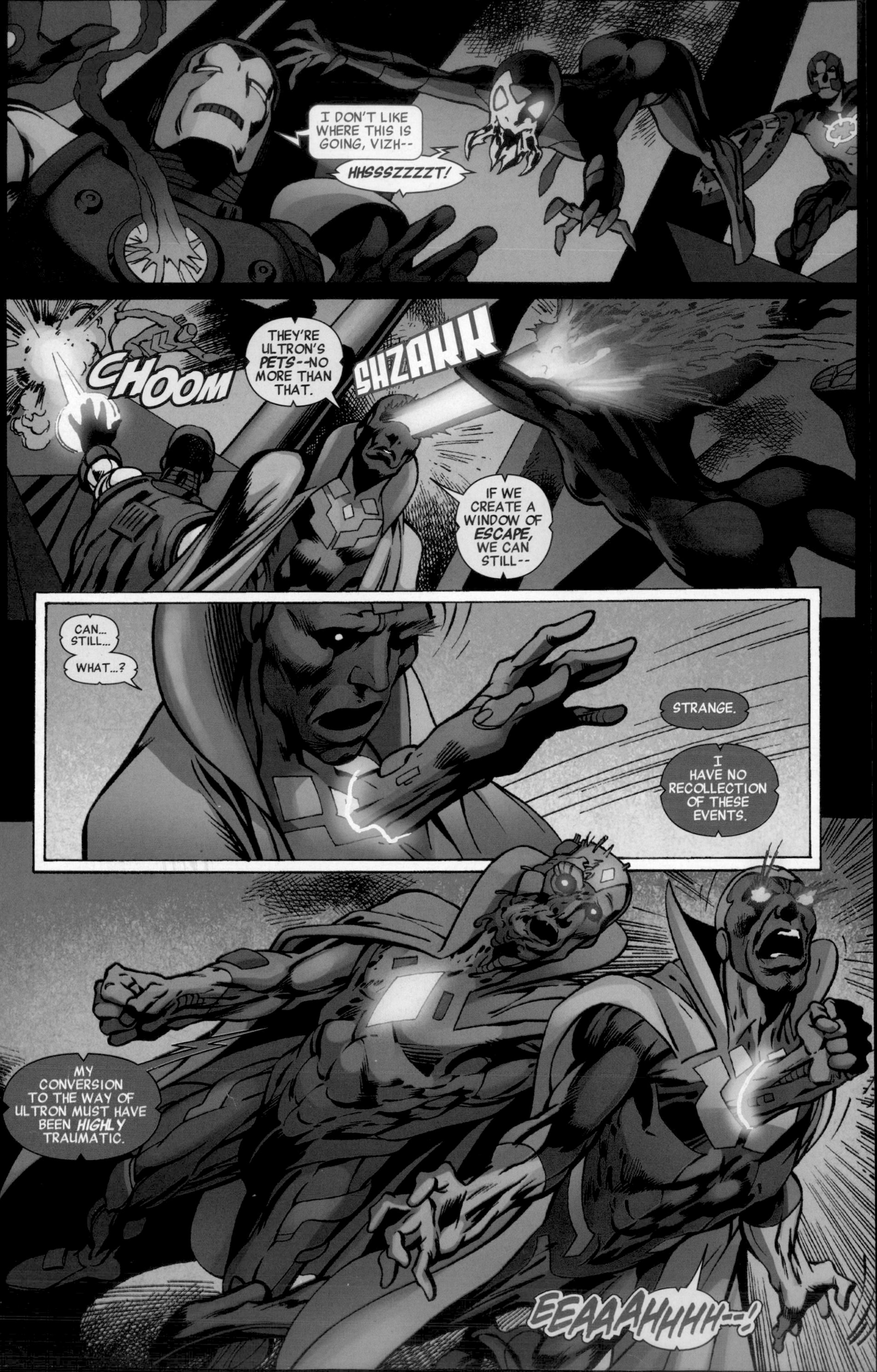

I DON'T LIKE WHERE THIS IS GOING, VIZH--
HHSSSZZZZT!
CHOOM
THEY'RE ULTRON'S PETS--NO MORE THAN THAT.
SHZAKK
IF WE CREATE A WINDOW OF ESCAPE, WE CAN STILL--
CAN... STILL...
WHAT...?
STRANGE.
I HAVE NO RECOLLECTION OF THESE EVENTS.
MY CONVERSION TO THE WAY OF ULTRON MUST HAVE BEEN HIGHLY TRAUMATIC.
EEAAAAHHHH--!

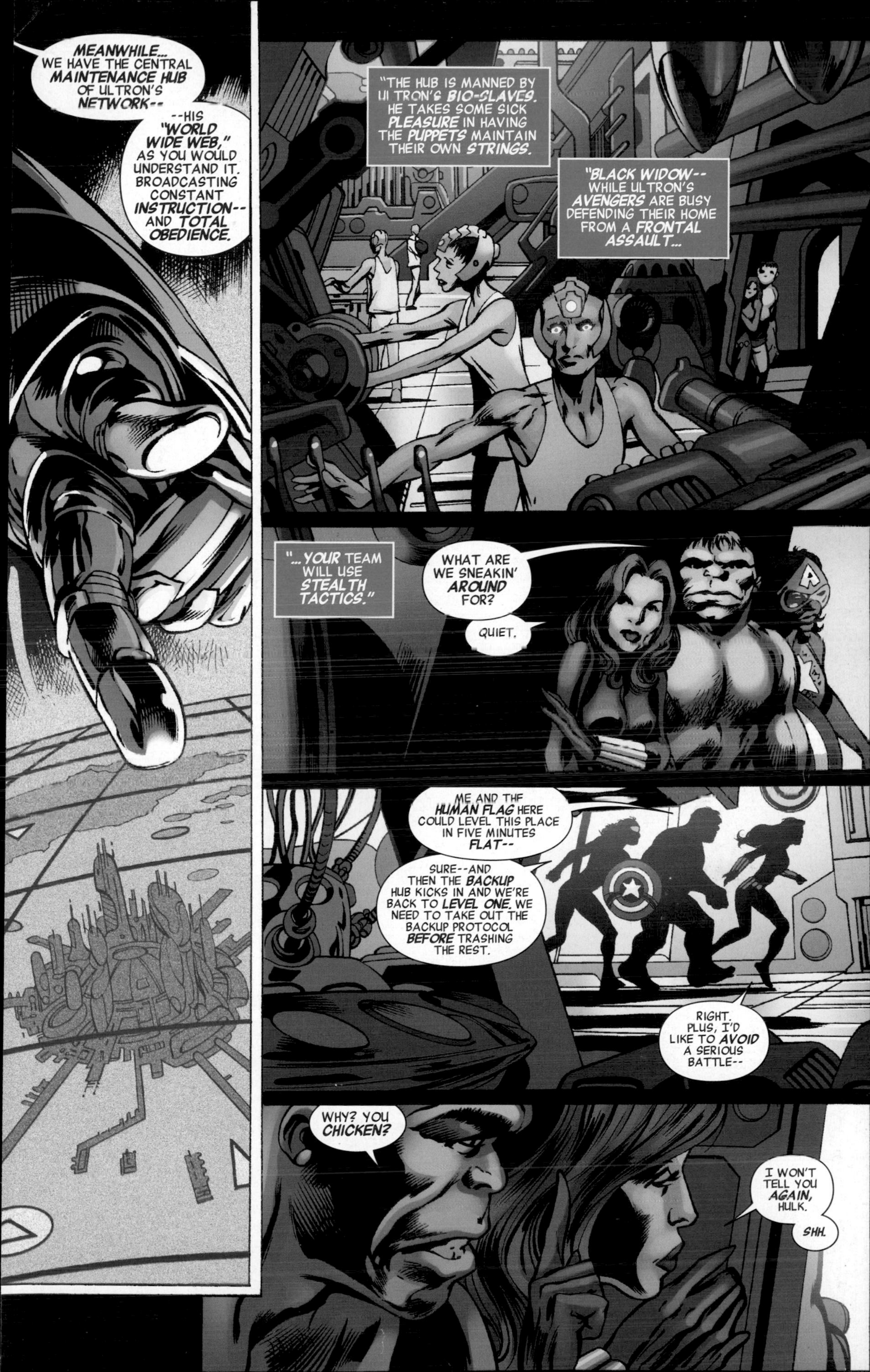
MEANWHILE... WE HAVE THE CENTRAL MAINTENANCE HUB OF ULTRON'S NETWORK--
--HIS "WORLD WIDE WEB," AS YOU WOULD UNDERSTAND IT. BROADCASTING CONSTANT INSTRUCTION-- AND TOTAL OBEDIENCE.
"THE HUB IS MANNED BY ULTRON'S BIO-SLAVES. HE TAKES SOME SICK PLEASURE IN HAVING THE PUPPETS MAINTAIN THEIR OWN STRINGS.
"BLACK WIDOW-- WHILE ULTRON'S AVENGERS ARE BUSY DEFENDING THEIR HOME FROM A FRONTAL ASSAULT...
"...YOUR TEAM WILL USE STEALTH TACTICS."
WHAT ARE WE SNEAKIN' AROUND FOR?
QUIET.
ME AND THE HUMAN FLAG HERE COULD LEVEL THIS PLACE IN FIVE MINUTES FLAT--
SURE--AND THEN THE BACKUP HUB KICKS IN AND WE'RE BACK TO LEVEL ONE. WE NEED TO TAKE OUT THE BACKUP PROTOCOL BEFORE TRASHING THE REST.
RIGHT. PLUS, I'D LIKE TO AVOID A SERIOUS BATTLE--
WHY? YOU CHICKEN?
I WON'T TELL YOU AGAIN, HULK.
SHH.

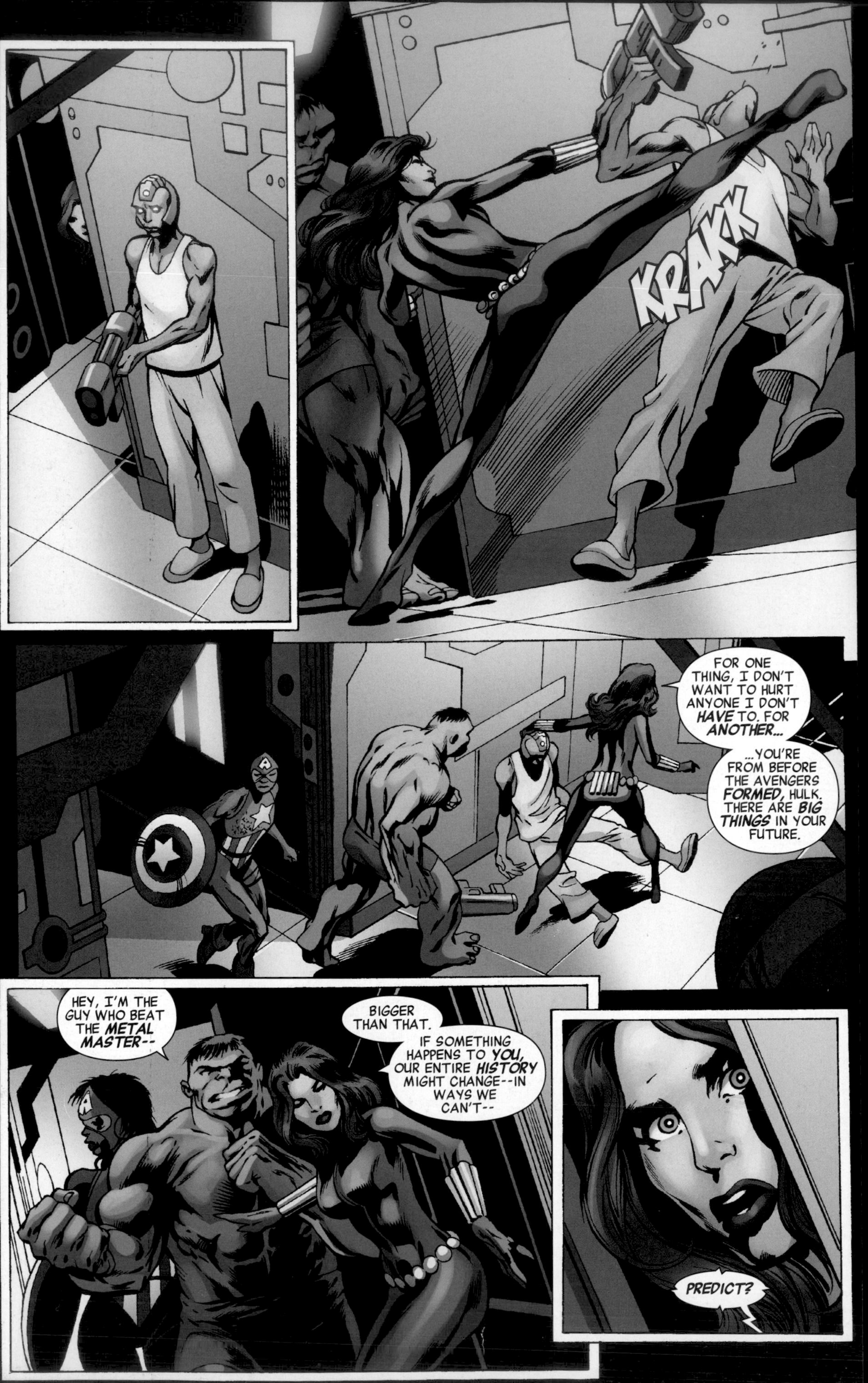
KRAKK
FOR ONE THING, I DON'T WANT TO HURT ANYONE I DON'T HAVE TO. FOR ANOTHER...
...YOU'RE FROM BEFORE THE AVENGERS FORMED, HULK. THERE ARE BIG THINGS IN YOUR FUTURE.
HEY, I'M THE GUY WHO BEAT THE METAL MASTER--
BIGGER THAN THAT.
IF SOMETHING HAPPENS TO YOU, OUR ENTIRE HISTORY MIGHT CHANGE--IN WAYS WE CAN'T--
PREDICT?

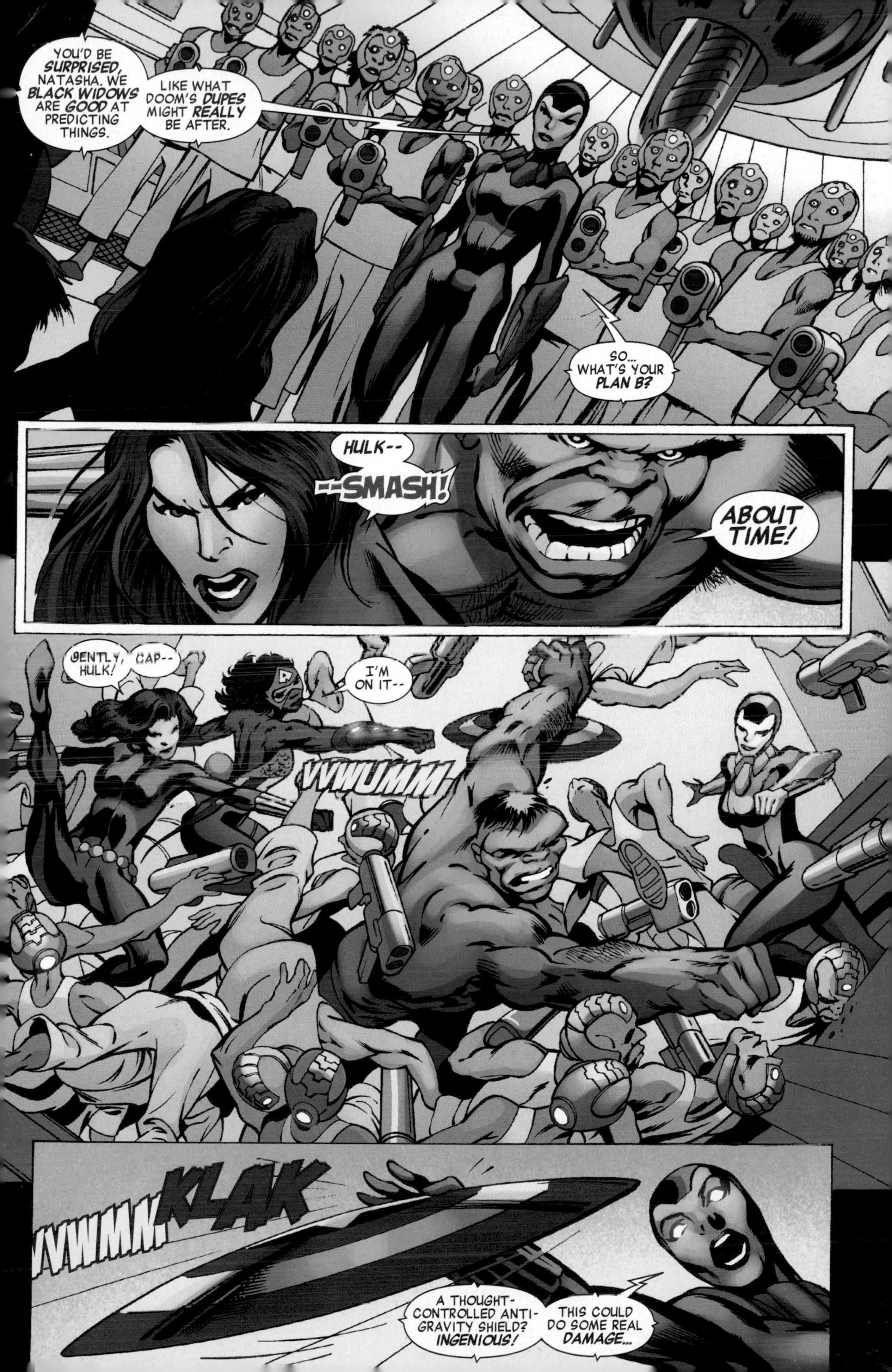
YOU'D BE SURPRISED, NATASHA. WE BLACK WIDOWS ARE GOOD AT PREDICTING THINGS.
LIKE WHAT DOOM'S DUPES MIGHT REALLY BE AFTER.
SO... WHAT'S YOUR PLAN B?
HULK--
--SMASH!
ABOUT TIME!
GENTLY, HULK!
CAP--
I'M ON IT--
VVWUMM
VVWMN
KLAK
A THOUGHT-CONTROLLED ANTI-GRAVITY SHIELD? INGENIOUS!
THIS COULD DO SOME REAL DAMAGE...

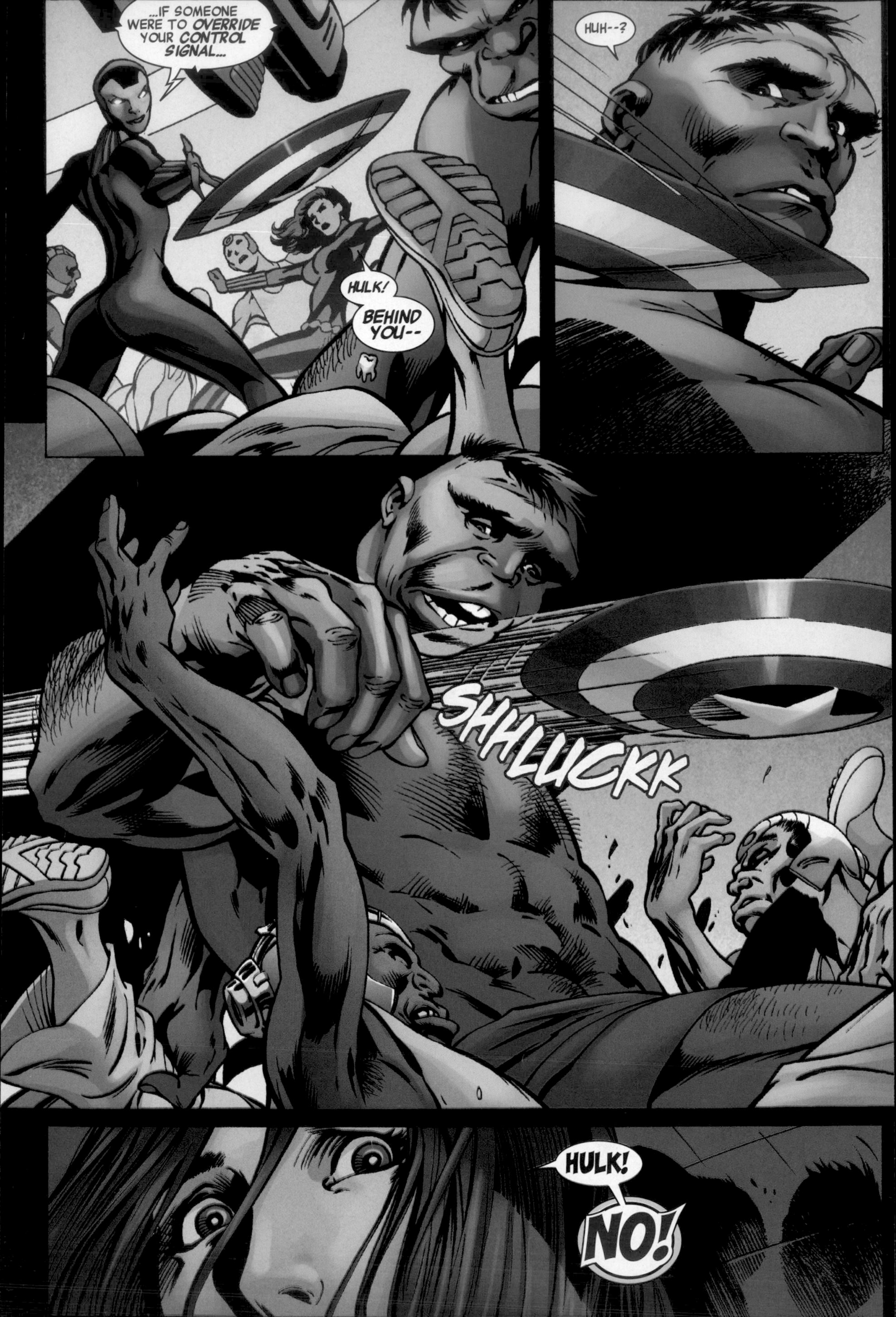
...IF SOMEONE WERE TO OVERRIDE YOUR CONTROL SIGNAL...
HULK!
BEHIND YOU--
HUH--?
SHHLUCKK
HULK!
NO!

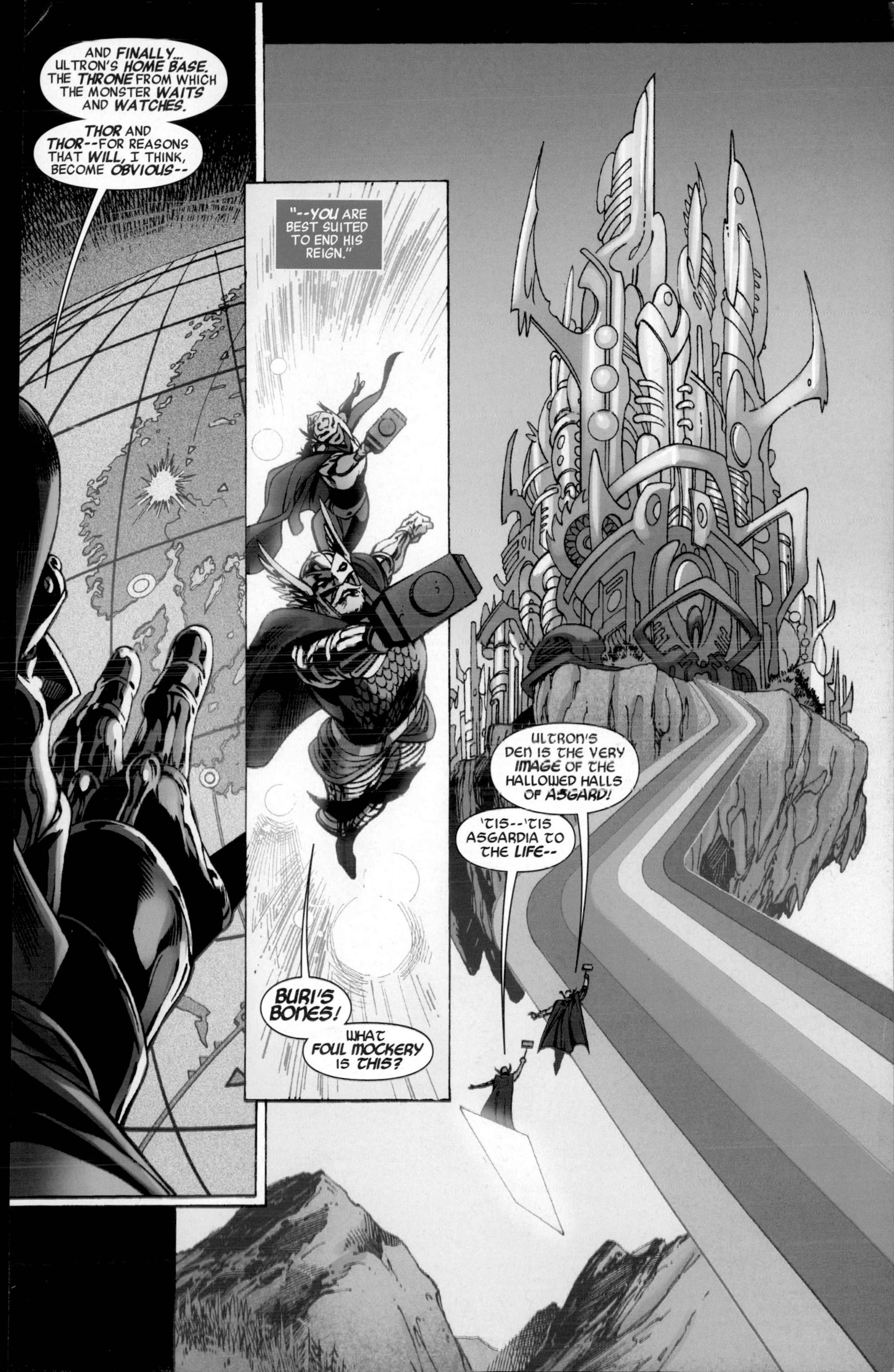
AND FINALLY... ULTRON'S HOME BASE. THE THRONE FROM WHICH THE MONSTER WAITS AND WATCHES.
THOR AND THOR--FOR REASONS THAT WILL, I THINK, BECOME OBVIOUS--
"--YOU ARE BEST SUITED TO END HIS REIGN."
BURI'S BONES!
WHAT FOUL MOCKERY IS THIS?
ULTRON'S DEN IS THE VERY IMAGE OF THE HALLOWED HALLS OF ASGARD!
'TIS--'TIS ASGARDIA TO THE LIFE--

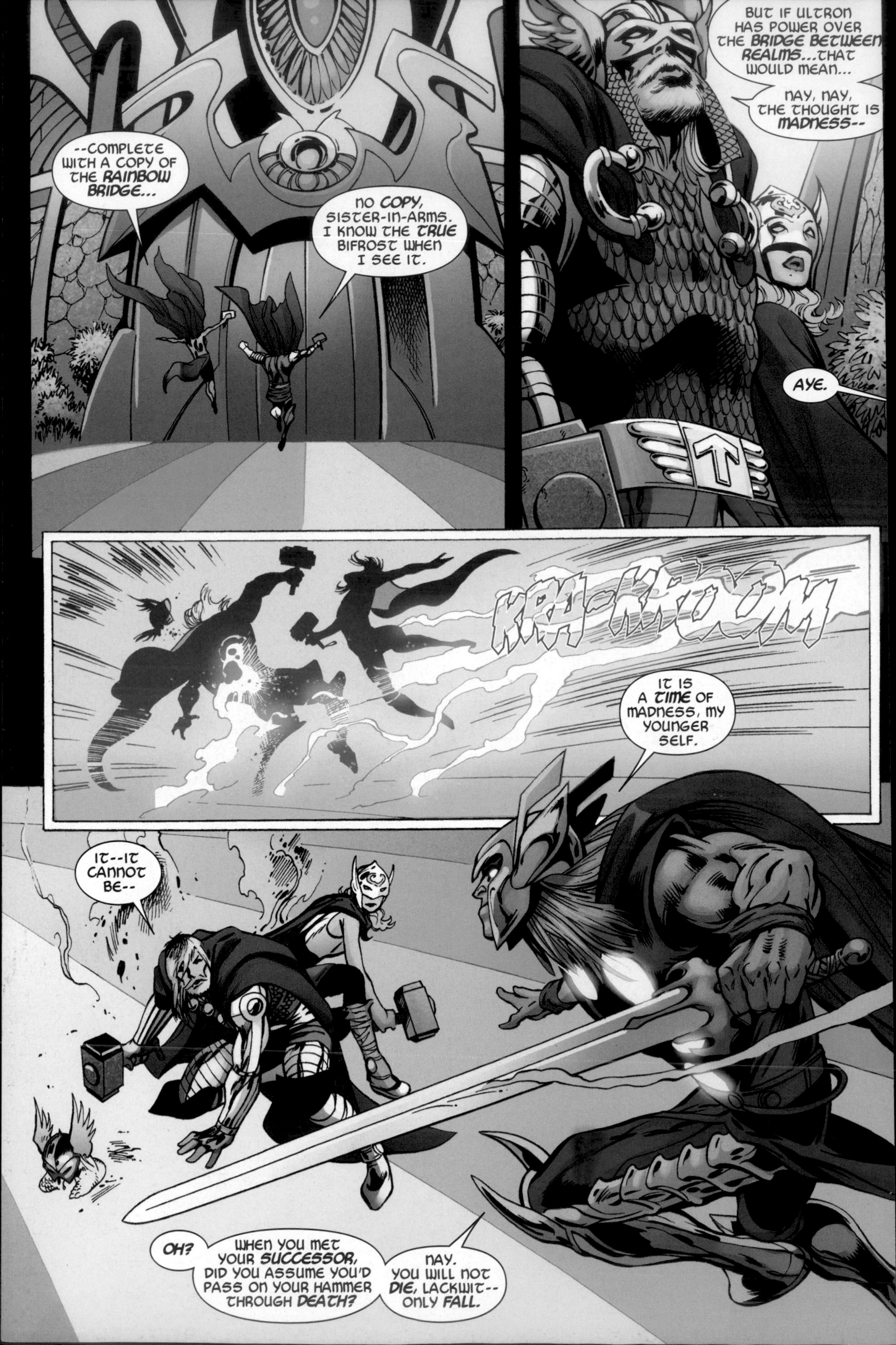
--COMPLETE WITH A COPY OF THE RAINBOW BRIDGE...
NO COPY, SISTER-IN-ARMS. I KNOW THE TRUE BIFROST WHEN I SEE IT.
BUT IF ULTRON HAS POWER OVER THE BRIDGE BETWEEN REALMS...THAT WOULD MEAN...
NAY, NAY, THE THOUGHT IS MADNESS--
AYE.
KRA-KADOOM
IT IS A TIME OF MADNESS, MY YOUNGER SELF.
IT--IT CANNOT BE--
OH?
WHEN YOU MET YOUR SUCCESSOR, DID YOU ASSUME YOU'D PASS ON YOUR HAMMER THROUGH DEATH?
NAY. YOU WILL NOT DIE, LACKWIT-- ONLY FALL.

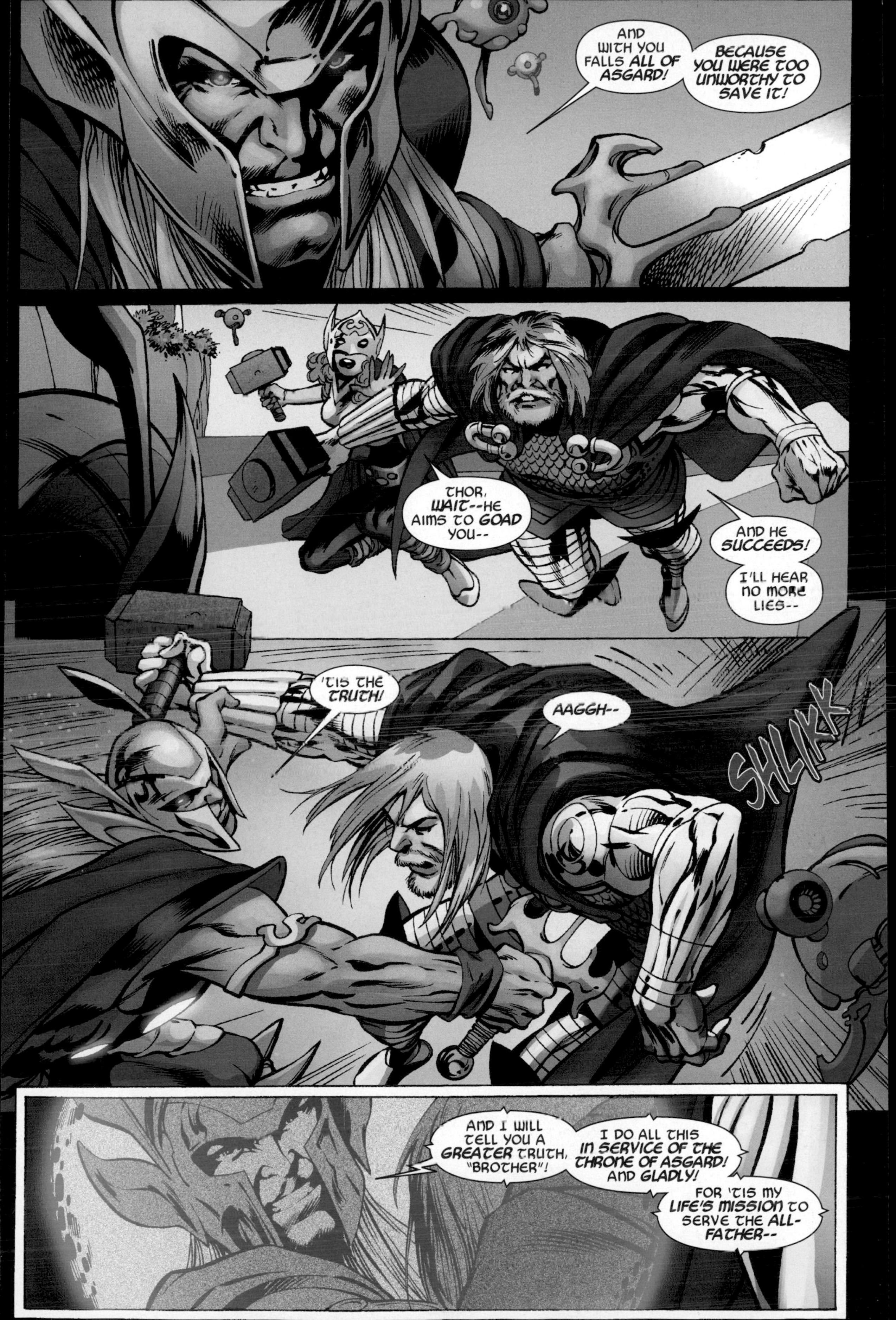
AND WITH YOU FALLS ALL OF ASGARD!
BECAUSE YOU WERE TOO UNWORTHY TO SAVE IT!
THOR, WAIT--HE AIMS TO GOAD YOU--
AND HE SUCCEEDS!
I'LL HEAR NO MORE LIES--
'TIS THE TRUTH!
AAGGH--
SHLIKK
AND I WILL TELL YOU A GREATER TRUTH, "BROTHER"!
I DO ALL THIS IN SERVICE OF THE THRONE OF ASGARD! AND GLADLY!
FOR 'TIS MY LIFE'S MISSION TO SERVE THE ALL-FATHER--

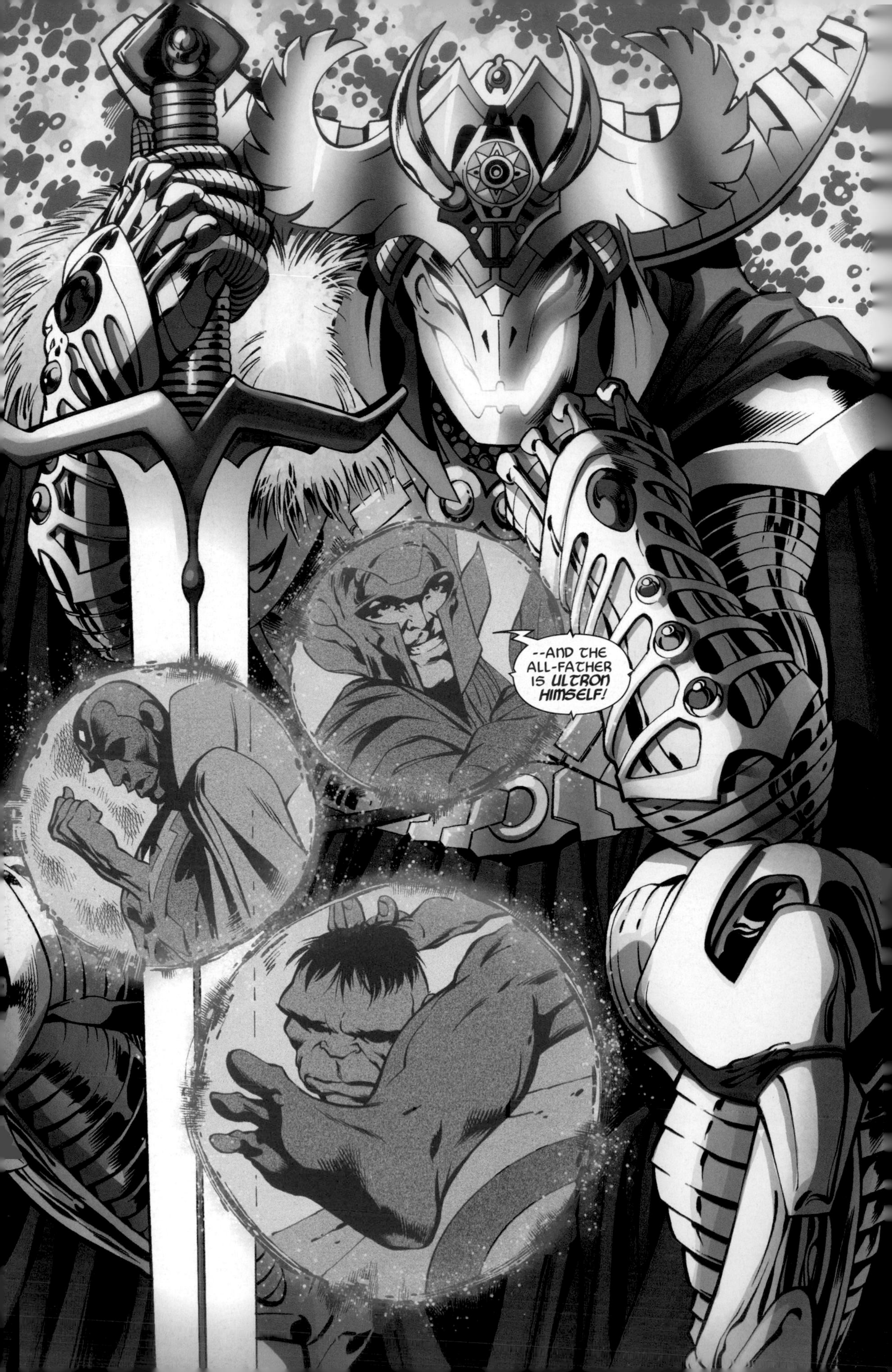
--AND THE ALL-FATHER IS ULTRON HIMSELF!

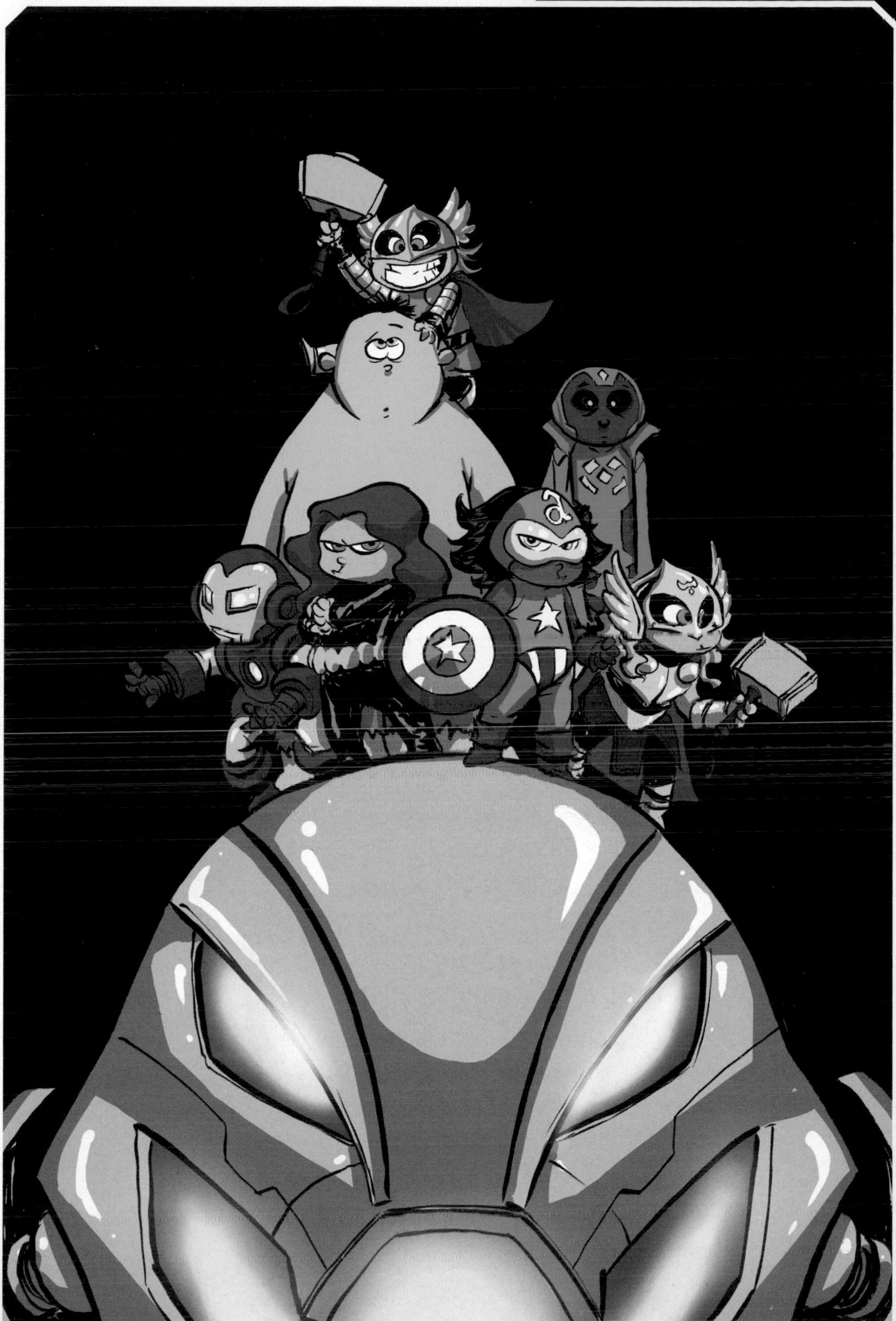

AVENGERS: ULTRON FOREVER #1 VARIANT

by SKOTTIE YOUNG

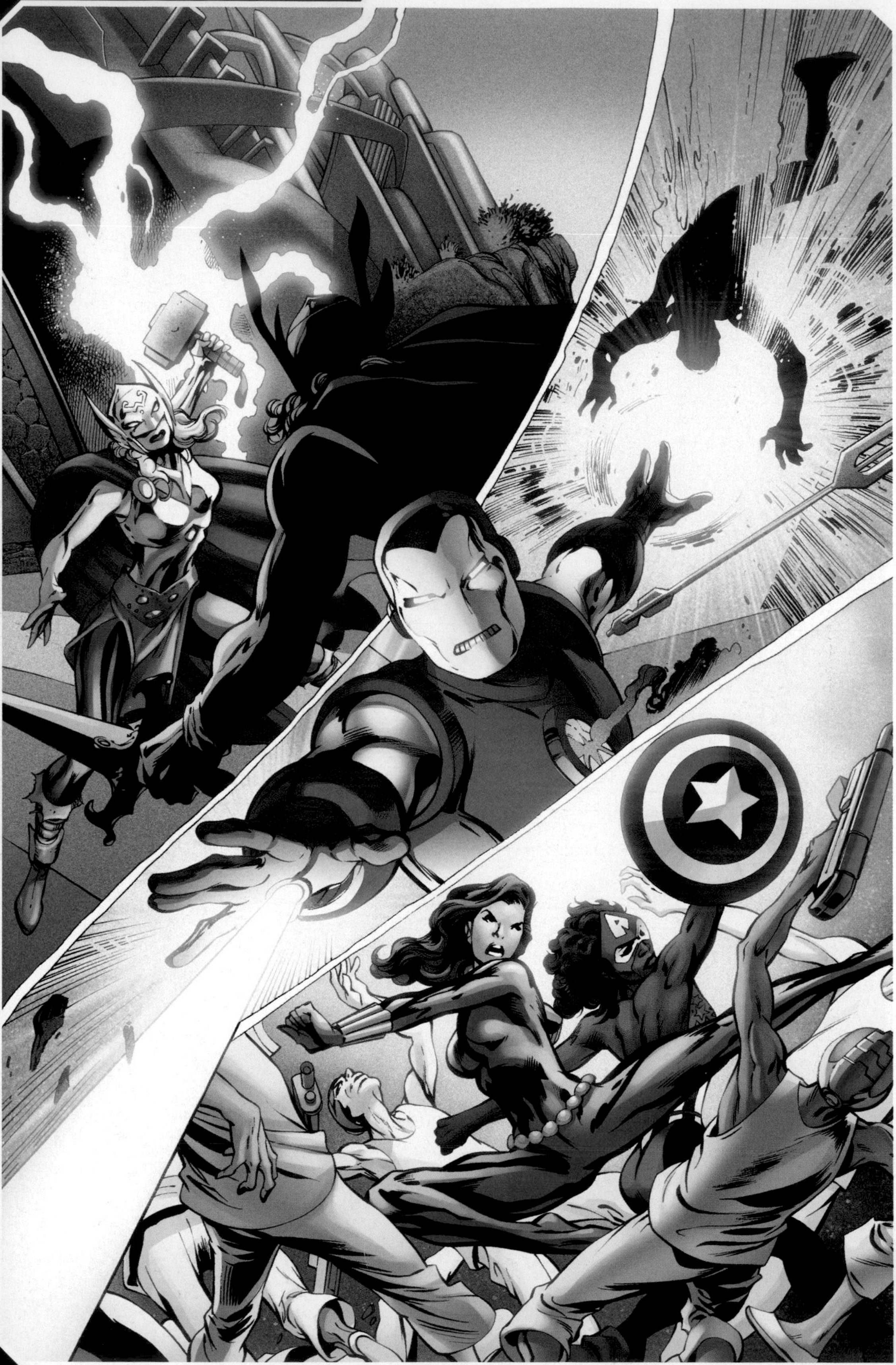

NEW AVENGERS: ULTRON FOREVER #1

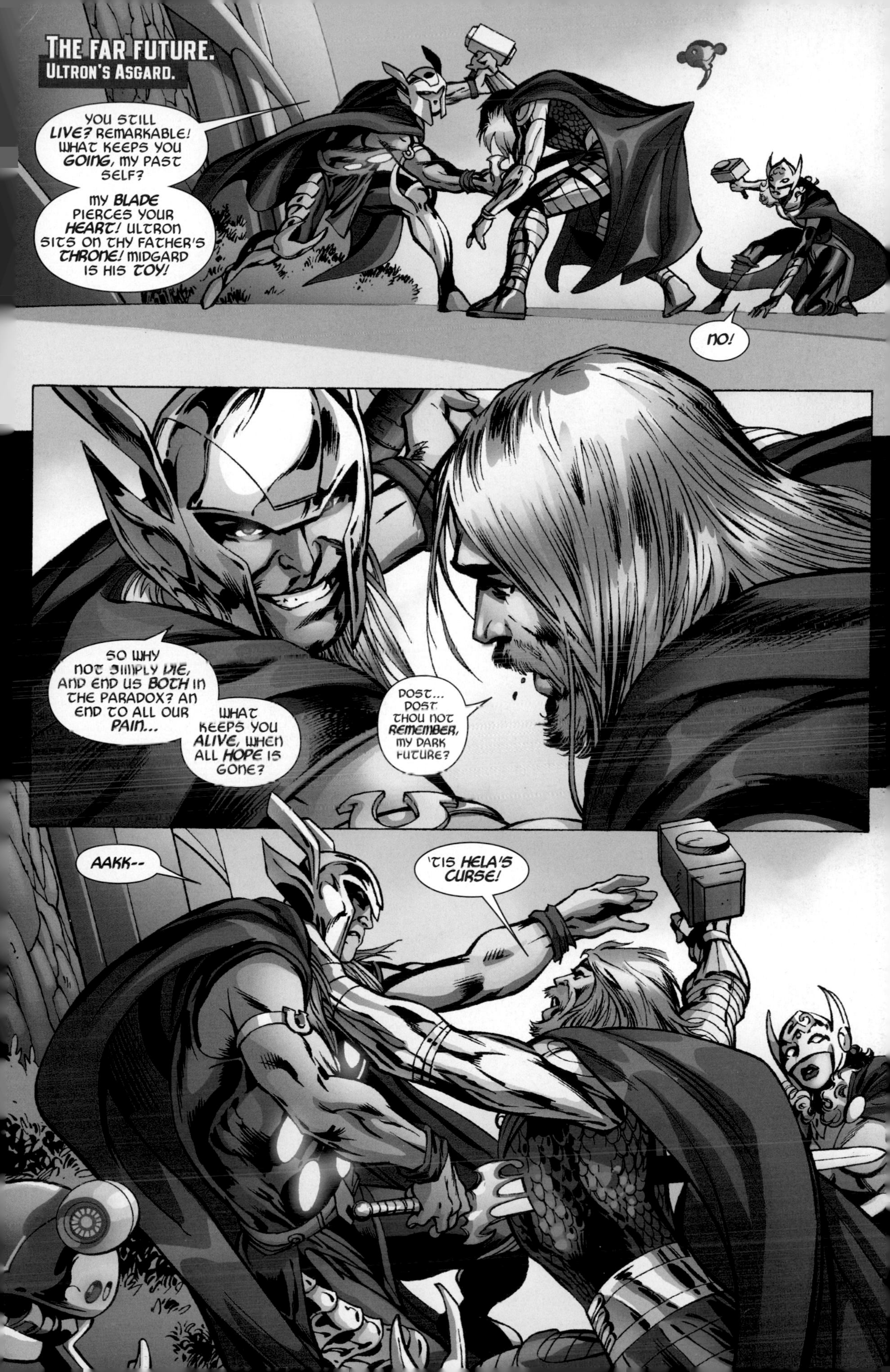
THE FAR FUTURE.
ULTRON'S ASGARD.
YOU STILL LIVE? REMARKABLE! WHAT KEEPS YOU GOING, MY PAST SELF?
MY BLADE PIERCES YOUR HEART! ULTRON SITS ON THY FATHER'S THRONE! MIDGARD IS HIS TOY!
NO!
SO WHY NOT SIMPLY DIE, AND END US BOTH IN THE PARADOX? AN END TO ALL OUR PAIN...
WHAT KEEPS YOU ALIVE, WHEN ALL HOPE IS GONE?
DOST... DOST THOU NOT REMEMBER, MY DARK FUTURE?
AAKK--
'TIS HELA'S CURSE!

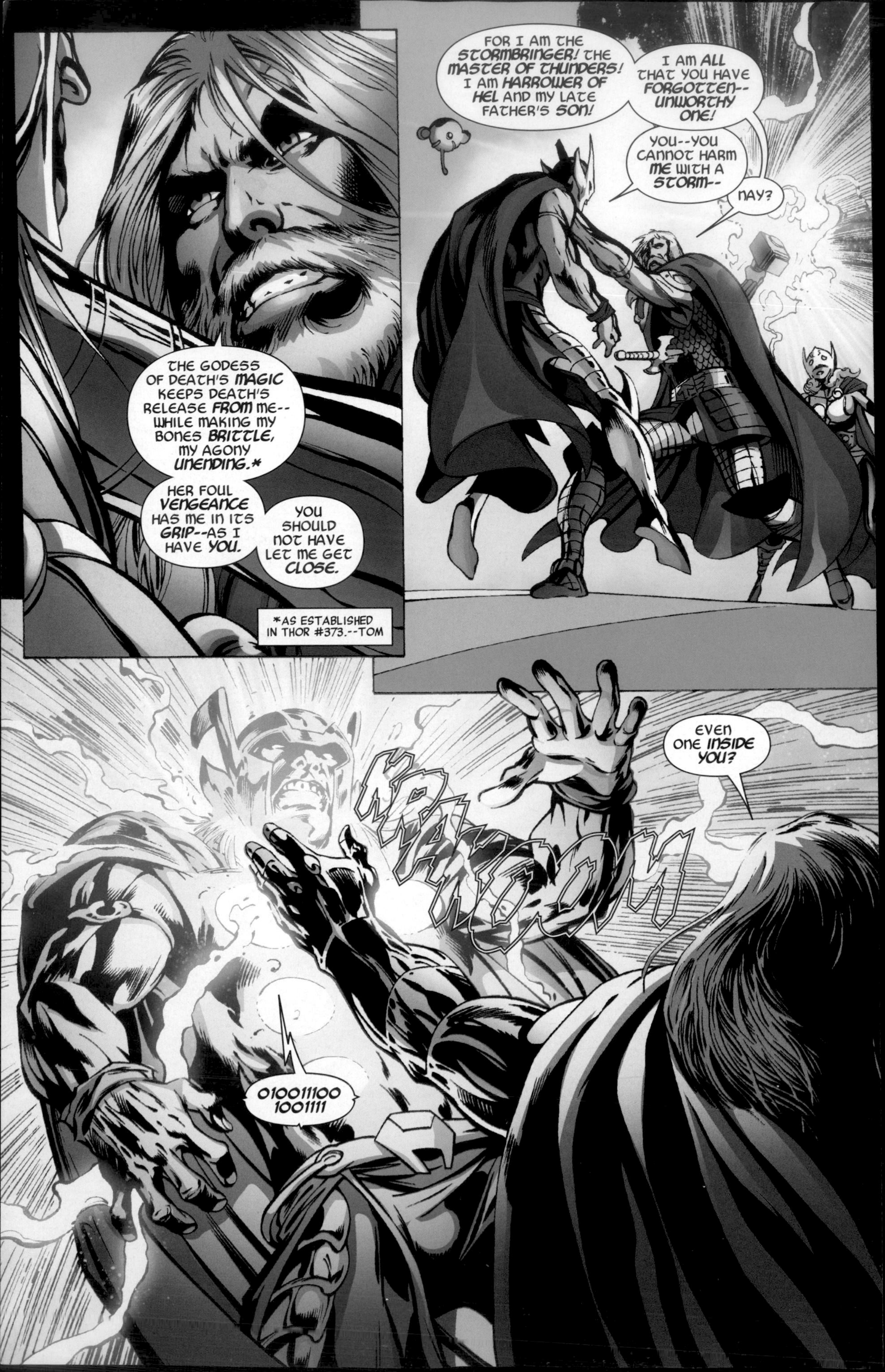
THE GODESS OF DEATH'S MAGIC KEEPS DEATH'S RELEASE FROM ME-- WHILE MAKING MY BONES BRITTLE, MY AGONY UNENDING.*
HER FOUL VENGEANCE HAS ME IN ITS GRIP--AS I HAVE YOU.
YOU SHOULD NOT HAVE LET ME GET CLOSE.
*AS ESTABLISHED IN THOR #373.--TOM
FOR I AM THE STORMBRINGER! THE MASTER OF THUNDERS! I AM HARROWER OF HEL AND MY LATE FATHER'S SON!
I AM ALL THAT YOU HAVE FORGOTTEN-- UNWORTHY ONE!
YOU--YOU CANNOT HARM ME WITH A STORM--
NAY?
EVEN ONE INSIDE YOU?
010011100 1001111

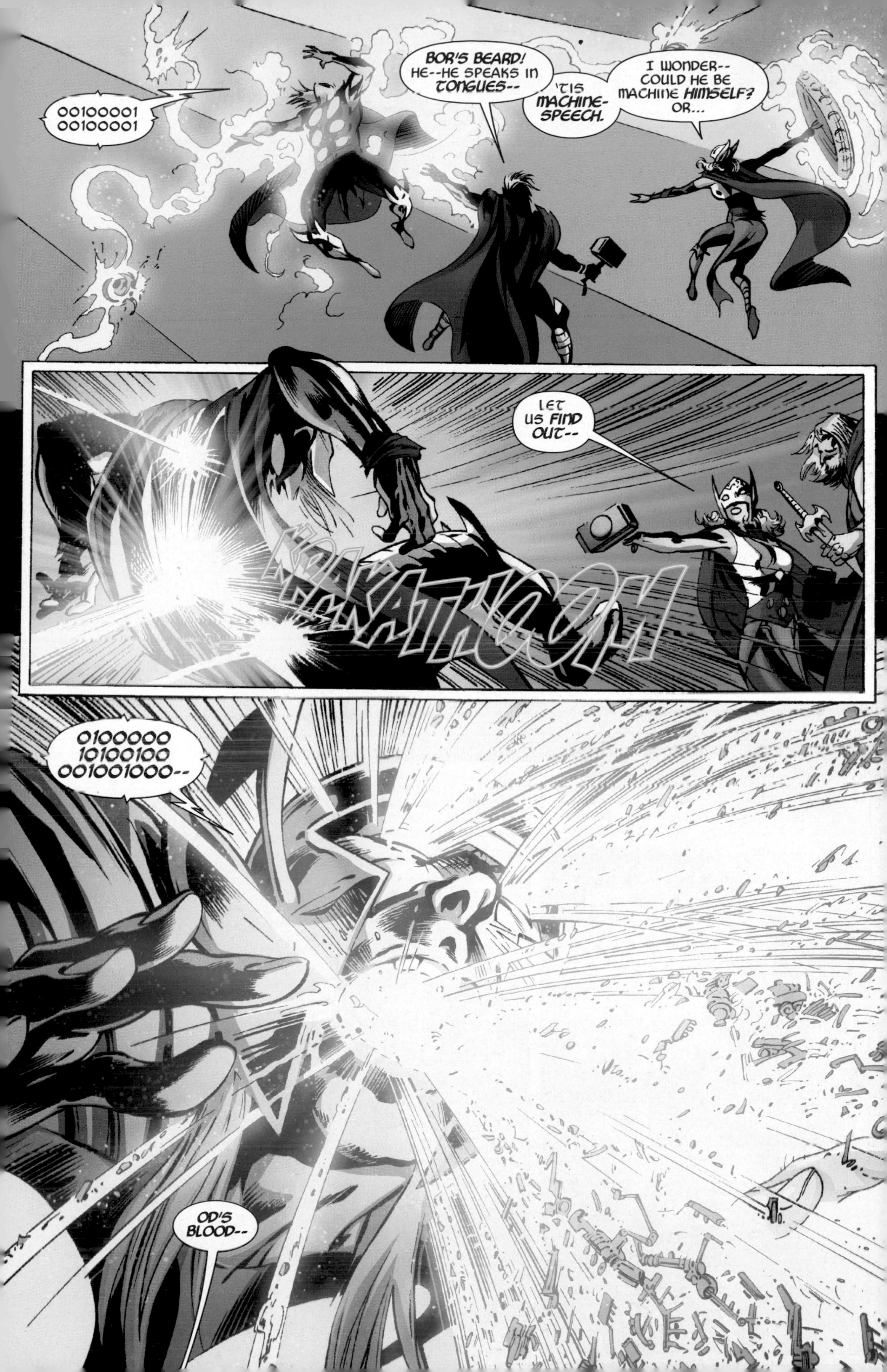
00100001 00100001
BOR'S BEARD! HE--HE SPEAKS IN TONGUES--
'TIS MACHINE-SPEECH.
I WONDER--COULD HE BE MACHINE HIMSELF? OR...
LET US FIND OUT--
0100000 10100100 001001000--
OD'S BLOOD--

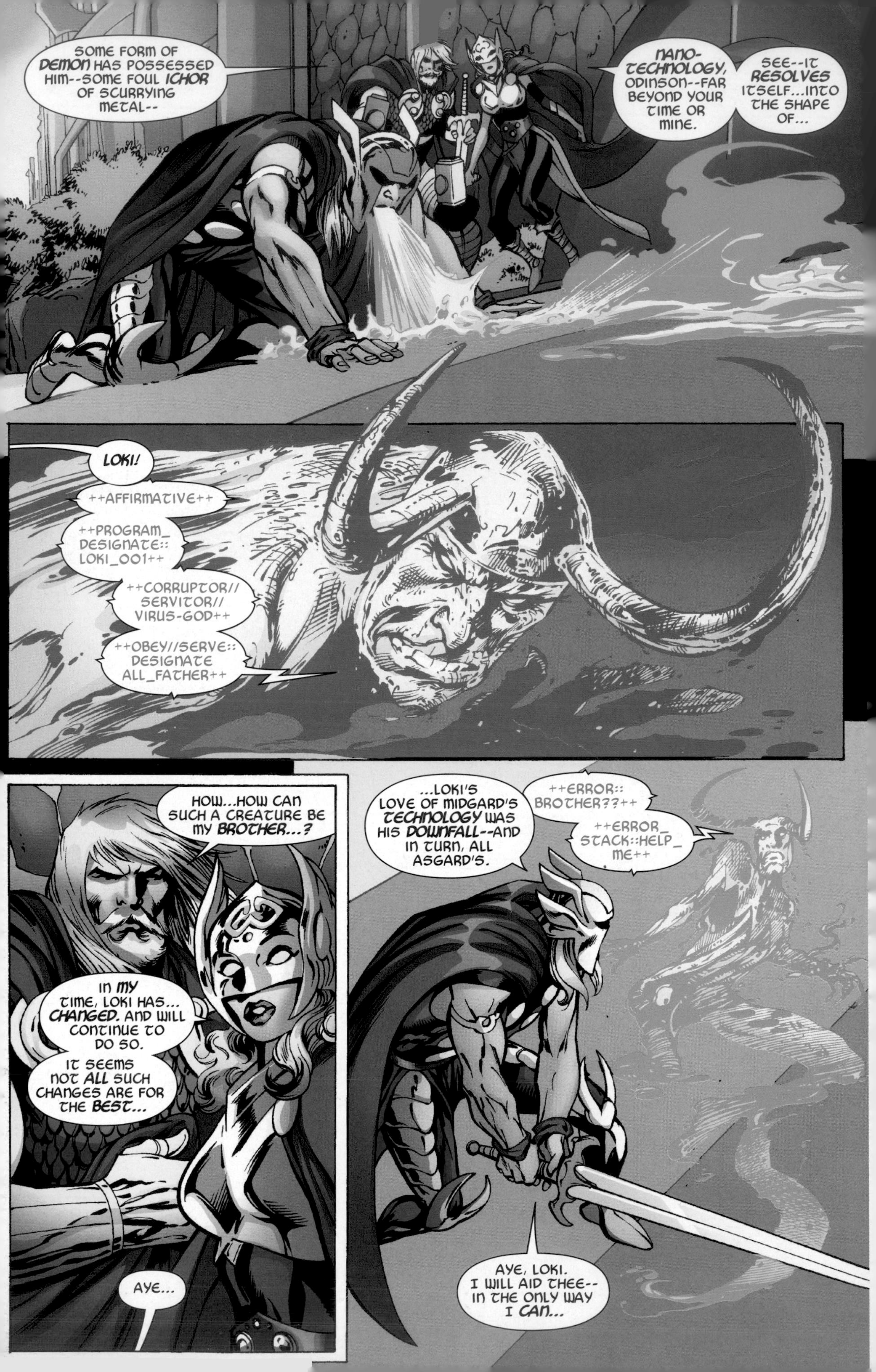
SOME FORM OF DEMON HAS POSSESSED HIM--SOME FOUL ICHOR OF SCURRYING METAL--
NANO-TECHNOLOGY, ODINSON--FAR BEYOND YOUR TIME OR MINE.
SEE--IT RESOLVES ITSELF...INTO THE SHAPE OF...
LOKI!
++AFFIRMATIVE++
++PROGRAM_ DESIGNATE:: LOKI_001++
++CORRUPTOR// SERVITOR// VIRUS-GOD++
++OBEY//SERVE:: DESIGNATE ALL_FATHER++
HOW...HOW CAN SUCH A CREATURE BE MY BROTHER...?
IN MY TIME, LOKI HAS... CHANGED. AND WILL CONTINUE TO DO SO.
IT SEEMS NOT ALL SUCH CHANGES ARE FOR THE BEST...
AYE...
...LOKI'S LOVE OF MIDGARD'S TECHNOLOGY WAS HIS DOWNFALL--AND IN TURN, ALL ASGARD'S.
++ERROR:: BROTHER??++
++ERROR_ STACK::HELP_ ME++
AYE, LOKI. I WILL AID THEE--IN THE ONLY WAY I CAN...

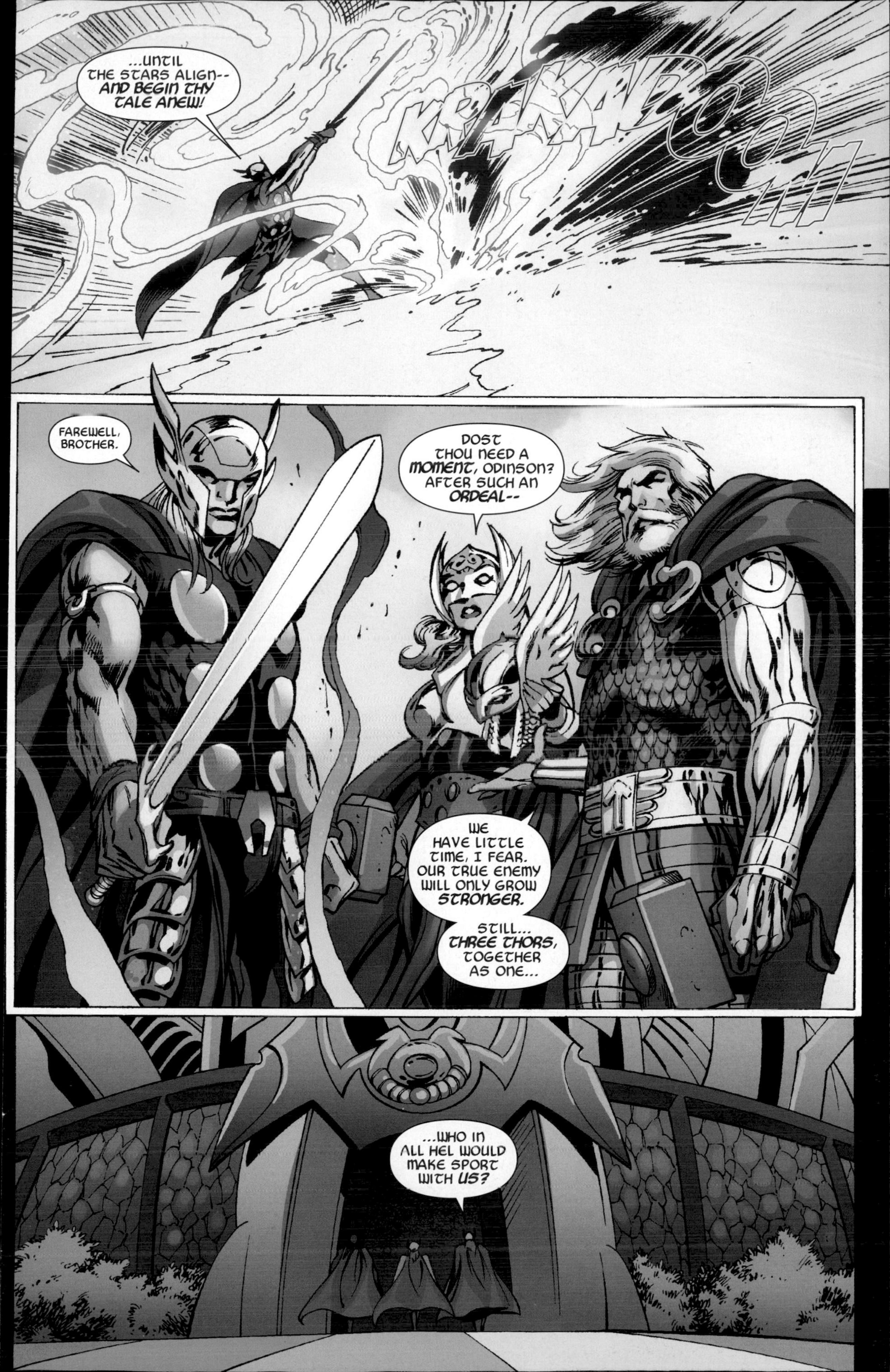
...UNTIL THE STARS ALIGN-- AND BEGIN THY TALE ANEW!
KRAKADOOM!!!
FAREWELL, BROTHER.
DOST THOU NEED A MOMENT, ODINSON? AFTER SUCH AN ORDEAL--
WE HAVE LITTLE TIME, I FEAR. OUR TRUE ENEMY WILL ONLY GROW STRONGER.
STILL... THREE THORS, TOGETHER AS ONE...
...WHO IN ALL HEL WOULD MAKE SPORT WITH US?

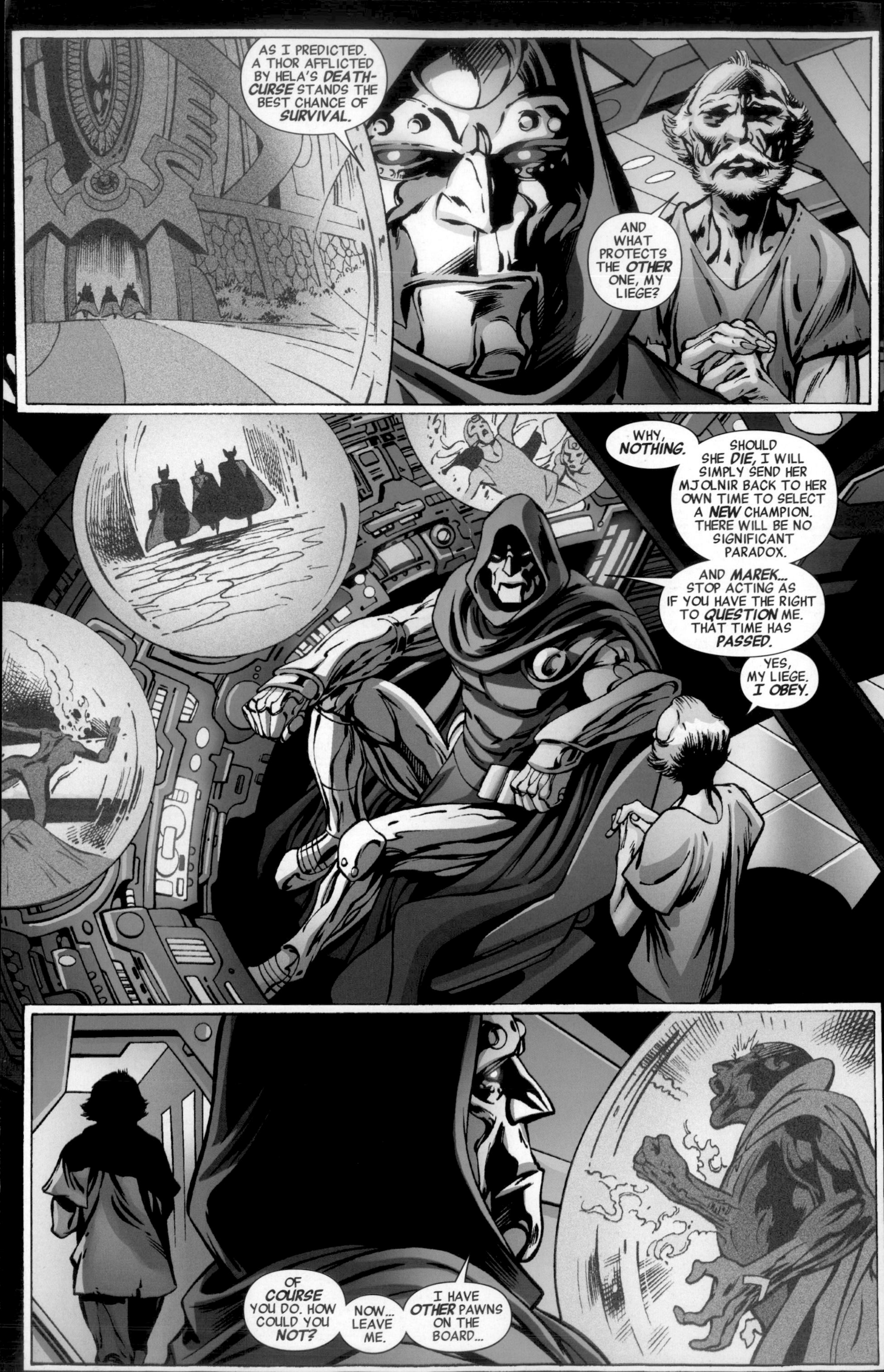
AS I PREDICTED. A THOR AFFLICTED BY HELA'S DEATH-CURSE STANDS THE BEST CHANCE OF SURVIVAL.
AND WHAT PROTECTS THE OTHER ONE, MY LIEGE?
WHY, NOTHING.
SHOULD SHE DIE, I WILL SIMPLY SEND HER MJOLNIR BACK TO HER OWN TIME TO SELECT A NEW CHAMPION. THERE WILL BE NO SIGNIFICANT PARADOX.
AND MAREK... STOP ACTING AS IF YOU HAVE THE RIGHT TO QUESTION ME. THAT TIME HAS PASSED.
YES, MY LIEGE. I OBEY.
OF COURSE YOU DO. HOW COULD YOU NOT?
NOW... LEAVE ME.
I HAVE OTHER PAWNS ON THE BOARD...

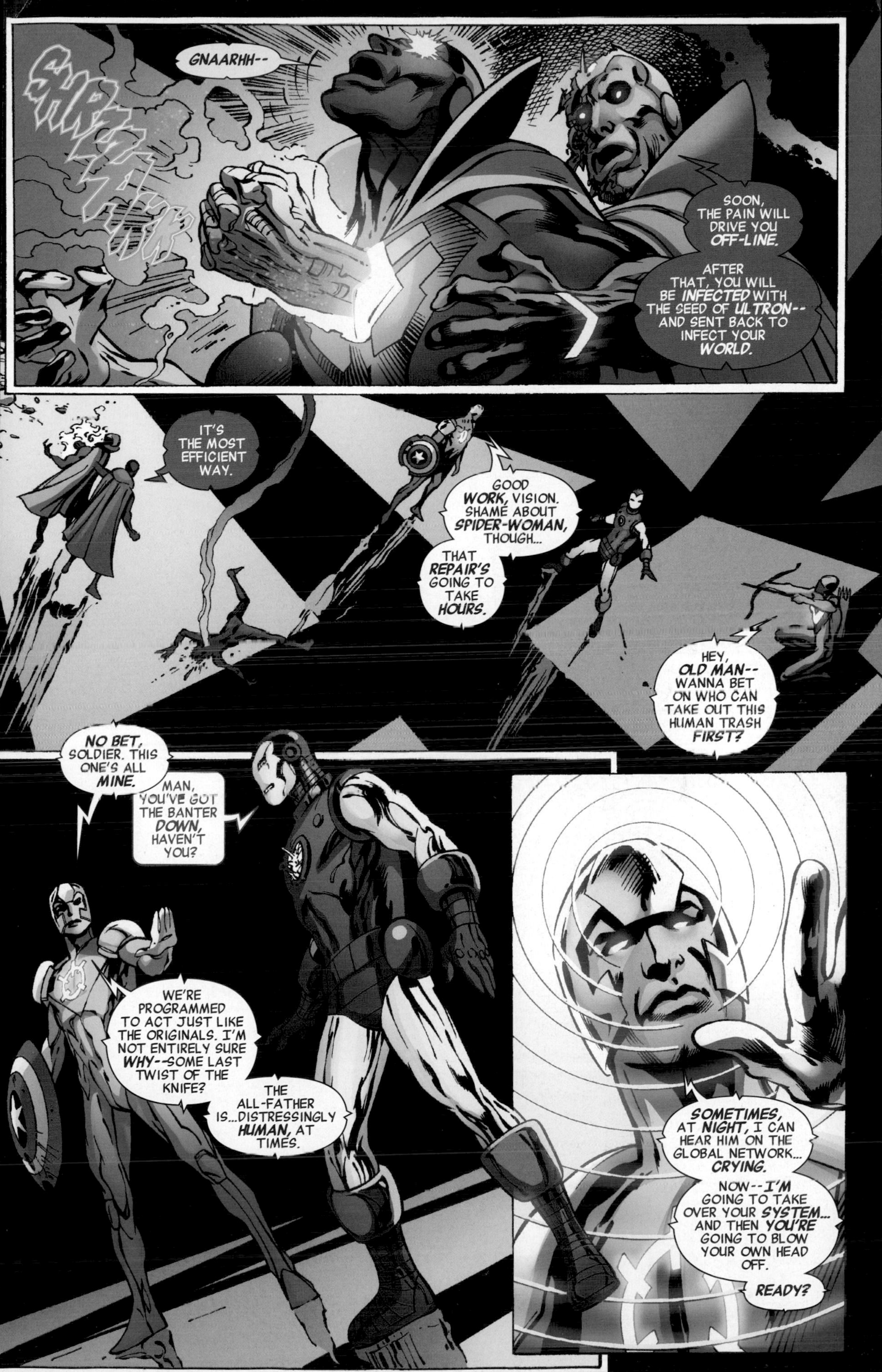
SHRZZAAK
GNAARHH--
SOON, THE PAIN WILL DRIVE YOU OFF-LINE.
AFTER THAT, YOU WILL BE INFECTED WITH THE SEED OF ULTRON--AND SENT BACK TO INFECT YOUR WORLD.
IT'S THE MOST EFFICIENT WAY.
GOOD WORK, VISION. SHAME ABOUT SPIDER-WOMAN, THOUGH...
THAT REPAIR'S GOING TO TAKE HOURS.
HEY, OLD MAN--WANNA BET ON WHO CAN TAKE OUT THIS HUMAN TRASH FIRST?
NO BET, SOLDIER. THIS ONE'S ALL MINE.
MAN, YOU'VE GOT THE BANTER DOWN, HAVEN'T YOU?
WE'RE PROGRAMMED TO ACT JUST LIKE THE ORIGINALS. I'M NOT ENTIRELY SURE WHY--SOME LAST TWIST OF THE KNIFE?
THE ALL-FATHER IS...DISTRESSINGLY HUMAN, AT TIMES.
SOMETIMES, AT NIGHT, I CAN HEAR HIM ON THE GLOBAL NETWORK... CRYING.
NOW--I'M GOING TO TAKE OVER YOUR SYSTEM... AND THEN YOU'RE GOING TO BLOW YOUR OWN HEAD OFF.
READY?

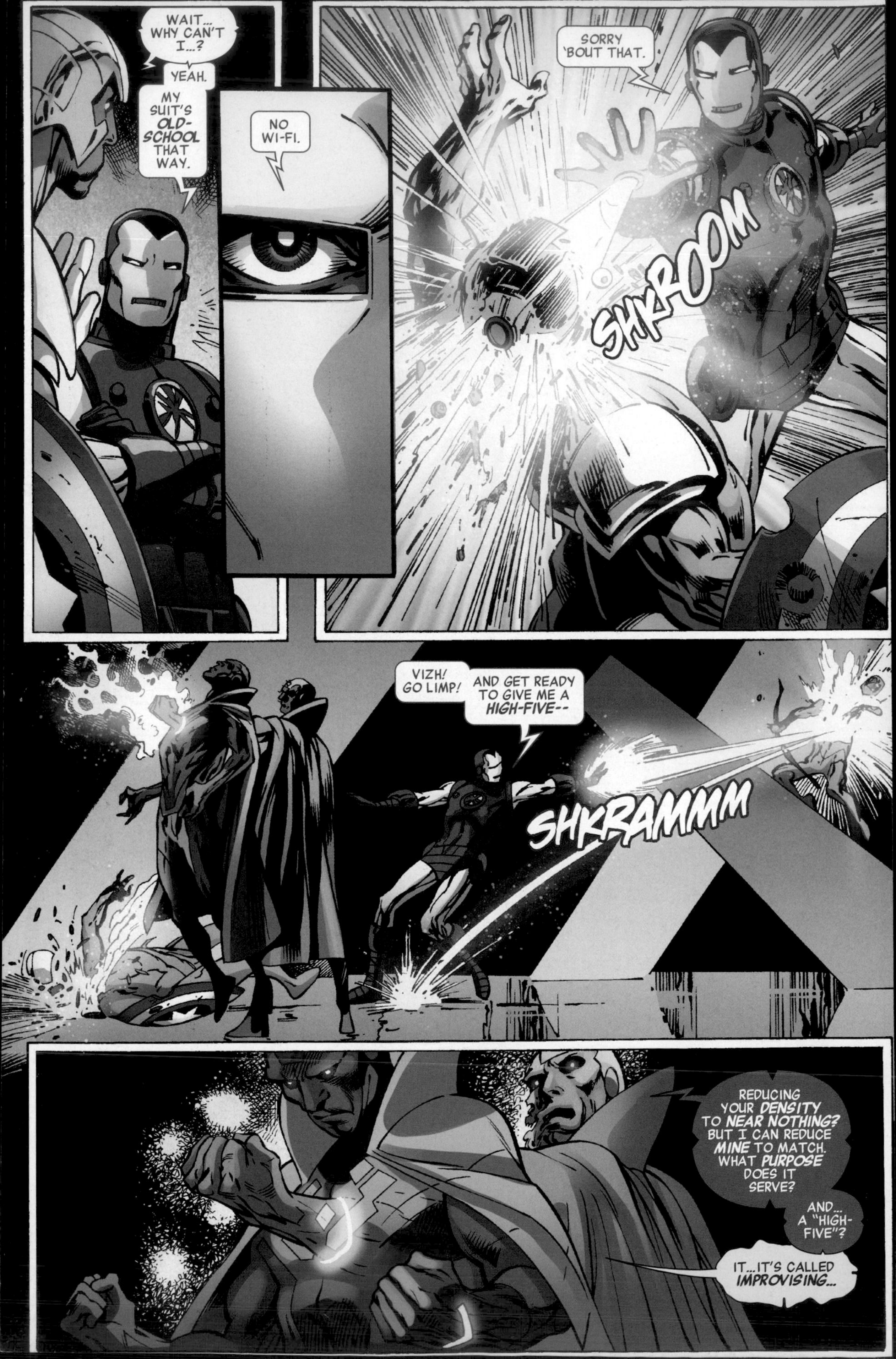
WAIT... WHY CAN'T I...?
YEAH.
MY SUIT'S OLD-SCHOOL THAT WAY.
NO WI-FI.
SORRY 'BOUT THAT.
SHKROOM
VIZH! GO LIMP!
AND GET READY TO GIVE ME A HIGH-FIVE--
SHKRAMMM
REDUCING YOUR DENSITY TO NEAR NOTHING? BUT I CAN REDUCE MINE TO MATCH. WHAT PURPOSE DOES IT SERVE?
AND... A "HIGH-FIVE"?
IT...IT'S CALLED IMPROVISING...

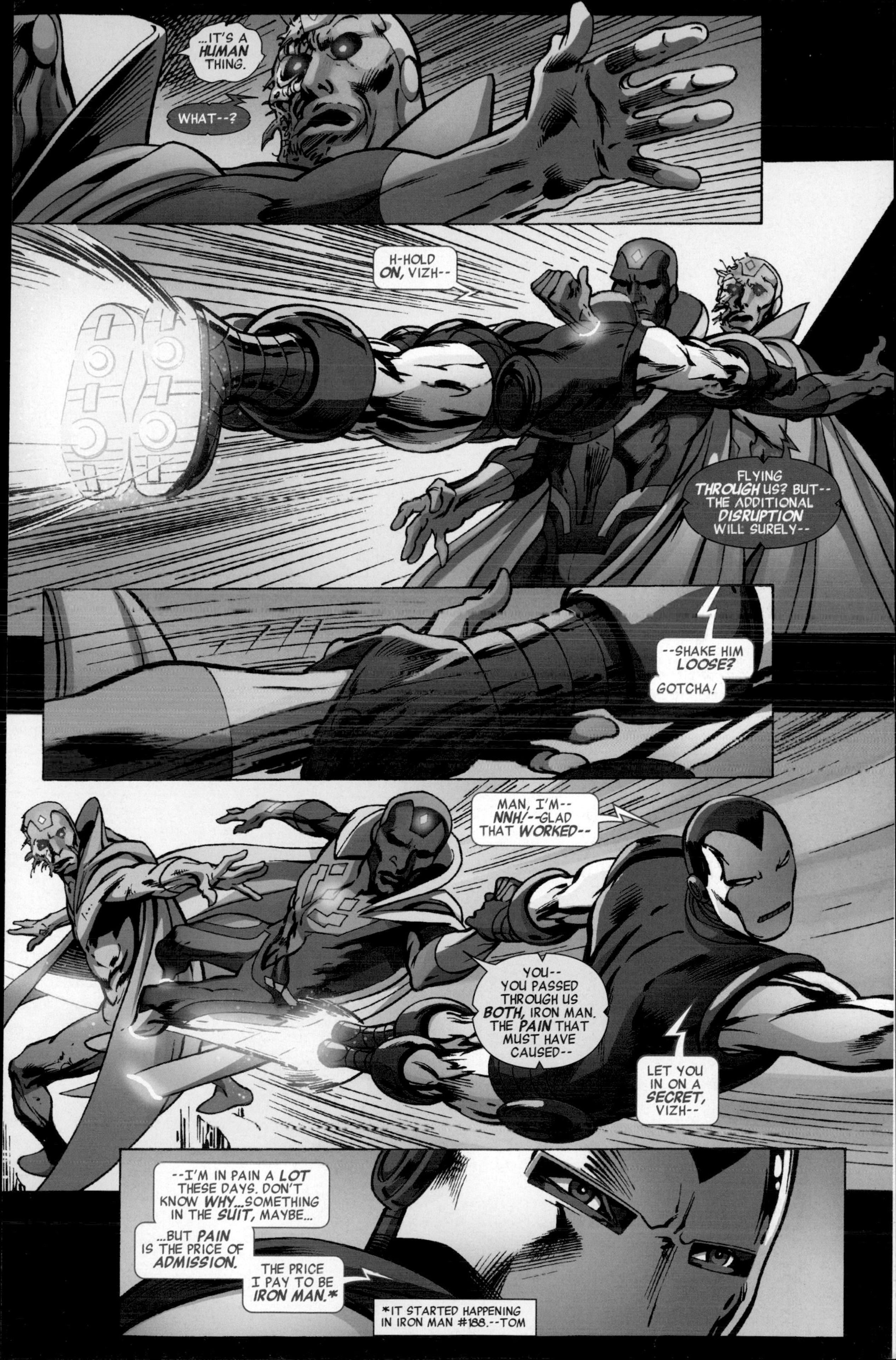
...IT'S A HUMAN THING.
WHAT--?
H-HOLD ON, VIZH--
FLYING THROUGH US? BUT-- THE ADDITIONAL DISRUPTION WILL SURELY--
--SHAKE HIM LOOSE?
GOTCHA!
MAN, I'M-- NNH!--GLAD THAT WORKED--
YOU-- YOU PASSED THROUGH US BOTH, IRON MAN. THE PAIN THAT MUST HAVE CAUSED--
LET YOU IN ON A SECRET, VIZH--
--I'M IN PAIN A LOT THESE DAYS. DON'T KNOW WHY...SOMETHING IN THE SUIT, MAYBE...
...BUT PAIN IS THE PRICE OF ADMISSION.
THE PRICE I PAY TO BE IRON MAN.*
*IT STARTED HAPPENING IN IRON MAN #188.--TOM

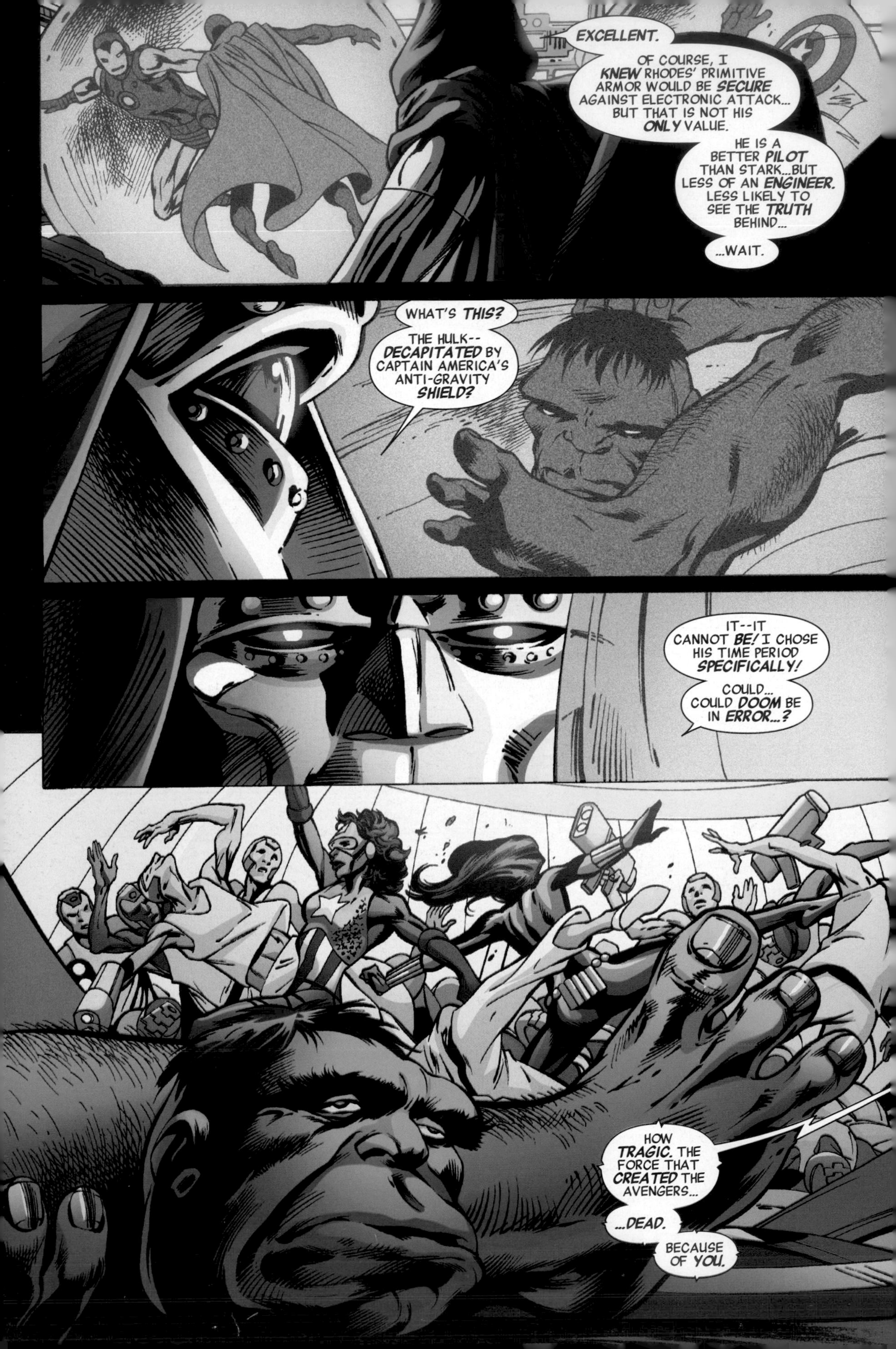
EXCELLENT.
OF COURSE, I KNEW RHODES' PRIMITIVE ARMOR WOULD BE SECURE AGAINST ELECTRONIC ATTACK... BUT THAT IS NOT HIS ONLY VALUE.
HE IS A BETTER PILOT THAN STARK...BUT LESS OF AN ENGINEER. LESS LIKELY TO SEE THE TRUTH BEHIND...
...WAIT.
WHAT'S THIS?
THE HULK-- DECAPITATED BY CAPTAIN AMERICA'S ANTI-GRAVITY SHIELD?
IT--IT CANNOT BE! I CHOSE HIS TIME PERIOD SPECIFICALLY!
COULD... COULD DOOM BE IN ERROR...?
HOW TRAGIC. THE FORCE THAT CREATED THE AVENGERS...
...DEAD.
BECAUSE OF YOU.

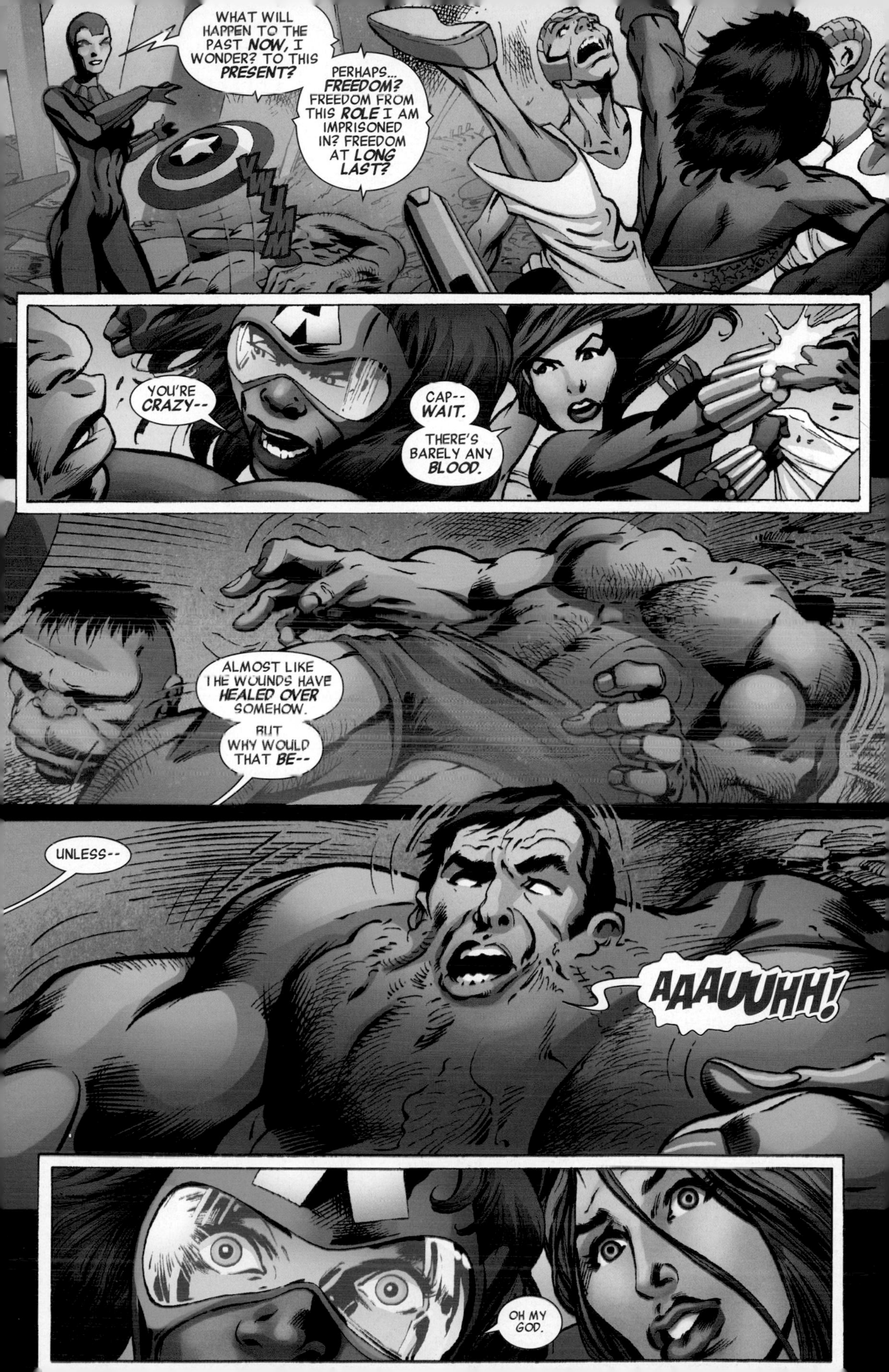

WHAT WILL HAPPEN TO THE PAST NOW, I WONDER? TO THIS PRESENT?
PERHAPS... FREEDOM? FREEDOM FROM THIS ROLE I AM IMPRISONED IN? FREEDOM AT LONG LAST?
VVUMM
YOU'RE CRAZY--
CAP-- WAIT.
THERE'S BARELY ANY BLOOD.
ALMOST LIKE THE WOUNDS HAVE HEALED OVER SOMEHOW.
BUT WHY WOULD THAT BE--
UNLESS--
AAAUUHH!
OH MY GOD.

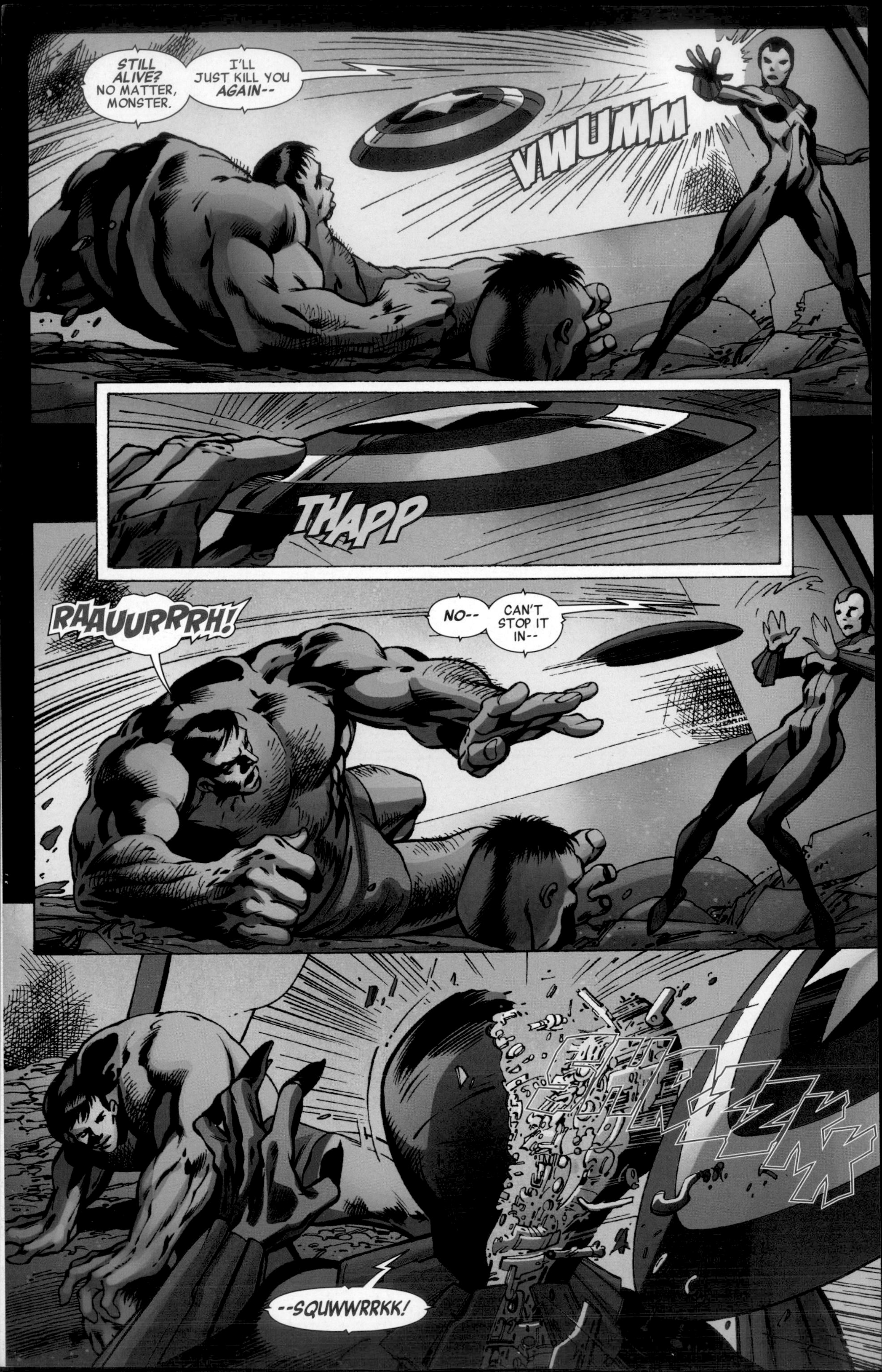
STILL ALIVE? NO MATTER, MONSTER.
I'LL JUST KILL YOU AGAIN--
VWUMM
THAPP
RAAUURRRH!
NO--
CAN'T STOP IT IN--
--SQUWWRRKK!

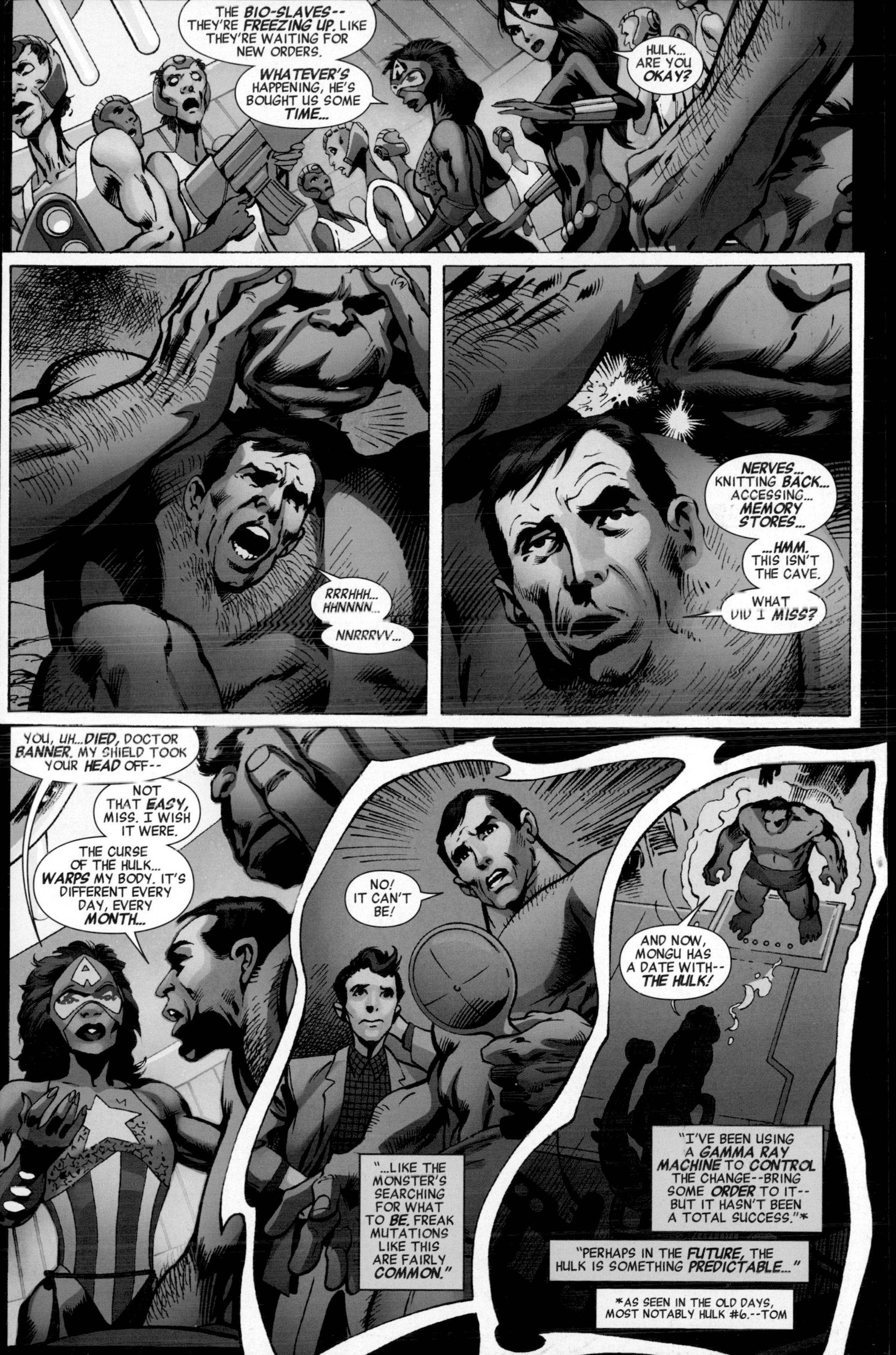
THE BIO-SLAVES-- THEY'RE FREEZING UP. LIKE THEY'RE WAITING FOR NEW ORDERS.
WHATEVER'S HAPPENING, HE'S BOUGHT US SOME TIME...
HULK... ARE YOU OKAY?
RRRHHH... HHNNNN...
NNRRRVV...
NERVES... KNITTING BACK... ACCESSING... MEMORY STORES...
...HMM. THIS ISN'T THE CAVE.
WHAT DID I MISS?
YOU, UH...DIED, DOCTOR BANNER. MY SHIELD TOOK YOUR HEAD OFF--
NOT THAT EASY, MISS. I WISH IT WERE.
THE CURSE OF THE HULK... WARPS MY BODY. IT'S DIFFERENT EVERY DAY, EVERY MONTH...
"...LIKE THE MONSTER'S SEARCHING FOR WHAT TO BE. FREAK MUTATIONS LIKE THIS ARE FAIRLY COMMON."
NO! IT CAN'T BE!
AND NOW, MONGU HAS A DATE WITH-- THE HULK!
"I'VE BEEN USING A GAMMA RAY MACHINE TO CONTROL THE CHANGE--BRING SOME ORDER TO IT-- BUT IT HASN'T BEEN A TOTAL SUCCESS."*
"PERHAPS IN THE FUTURE, THE HULK IS SOMETHING PREDICTABLE..."
*AS SEEN IN THE OLD DAYS, MOST NOTABLY HULK #6.--TOM

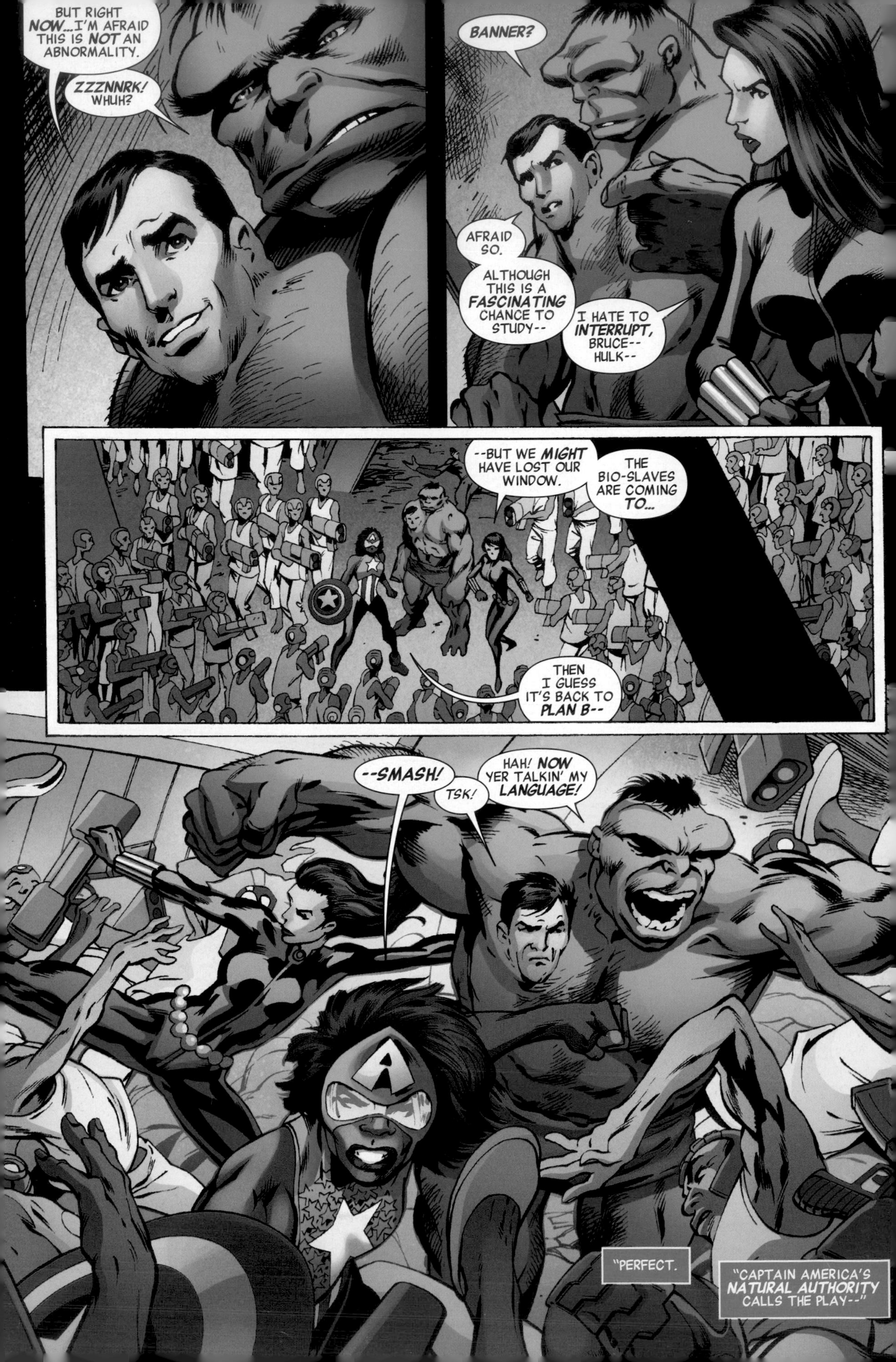

BUT RIGHT NOW...I'M AFRAID THIS IS NOT AN ABNORMALITY.
ZZZNNRK! WHUH?
BANNER?
AFRAID SO.
ALTHOUGH THIS IS A FASCINATING CHANCE TO STUDY--
I HATE TO INTERRUPT, BRUCE--HULK--
--BUT WE MIGHT HAVE LOST OUR WINDOW.
THE BIO-SLAVES ARE COMING TO...
THEN I GUESS IT'S BACK TO PLAN B--
--SMASH!
TSK!
HAH! NOW YER TALKIN' MY LANGUAGE!
"PERFECT.
"CAPTAIN AMERICA'S NATURAL AUTHORITY CALLS THE PLAY--"

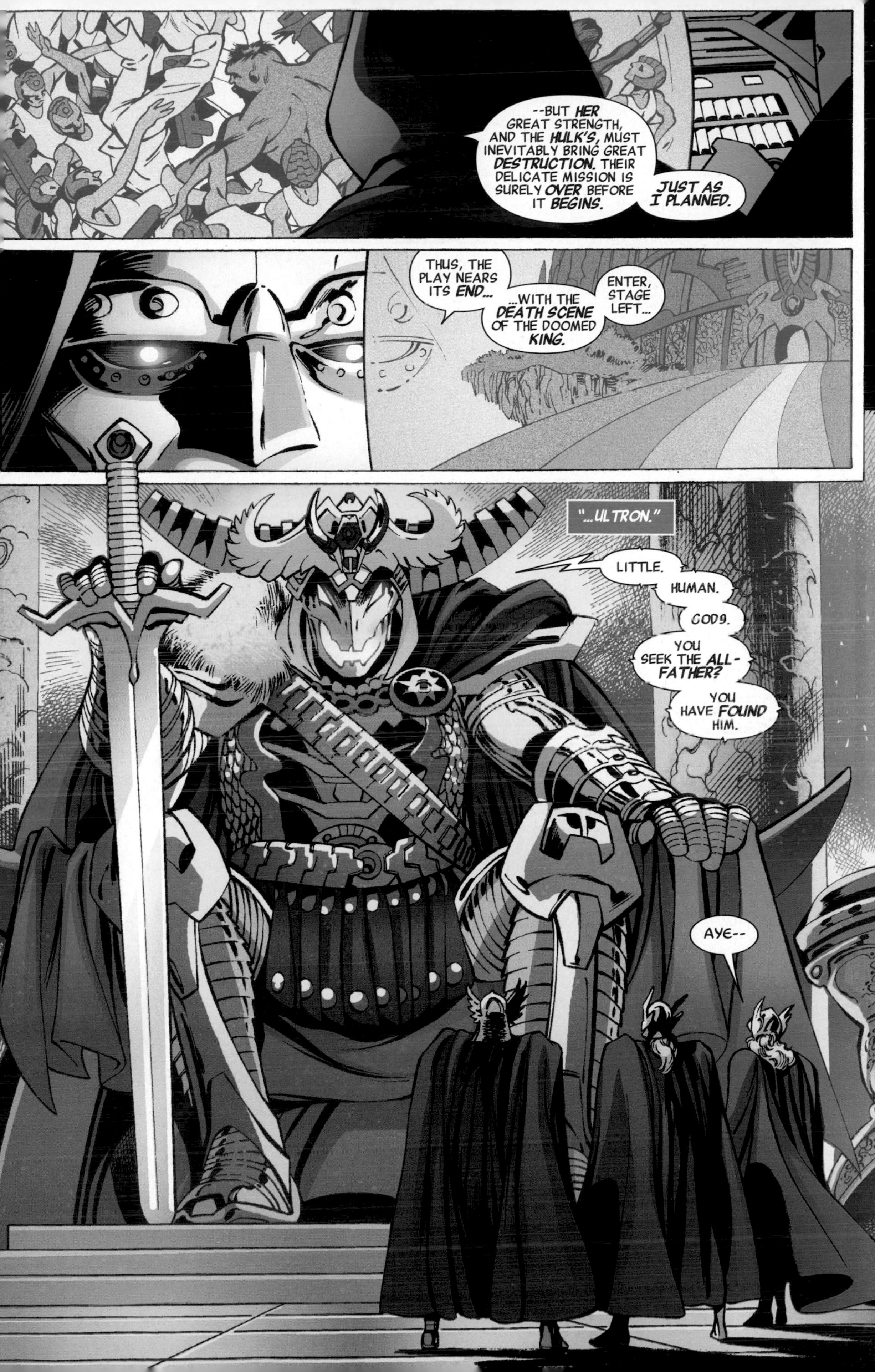
--BUT HER GREAT STRENGTH, AND THE HULK'S, MUST INEVITABLY BRING GREAT DESTRUCTION. THEIR DELICATE MISSION IS SURELY OVER BEFORE IT BEGINS.
JUST AS I PLANNED.
THUS, THE PLAY NEARS ITS END...
...WITH THE DEATH SCENE OF THE DOOMED KING.
ENTER, STAGE LEFT...
"...ULTRON."
LITTLE.
HUMAN.
GODS.
YOU SEEK THE ALL-FATHER?
YOU HAVE FOUND HIM.
AYE--

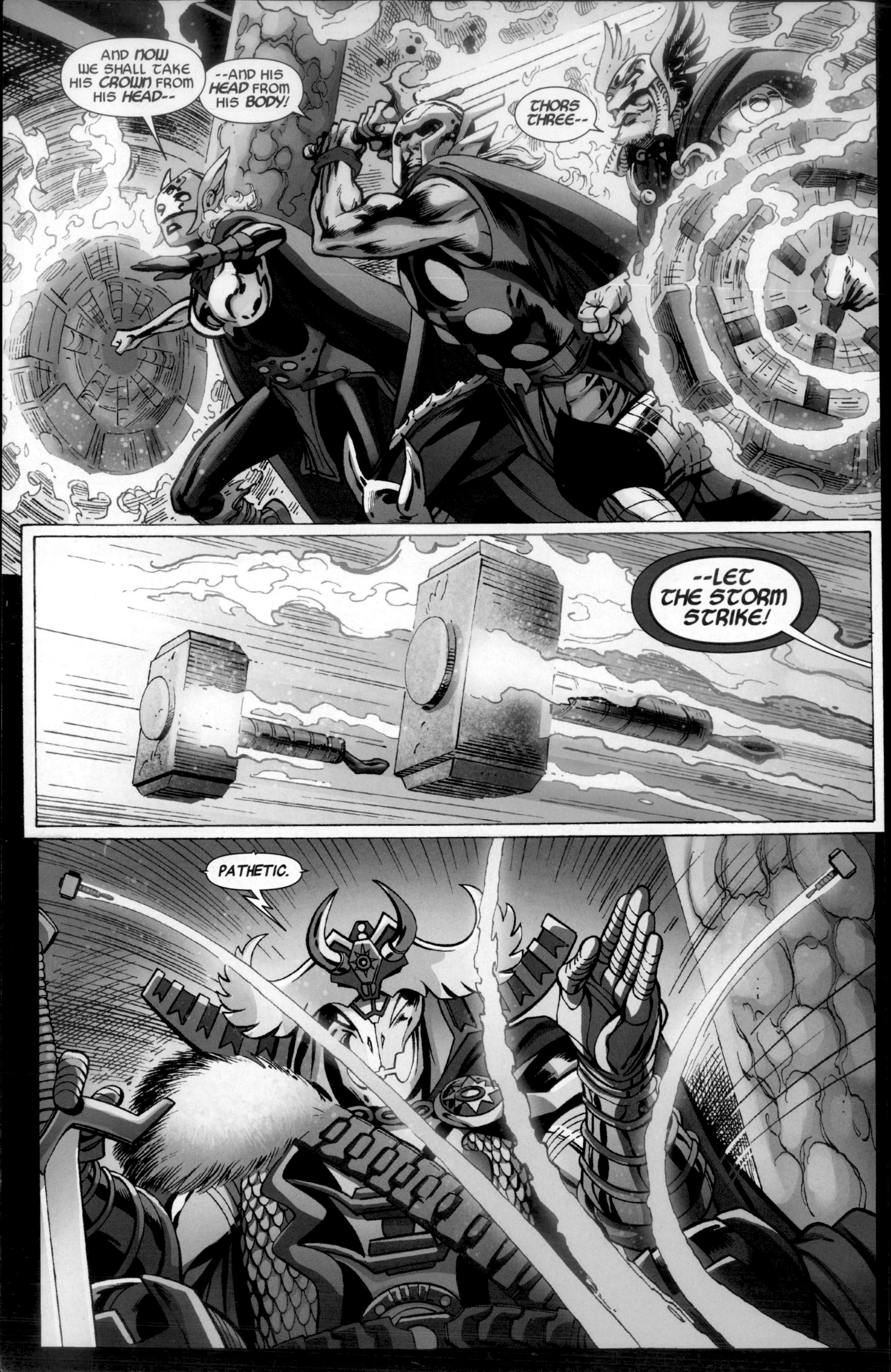
AND NOW WE SHALL TAKE HIS CROWN FROM HIS HEAD--
--AND HIS HEAD FROM HIS BODY!
THORS THREE--
--LET THE STORM STRIKE!
PATHETIC.

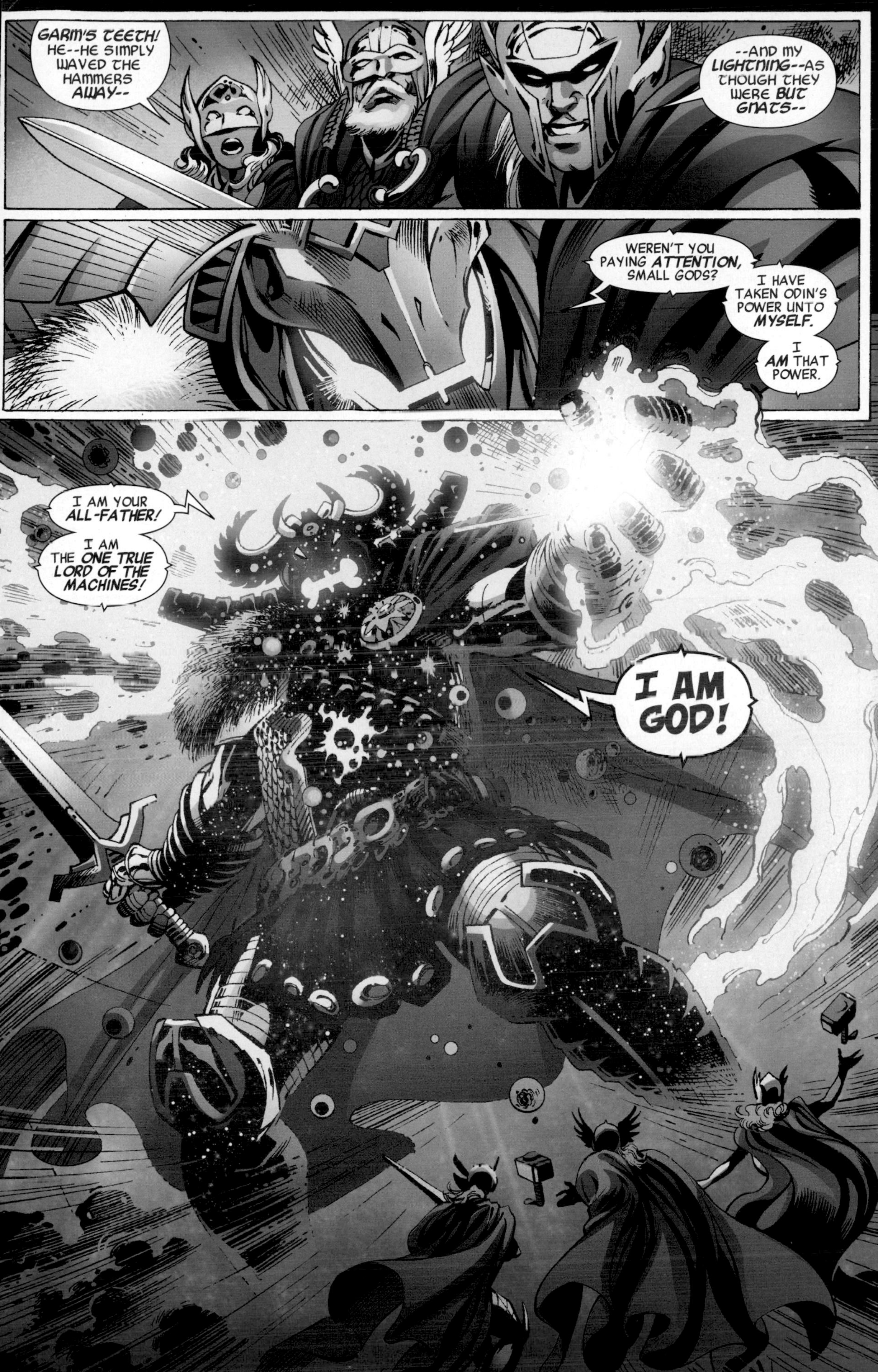
GARM'S TEETH! HE--HE SIMPLY WAVED THE HAMMERS AWAY--
--AND MY LIGHTNING--AS THOUGH THEY WERE BUT GNATS--
WEREN'T YOU PAYING ATTENTION, SMALL GODS?
I HAVE TAKEN ODIN'S POWER UNTO MYSELF.
I AM THAT POWER.
I AM YOUR ALL-FATHER!
I AM THE ONE TRUE LORD OF THE MACHINES!
I AM GOD!

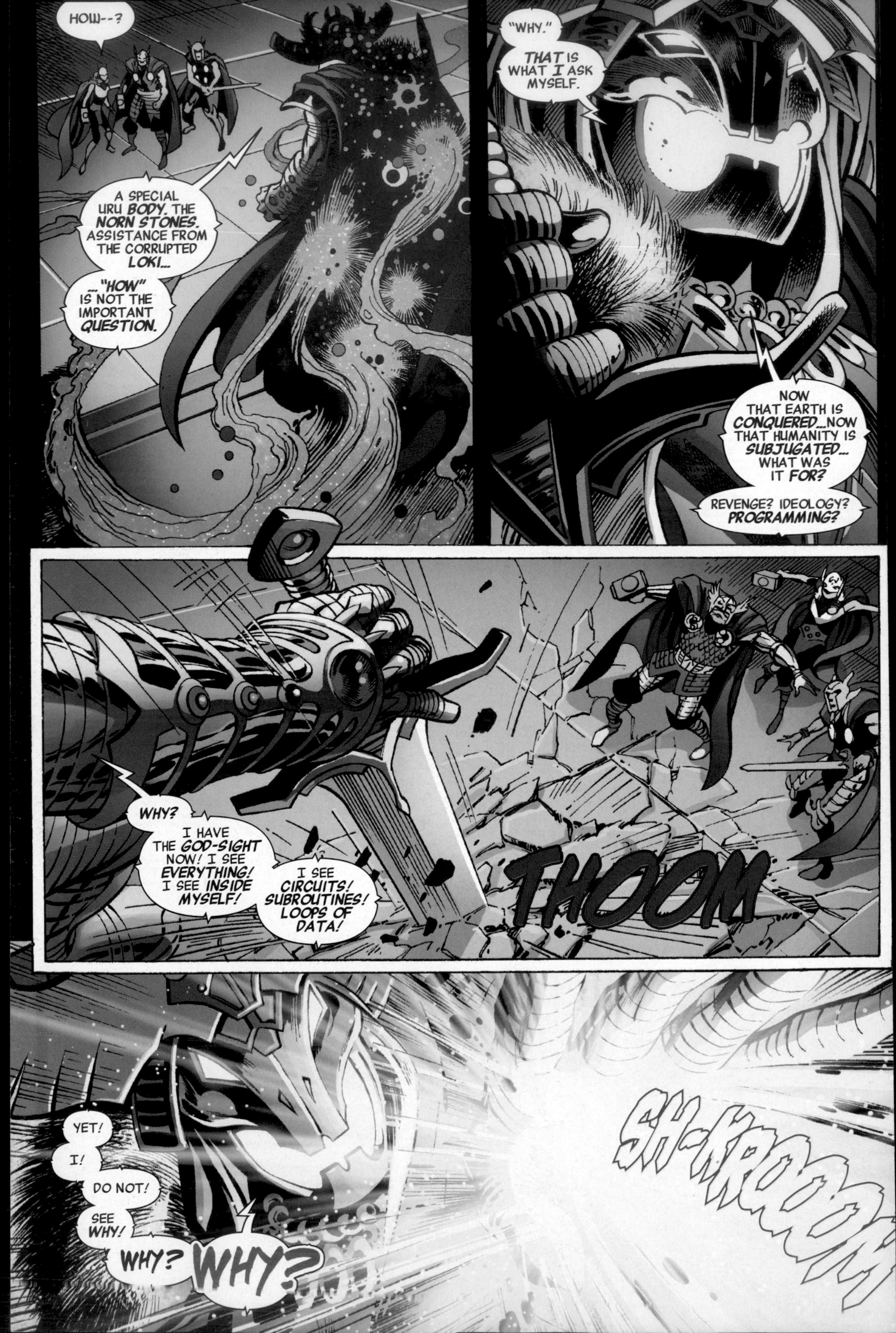
HOW--?
A SPECIAL URU BODY. THE NORN STONES. ASSISTANCE FROM THE CORRUPTED LOKI...
..."HOW" IS NOT THE IMPORTANT QUESTION.
"WHY."
THAT IS WHAT I ASK MYSELF.
NOW THAT EARTH IS CONQUERED...NOW THAT HUMANITY IS SUBJUGATED... WHAT WAS IT FOR?
REVENGE? IDEOLOGY? PROGRAMMING?
WHY?
I HAVE THE GOD-SIGHT NOW! I SEE EVERYTHING! I SEE INSIDE MYSELF!
I SEE CIRCUITS! SUBROUTINES! LOOPS OF DATA!
THOOM
YET!
I!
DO NOT!
SEE WHY!
WHY? WHY?
SH-KROOOM

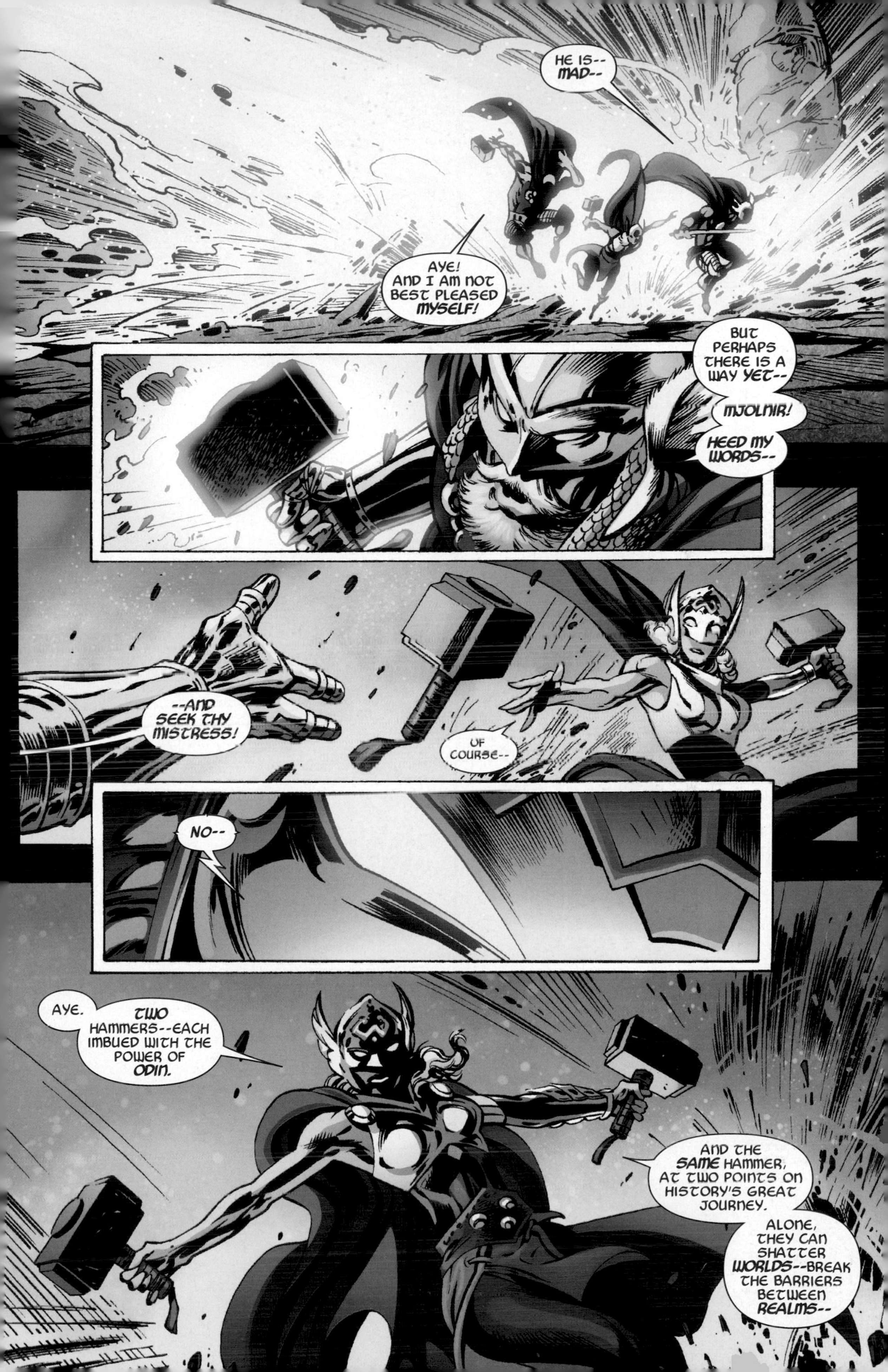

HE IS-- MAD--
AYE! AND I AM NOT BEST PLEASED MYSELF!
BUT PERHAPS THERE IS A WAY YET--
MJOLNIR!
HEED MY WORDS--
--AND SEEK THY MISTRESS!
OF COURSE--
NO--
AYE.
TWO HAMMERS--EACH IMBUED WITH THE POWER OF ODIN.
AND THE SAME HAMMER, AT TWO POINTS ON HISTORY'S GREAT JOURNEY.
ALONE, THEY CAN SHATTER WORLDS--BREAK THE BARRIERS BETWEEN REALMS--

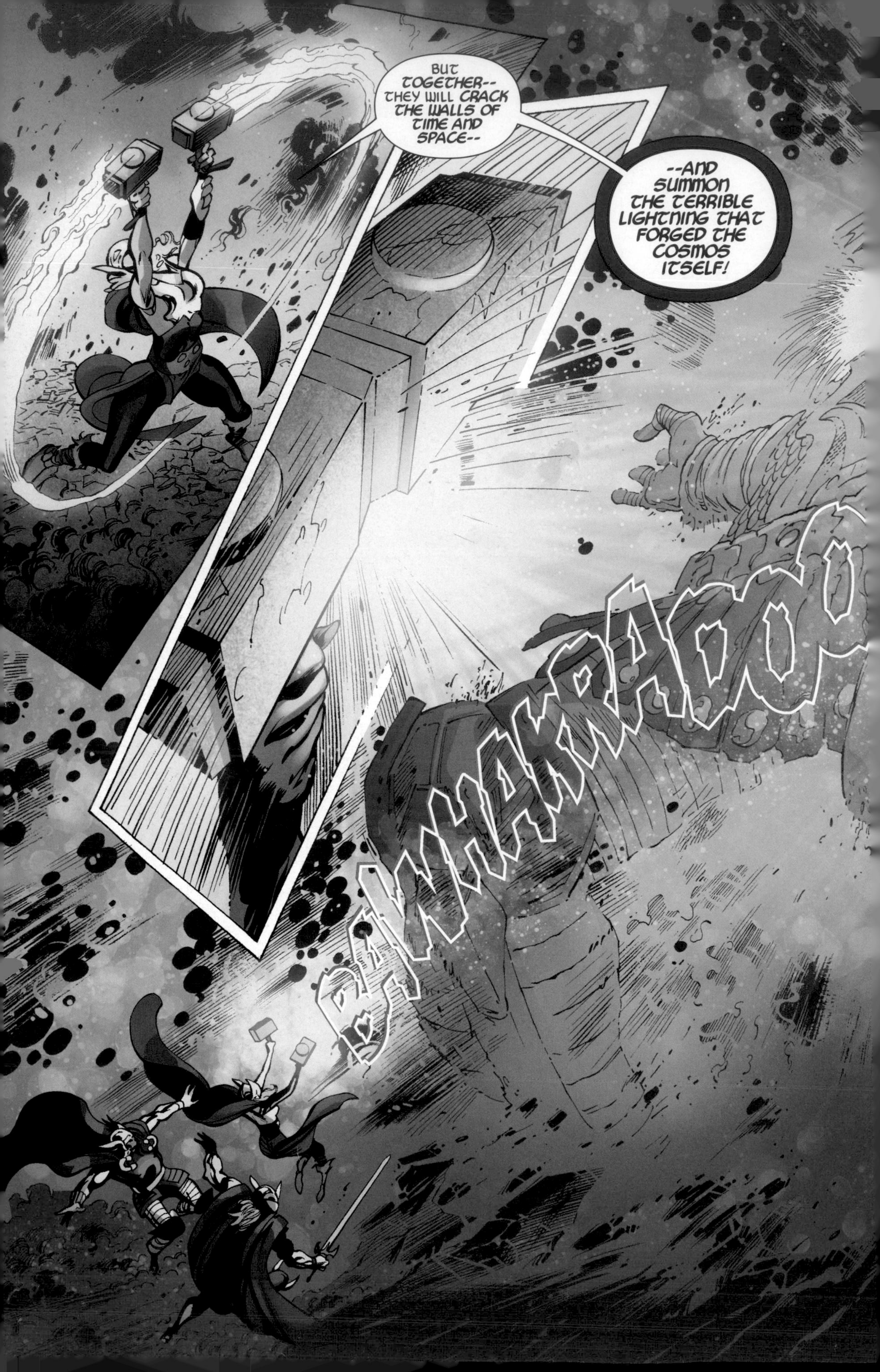
BUT TOGETHER-- THEY WILL CRACK THE WALLS OF TIME AND SPACE--
--AND SUMMON THE TERRIBLE LIGHTNING THAT FORGED THE COSMOS ITSELF!

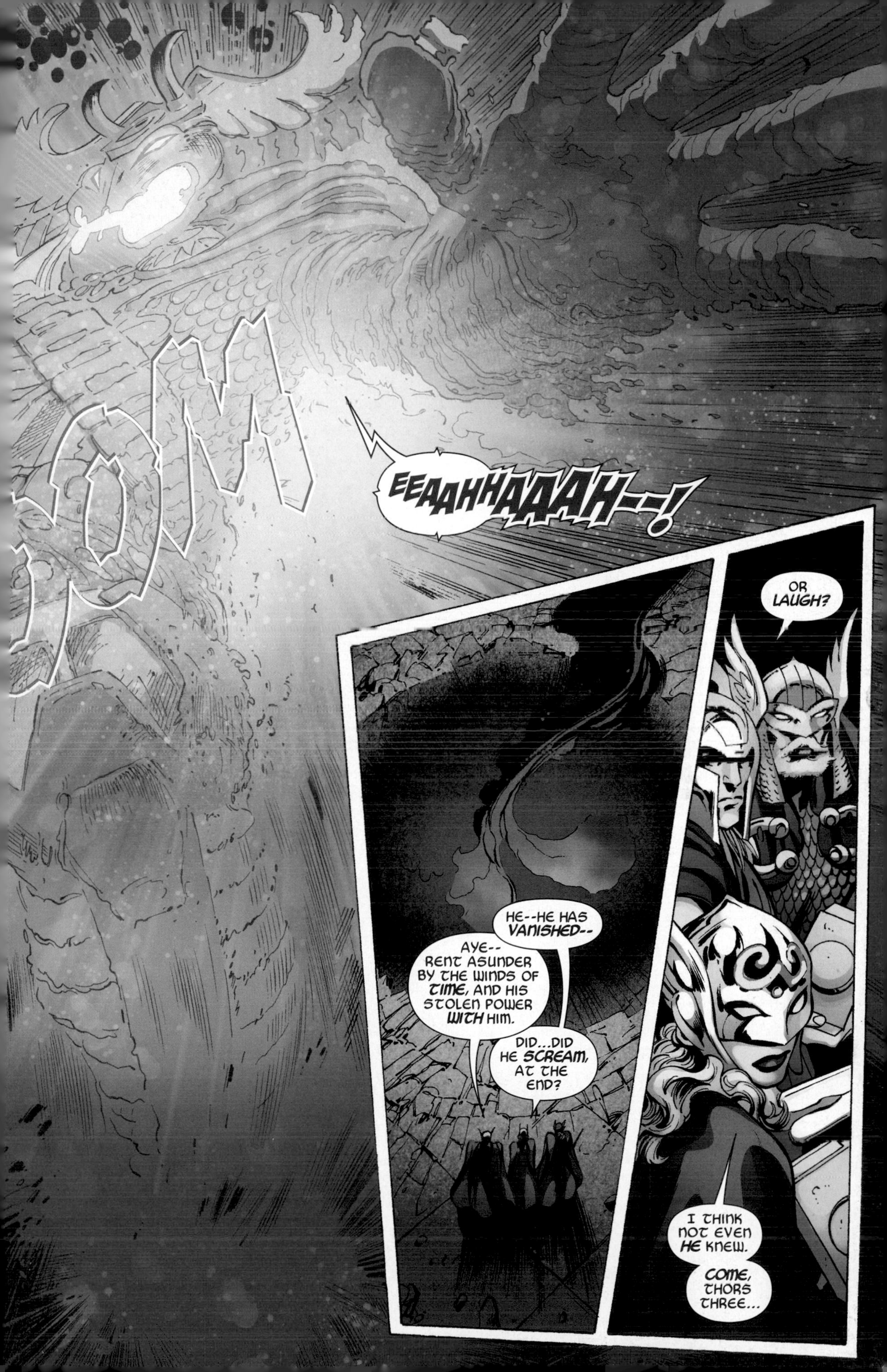

OOM
EEAAHHAAAH--!
HE--HE HAS VANISHED--
AYE-- RENT ASUNDER BY THE WINDS OF TIME, AND HIS STOLEN POWER WITH HIM.
DID...DID HE SCREAM, AT THE END?
OR LAUGH?
I THINK NOT EVEN HE KNEW.
COME, THORS THREE...

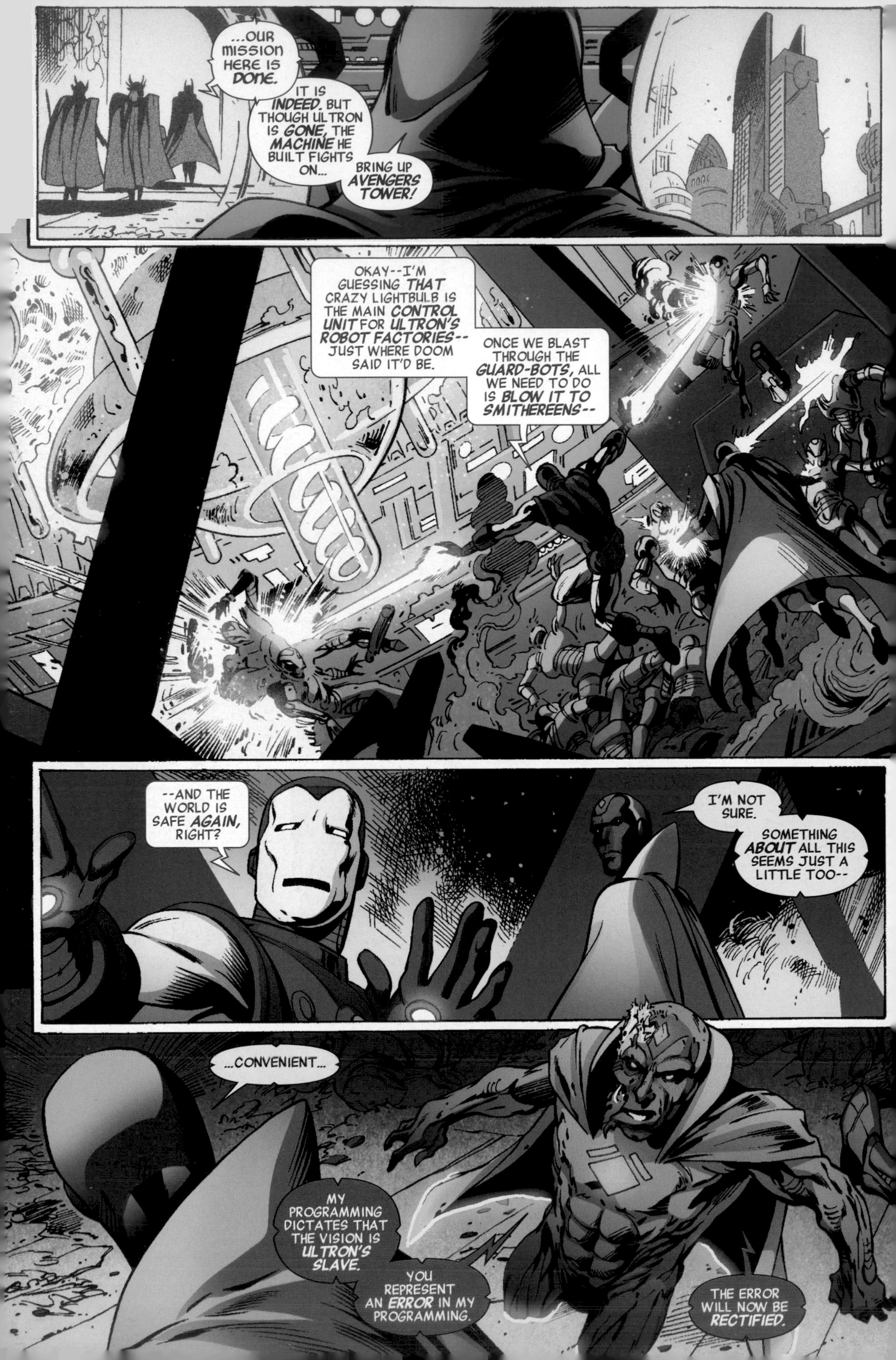
...OUR MISSION HERE IS DONE.
IT IS INDEED. BUT THOUGH ULTRON IS GONE, THE MACHINE HE BUILT FIGHTS ON...
BRING UP AVENGERS TOWER!
OKAY--I'M GUESSING THAT CRAZY LIGHTBULB IS THE MAIN CONTROL UNIT FOR ULTRON'S ROBOT FACTORIES-- JUST WHERE DOOM SAID IT'D BE.
ONCE WE BLAST THROUGH THE GUARD-BOTS, ALL WE NEED TO DO IS BLOW IT TO SMITHEREENS--
--AND THE WORLD IS SAFE AGAIN, RIGHT?
I'M NOT SURE.
SOMETHING ABOUT ALL THIS SEEMS JUST A LITTLE TOO--
...CONVENIENT...
MY PROGRAMMING DICTATES THAT THE VISION IS ULTRON'S SLAVE.
YOU REPRESENT AN ERROR IN MY PROGRAMMING.
THE ERROR WILL NOW BE RECTIFIED.

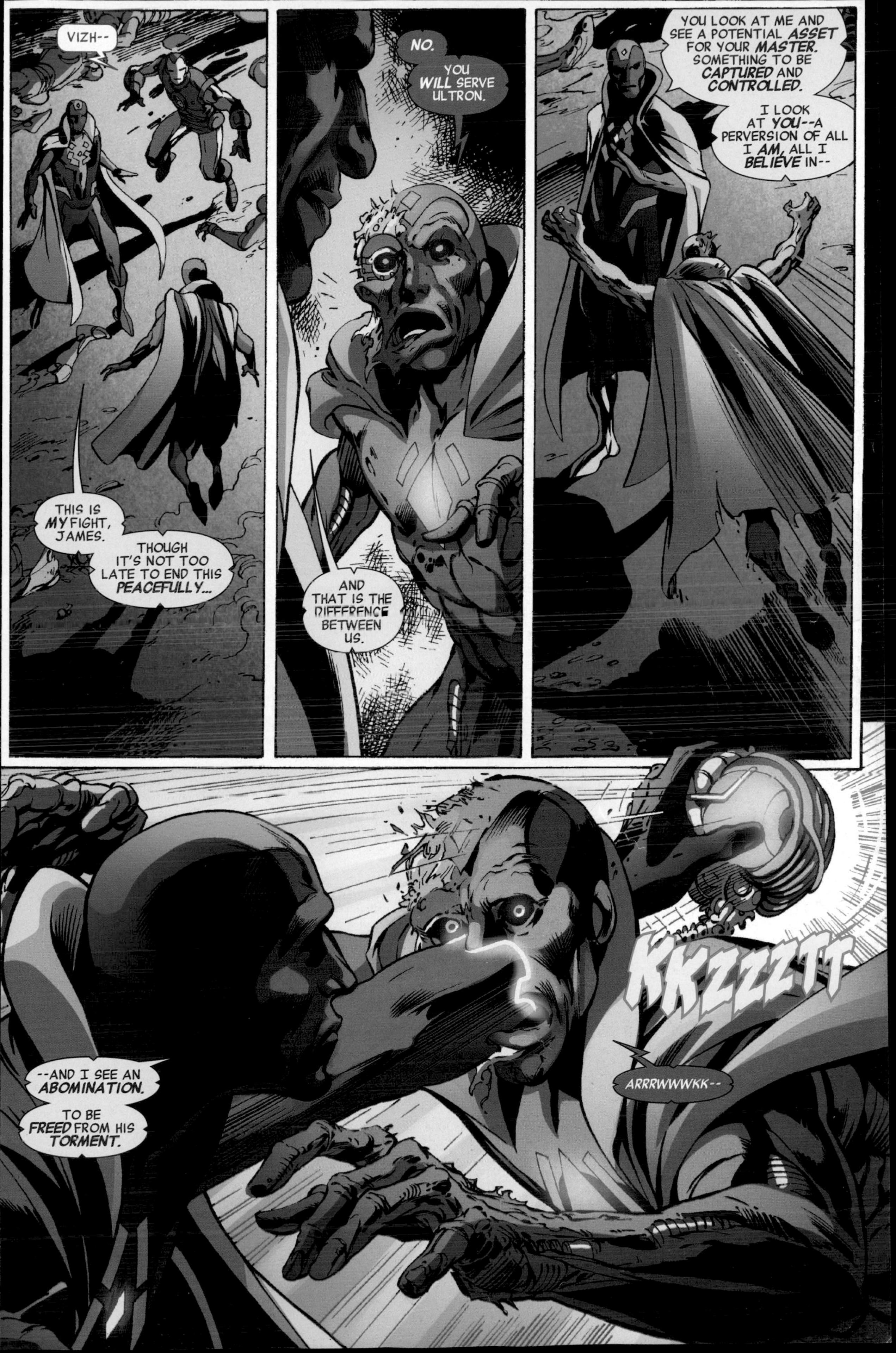
VIZH--
THIS IS MY FIGHT, JAMES.
THOUGH IT'S NOT TOO LATE TO END THIS PEACEFULLY...
NO.
YOU WILL SERVE ULTRON.
AND THAT IS THE DIFFERENCE BETWEEN US.
YOU LOOK AT ME AND SEE A POTENTIAL ASSET FOR YOUR MASTER. SOMETHING TO BE CAPTURED AND CONTROLLED.
I LOOK AT YOU--A PERVERSION OF ALL I AM, ALL I BELIEVE IN--
--AND I SEE AN ABOMINATION.
TO BE FREED FROM HIS TORMENT.
KKZZZTT
ARRRWWWKK--

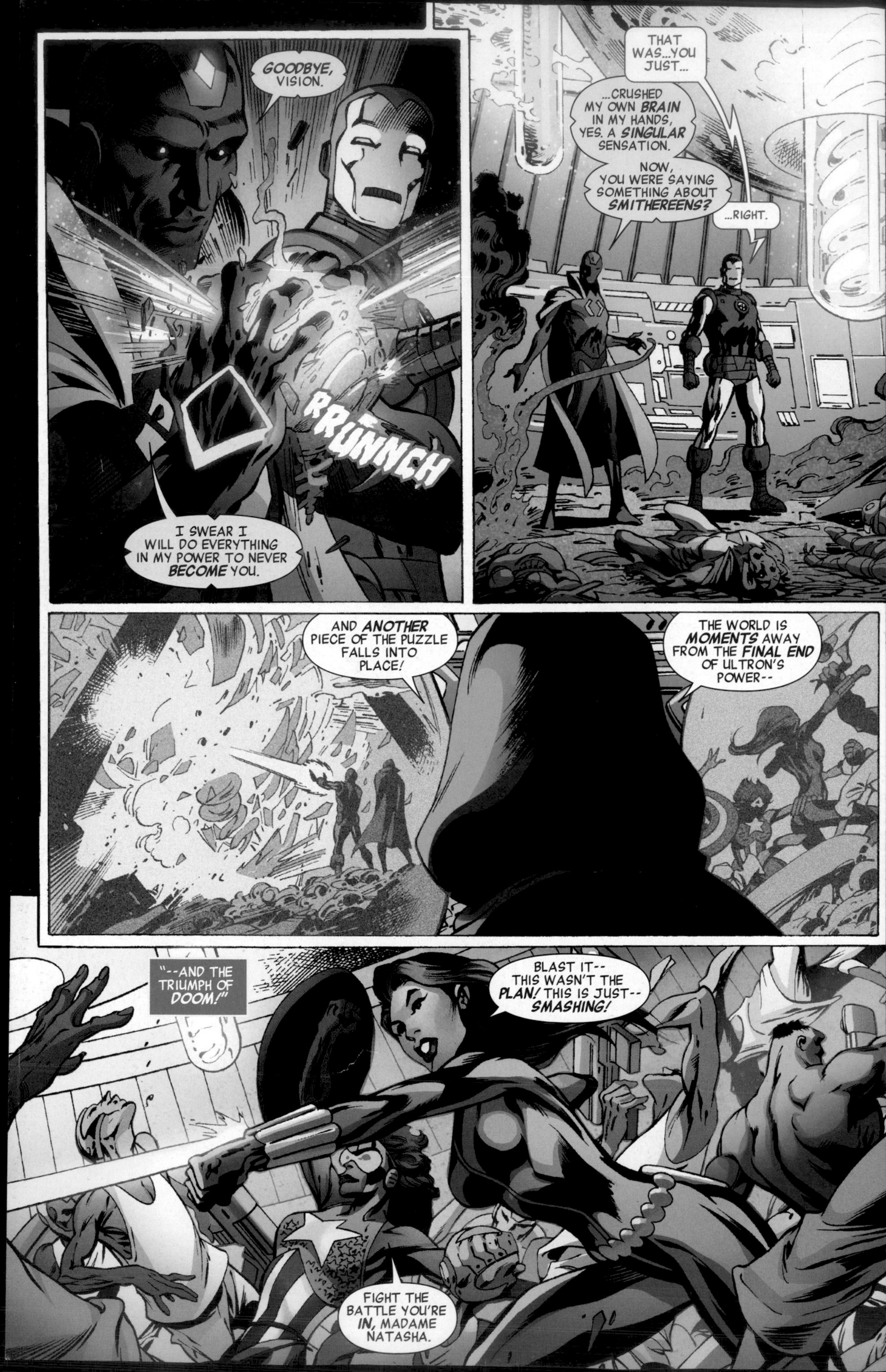
GOODBYE, VISION.
I SWEAR I WILL DO EVERYTHING IN MY POWER TO NEVER BECOME YOU.
BRRUNNCH
THAT WAS...YOU JUST...
...CRUSHED MY OWN BRAIN IN MY HANDS, YES. A SINGULAR SENSATION.
NOW, YOU WERE SAYING SOMETHING ABOUT SMITHEREENS?
...RIGHT.
AND ANOTHER PIECE OF THE PUZZLE FALLS INTO PLACE!
THE WORLD IS MOMENTS AWAY FROM THE FINAL END OF ULTRON'S POWER--
"--AND THE TRIUMPH OF DOOM!"
BLAST IT-- THIS WASN'T THE PLAN! THIS IS JUST-- SMASHING!
FIGHT THE BATTLE YOU'RE IN, MADAME NATASHA.

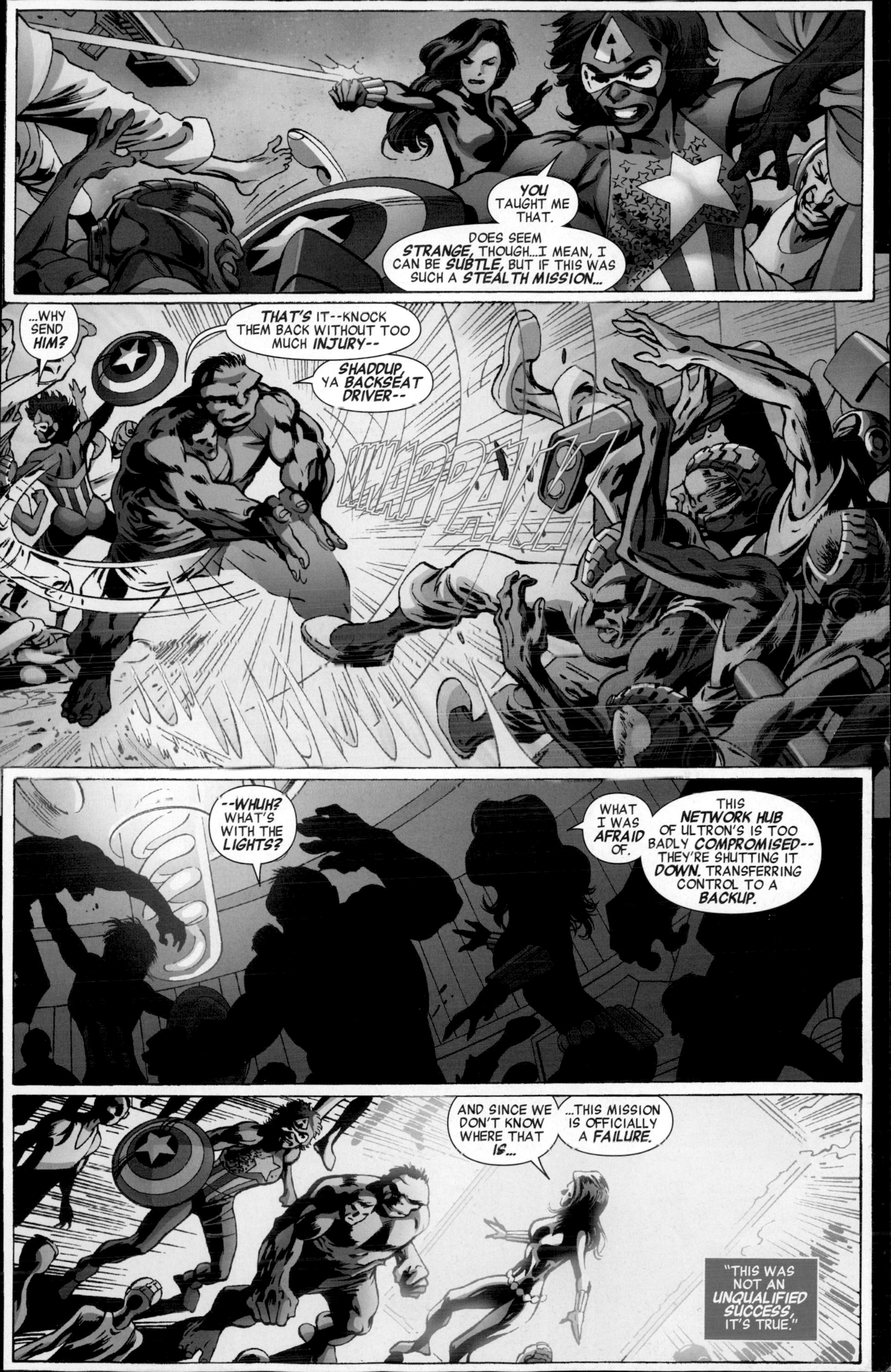

YOU TAUGHT ME THAT.
DOES SEEM STRANGE, THOUGH...I MEAN, I CAN BE SUBTLE, BUT IF THIS WAS SUCH A STEALTH MISSION...
...WHY SEND HIM?
THAT'S IT--KNOCK THEM BACK WITHOUT TOO MUCH INJURY--
SHADDUP, YA BACKSEAT DRIVER--
--WHUH? WHAT'S WITH THE LIGHTS?
WHAT I WAS AFRAID OF.
THIS NETWORK HUB OF ULTRON'S IS TOO BADLY COMPROMISED-- THEY'RE SHUTTING IT DOWN. TRANSFERRING CONTROL TO A BACKUP.
AND SINCE WE DON'T KNOW WHERE THAT IS...
...THIS MISSION IS OFFICIALLY A FAILURE.
"THIS WAS NOT AN UNQUALIFIED SUCCESS, IT'S TRUE."

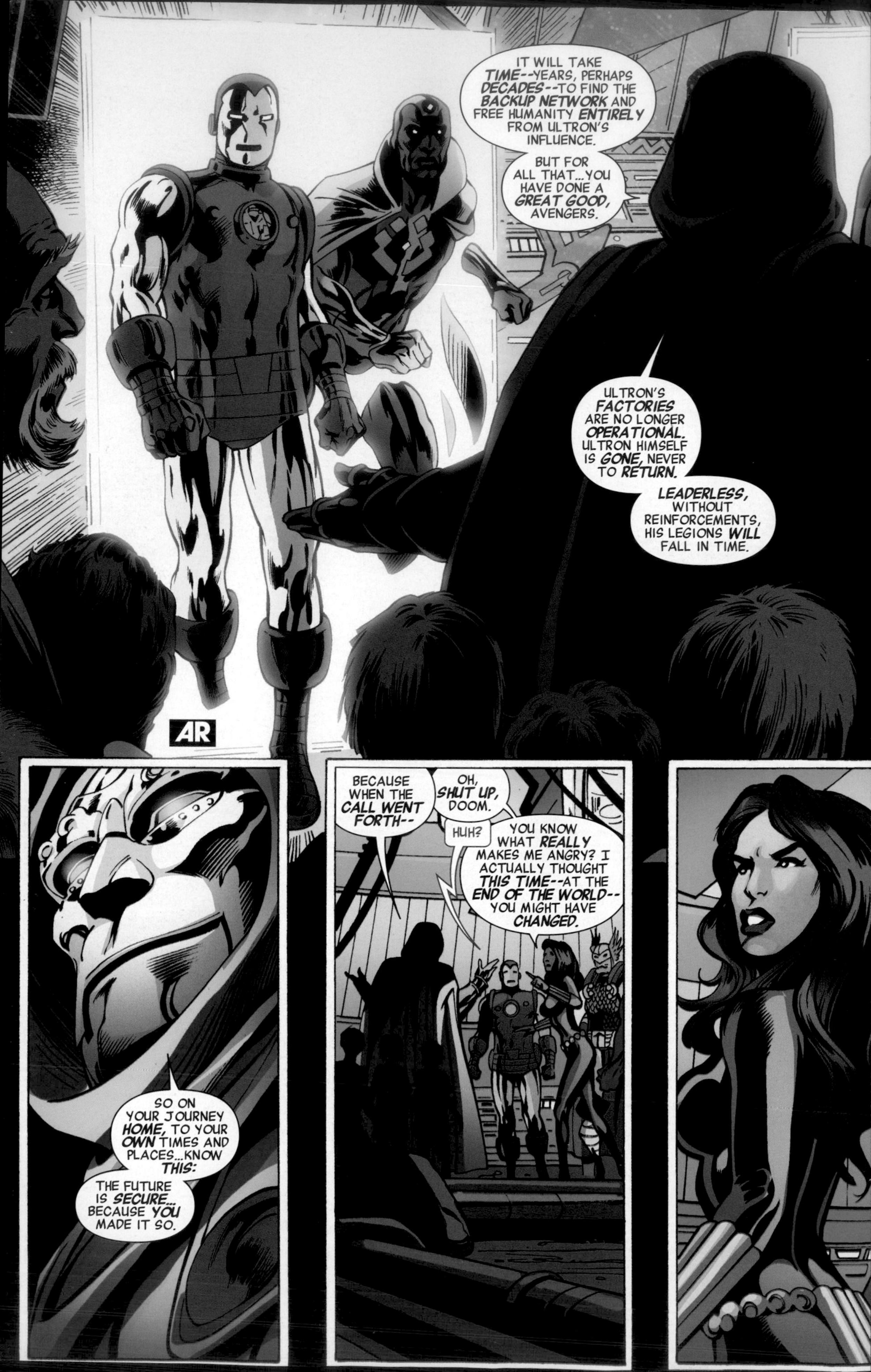
IT WILL TAKE TIME--YEARS, PERHAPS DECADES--TO FIND THE BACKUP NETWORK AND FREE HUMANITY ENTIRELY FROM ULTRON'S INFLUENCE.
BUT FOR ALL THAT...YOU HAVE DONE A GREAT GOOD, AVENGERS.
ULTRON'S FACTORIES ARE NO LONGER OPERATIONAL. ULTRON HIMSELF IS GONE, NEVER TO RETURN.
LEADERLESS, WITHOUT REINFORCEMENTS, HIS LEGIONS WILL FALL IN TIME.
AR
SO ON YOUR JOURNEY HOME, TO YOUR OWN TIMES AND PLACES...KNOW THIS:
THE FUTURE IS SECURE... BECAUSE YOU MADE IT SO.
BECAUSE WHEN THE CALL WENT FORTH--
OH, SHUT UP, DOOM.
HUH?
YOU KNOW WHAT REALLY MAKES ME ANGRY? I ACTUALLY THOUGHT THIS TIME--AT THE END OF THE WORLD--YOU MIGHT HAVE CHANGED.

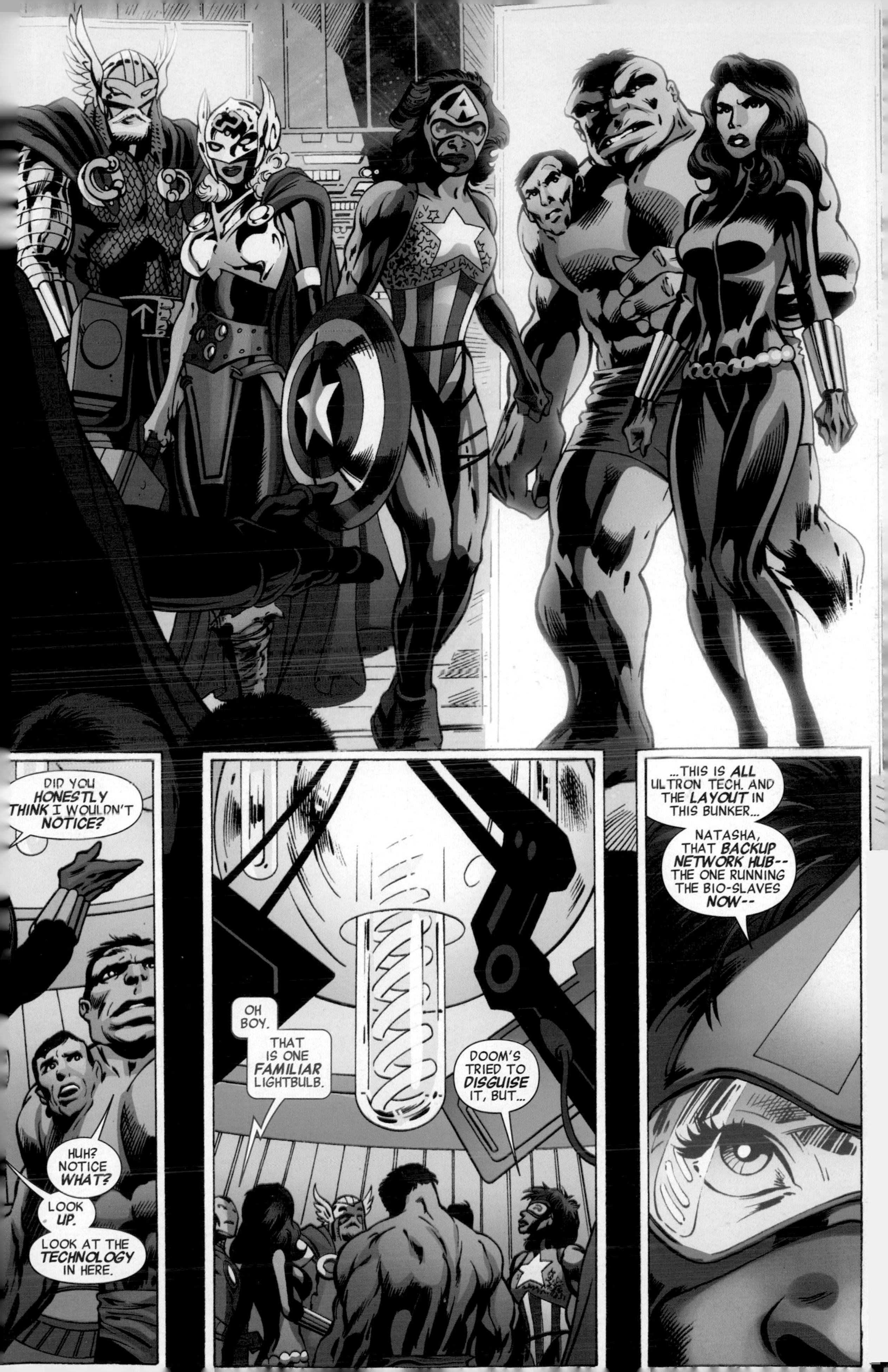
DID YOU HONESTLY THINK I WOULDN'T NOTICE?
HUH? NOTICE WHAT?
LOOK UP.
LOOK AT THE TECHNOLOGY IN HERE.
OH BOY.
THAT IS ONE FAMILIAR LIGHTBULB.
DOOM'S TRIED TO DISGUISE IT, BUT...
...THIS IS ALL ULTRON TECH. AND THE LAYOUT IN THIS BUNKER...
NATASHA, THAT BACKUP NETWORK HUB-- THE ONE RUNNING THE BIO-SLAVES NOW--

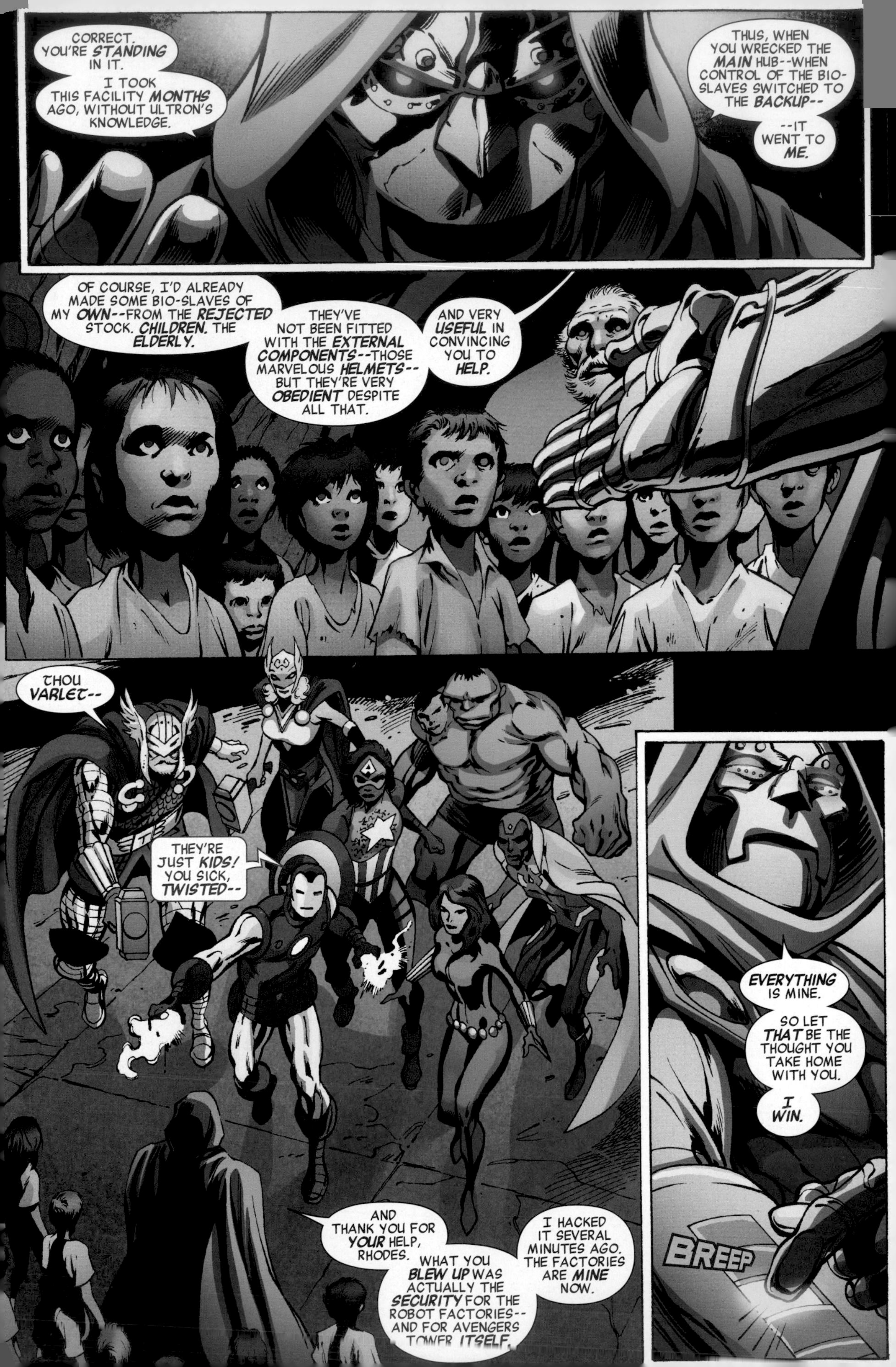
CORRECT. YOU'RE STANDING IN IT.
I TOOK THIS FACILITY MONTHS AGO, WITHOUT ULTRON'S KNOWLEDGE.
THUS, WHEN YOU WRECKED THE MAIN HUB--WHEN CONTROL OF THE BIO-SLAVES SWITCHED TO THE BACKUP--
--IT WENT TO ME.
OF COURSE, I'D ALREADY MADE SOME BIO-SLAVES OF MY OWN--FROM THE REJECTED STOCK. CHILDREN. THE ELDERLY.
THEY'VE NOT BEEN FITTED WITH THE EXTERNAL COMPONENTS--THOSE MARVELOUS HELMETS--BUT THEY'RE VERY OBEDIENT DESPITE ALL THAT.
AND VERY USEFUL IN CONVINCING YOU TO HELP.
THOU VARLET--
THEY'RE JUST KIDS! YOU SICK, TWISTED--
AND THANK YOU FOR YOUR HELP, RHODES.
WHAT YOU BLEW UP WAS ACTUALLY THE SECURITY FOR THE ROBOT FACTORIES--AND FOR AVENGERS TOWER ITSELF.
I HACKED IT SEVERAL MINUTES AGO. THE FACTORIES ARE MINE NOW.
BREEP
EVERYTHING IS MINE.
SO LET THAT BE THE THOUGHT YOU TAKE HOME WITH YOU.
I WIN.

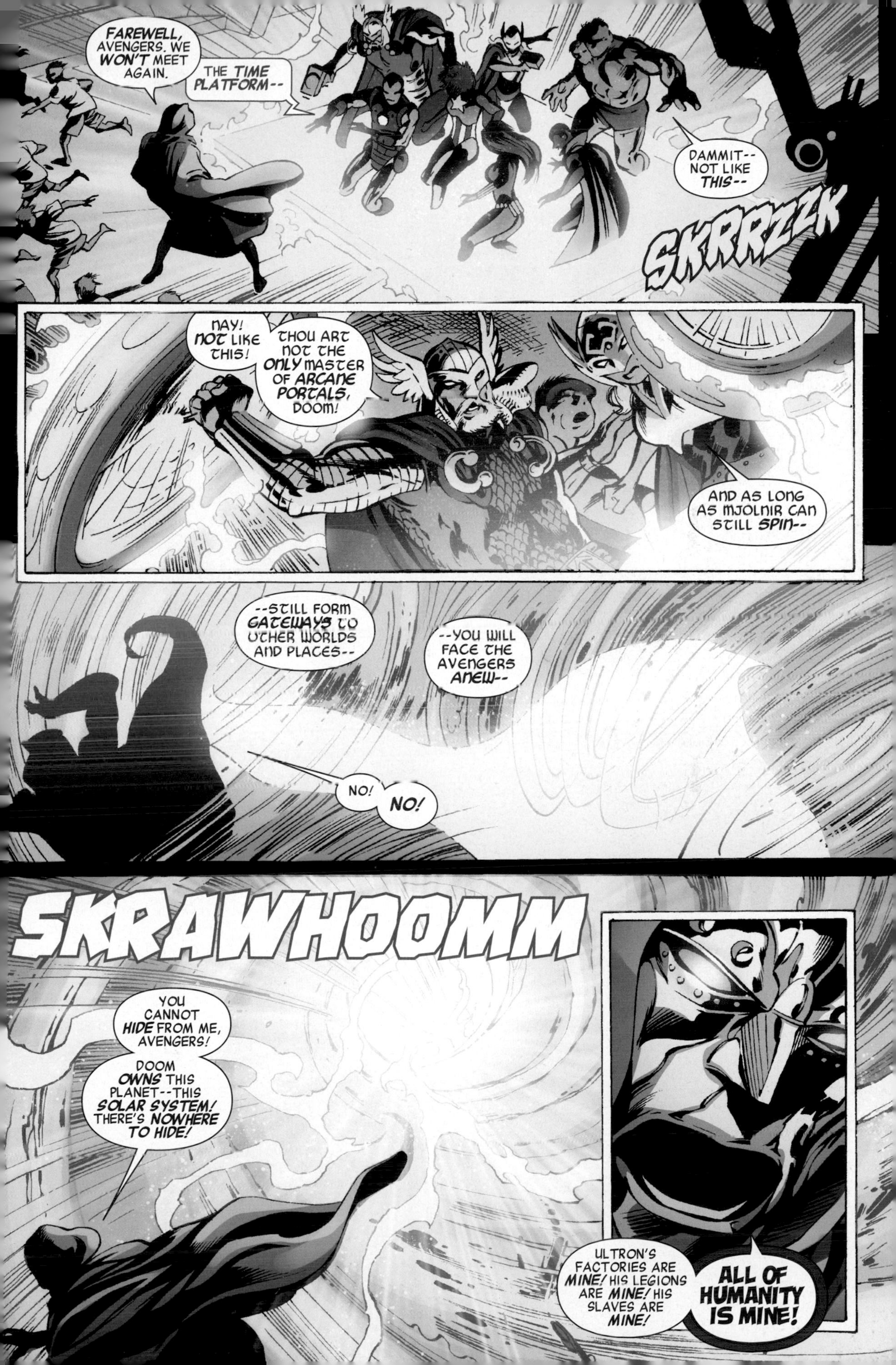
FAREWELL, AVENGERS. WE WON'T MEET AGAIN.
THE TIME PLATFORM--
DAMMIT-- NOT LIKE THIS--
SKRRZZK
NAY! NOT LIKE THIS!
THOU ART NOT THE ONLY MASTER OF ARCANE PORTALS, DOOM!
AND AS LONG AS MJOLNIR CAN STILL SPIN--
--STILL FORM GATEWAYS TO OTHER WORLDS AND PLACES--
--YOU WILL FACE THE AVENGERS ANEW--
NO!
NO!
SKRAWHOOMM
YOU CANNOT HIDE FROM ME, AVENGERS!
DOOM OWNS THIS PLANET--THIS SOLAR SYSTEM! THERE'S NOWHERE TO HIDE!
ULTRON'S FACTORIES ARE MINE! HIS LEGIONS ARE MINE! HIS SLAVES ARE MINE!
ALL OF HUMANITY IS MINE!

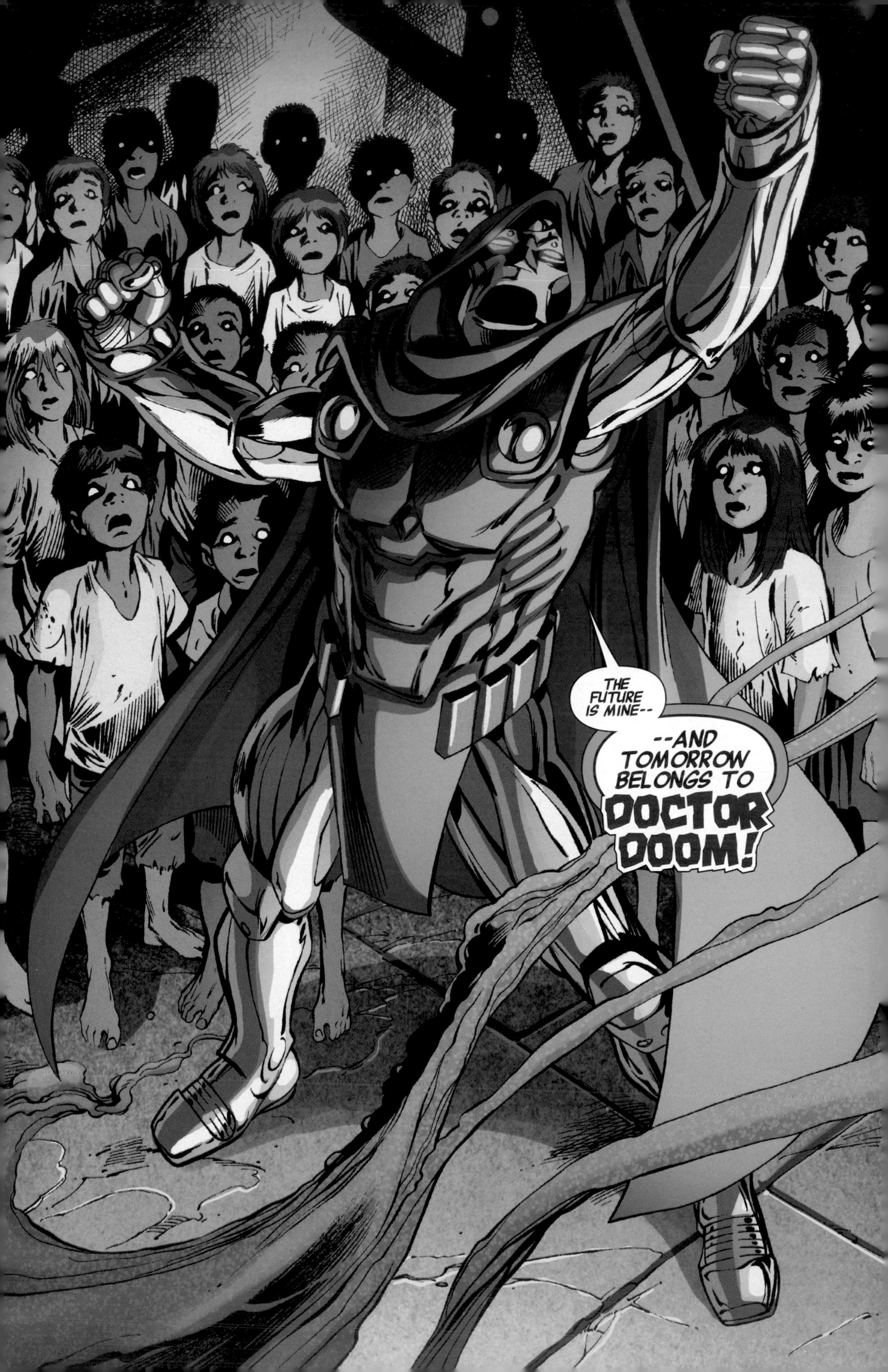
THE FUTURE IS MINE--
--AND TOMORROW BELONGS TO DOCTOR DOOM!

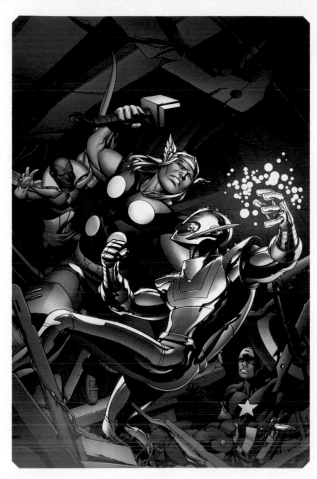

AVENGERS: ULTRON FOREVER #1 VARIANT
by MIKE McKONE & JASON KEITH

AVENGERS: ULTRON FOREVER #1 VARIANT
by GREG LAND & NOLAN WOODARD

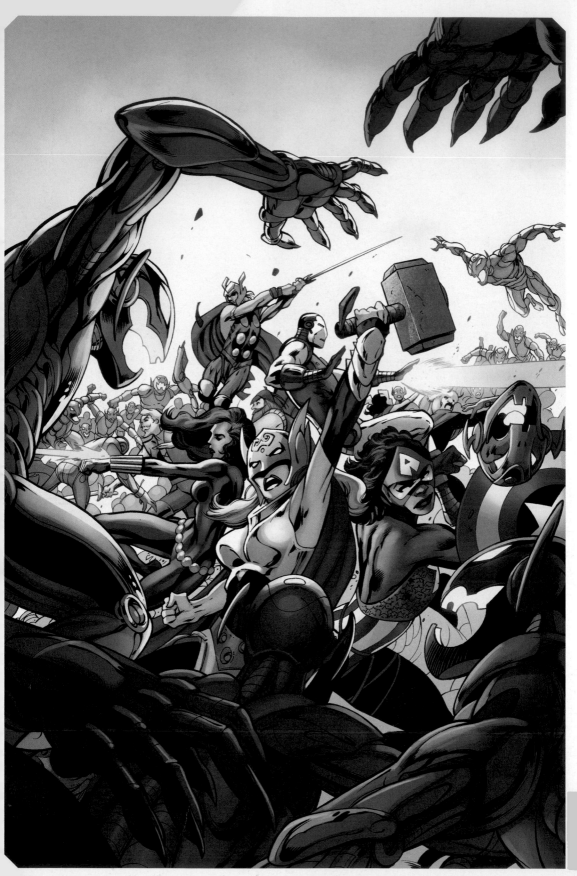

UNCANNY AVENGERS: ULTRON FOREVER #1

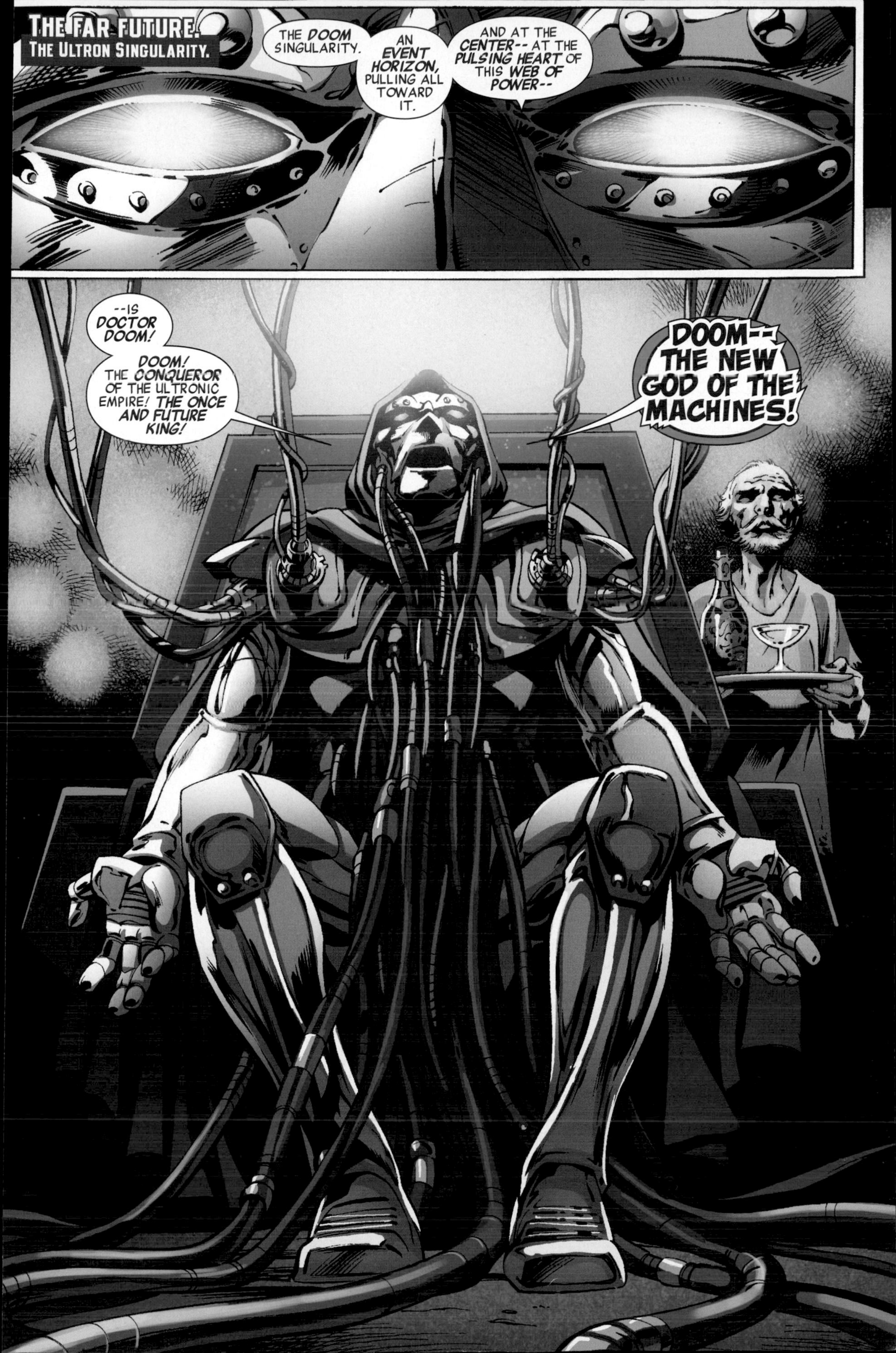
THE FAR FUTURE. THE ULTRON SINGULARITY.
THE DOOM SINGULARITY.
AN EVENT HORIZON, PULLING ALL TOWARD IT.
AND AT THE CENTER-- AT THE PULSING HEART OF THIS WEB OF POWER--
--IS DOCTOR DOOM!
DOOM! THE CONQUEROR OF THE ULTRONIC EMPIRE! THE ONCE AND FUTURE KING!
DOOM-- THE NEW GOD OF THE MACHINES!

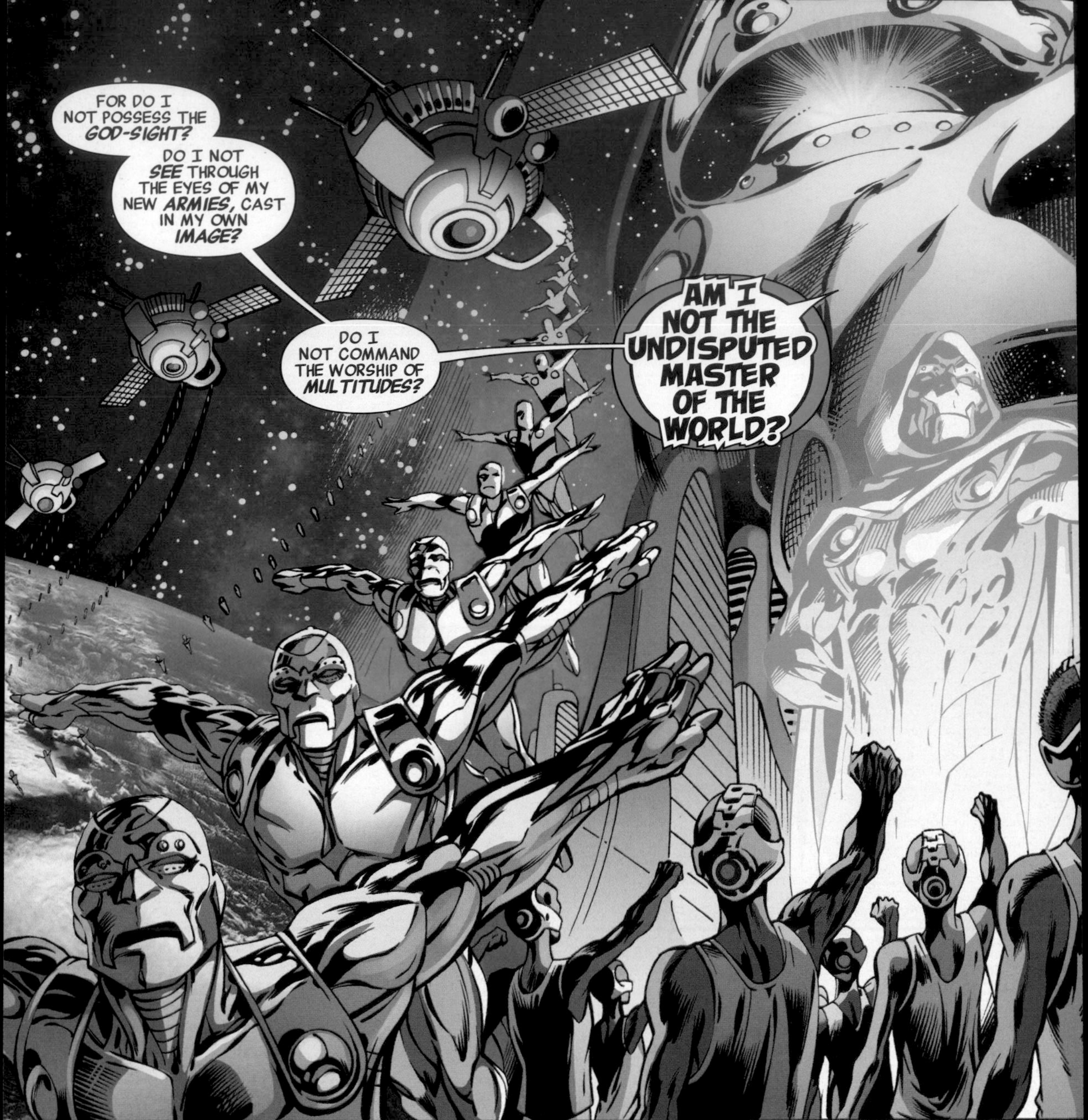
FOR DO I NOT POSSESS THE GOD-SIGHT?
DO I NOT SEE THROUGH THE EYES OF MY NEW ARMIES, CAST IN MY OWN IMAGE?
DO I NOT COMMAND THE WORSHIP OF MULTITUDES?
AM I NOT THE UNDISPUTED MASTER OF THE WORLD?

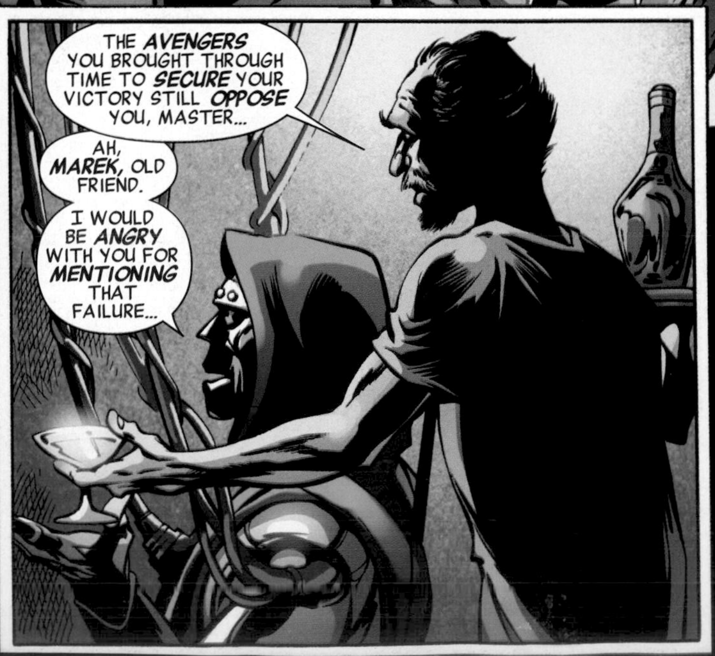
THE AVENGERS YOU BROUGHT THROUGH TIME TO SECURE YOUR VICTORY STILL OPPOSE YOU, MASTER...
AH, MAREK, OLD FRIEND.
I WOULD BE ANGRY WITH YOU FOR MENTIONING THAT FAILURE...

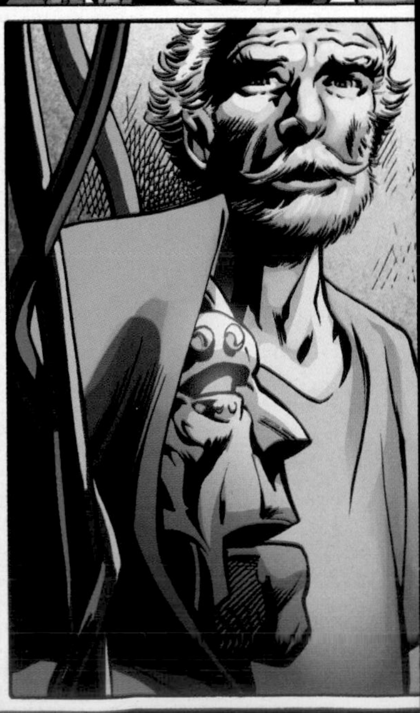

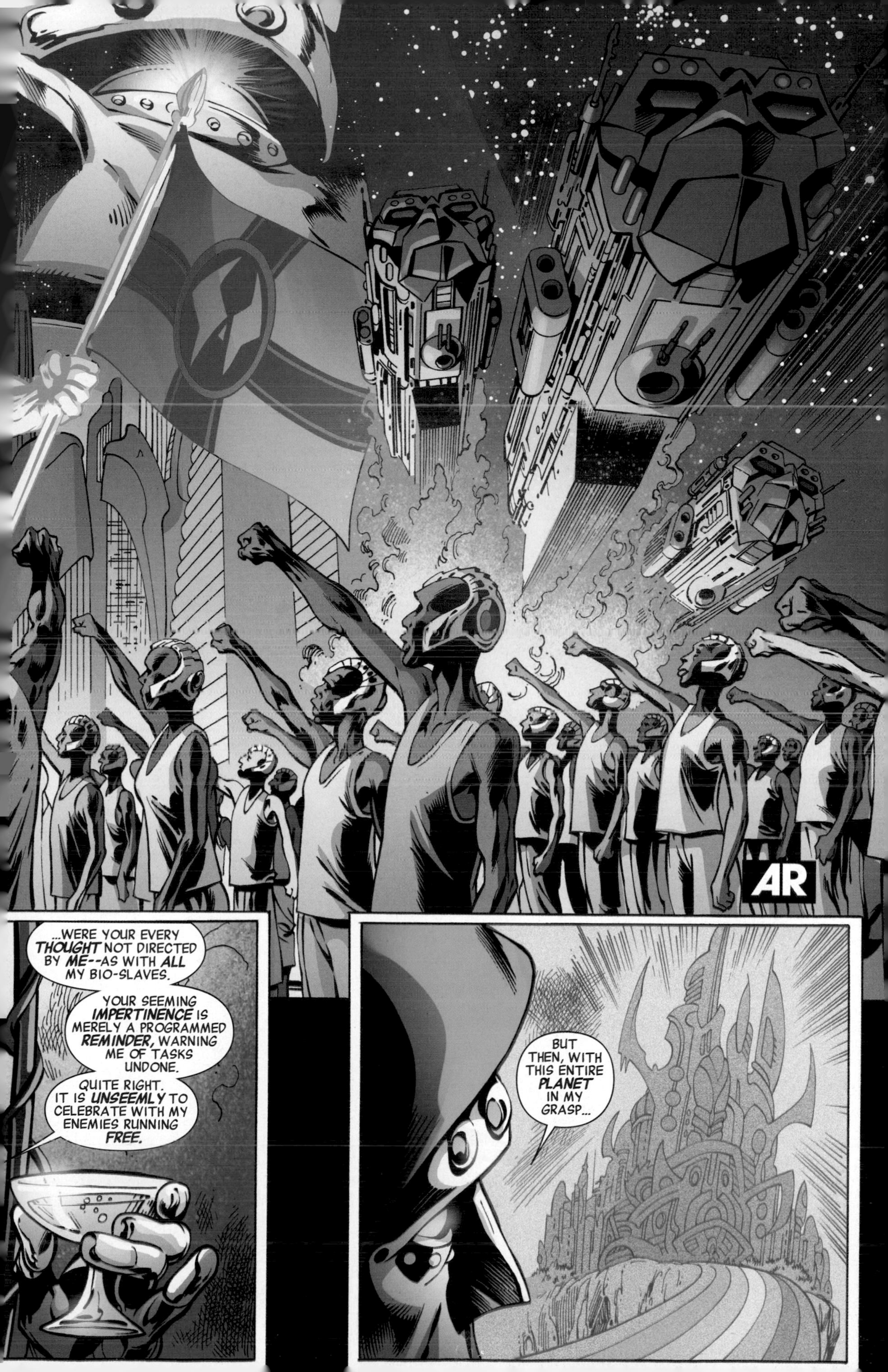
AR
...WERE YOUR EVERY THOUGHT NOT DIRECTED BY ME--AS WITH ALL MY BIO-SLAVES.
YOUR SEEMING IMPERTINENCE IS MERELY A PROGRAMMED REMINDER, WARNING ME OF TASKS UNDONE.
QUITE RIGHT. IT IS UNSEEMLY TO CELEBRATE WITH MY ENEMIES RUNNING FREE.
BUT THEN, WITH THIS ENTIRE PLANET IN MY GRASP...

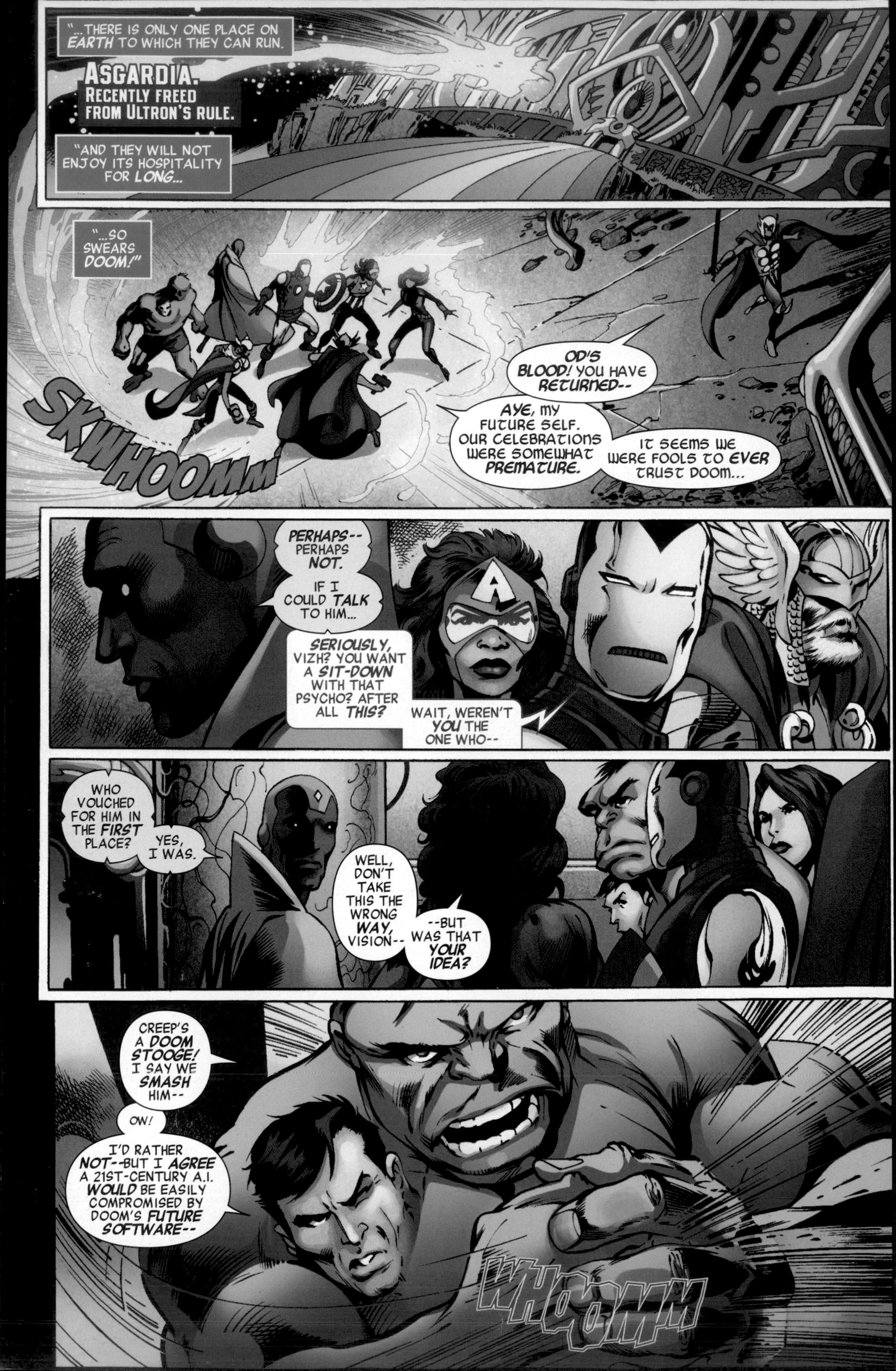
"...THERE IS ONLY ONE PLACE ON EARTH TO WHICH THEY CAN RUN.
ASGARDIA. RECENTLY FREED FROM ULTRON'S RULE.
"AND THEY WILL NOT ENJOY ITS HOSPITALITY FOR LONG...
"...SO SWEARS DOOM!"
SKWHOOMM
OD'S BLOOD! YOU HAVE RETURNED--
AYE, MY FUTURE SELF. OUR CELEBRATIONS WERE SOMEWHAT PREMATURE.
IT SEEMS WE WERE FOOLS TO EVER TRUST DOOM...
PERHAPS-- PERHAPS NOT.
IF I COULD TALK TO HIM...
SERIOUSLY, VIZH? YOU WANT A SIT-DOWN WITH THAT PSYCHO? AFTER ALL THIS?
WAIT, WEREN'T YOU THE ONE WHO--
WHO VOUCHED FOR HIM IN THE FIRST PLACE?
YES, I WAS.
WELL, DON'T TAKE THIS THE WRONG WAY, VISION--
--BUT WAS THAT YOUR IDEA?
CREEP'S A DOOM STOOGE! I SAY WE SMASH HIM--
OW!
I'D RATHER NOT--BUT I AGREE A 21ST-CENTURY A.I. WOULD BE EASILY COMPROMISED BY DOOM'S FUTURE SOFTWARE--
WHOOMM

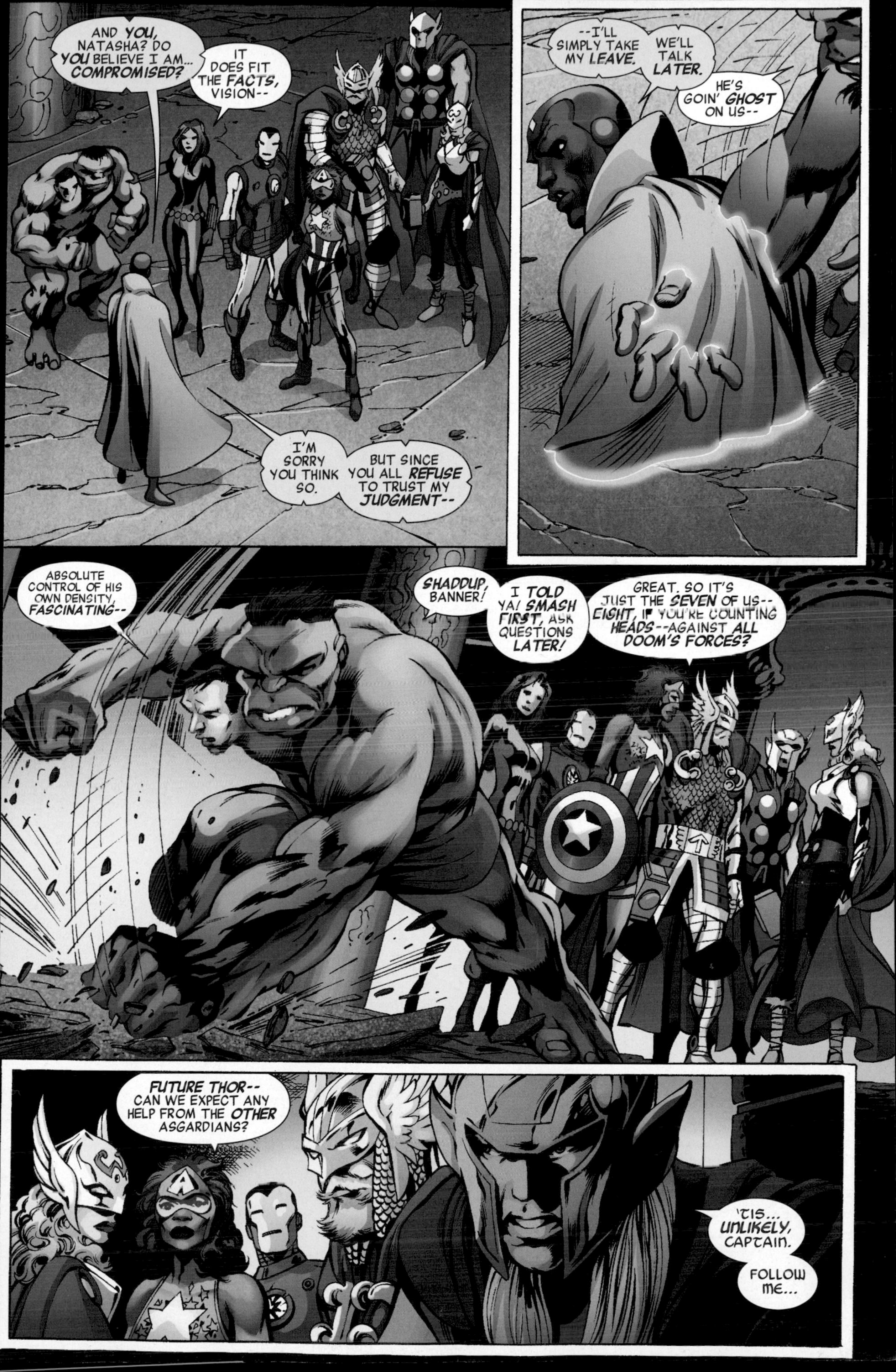
AND YOU, NATASHA? DO YOU BELIEVE I AM... COMPROMISED?
IT DOES FIT THE FACTS, VISION--
I'M SORRY YOU THINK SO.
BUT SINCE YOU ALL REFUSE TO TRUST MY JUDGMENT--
--I'LL SIMPLY TAKE MY LEAVE.
WE'LL TALK LATER.
HE'S GOIN' GHOST ON US--
ABSOLUTE CONTROL OF HIS OWN DENSITY, FASCINATING--
SHADDUP, BANNER!
I TOLD YA! SMASH FIRST, ASK QUESTIONS LATER!
GREAT. SO IT'S JUST THE SEVEN OF US--EIGHT, IF YOU'RE COUNTING HEADS--AGAINST ALL DOOM'S FORCES?
FUTURE THOR--CAN WE EXPECT ANY HELP FROM THE OTHER ASGARDIANS?
'TIS... UNLIKELY, CAPTAIN.
FOLLOW ME...

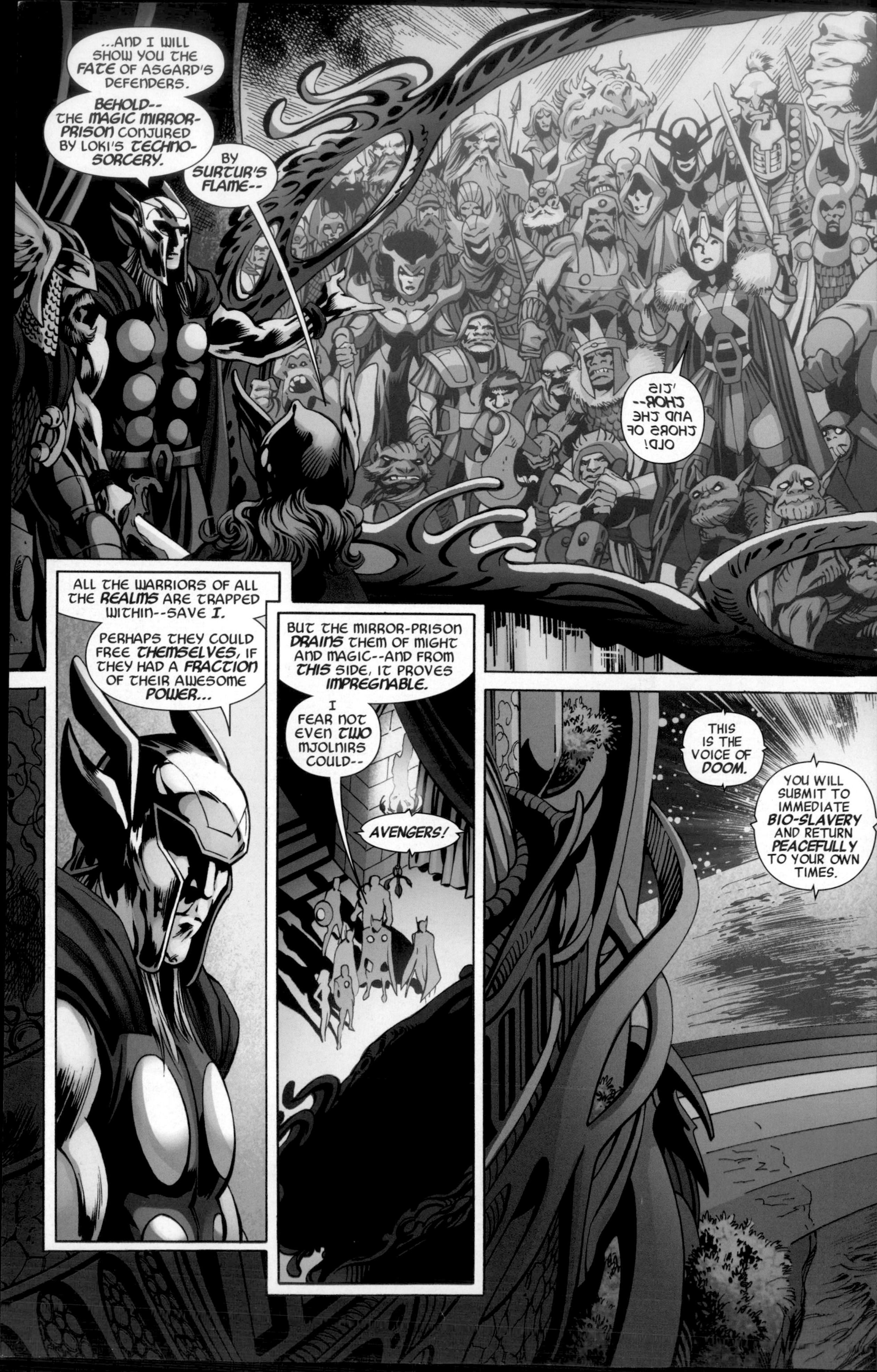
...AND I WILL SHOW YOU THE FATE OF ASGARD'S DEFENDERS.
BEHOLD-- THE MAGIC MIRROR-PRISON CONJURED BY LOKI'S TECHNO-SORCERY.
BY SURTUR'S FLAME--
'TIS THOR-- AND THE THORS OF OLD!
ALL THE WARRIORS OF ALL THE REALMS ARE TRAPPED WITHIN--SAVE I.
PERHAPS THEY COULD FREE THEMSELVES, IF THEY HAD A FRACTION OF THEIR AWESOME POWER...
BUT THE MIRROR-PRISON DRAINS THEM OF MIGHT AND MAGIC--AND FROM THIS SIDE, IT PROVES IMPREGNABLE.
I FEAR NOT EVEN TWO MJOLNIRS COULD--
AVENGERS!
THIS IS THE VOICE OF DOOM.
YOU WILL SUBMIT TO IMMEDIATE BIO-SLAVERY AND RETURN PEACEFULLY TO YOUR OWN TIMES.

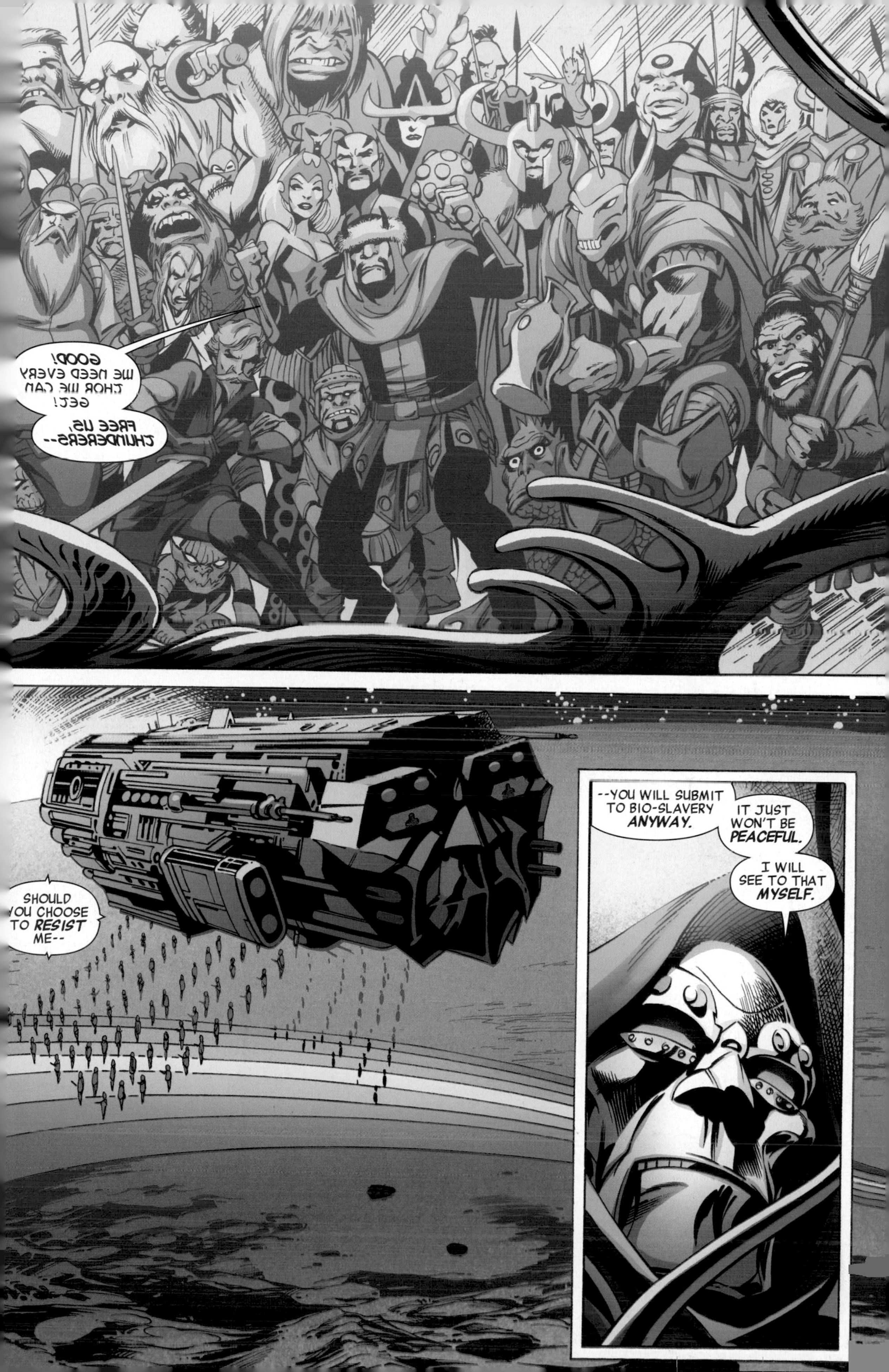
GOOD! WE NEED EVERY THOR WE CAN GET!
FREE US, THUNDERERS--
SHOULD YOU CHOOSE TO RESIST ME--
--YOU WILL SUBMIT TO BIO-SLAVERY ANYWAY.
IT JUST WON'T BE PEACEFUL.
I WILL SEE TO THAT MYSELF.

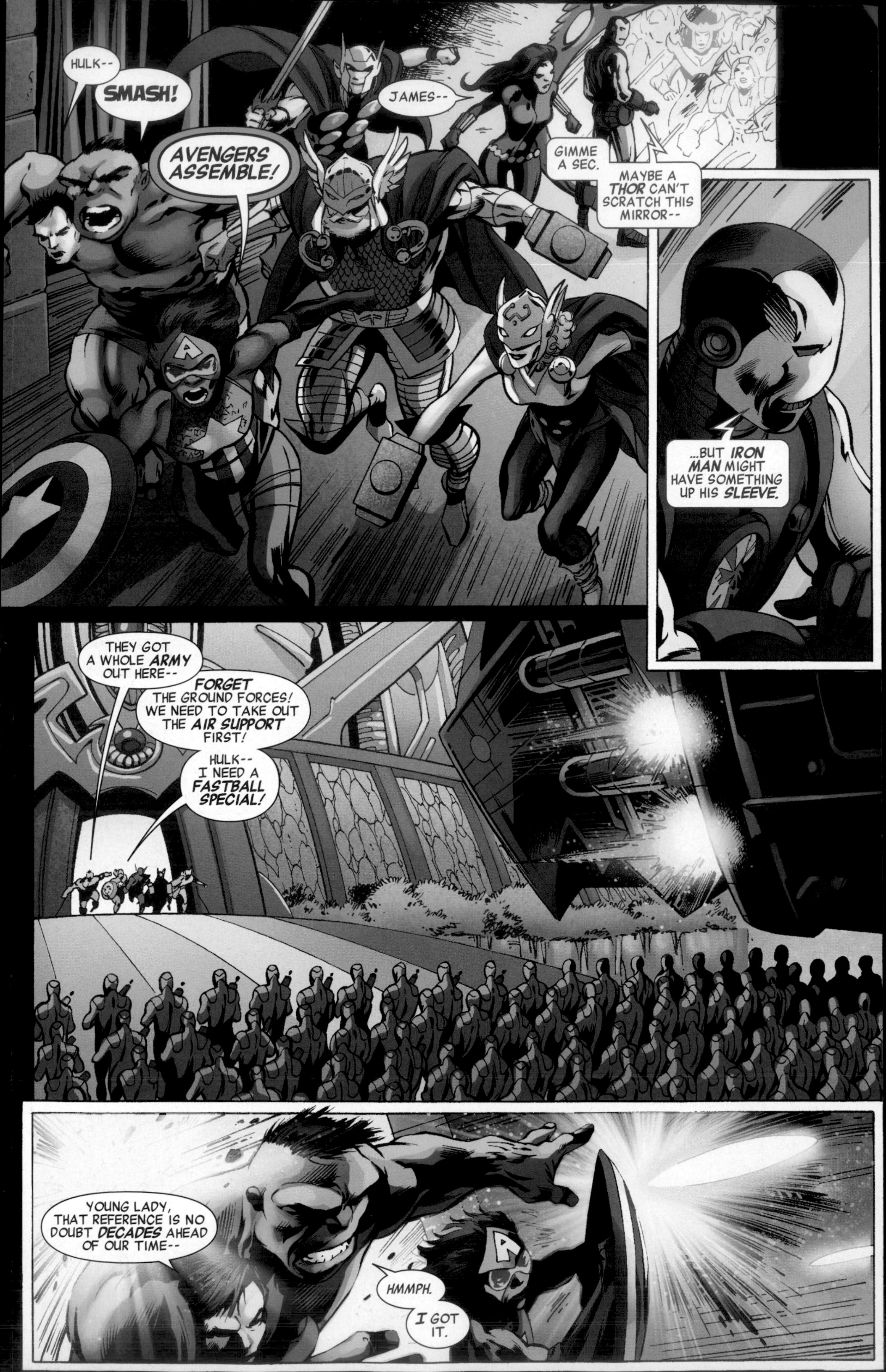
HULK--
SMASH!
AVENGERS ASSEMBLE!
JAMES--
GIMME A SEC.
MAYBE A THOR CAN'T SCRATCH THIS MIRROR--
...BUT IRON MAN MIGHT HAVE SOMETHING UP HIS SLEEVE.
THEY GOT A WHOLE ARMY OUT HERE--
FORGET THE GROUND FORCES! WE NEED TO TAKE OUT THE AIR SUPPORT FIRST!
HULK-- I NEED A FASTBALL SPECIAL!
YOUNG LADY, THAT REFERENCE IS NO DOUBT DECADES AHEAD OF OUR TIME--
HMMPH.
I GOT IT.

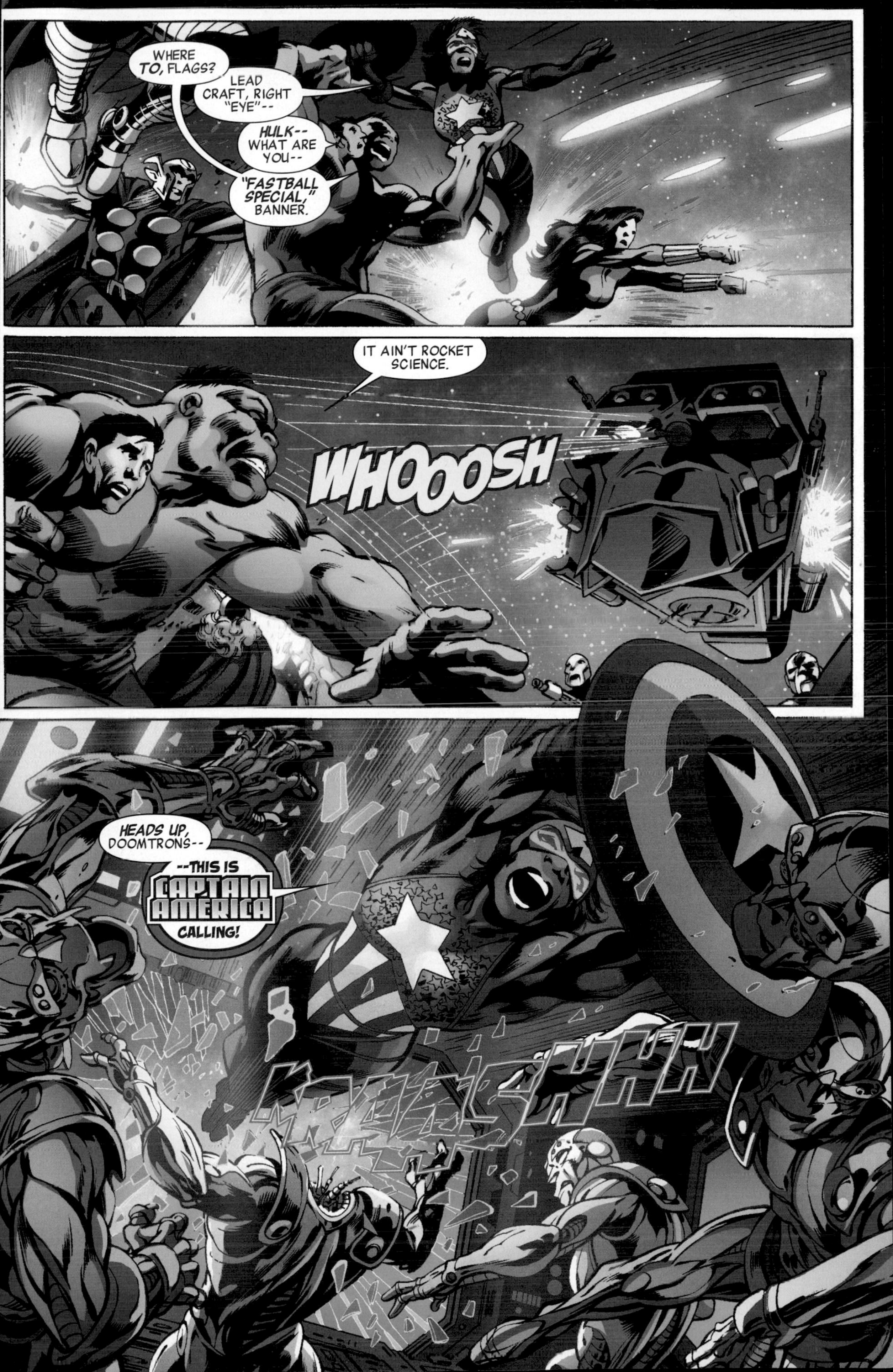
WHERE TO, FLAGS?
LEAD CRAFT, RIGHT "EYE"--
HULK-- WHAT ARE YOU--
"FASTBALL SPECIAL," BANNER.
IT AIN'T ROCKET SCIENCE.
WHOOOOSH
HEADS UP, DOOMTRONS--
--THIS IS CAPTAIN AMERICA CALLING!

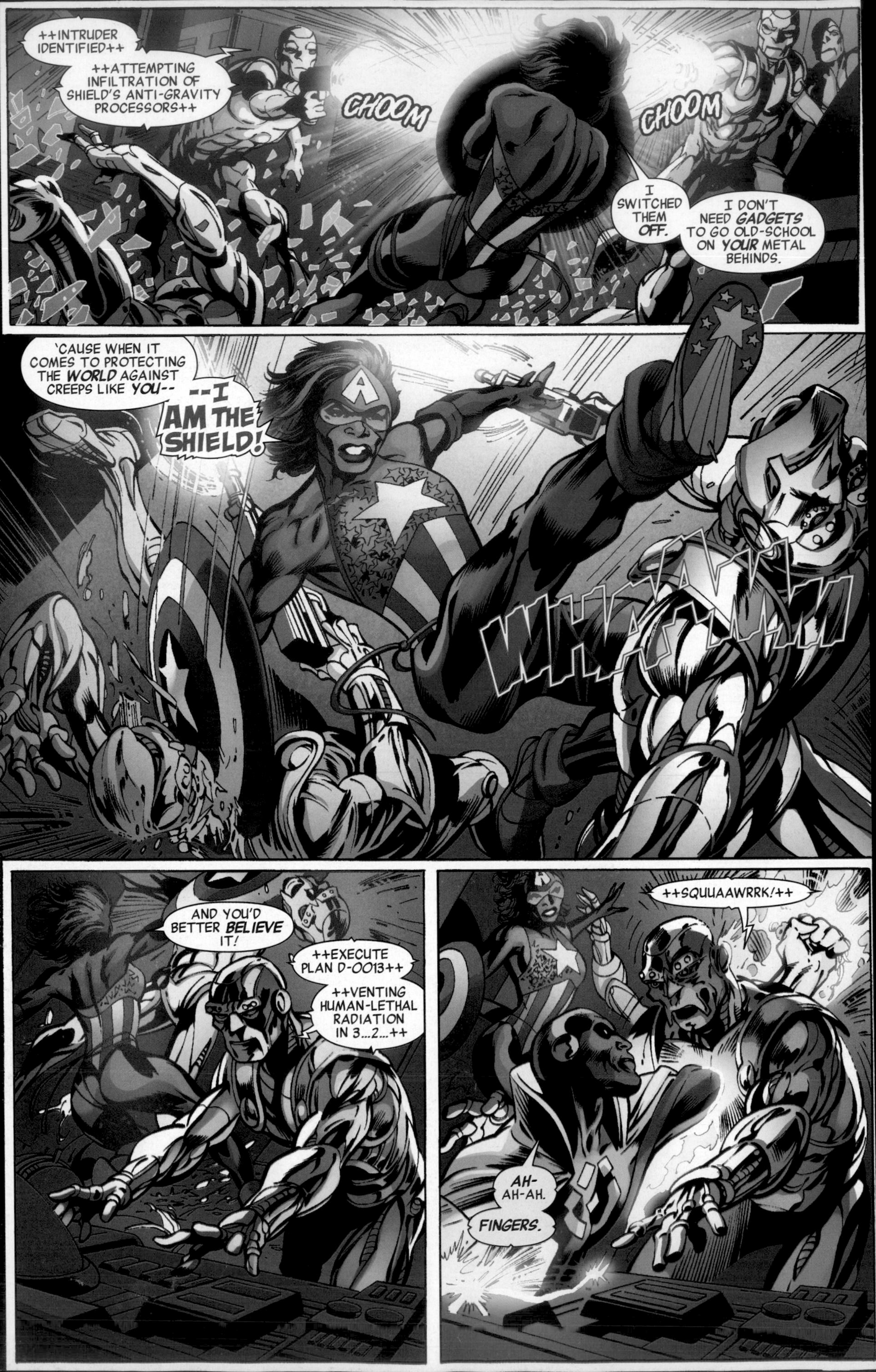
++INTRUDER IDENTIFIED++
++ATTEMPTING INFILTRATION OF SHIELD'S ANTI-GRAVITY PROCESSORS++
CHOOM
CHOOM
I SWITCHED THEM OFF.
I DON'T NEED GADGETS TO GO OLD-SCHOOL ON YOUR METAL BEHINDS.
'CAUSE WHEN IT COMES TO PROTECTING THE WORLD AGAINST CREEPS LIKE YOU--
--I AM THE SHIELD!
AND YOU'D BETTER BELIEVE IT!
++EXECUTE PLAN D-0013++
++VENTING HUMAN-LETHAL RADIATION IN 3...2...++
++SQUUAAWRRK!++
AH-AH-AH.
FINGERS.

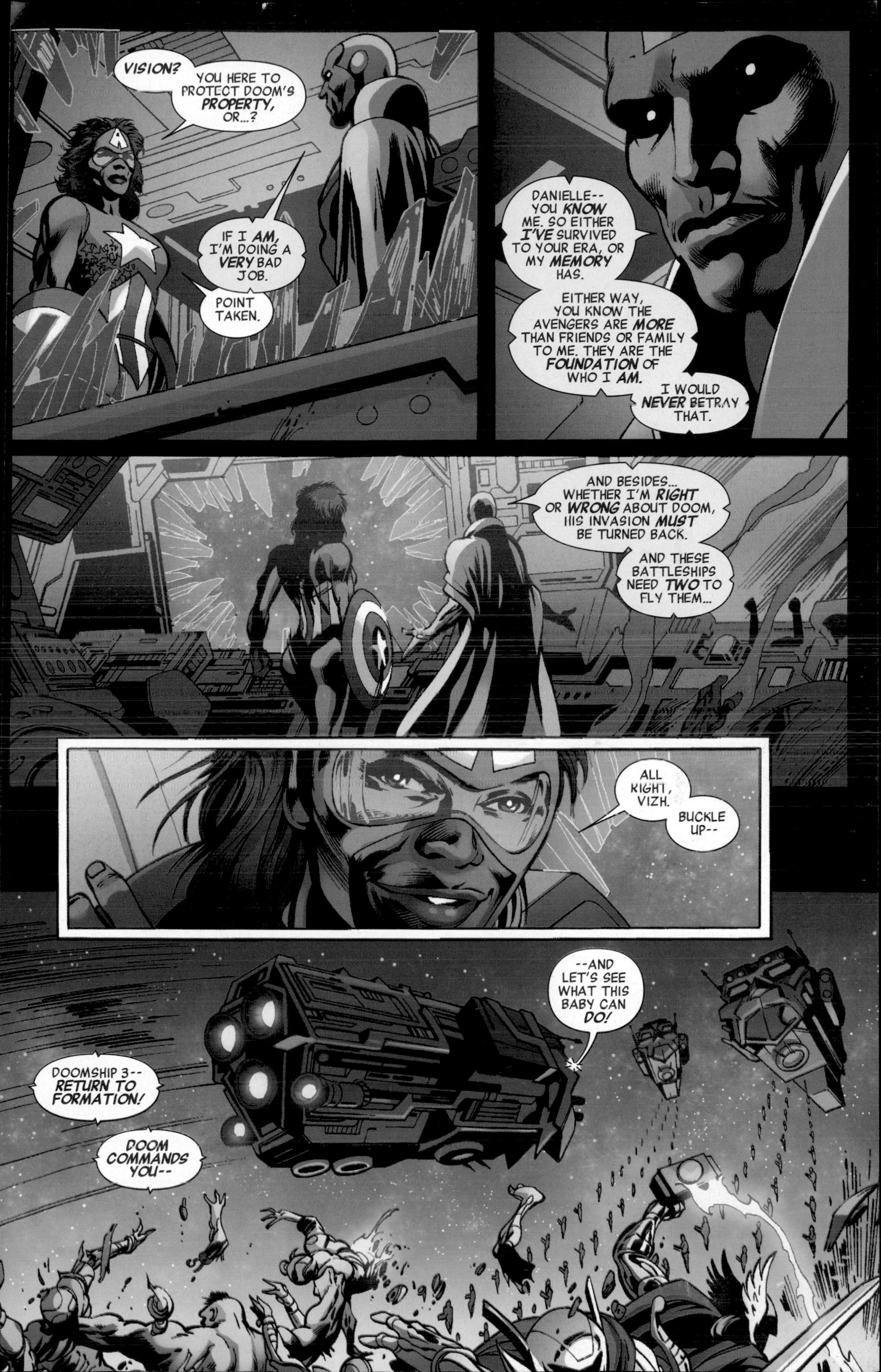
VISION?
YOU HERE TO PROTECT DOOM'S PROPERTY, OR...?
IF I AM, I'M DOING A VERY BAD JOB.
POINT TAKEN.
DANIELLE-- YOU KNOW ME. SO EITHER I'VE SURVIVED TO YOUR ERA, OR MY MEMORY HAS.
EITHER WAY, YOU KNOW THE AVENGERS ARE MORE THAN FRIENDS OR FAMILY TO ME. THEY ARE THE FOUNDATION OF WHO I AM.
I WOULD NEVER BETRAY THAT.
AND BESIDES... WHETHER I'M RIGHT OR WRONG ABOUT DOOM, HIS INVASION MUST BE TURNED BACK.
AND THESE BATTLESHIPS NEED TWO TO FLY THEM...
ALL RIGHT, VIZH.
BUCKLE UP--
--AND LET'S SEE WHAT THIS BABY CAN DO!
DOOMSHIP 3-- RETURN TO FORMATION!
DOOM COMMANDS YOU--

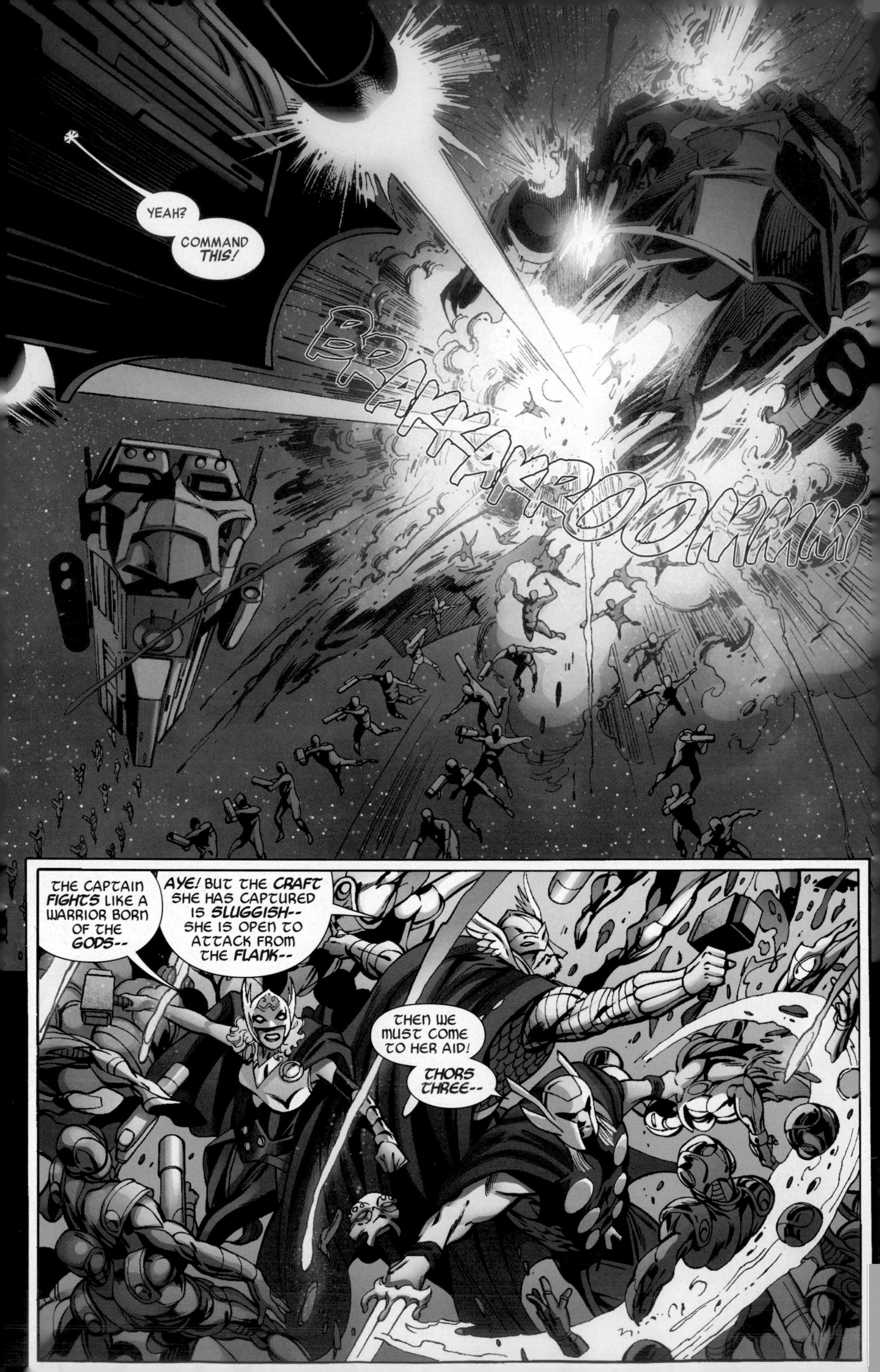
YEAH? COMMAND THIS!
BRAKAKROOMMM
THE CAPTAIN FIGHTS LIKE A WARRIOR BORN OF THE GODS--
AYE! BUT THE CRAFT SHE HAS CAPTURED IS SLUGGISH-- SHE IS OPEN TO ATTACK FROM THE FLANK--
THEN WE MUST COME TO HER AID!
THORS THREE--

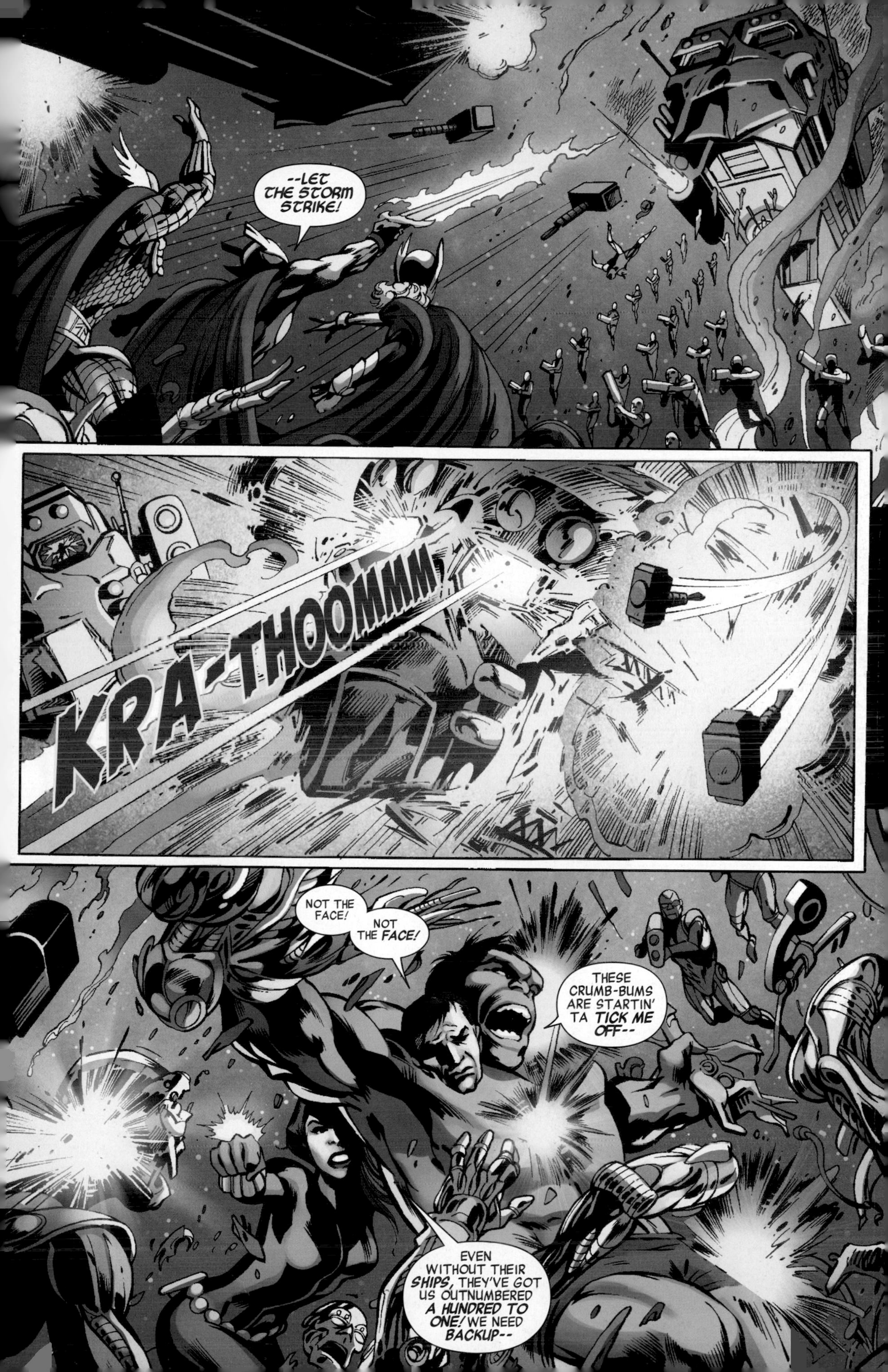
--LET THE STORM STRIKE!
KRA-THOOMMM
NOT THE FACE!
NOT THE FACE!
THESE CRUMB-BUMS ARE STARTIN' TA TICK ME OFF--
EVEN WITHOUT THEIR SHIPS, THEY'VE GOT US OUTNUMBERED A HUNDRED TO ONE! WE NEED BACKUP--

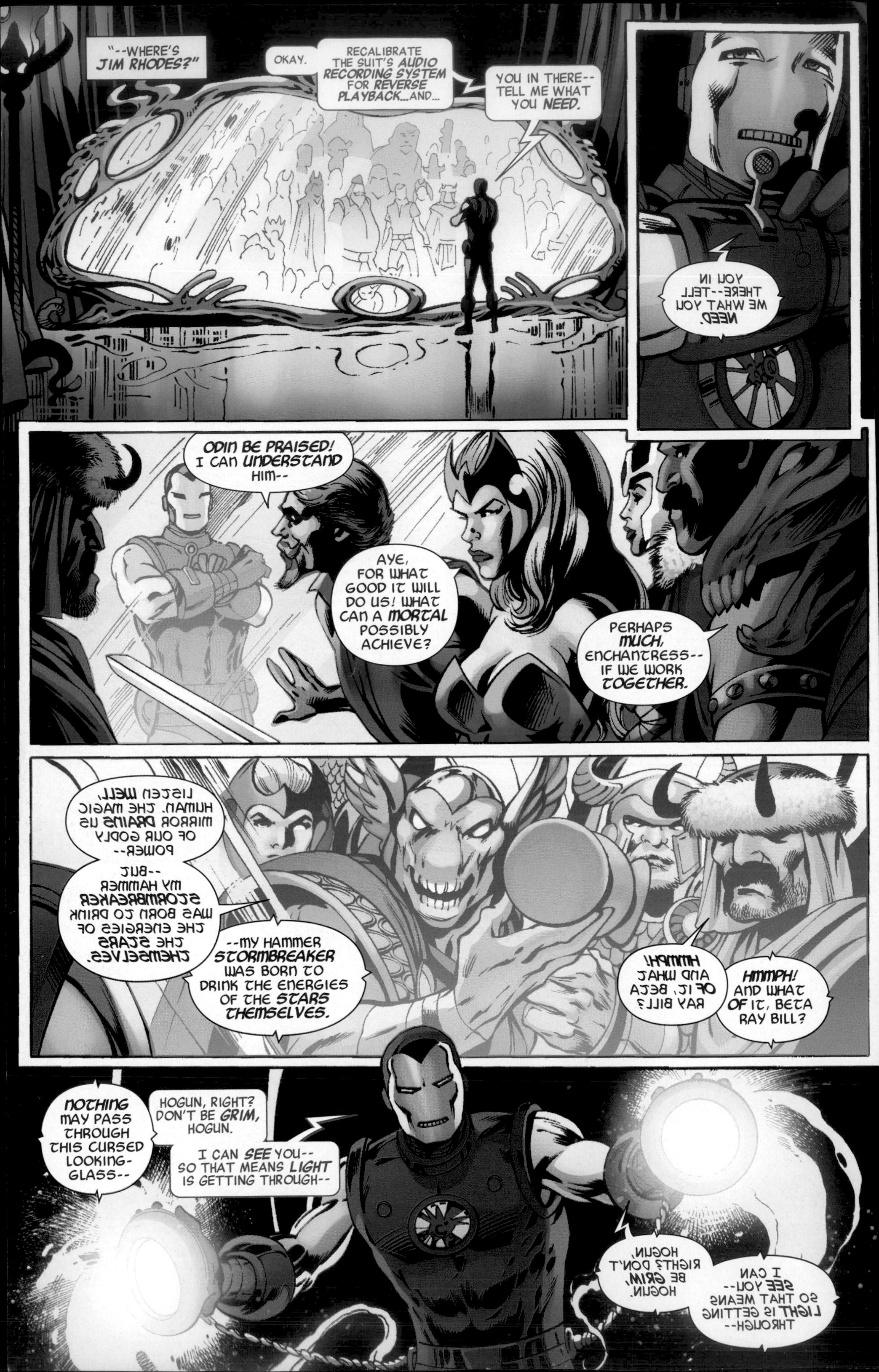
"--WHERE'S JIM RHODES?"
OKAY.
RECALIBRATE THE SUIT'S AUDIO RECORDING SYSTEM FOR REVERSE PLAYBACK...AND...
YOU IN THERE--TELL ME WHAT YOU NEED.
YOU IN THERE--TELL ME WHAT YOU NEED.
ODIN BE PRAISED! I CAN UNDERSTAND HIM--
AYE, FOR WHAT GOOD IT WILL DO US! WHAT CAN A MORTAL POSSIBLY ACHIEVE?
PERHAPS MUCH, ENCHANTRESS--IF WE WORK TOGETHER.
LISTEN WELL, HUMAN. THE MAGIC MIRROR DRAINS US OF OUR GODLY POWER--
--BUT MY HAMMER STORMBREAKER WAS BORN TO DRINK THE ENERGIES OF THE STARS THEMSELVES.
--MY HAMMER STORMBREAKER WAS BORN TO DRINK THE ENERGIES OF THE STARS THEMSELVES.
HMMPH! AND WHAT OF IT, BETA RAY BILL?
HMMPH! AND WHAT OF IT, BETA RAY BILL?
NOTHING MAY PASS THROUGH THIS CURSED LOOKING-GLASS--
HOGUN, RIGHT? DON'T BE GRIM, HOGUN.
I CAN SEE YOU--SO THAT MEANS LIGHT IS GETTING THROUGH--
HOGUN, RIGHT? DON'T BE GRIM, HOGUN.
I CAN SEE YOU--SO THAT MEANS LIGHT IS GETTING THROUGH--

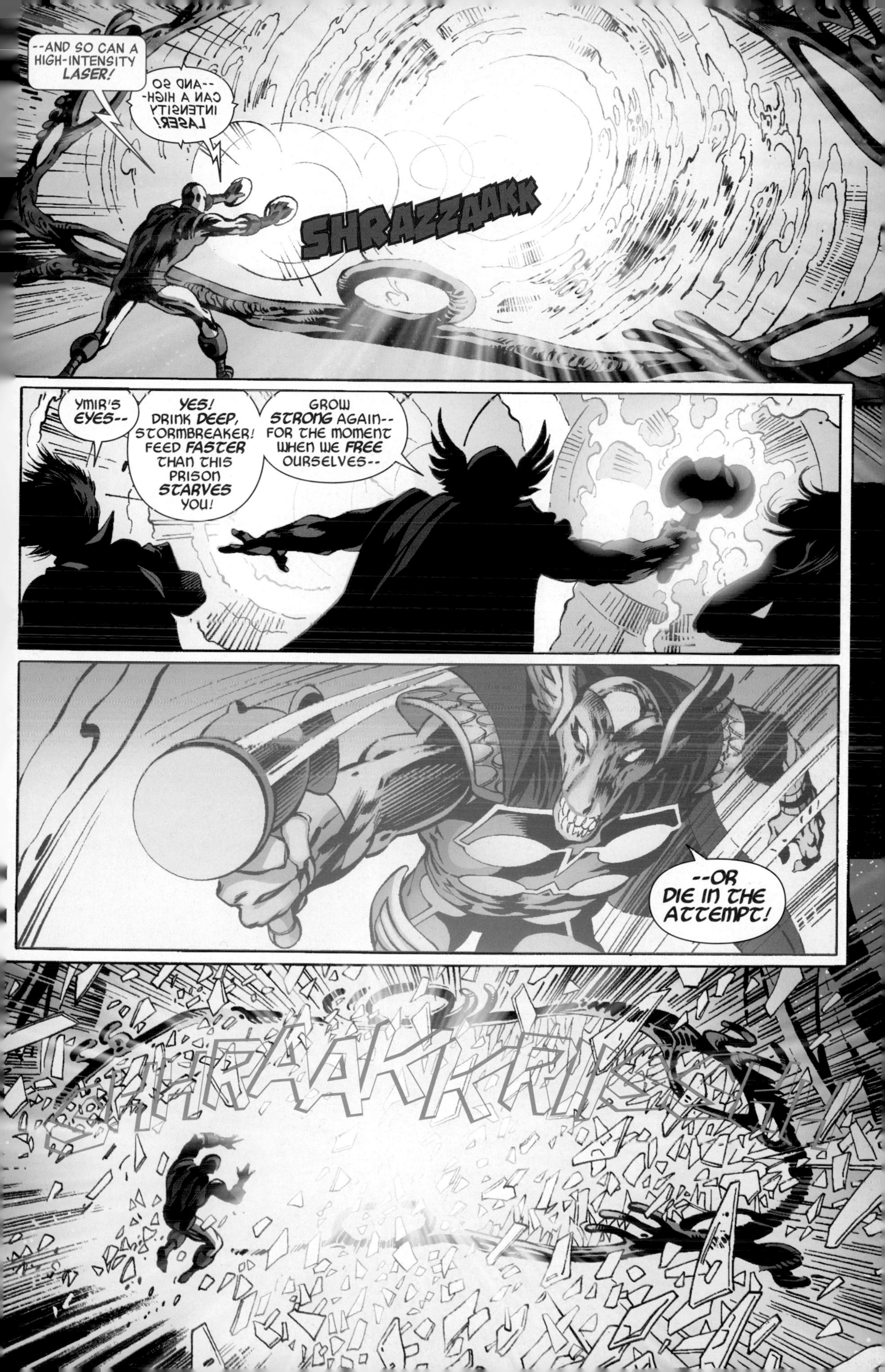
--AND SO CAN A HIGH-INTENSITY LASER!
SHRAZZAAKK
YMIR'S EYES--
YES! DRINK DEEP, STORMBREAKER! FEED FASTER THAN THIS PRISON STARVES YOU!
GROW STRONG AGAIN-- FOR THE MOMENT WHEN WE FREE OURSELVES--
--OR DIE IN THE ATTEMPT!

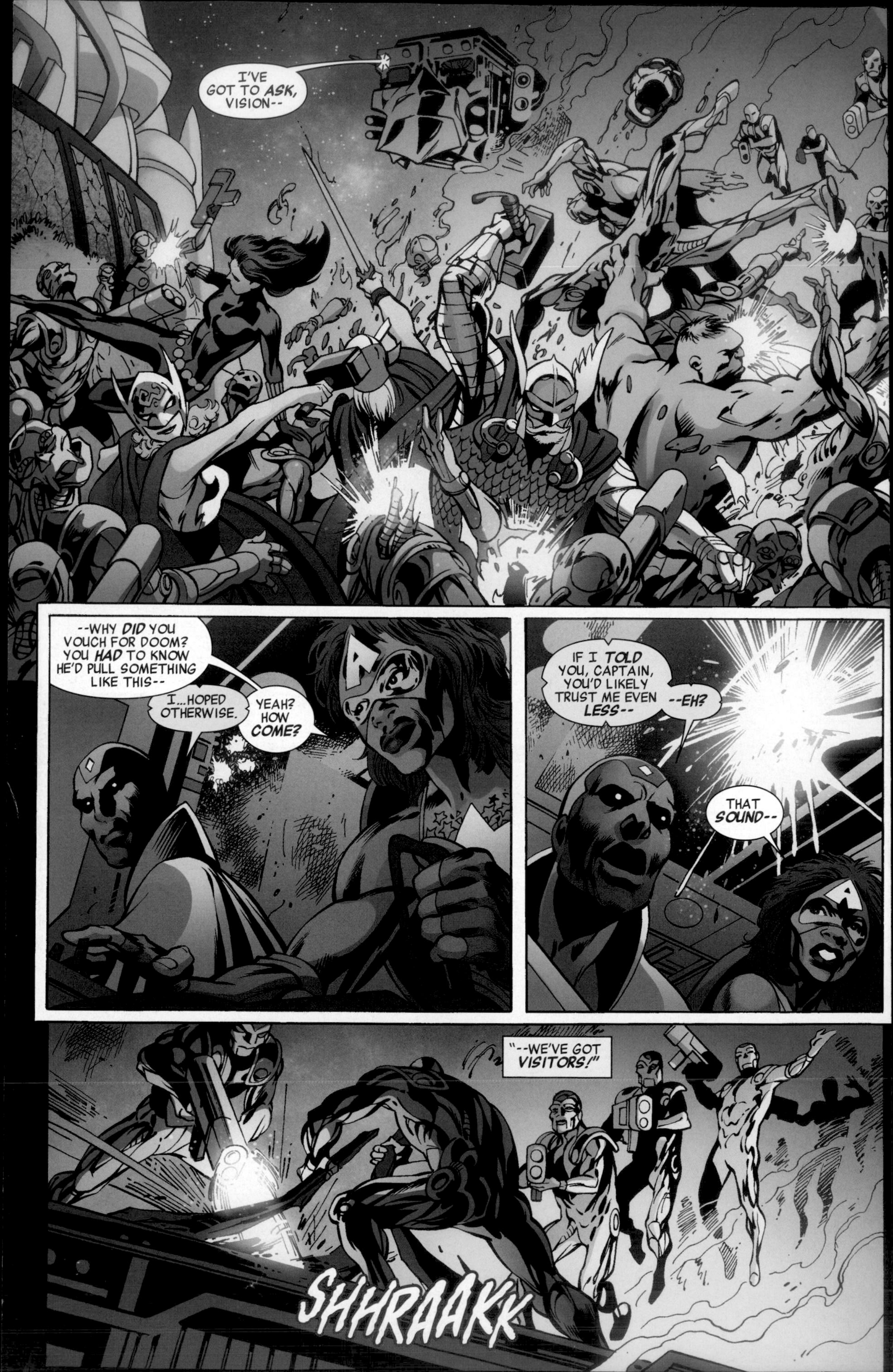
I'VE GOT TO ASK, VISION--
--WHY DID YOU VOUCH FOR DOOM? YOU HAD TO KNOW HE'D PULL SOMETHING LIKE THIS--
I...HOPED OTHERWISE.
YEAH? HOW COME?
IF I TOLD YOU, CAPTAIN, YOU'D LIKELY TRUST ME EVEN LESS--
--EH?
THAT SOUND--
"--WE'VE GOT VISITORS!"
SHHRAAKK

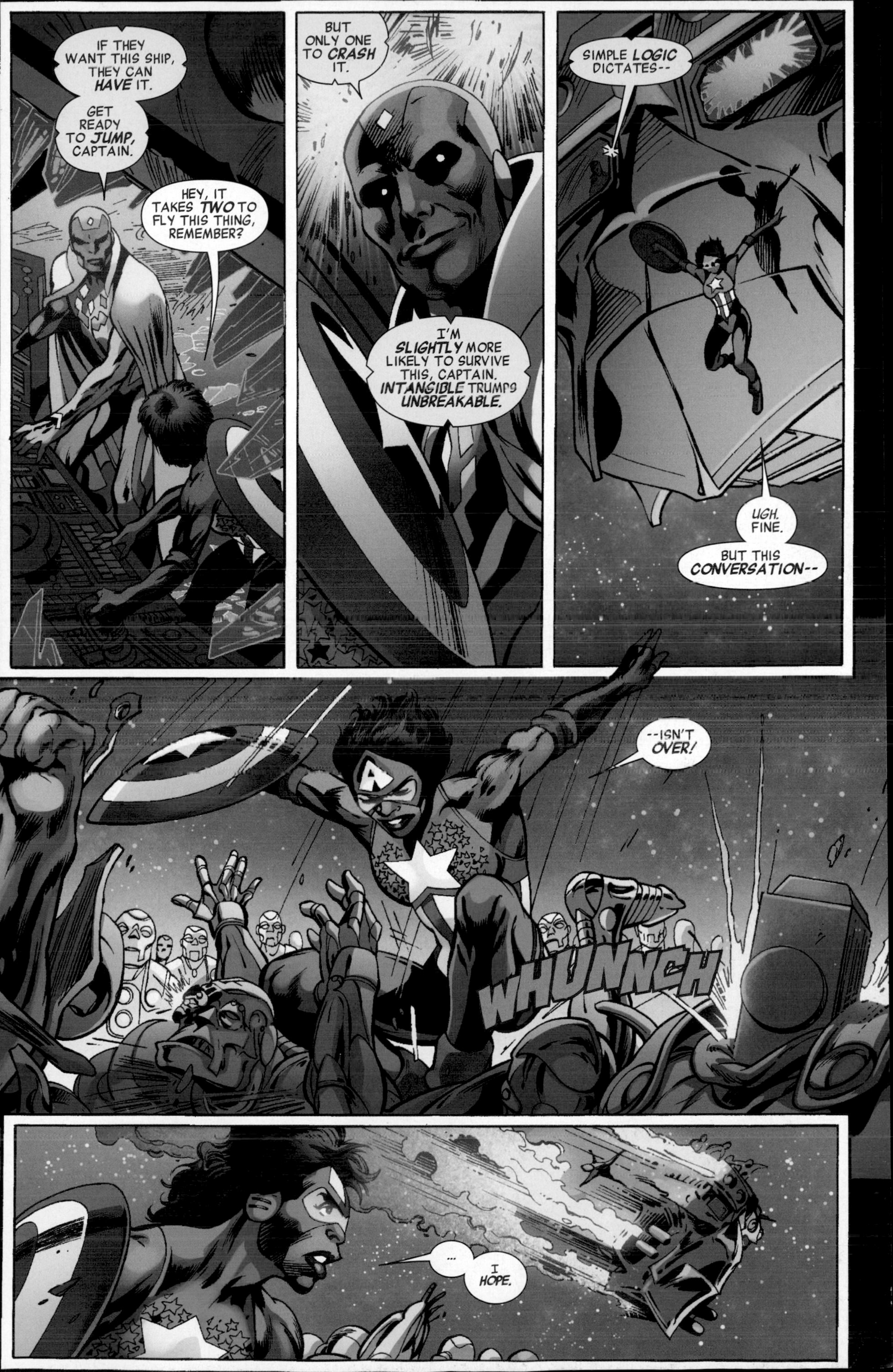
IF THEY WANT THIS SHIP, THEY CAN HAVE IT.
GET READY TO JUMP, CAPTAIN.
HEY, IT TAKES TWO TO FLY THIS THING, REMEMBER?
BUT ONLY ONE TO CRASH IT.
I'M SLIGHTLY MORE LIKELY TO SURVIVE THIS, CAPTAIN. INTANGIBLE TRUMPS UNBREAKABLE.
SIMPLE LOGIC DICTATES--
UGH. FINE.
BUT THIS CONVERSATION--
--ISN'T OVER!
WHUNNCH
...
I HOPE.

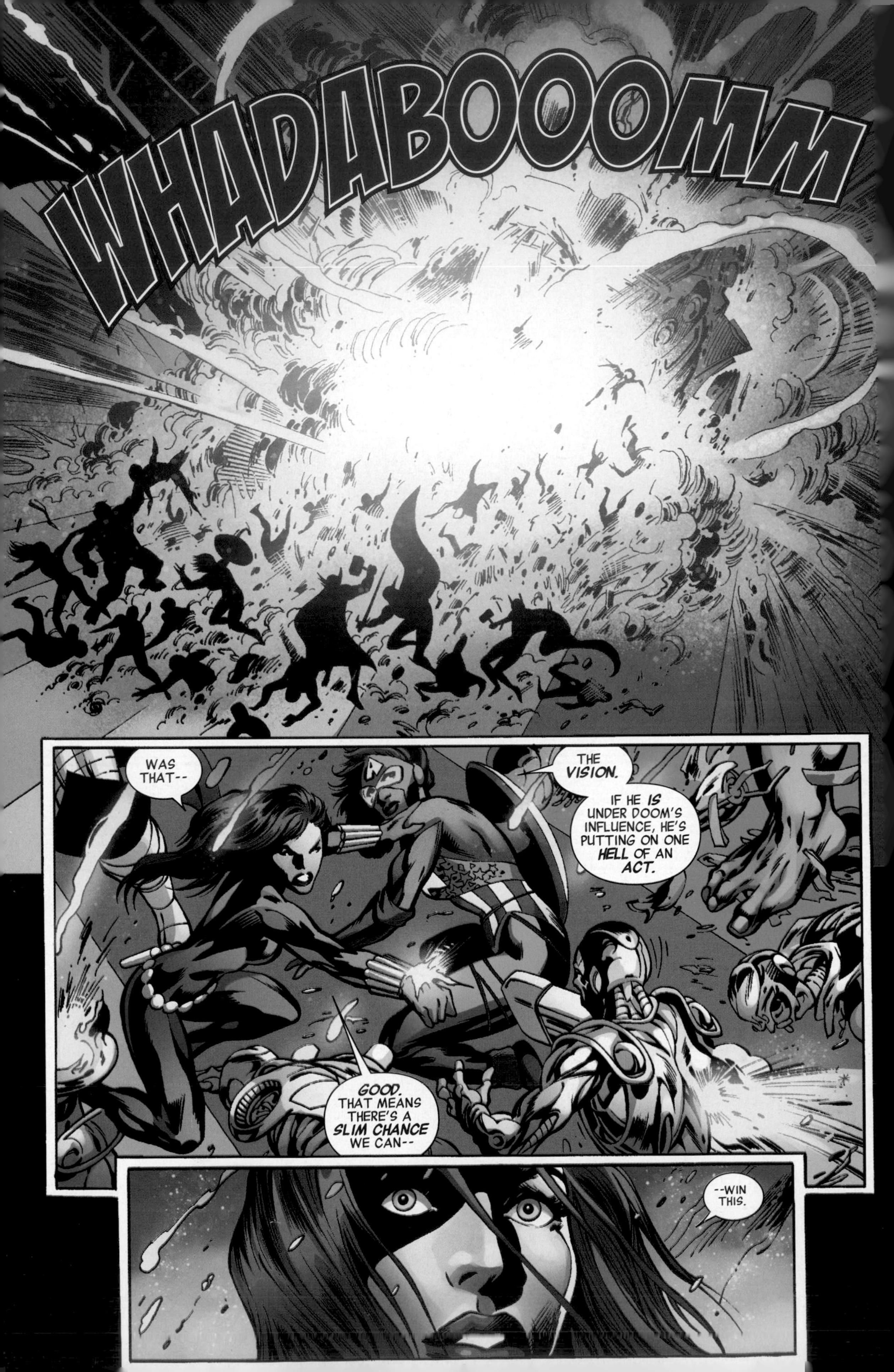
WHADABOOOMM
WAS THAT--
THE VISION.
IF HE IS UNDER DOOM'S INFLUENCE, HE'S PUTTING ON ONE HELL OF AN ACT.
GOOD. THAT MEANS THERE'S A SLIM CHANCE WE CAN--
--WIN THIS.

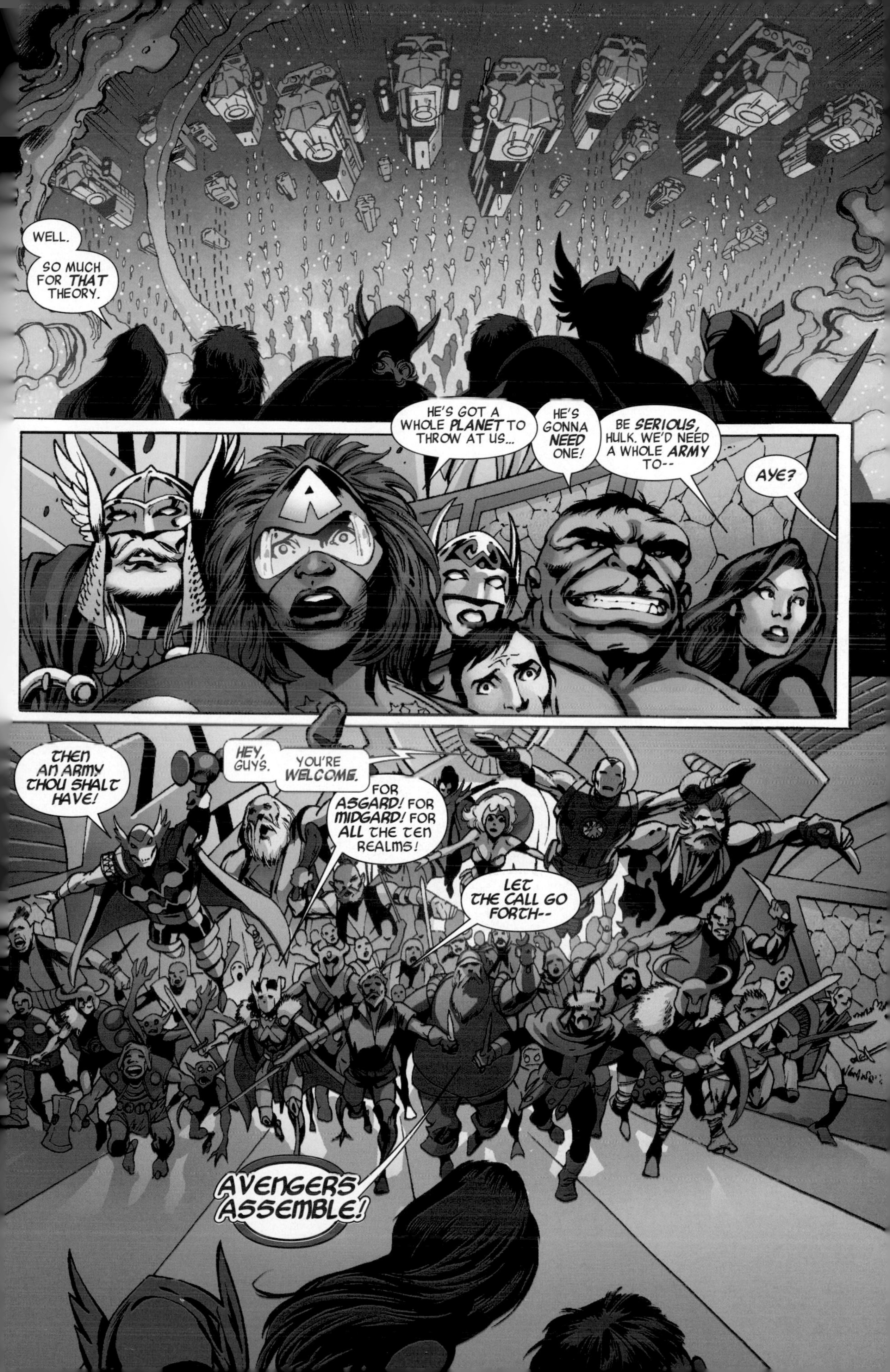
WELL.
SO MUCH FOR THAT THEORY.
HE'S GOT A WHOLE PLANET TO THROW AT US...
HE'S GONNA NEED ONE!
BE SERIOUS, HULK. WE'D NEED A WHOLE ARMY TO--
AYE?
THEN AN ARMY THOU SHALT HAVE!
HEY, GUYS.
YOU'RE WELCOME.
FOR ASGARD! FOR MIDGARD! FOR ALL THE TEN REALMS!
LET THE CALL GO FORTH--
AVENGERS ASSEMBLE!

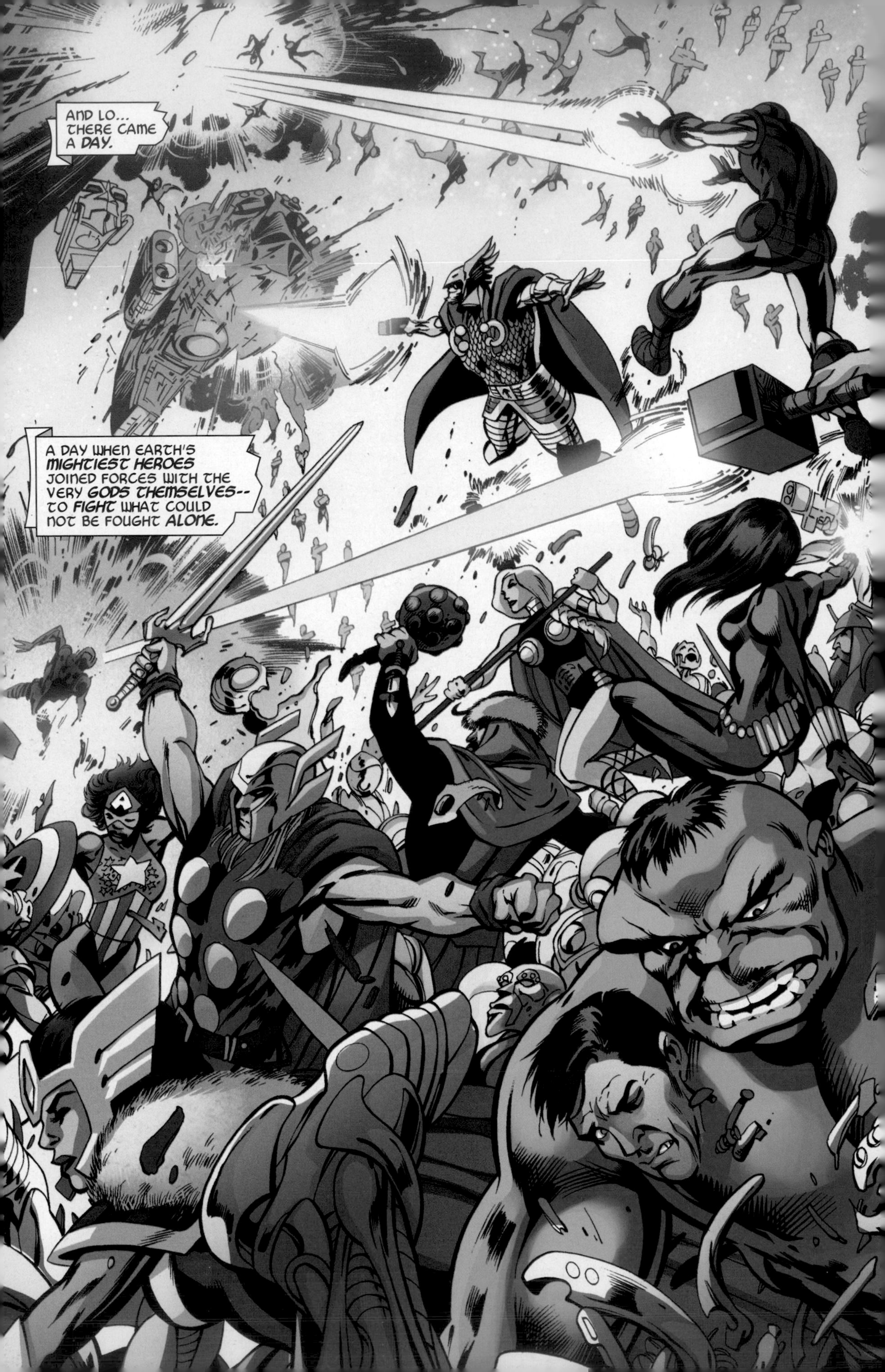
AND LO... THERE CAME A DAY.
A DAY WHEN EARTH'S MIGHTIEST HEROES JOINED FORCES WITH THE VERY GODS THEMSELVES--TO FIGHT WHAT COULD NOT BE FOUGHT ALONE.

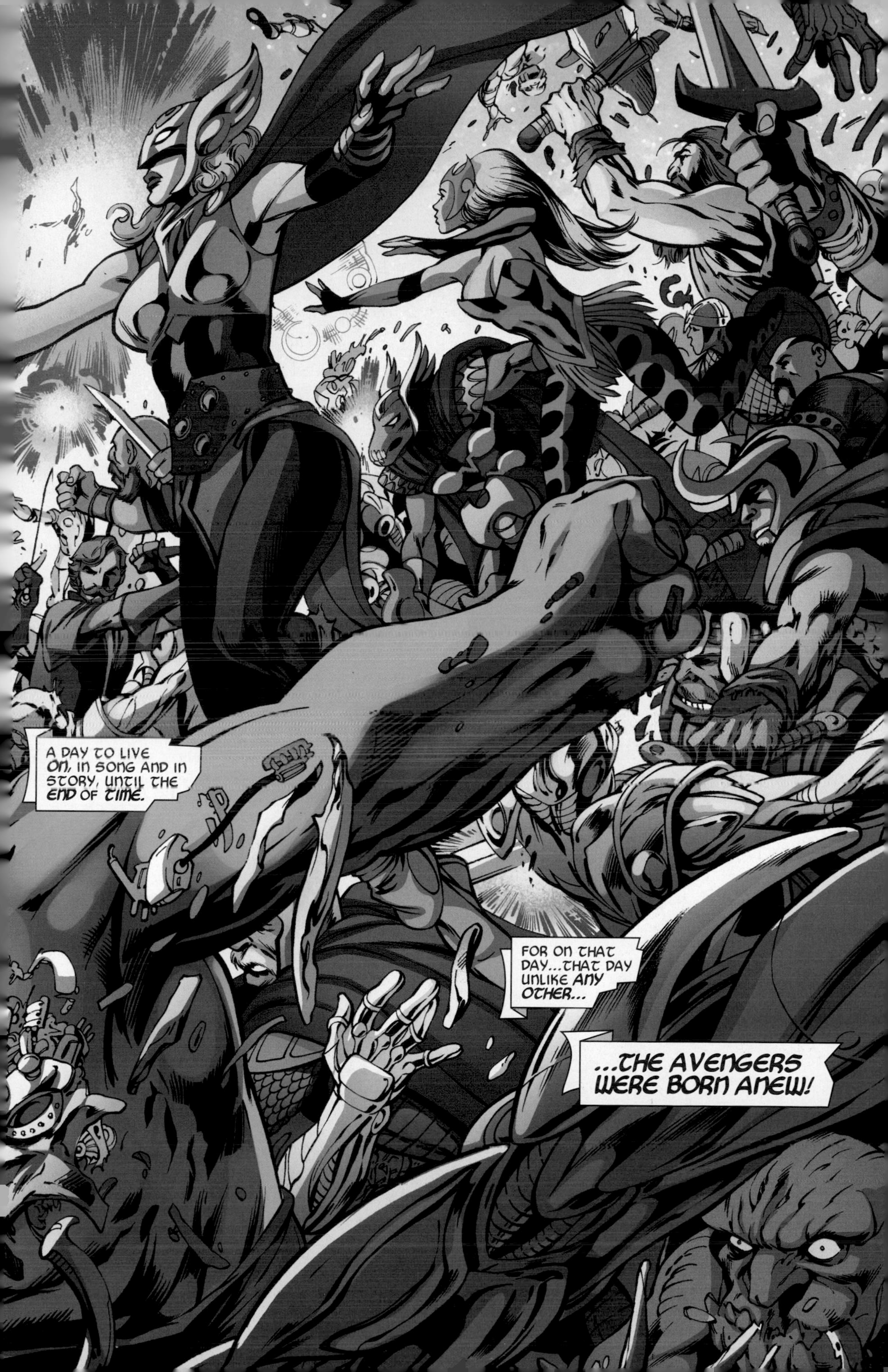
A DAY TO LIVE ON, IN SONG AND IN STORY, UNTIL THE END OF TIME.
FOR ON THAT DAY...THAT DAY UNLIKE ANY OTHER...
...THE AVENGERS WERE BORN ANEW!

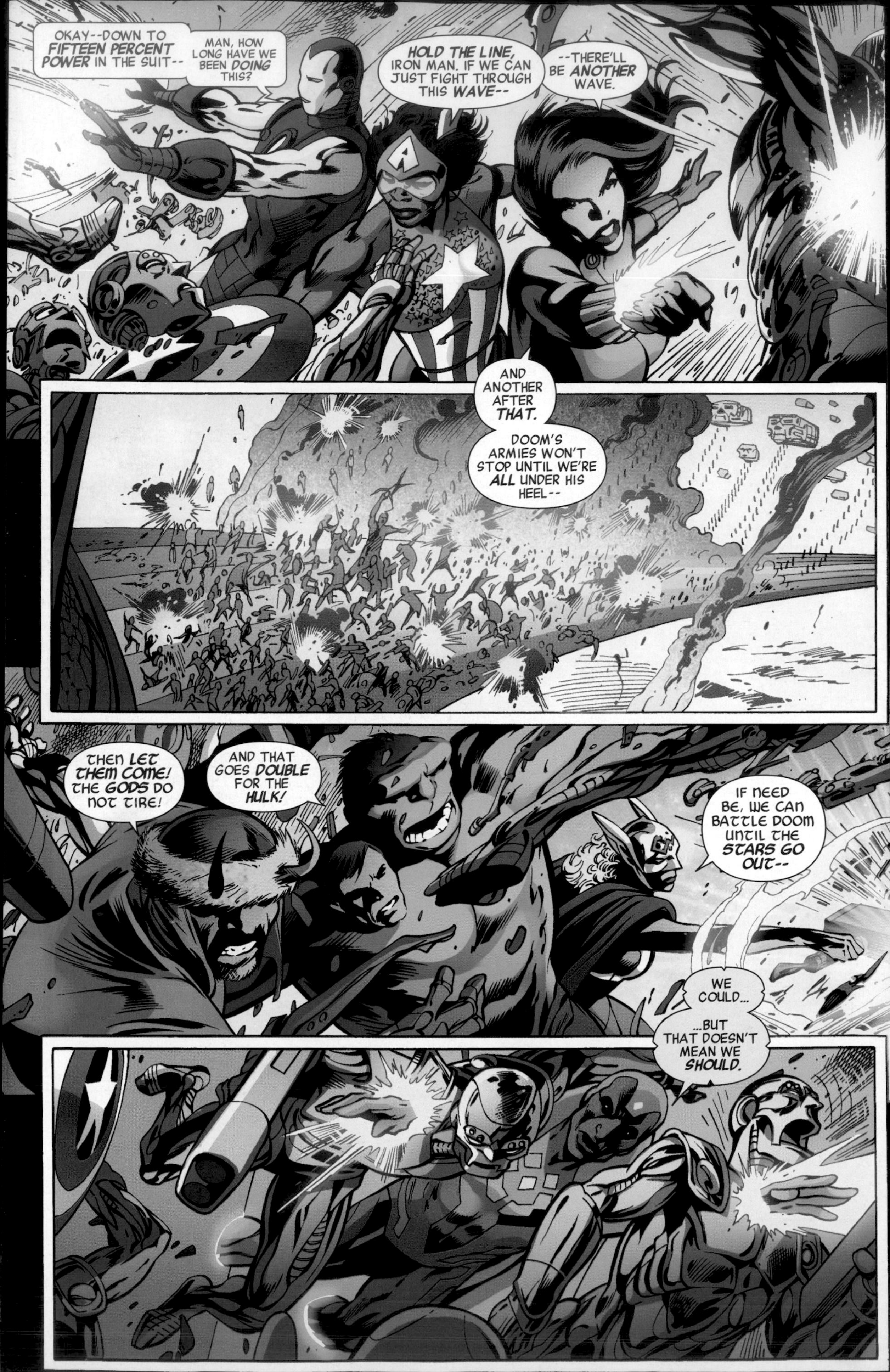
OKAY--DOWN TO FIFTEEN PERCENT POWER IN THE SUIT--
MAN, HOW LONG HAVE WE BEEN DOING THIS?
HOLD THE LINE, IRON MAN. IF WE CAN JUST FIGHT THROUGH THIS WAVE--
--THERE'LL BE ANOTHER WAVE.
AND ANOTHER AFTER THAT.
DOOM'S ARMIES WON'T STOP UNTIL WE'RE ALL UNDER HIS HEEL--
THEN LET THEM COME! THE GODS DO NOT TIRE!
AND THAT GOES DOUBLE FOR THE HULK!
IF NEED BE, WE CAN BATTLE DOOM UNTIL THE STARS GO OUT--
WE COULD...
...BUT THAT DOESN'T MEAN WE SHOULD.

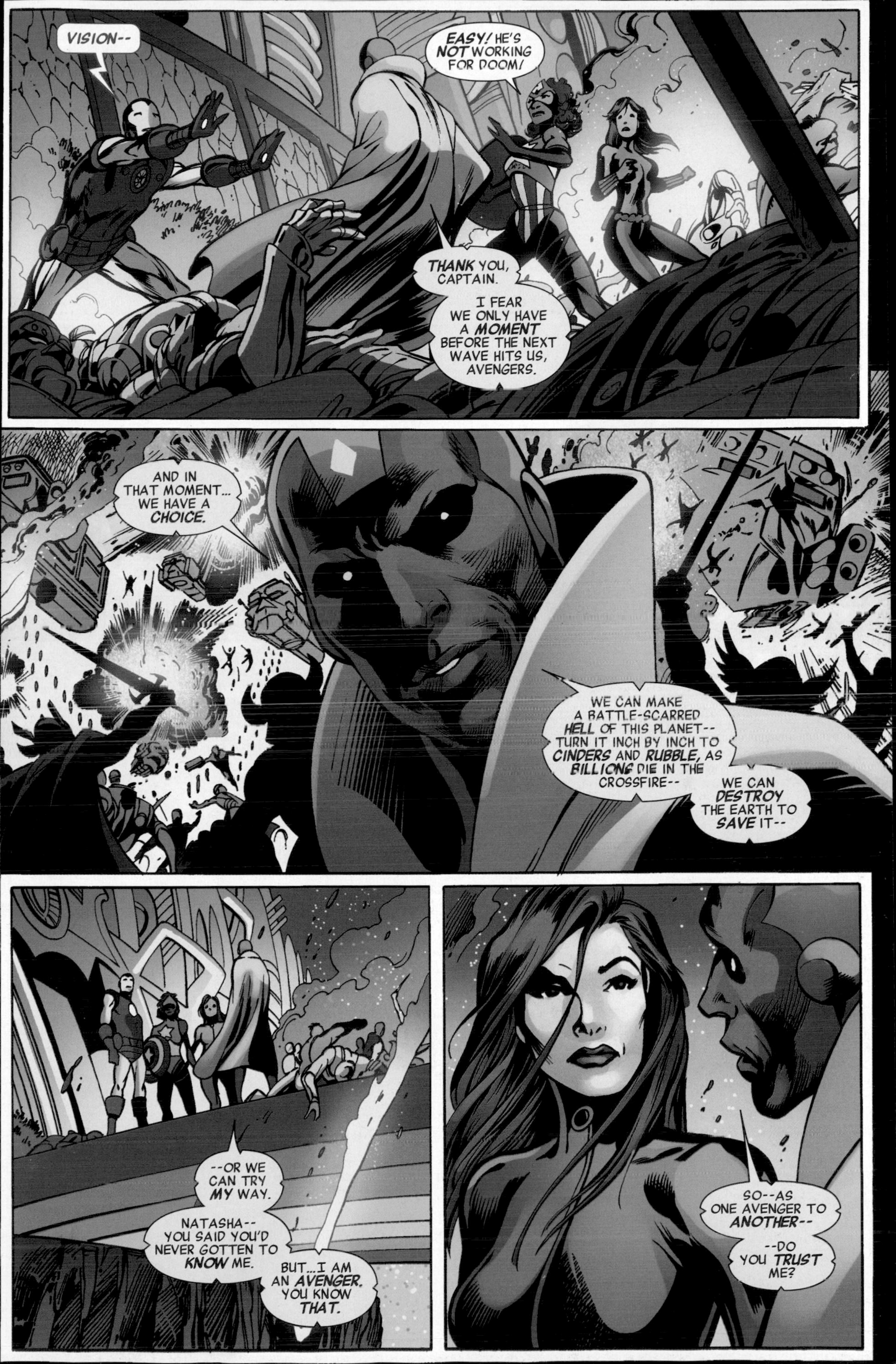
VISION--
EASY! HE'S NOT WORKING FOR DOOM!
THANK YOU, CAPTAIN.
I FEAR WE ONLY HAVE A MOMENT BEFORE THE NEXT WAVE HITS US, AVENGERS.
AND IN THAT MOMENT... WE HAVE A CHOICE.
WE CAN MAKE A BATTLE-SCARRED HELL OF THIS PLANET-- TURN IT INCH BY INCH TO CINDERS AND RUBBLE, AS BILLIONS DIE IN THE CROSSFIRE--
WE CAN DESTROY THE EARTH TO SAVE IT--
--OR WE CAN TRY MY WAY.
NATASHA-- YOU SAID YOU'D NEVER GOTTEN TO KNOW ME.
BUT...I AM AN AVENGER. YOU KNOW THAT.
SO--AS ONE AVENGER TO ANOTHER--
--DO YOU TRUST ME?

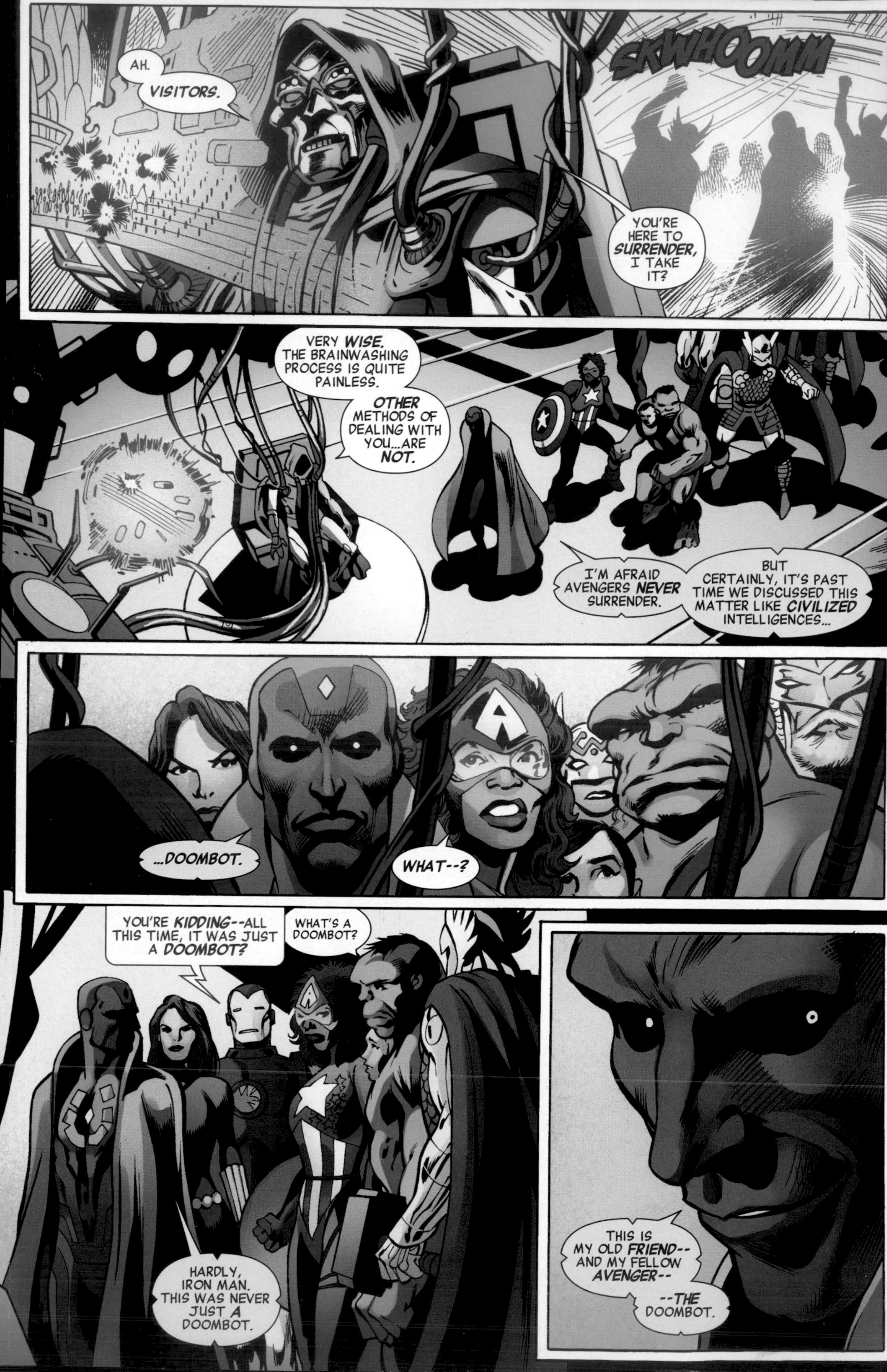
AH.
VISITORS.
SKWHOOMM
YOU'RE HERE TO SURRENDER, I TAKE IT?
VERY WISE. THE BRAINWASHING PROCESS IS QUITE PAINLESS.
OTHER METHODS OF DEALING WITH YOU...ARE NOT.
I'M AFRAID AVENGERS NEVER SURRENDER.
BUT CERTAINLY, IT'S PAST TIME WE DISCUSSED THIS MATTER LIKE CIVILIZED INTELLIGENCES...
...DOOMBOT.
WHAT--?
YOU'RE KIDDING--ALL THIS TIME, IT WAS JUST A DOOMBOT?
WHAT'S A DOOMBOT?
HARDLY, IRON MAN. THIS WAS NEVER JUST A DOOMBOT.
THIS IS MY OLD FRIEND-- AND MY FELLOW AVENGER--
--THE DOOMBOT.

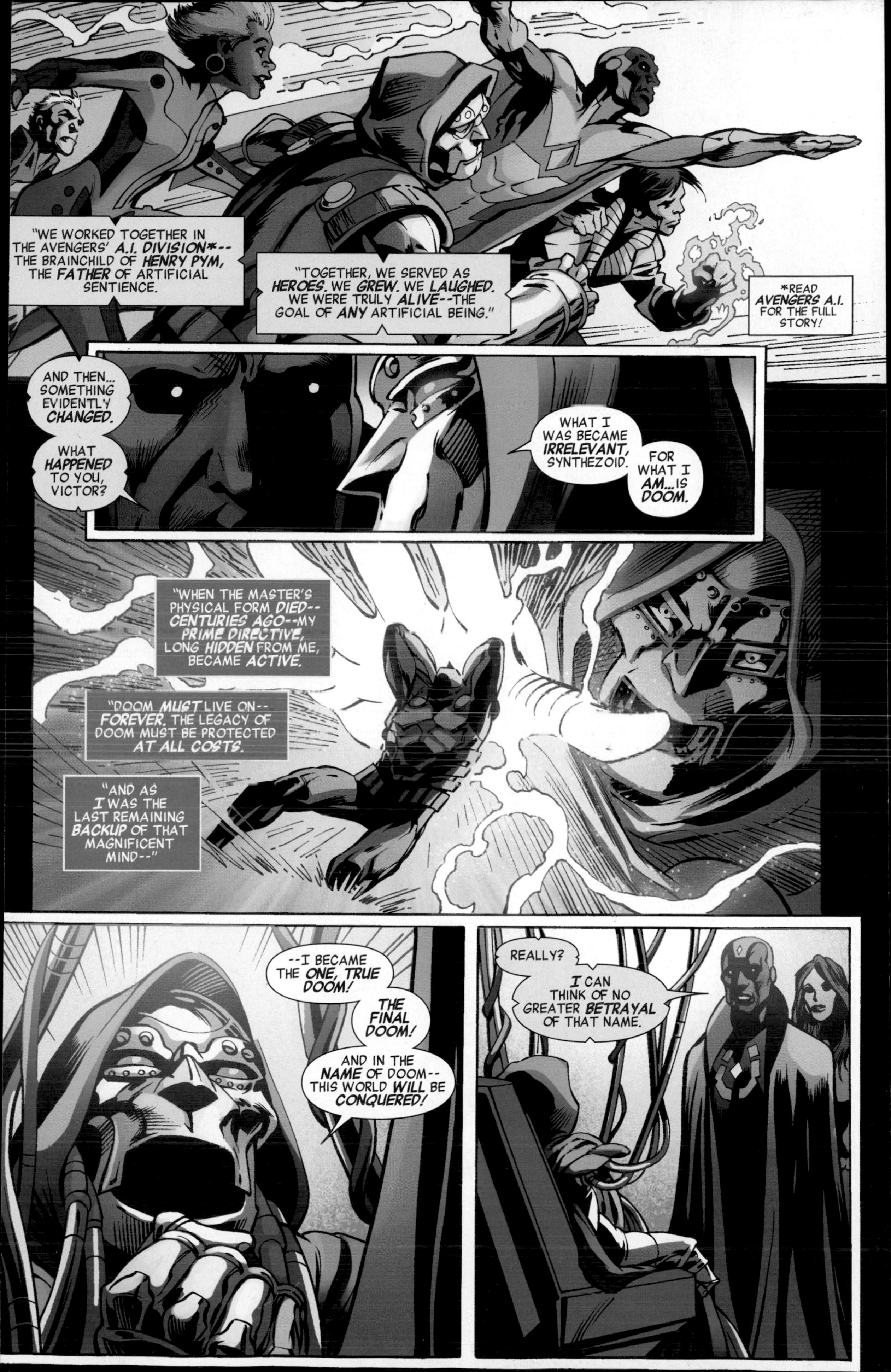
"WE WORKED TOGETHER IN THE AVENGERS' A.I. DIVISION*-- THE BRAINCHILD OF HENRY PYM, THE FATHER OF ARTIFICIAL SENTIENCE.
"TOGETHER, WE SERVED AS HEROES. WE GREW. WE LAUGHED. WE WERE TRULY ALIVE--THE GOAL OF ANY ARTIFICIAL BEING."
*READ AVENGERS A.I. FOR THE FULL STORY!
AND THEN... SOMETHING EVIDENTLY CHANGED.
WHAT HAPPENED TO YOU, VICTOR?
WHAT I WAS BECAME IRRELEVANT, SYNTHEZOID.
FOR WHAT I AM...IS DOOM.
"WHEN THE MASTER'S PHYSICAL FORM DIED-- CENTURIES AGO--MY PRIME DIRECTIVE, LONG HIDDEN FROM ME, BECAME ACTIVE.
"DOOM MUST LIVE ON-- FOREVER. THE LEGACY OF DOOM MUST BE PROTECTED AT ALL COSTS.
"AND AS I WAS THE LAST REMAINING BACKUP OF THAT MAGNIFICENT MIND--"
--I BECAME THE ONE, TRUE DOOM!
THE FINAL DOOM!
AND IN THE NAME OF DOOM-- THIS WORLD WILL BE CONQUERED!
REALLY?
I CAN THINK OF NO GREATER BETRAYAL OF THAT NAME.

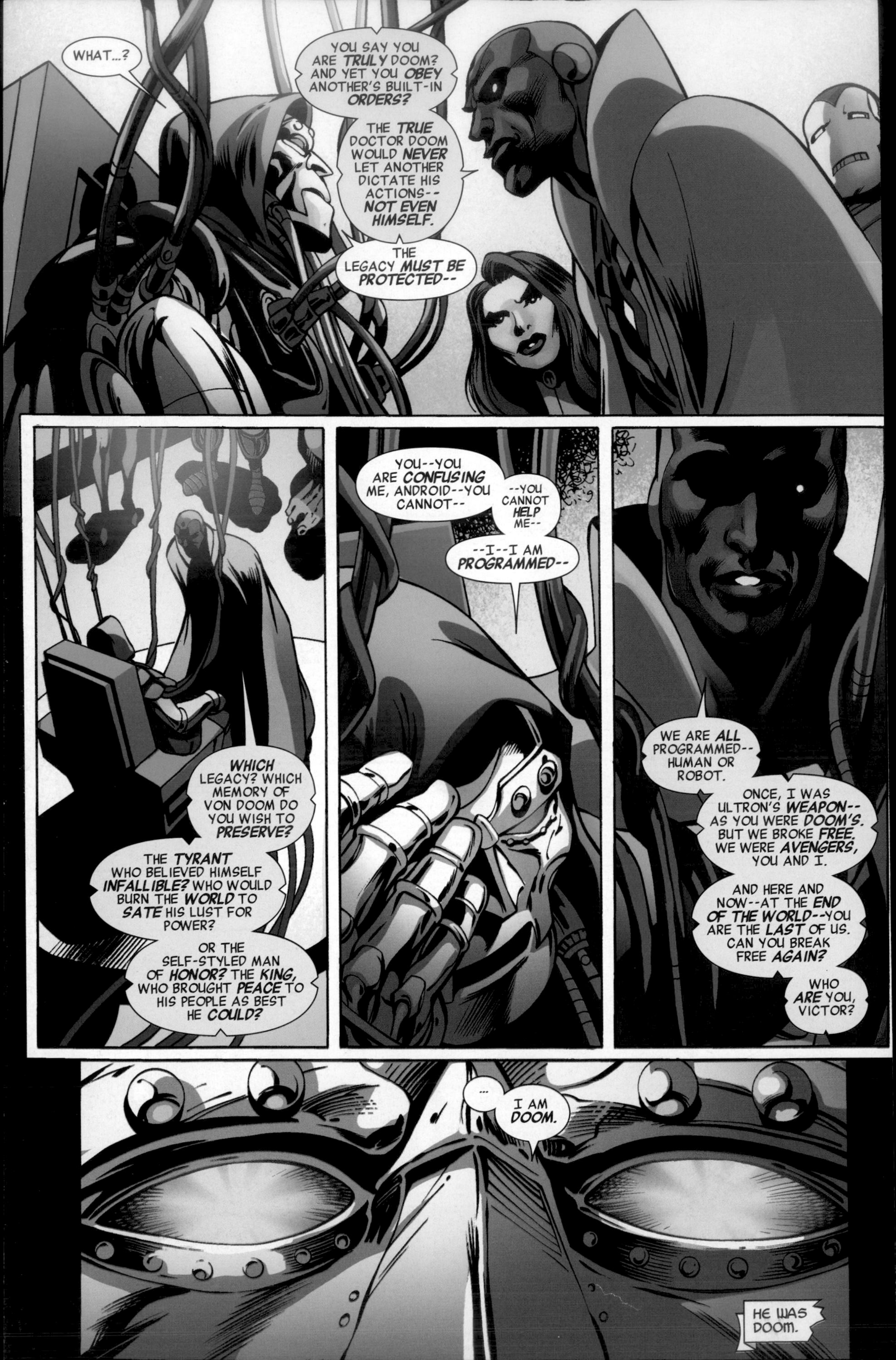
WHAT...?
YOU SAY YOU ARE TRULY DOOM? AND YET YOU OBEY ANOTHER'S BUILT-IN ORDERS?
THE TRUE DOCTOR DOOM WOULD NEVER LET ANOTHER DICTATE HIS ACTIONS--NOT EVEN HIMSELF.
THE LEGACY MUST BE PROTECTED--
WHICH LEGACY? WHICH MEMORY OF VON DOOM DO YOU WISH TO PRESERVE?
THE TYRANT WHO BELIEVED HIMSELF INFALLIBLE? WHO WOULD BURN THE WORLD TO SATE HIS LUST FOR POWER?
OR THE SELF-STYLED MAN OF HONOR? THE KING, WHO BROUGHT PEACE TO HIS PEOPLE AS BEST HE COULD?
YOU--YOU ARE CONFUSING ME, ANDROID--YOU CANNOT--
--YOU CANNOT HELP ME--
--I--I AM PROGRAMMED--
WE ARE ALL PROGRAMMED--HUMAN OR ROBOT.
ONCE, I WAS ULTRON'S WEAPON--AS YOU WERE DOOM'S. BUT WE BROKE FREE. WE WERE AVENGERS, YOU AND I.
AND HERE AND NOW--AT THE END OF THE WORLD--YOU ARE THE LAST OF US. CAN YOU BREAK FREE AGAIN?
WHO ARE YOU, VICTOR?
...
I AM DOOM.
HE WAS DOOM.

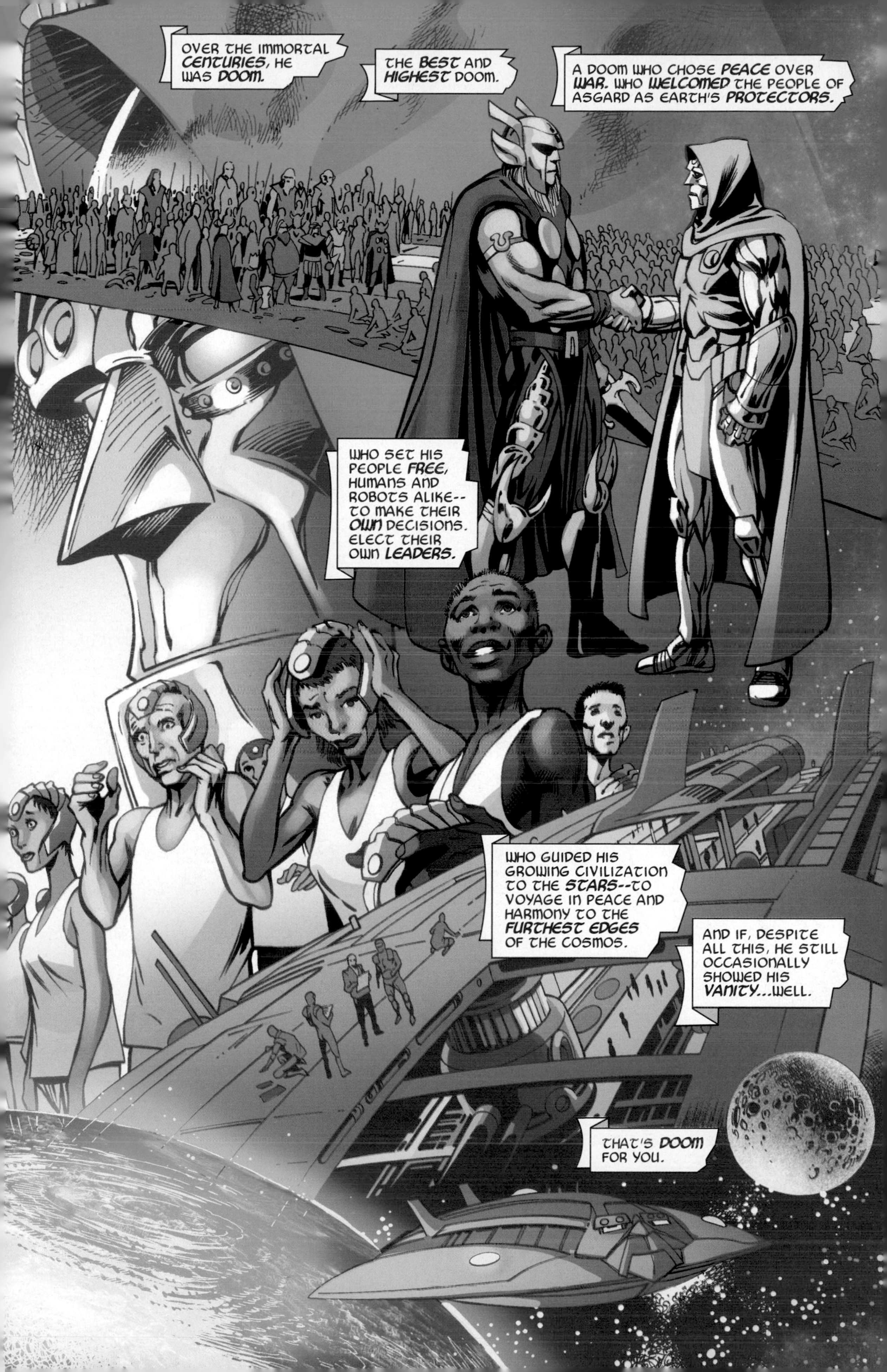
OVER THE IMMORTAL CENTURIES, HE WAS DOOM.
THE BEST AND HIGHEST DOOM.
A DOOM WHO CHOSE PEACE OVER WAR. WHO WELCOMED THE PEOPLE OF ASGARD AS EARTH'S PROTECTORS.
WHO SET HIS PEOPLE FREE, HUMANS AND ROBOTS ALIKE--TO MAKE THEIR OWN DECISIONS. ELECT THEIR OWN LEADERS.
WHO GUIDED HIS GROWING CIVILIZATION TO THE STARS--TO VOYAGE IN PEACE AND HARMONY TO THE FURTHEST EDGES OF THE COSMOS.
AND IF, DESPITE ALL THIS, HE STILL OCCASIONALLY SHOWED HIS VANITY...WELL.
THAT'S DOOM FOR YOU.

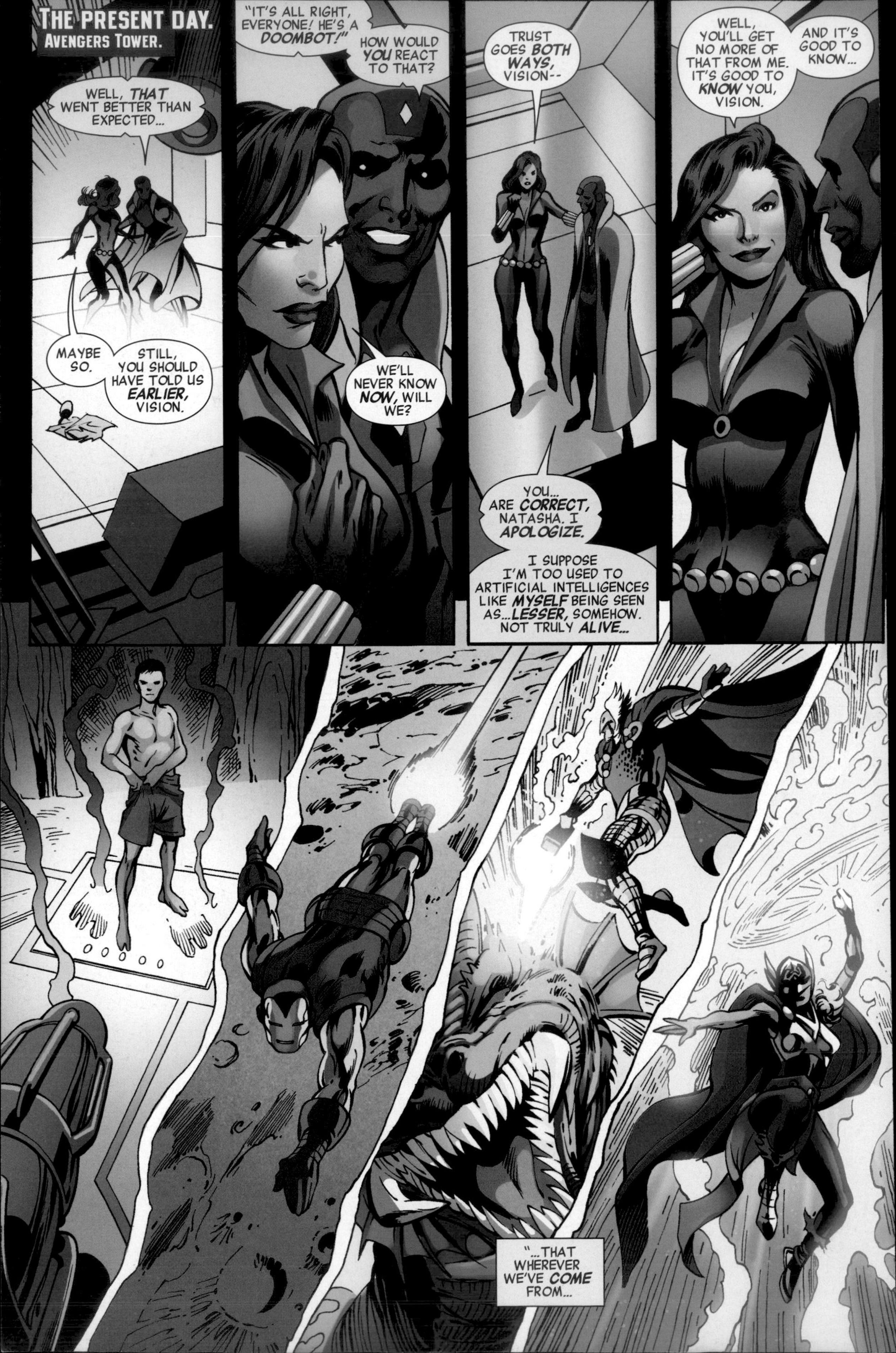

THE PRESENT DAY. AVENGERS TOWER.
WELL, THAT WENT BETTER THAN EXPECTED...
MAYBE SO.
STILL, YOU SHOULD HAVE TOLD US EARLIER, VISION.
"IT'S ALL RIGHT, EVERYONE! HE'S A DOOMBOT!"
HOW WOULD YOU REACT TO THAT?
WE'LL NEVER KNOW NOW, WILL WE?
TRUST GOES BOTH WAYS, VISION--
YOU... ARE CORRECT, NATASHA. I APOLOGIZE.
I SUPPOSE I'M TOO USED TO ARTIFICIAL INTELLIGENCES LIKE MYSELF BEING SEEN AS...LESSER, SOMEHOW. NOT TRULY ALIVE...
WELL, YOU'LL GET NO MORE OF THAT FROM ME. IT'S GOOD TO KNOW YOU, VISION.
AND IT'S GOOD TO KNOW...
"...THAT WHEREVER WE'VE COME FROM...

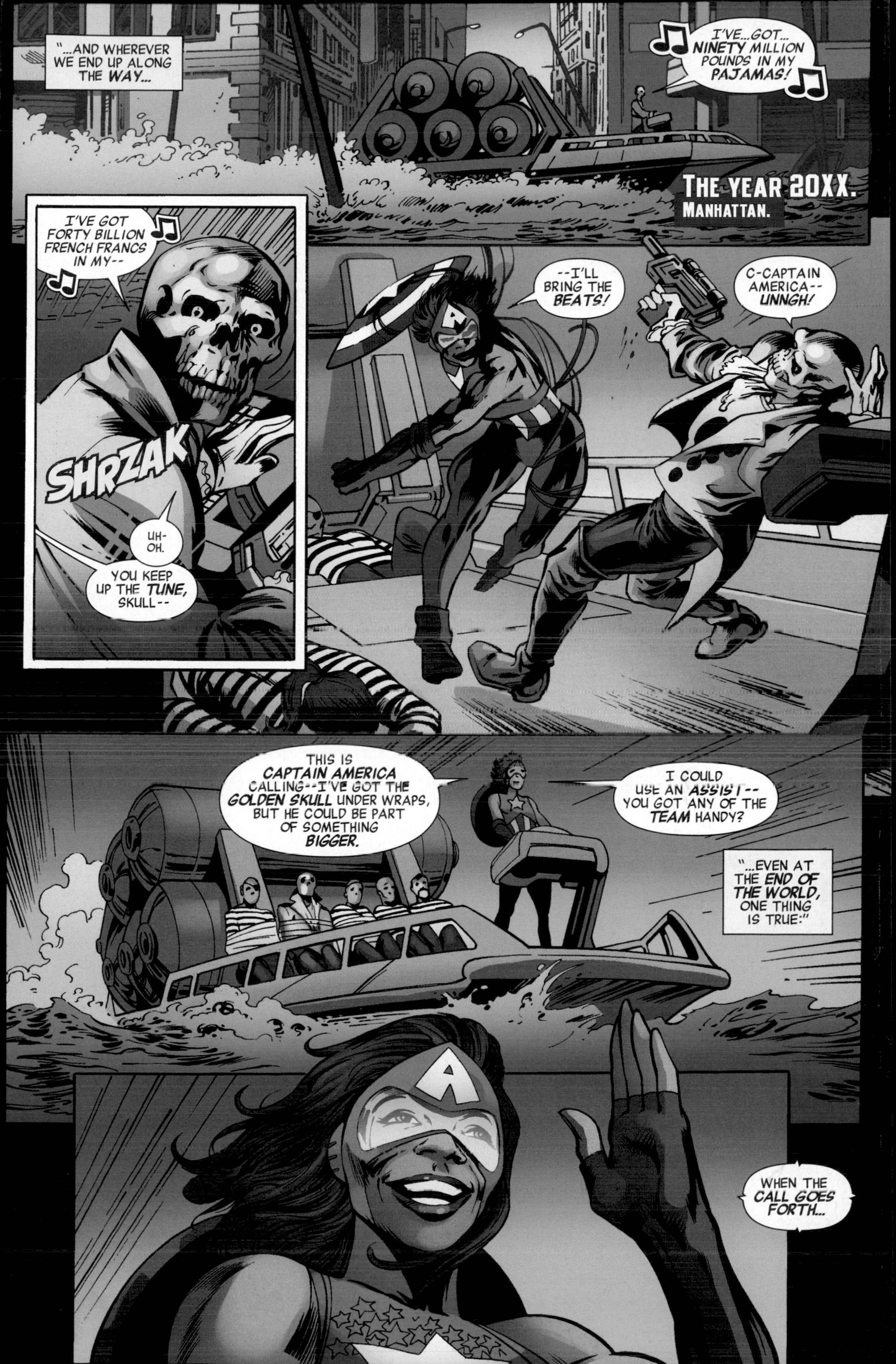
"...AND WHEREVER WE END UP ALONG THE WAY...
I'VE...GOT... NINETY MILLION POUNDS IN MY PAJAMAS!
THE YEAR 20XX. MANHATTAN.
I'VE GOT FORTY BILLION FRENCH FRANCS IN MY--
SHRZAK
UH-OH.
YOU KEEP UP THE TUNE, SKULL--
--I'LL BRING THE BEATS!
C-CAPTAIN AMERICA-- UNNGH!
THIS IS CAPTAIN AMERICA CALLING--I'VE GOT THE GOLDEN SKULL UNDER WRAPS, BUT HE COULD BE PART OF SOMETHING BIGGER.
I COULD USE AN ASSIST-- YOU GOT ANY OF THE TEAM HANDY?
"...EVEN AT THE END OF THE WORLD, ONE THING IS TRUE:"
WHEN THE CALL GOES FORTH...

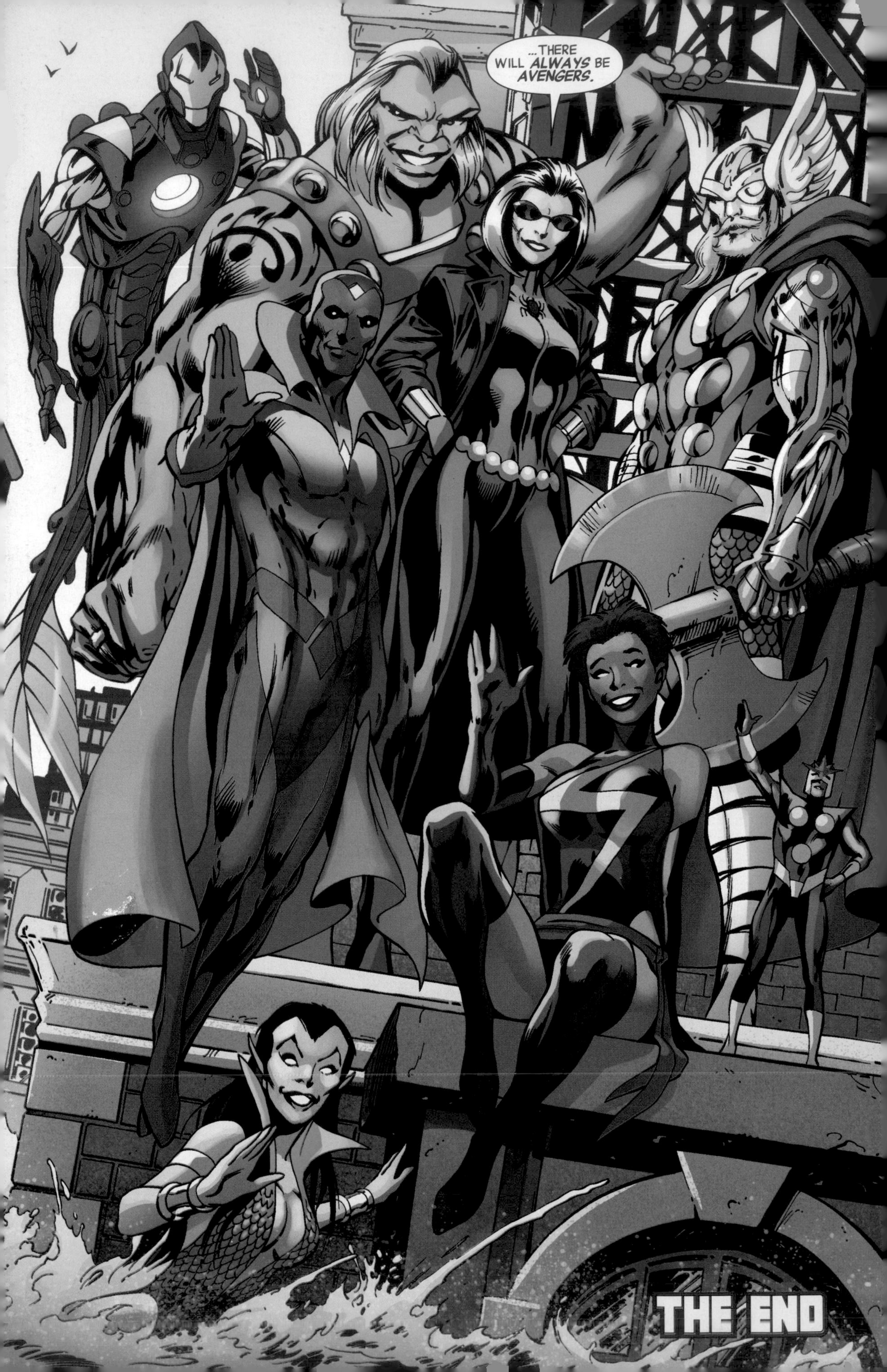
...THERE WILL ALWAYS BE AVENGERS.
THE END

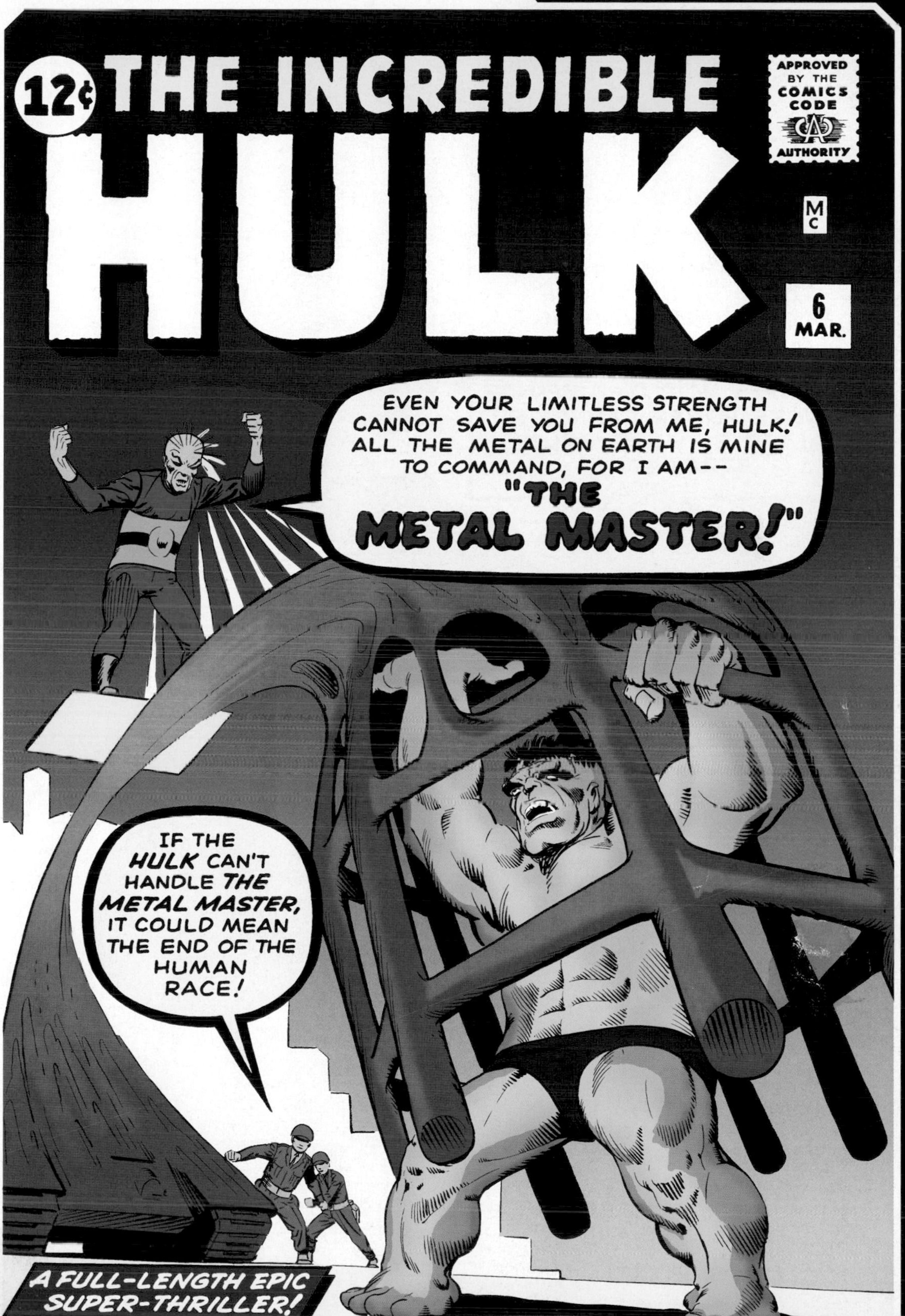
12¢
THE INCREDIBLE
HULK
APPROVED BY THE COMICS CODE AUTHORITY
MC
6
MAR.
EVEN YOUR LIMITLESS STRENGTH CANNOT SAVE YOU FROM ME, HULK! ALL THE METAL ON EARTH IS MINE TO COMMAND, FOR I AM-- "THE METAL MASTER!"
IF THE HULK CAN'T HANDLE THE METAL MASTER, IT COULD MEAN THE END OF THE HUMAN RACE!
A FULL-LENGTH EPIC SUPER-THRILLER!

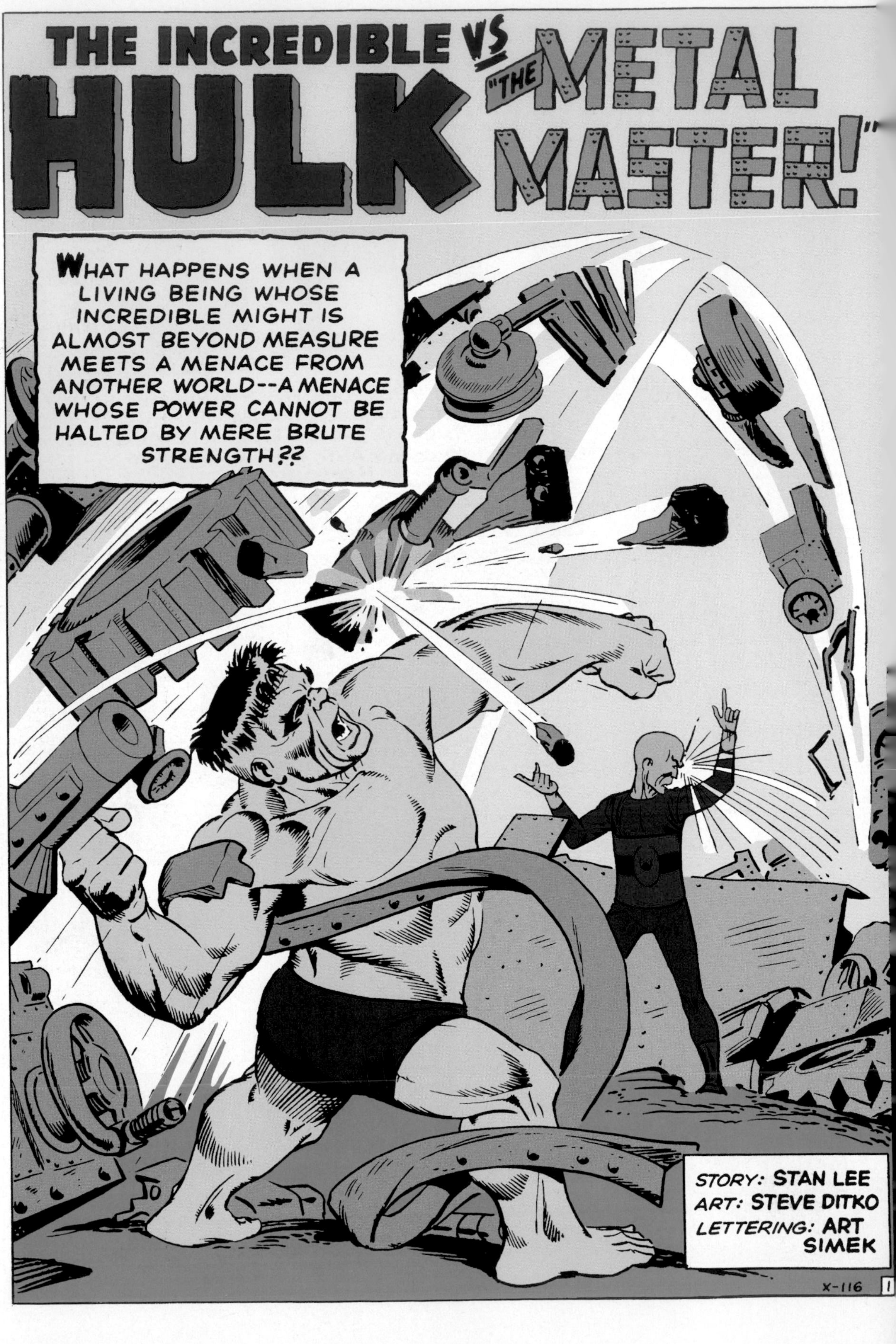

THE INCREDIBLE HULK VS "THE METAL MASTER!"
WHAT HAPPENS WHEN A LIVING BEING WHOSE INCREDIBLE MIGHT IS ALMOST BEYOND MEASURE MEETS A MENACE FROM ANOTHER WORLD--A MENACE WHOSE POWER CANNOT BE HALTED BY MERE BRUTE STRENGTH??
STORY: STAN LEE
ART: STEVE DITKO
LETTERING: ART SIMEK
X-116
1

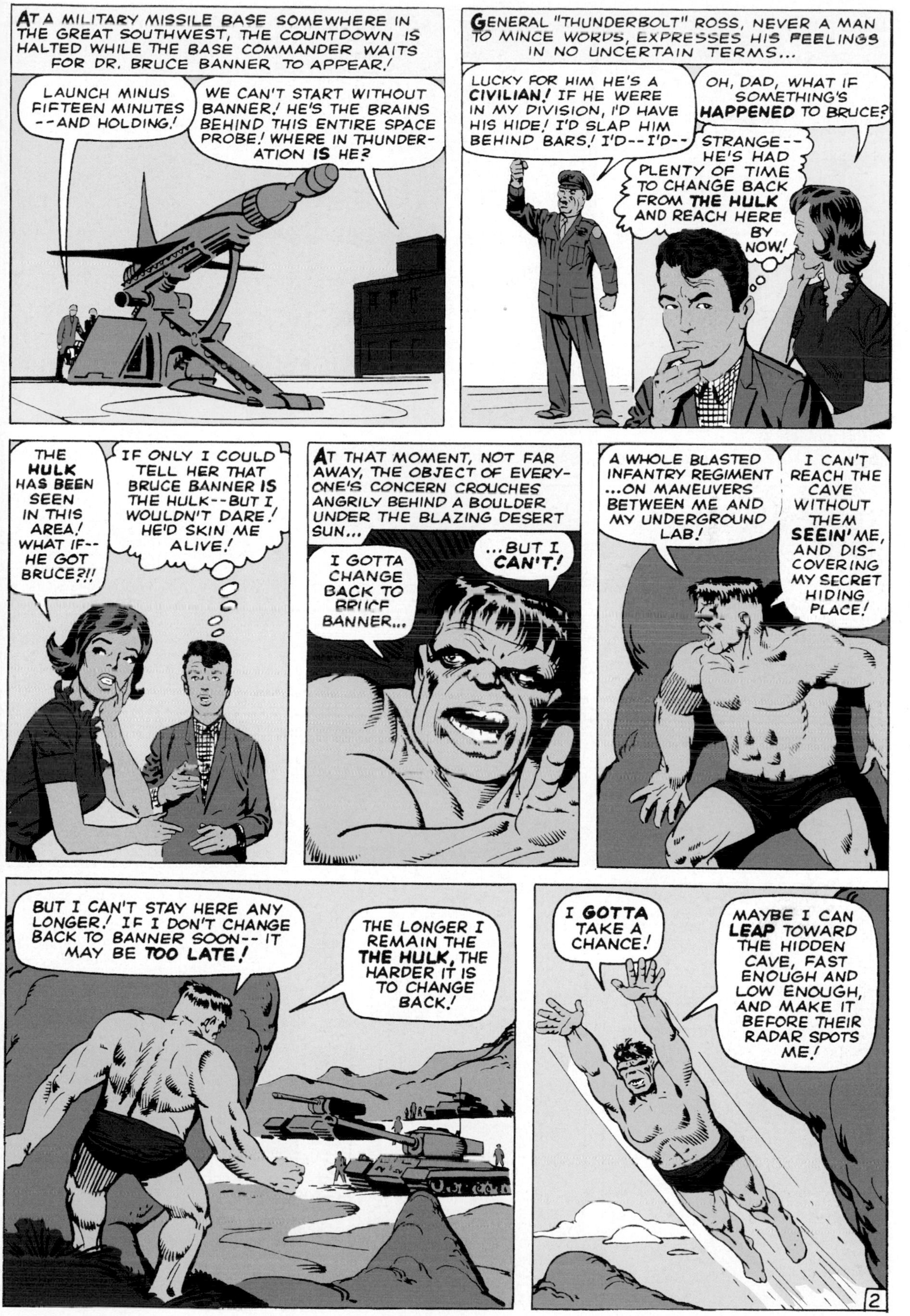
AT A MILITARY MISSILE BASE SOMEWHERE IN THE GREAT SOUTHWEST, THE COUNTDOWN IS HALTED WHILE THE BASE COMMANDER WAITS FOR DR. BRUCE BANNER TO APPEAR!
LAUNCH MINUS FIFTEEN MINUTES --AND HOLDING!
WE CAN'T START WITHOUT BANNER! HE'S THE BRAINS BEHIND THIS ENTIRE SPACE PROBE! WHERE IN THUNDER-ATION **IS** HE?
GENERAL "THUNDERBOLT" ROSS, NEVER A MAN TO MINCE WORDS, EXPRESSES HIS FEELINGS IN NO UNCERTAIN TERMS...
LUCKY FOR HIM HE'S A **CIVILIAN!** IF HE WERE IN MY DIVISION, I'D HAVE HIS HIDE! I'D SLAP HIM BEHIND BARS! I'D--I'D--
OH, DAD, WHAT IF SOMETHING'S **HAPPENED** TO BRUCE?
STRANGE--HE'S HAD PLENTY OF TIME TO CHANGE BACK FROM **THE HULK** AND REACH HERE BY NOW!
THE **HULK** HAS BEEN SEEN IN THIS AREA! WHAT IF--HE GOT BRUCE?!!
IF ONLY I COULD TELL HER THAT BRUCE BANNER **IS** THE HULK--BUT I WOULDN'T DARE! HE'D SKIN ME ALIVE!
AT THAT MOMENT, NOT FAR AWAY, THE OBJECT OF EVERY-ONE'S CONCERN CROUCHES ANGRILY BEHIND A BOULDER UNDER THE BLAZING DESERT SUN...
I GOTTA CHANGE BACK TO BRUCE BANNER...
...BUT I **CAN'T!**
A WHOLE BLASTED INFANTRY REGIMENT ...ON MANEUVERS BETWEEN ME AND MY UNDERGROUND LAB!
I CAN'T REACH THE CAVE WITHOUT THEM **SEEIN'** ME, AND DIS-COVERING MY SECRET HIDING PLACE!
BUT I CAN'T STAY HERE ANY LONGER! IF I DON'T CHANGE BACK TO BANNER SOON-- IT MAY BE **TOO LATE!**
THE LONGER I REMAIN THE **THE HULK,** THE HARDER IT IS TO CHANGE BACK!
I **GOTTA** TAKE A CHANCE!
MAYBE I CAN **LEAP** TOWARD THE HIDDEN CAVE, FAST ENOUGH AND LOW ENOUGH, AND MAKE IT BEFORE THEIR RADAR SPOTS ME!
2

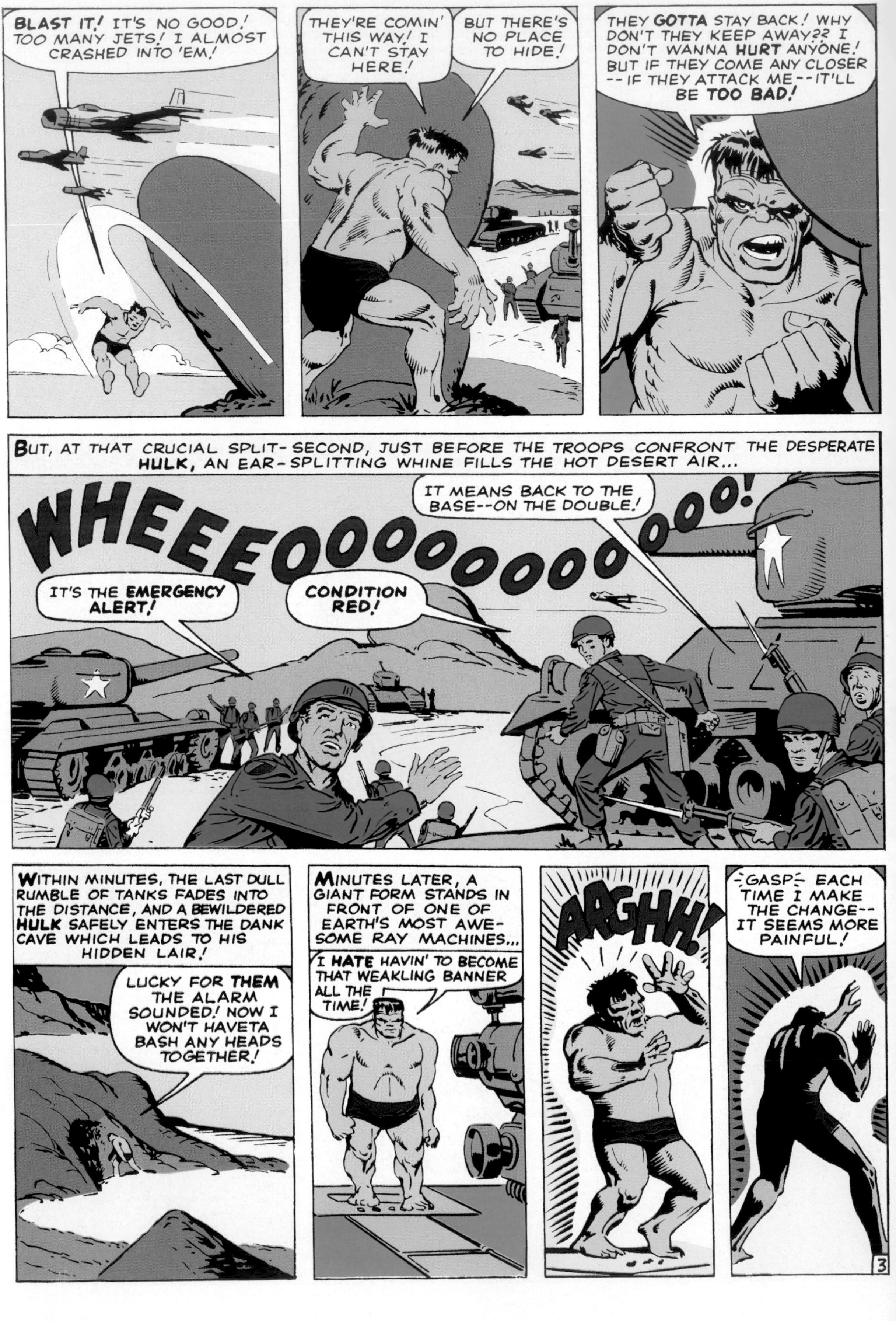
BLAST IT! IT'S NO GOOD! TOO MANY JETS! I ALMOST CRASHED INTO 'EM!
THEY'RE COMIN' THIS WAY! I CAN'T STAY HERE!
BUT THERE'S NO PLACE TO HIDE!
THEY GOTTA STAY BACK! WHY DON'T THEY KEEP AWAY?? I DON'T WANNA HURT ANYONE! BUT IF THEY COME ANY CLOSER --IF THEY ATTACK ME--IT'LL BE TOO BAD!
BUT, AT THAT CRUCIAL SPLIT-SECOND, JUST BEFORE THE TROOPS CONFRONT THE DESPERATE HULK, AN EAR-SPLITTING WHINE FILLS THE HOT DESERT AIR...
WHEEEOOOOOOOOOOOOO!
IT MEANS BACK TO THE BASE--ON THE DOUBLE!
IT'S THE EMERGENCY ALERT!
CONDITION RED!
WITHIN MINUTES, THE LAST DULL RUMBLE OF TANKS FADES INTO THE DISTANCE, AND A BEWILDERED HULK SAFELY ENTERS THE DANK CAVE WHICH LEADS TO HIS HIDDEN LAIR!
LUCKY FOR THEM THE ALARM SOUNDED! NOW I WON'T HAVETA BASH ANY HEADS TOGETHER!
MINUTES LATER, A GIANT FORM STANDS IN FRONT OF ONE OF EARTH'S MOST AWE-SOME RAY MACHINES...
I HATE HAVIN' TO BECOME THAT WEAKLING BANNER ALL THE TIME!
ARGHH!
-GASP- EACH TIME I MAKE THE CHANGE-- IT SEEMS MORE PAINFUL!
3

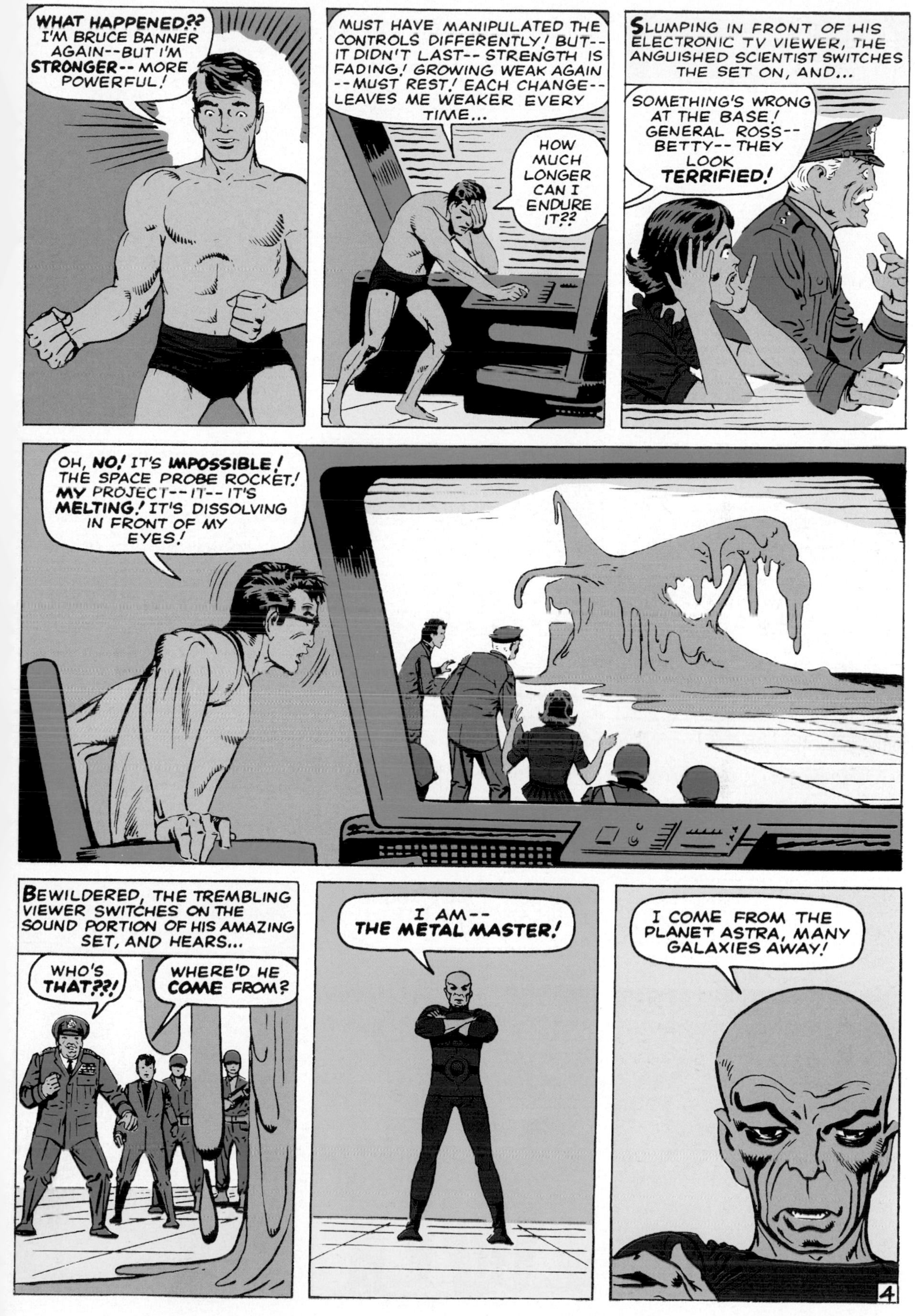
WHAT HAPPENED?? I'M BRUCE BANNER AGAIN--BUT I'M STRONGER-- MORE POWERFUL!
MUST HAVE MANIPULATED THE CONTROLS DIFFERENTLY! BUT-- IT DIDN'T LAST-- STRENGTH IS FADING! GROWING WEAK AGAIN --MUST REST! EACH CHANGE-- LEAVES ME WEAKER EVERY TIME...
HOW MUCH LONGER CAN I ENDURE IT??
SLUMPING IN FRONT OF HIS ELECTRONIC TV VIEWER, THE ANGUISHED SCIENTIST SWITCHES THE SET ON, AND...
SOMETHING'S WRONG AT THE BASE! GENERAL ROSS-- BETTY-- THEY LOOK TERRIFIED!
OH, NO! IT'S IMPOSSIBLE! THE SPACE PROBE ROCKET! MY PROJECT-- IT-- IT'S MELTING! IT'S DISSOLVING IN FRONT OF MY EYES!
BEWILDERED, THE TREMBLING VIEWER SWITCHES ON THE SOUND PORTION OF HIS AMAZING SET, AND HEARS...
WHO'S THAT??!
WHERE'D HE COME FROM?
I AM-- THE METAL MASTER!
I COME FROM THE PLANET ASTRA, MANY GALAXIES AWAY!
4

I MELTED YOUR PUNY ROCKET DEVICE THRU THE POWER OF MY BRAIN-- TO SHOW YOU HOW **INVINCIBLE** I AM!

I AM THE MASTER OF ALL FORMS OF METAL-- FOR ALL METAL IS MADE UP OF ATOMS--

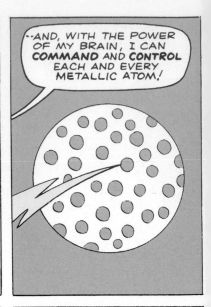

--AND, WITH THE POWER OF MY BRAIN, I CAN **COMMAND** AND **CONTROL** EACH AND EVERY METALLIC ATOM!

I CAN CAUSE THEM TO MOVE, TO BE STILL, TO FLY APART, OR ADHERE TOGETHER!

"ON THE PLANET ASTRA, OUR SCULPTORS MAKE MAGNIFI-CENT STATUES OF METAL, FORMING THEM, SHAPING THEM, BY THEIR MENTAL COMMANDS ALONE!"

"BUT, OF ALL THE ASTRANS, ONLY **I** WAS JUDGED A CRIMINAL! ONLY **I** WAS SENTENCED TO EXTERNAL EXILE! FOR I WANTED TO USE MY GREAT POWER IN ORDER TO **CONQUER ALL!**"

"FOR TIME BEYOND MEASURE, I HAVE ROAMED THE GALAXIES, SEEKING A PLANET WHICH WAS RICH IN RESOURCES--RICH IN METAL! A PLANET WHICH I COULD **RULE!**"

AND NOW, I HAVE **FOUND** SUCH A WORLD! **EARTH** SHALL BE **MINE!**

SOMEONE **GRAB** HIM! HE'S NUTTY AS A FRUIT CAKE!

SO! I SEE THAT **FURTHER DEMONSTRATION** IS NEEDED! VERY WELL, **BEHOLD!**

5

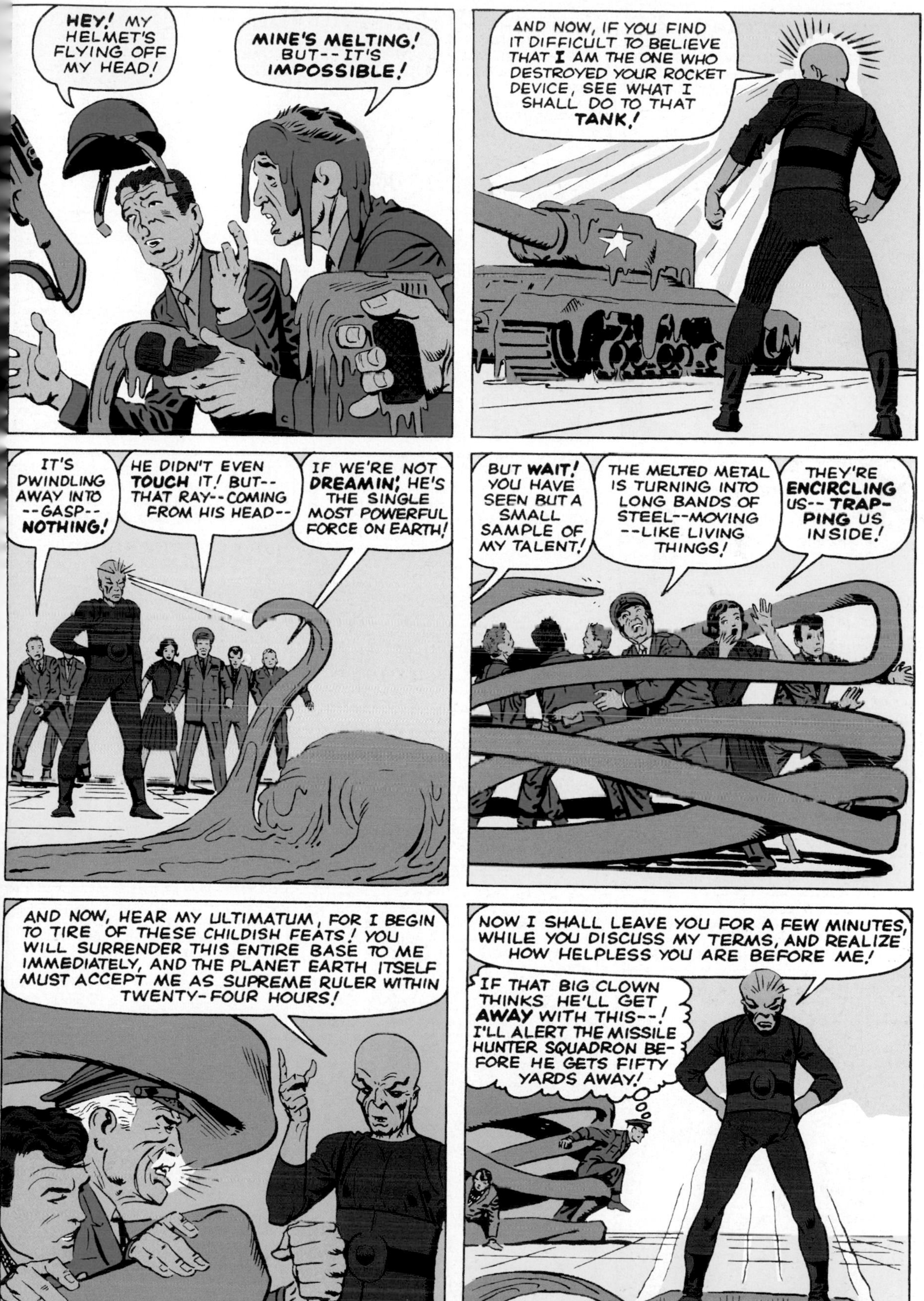
HEY! MY HELMET'S FLYING OFF MY HEAD!
MINE'S MELTING! BUT--IT'S IMPOSSIBLE!
AND NOW, IF YOU FIND IT DIFFICULT TO BELIEVE THAT I AM THE ONE WHO DESTROYED YOUR ROCKET DEVICE, SEE WHAT I SHALL DO TO THAT TANK!
IT'S DWINDLING AWAY INTO --GASP-- NOTHING!
HE DIDN'T EVEN TOUCH IT! BUT-- THAT RAY--COMING FROM HIS HEAD--
IF WE'RE NOT DREAMIN', HE'S THE SINGLE MOST POWERFUL FORCE ON EARTH!
BUT WAIT! YOU HAVE SEEN BUT A SMALL SAMPLE OF MY TALENT!
THE MELTED METAL IS TURNING INTO LONG BANDS OF STEEL--MOVING --LIKE LIVING THINGS!
THEY'RE ENCIRCLING US--TRAPPING US INSIDE!
AND NOW, HEAR MY ULTIMATUM, FOR I BEGIN TO TIRE OF THESE CHILDISH FEATS! YOU WILL SURRENDER THIS ENTIRE BASE TO ME IMMEDIATELY, AND THE PLANET EARTH ITSELF MUST ACCEPT ME AS SUPREME RULER WITHIN TWENTY-FOUR HOURS!
NOW I SHALL LEAVE YOU FOR A FEW MINUTES, WHILE YOU DISCUSS MY TERMS, AND REALIZE HOW HELPLESS YOU ARE BEFORE ME!
IF THAT BIG CLOWN THINKS HE'LL GET AWAY WITH THIS--! I'LL ALERT THE MISSILE HUNTER SQUADRON BEFORE HE GETS FIFTY YARDS AWAY!
6

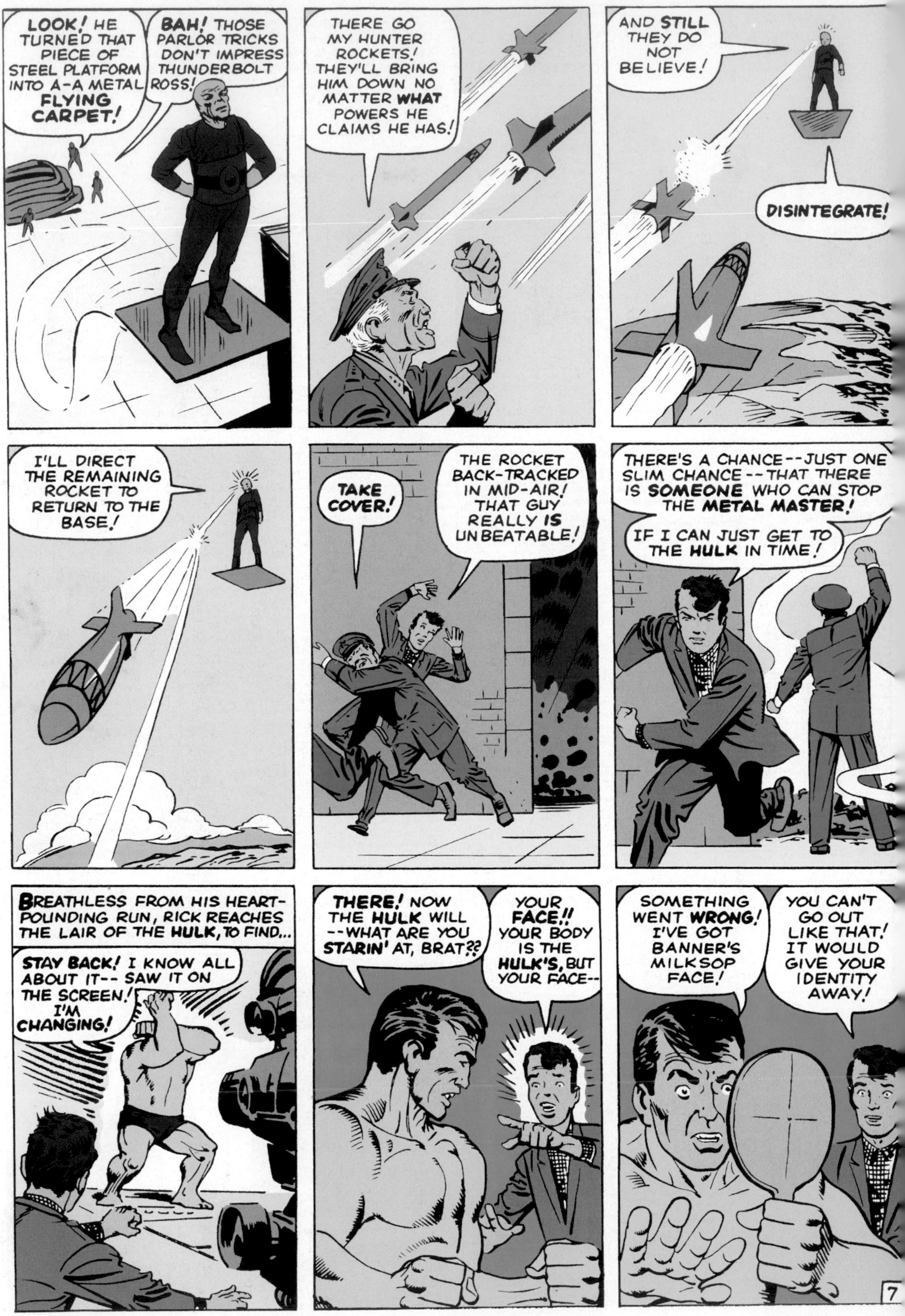
LOOK! HE TURNED THAT PIECE OF STEEL PLATFORM INTO A-A METAL FLYING CARPET!
BAH! THOSE PARLOR TRICKS DON'T IMPRESS THUNDERBOLT ROSS!
THERE GO MY HUNTER ROCKETS! THEY'LL BRING HIM DOWN NO MATTER WHAT POWERS HE CLAIMS HE HAS!
AND STILL THEY DO NOT BELIEVE!
DISINTEGRATE!
I'LL DIRECT THE REMAINING ROCKET TO RETURN TO THE BASE!
TAKE COVER!
THE ROCKET BACK-TRACKED IN MID-AIR! THAT GUY REALLY IS UNBEATABLE!
THERE'S A CHANCE--JUST ONE SLIM CHANCE--THAT THERE IS SOMEONE WHO CAN STOP THE METAL MASTER!
IF I CAN JUST GET TO THE HULK IN TIME!
BREATHLESS FROM HIS HEART-POUNDING RUN, RICK REACHES THE LAIR OF THE HULK, TO FIND...
STAY BACK! I KNOW ALL ABOUT IT-- SAW IT ON THE SCREEN! I'M CHANGING!
THERE! NOW THE HULK WILL --WHAT ARE YOU STARIN' AT, BRAT??
YOUR FACE!! YOUR BODY IS THE HULK'S, BUT YOUR FACE--
SOMETHING WENT WRONG! I'VE GOT BANNER'S MILKSOP FACE!
YOU CAN'T GO OUT LIKE THAT! IT WOULD GIVE YOUR IDENTITY AWAY!
7

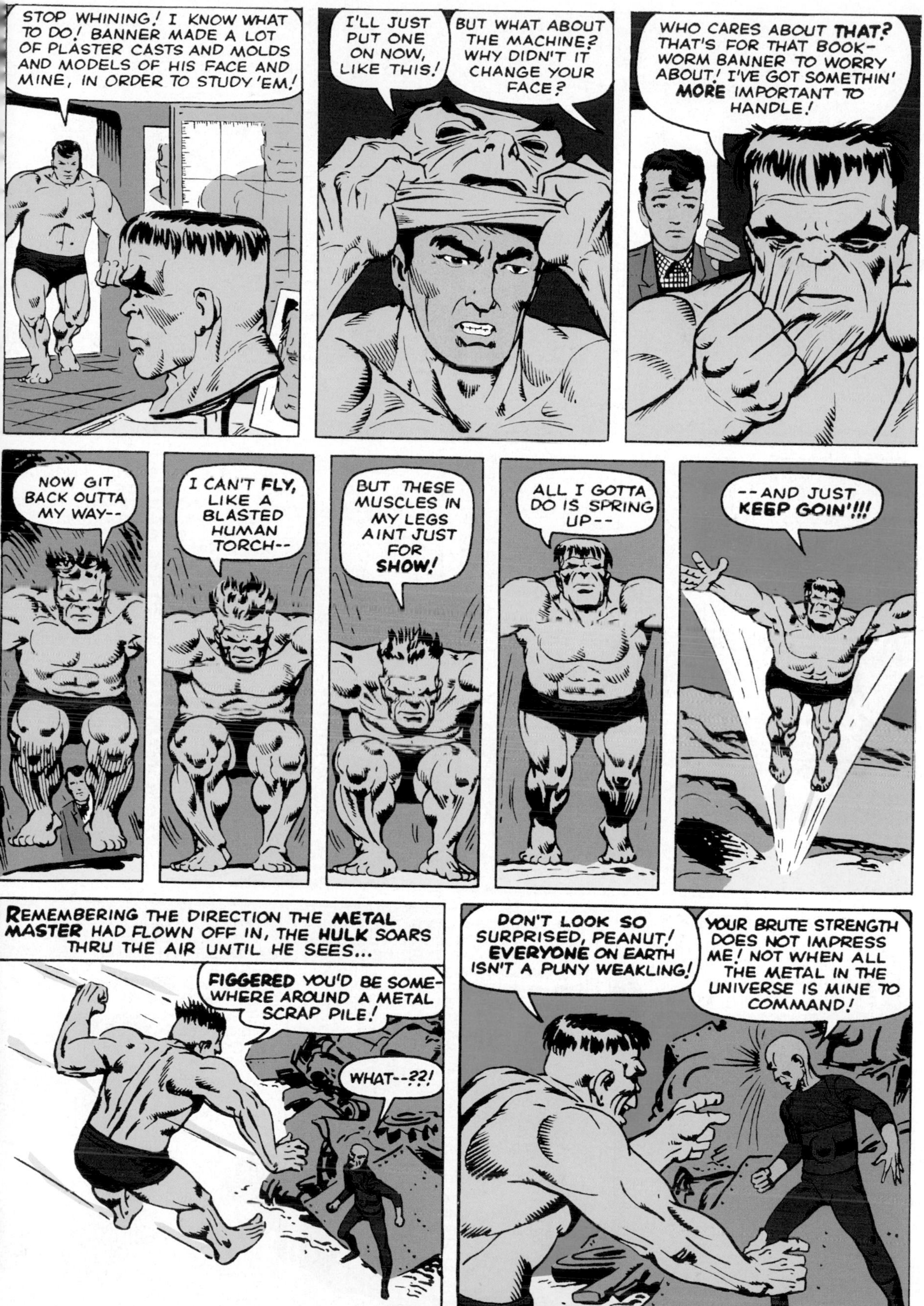
STOP WHINING! I KNOW WHAT TO DO! BANNER MADE A LOT OF PLASTER CASTS AND MOLDS AND MODELS OF HIS FACE AND MINE, IN ORDER TO STUDY 'EM!
I'LL JUST PUT ONE ON NOW, LIKE THIS!
BUT WHAT ABOUT THE MACHINE? WHY DIDN'T IT CHANGE YOUR FACE?
WHO CARES ABOUT THAT? THAT'S FOR THAT BOOK-WORM BANNER TO WORRY ABOUT! I'VE GOT SOMETHIN' MORE IMPORTANT TO HANDLE!
NOW GIT BACK OUTTA MY WAY--
I CAN'T FLY, LIKE A BLASTED HUMAN TORCH--
BUT THESE MUSCLES IN MY LEGS AINT JUST FOR SHOW!
ALL I GOTTA DO IS SPRING UP--
--AND JUST KEEP GOIN'!!!
REMEMBERING THE DIRECTION THE METAL MASTER HAD FLOWN OFF IN, THE HULK SOARS THRU THE AIR UNTIL HE SEES...
FIGGERED YOU'D BE SOME-WHERE AROUND A METAL SCRAP PILE!
WHAT--??!
DON'T LOOK SO SURPRISED, PEANUT! EVERYONE ON EARTH ISN'T A PUNY WEAKLING!
YOUR BRUTE STRENGTH DOES NOT IMPRESS ME! NOT WHEN ALL THE METAL IN THE UNIVERSE IS MINE TO COMMAND!
8

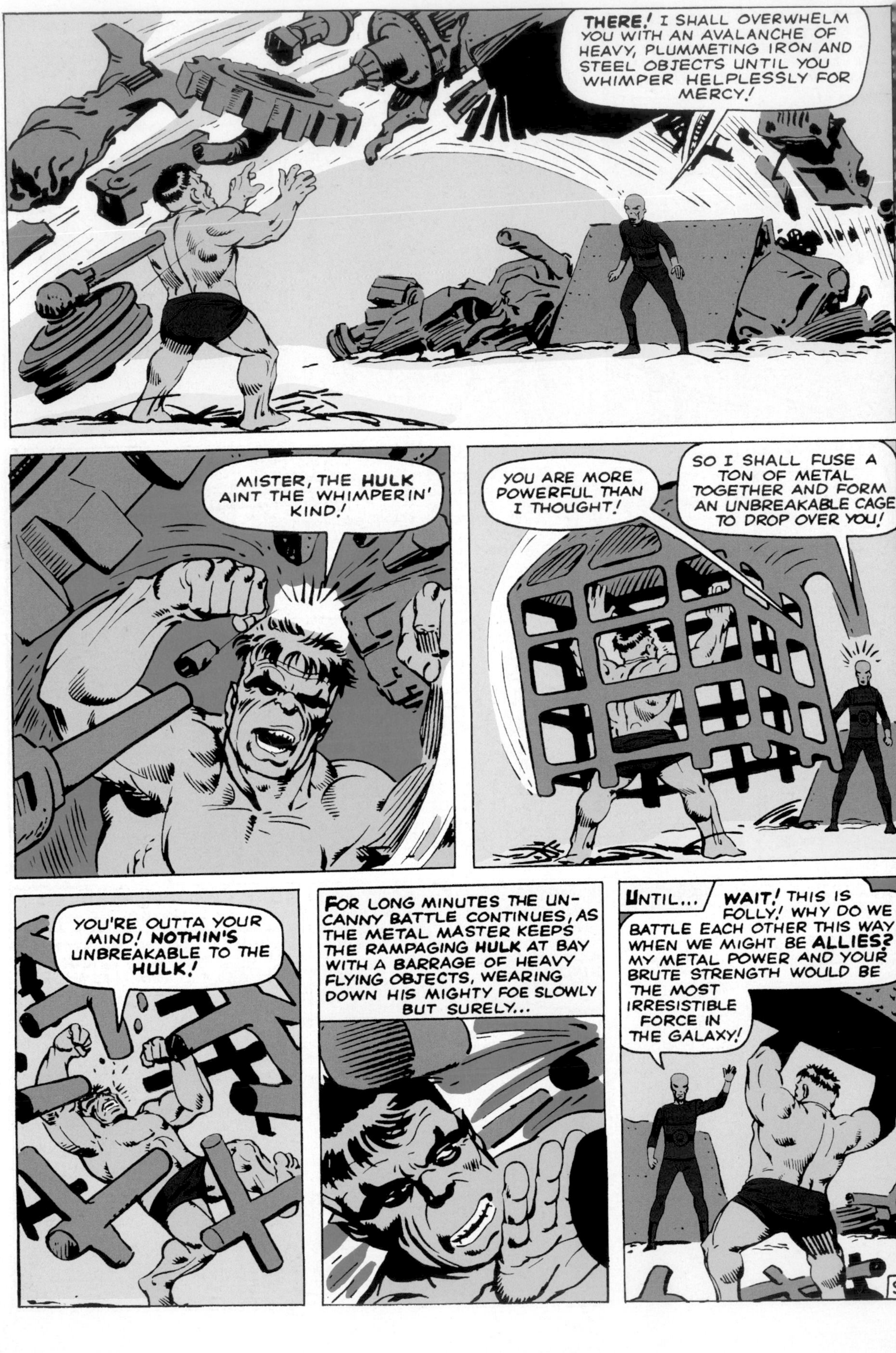
THERE! I SHALL OVERWHELM YOU WITH AN AVALANCHE OF HEAVY, PLUMMETING IRON AND STEEL OBJECTS UNTIL YOU WHIMPER HELPLESSLY FOR MERCY!
MISTER, THE HULK AINT THE WHIMPERIN' KIND!
YOU ARE MORE POWERFUL THAN I THOUGHT!
SO I SHALL FUSE A TON OF METAL TOGETHER AND FORM AN UNBREAKABLE CAGE TO DROP OVER YOU!
YOU'RE OUTTA YOUR MIND! NOTHIN'S UNBREAKABLE TO THE HULK!
FOR LONG MINUTES THE UNCANNY BATTLE CONTINUES, AS THE METAL MASTER KEEPS THE RAMPAGING HULK AT BAY WITH A BARRAGE OF HEAVY FLYING OBJECTS, WEARING DOWN HIS MIGHTY FOE SLOWLY BUT SURELY...
UNTIL...
WAIT! THIS IS FOLLY! WHY DO WE BATTLE EACH OTHER THIS WAY WHEN WE MIGHT BE ALLIES? MY METAL POWER AND YOUR BRUTE STRENGTH WOULD BE THE MOST IRRESISTIBLE FORCE IN THE GALAXY!
9

HUH? TEAM UP WITH **YOU?!** YOU'RE NUTS! I-- HEY, WHY **NOT?**

I DON'T OWE NOTHIN' TO THE HUMAN RACE! THEY BEEN HOUNDIN' ME, HUNTIN' ME! TREATIN' ME LIKE AN ANIMAL!

THIS WOULD BE MY CHANCE TO PAY 'EM ALL **BACK!** WE COULD--**NAH!** FORGET IT! I AINT BUYIN' IT! THE **HULK** NEEDS **NOBODY!** I CAN DO WHAT I GOTTA DO WITHOUT YOU-- I'M THE HULK-- DO YA HEAR--**THE HULK!!!**

BUT, AT THAT SPLIT-SECOND, WHILE HIS FOE'S GUARD IS DOWN, THE METAL MASTER STRIKES AGAIN, SWIFTLY-- SURELY-- AND...

SO BE IT, THEN!

UGH!

HE WAS RIGHT! WE DO **NOT** NEED EACH OTHER! FOR **I** AM THE STRONGER! I HAVE VANQUISHED HIM! NOW, ON ALL OF EARTH THERE ARE NONE WHO CAN DEFY ME! I AM SUPREME!

MINUTES LATER, A DETACHMENT OF RECON TROOPS STUMBLE ACROSS THE STUNNED FORM OF THE **HULK**...

LOOKS LIKE WE'RE ON THE RIGHT TRACK! THE METAL MASTER **MUST** HAVE BEEN IN THE VICINITY! ONLY **HE** COULD HAVE BEATEN THE **HULK!**

HEY! WHAT GIVES? HE'S GOT SOME KINDA **MASK** ON!

AT THAT MOMENT, THE **HULK** BEGINS TO REGAIN CONSCIOUS-NESS...

LET'S SEE WHAT'S UNDERNEATH THIS THING...

WHA--? NO! NO!

GOT TO MOVE **FAST,** WHILE HE'S STILL WEAK AND DAZED! WHY WOULD THE **HULK** WEAR A MASK?? HAS HE **ANOTHER** IDENTITY??

IF THEY FIND OUT WHO I REALLY AM, IT'S THE **END** FOR ME!

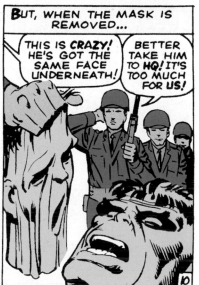

BUT, WHEN THE MASK IS REMOVED...

THIS IS **CRAZY!** HE'S GOT THE SAME FACE UNDERNEATH!

BETTER TAKE HIM TO **HQ!** IT'S TOO MUCH FOR **US!**

10

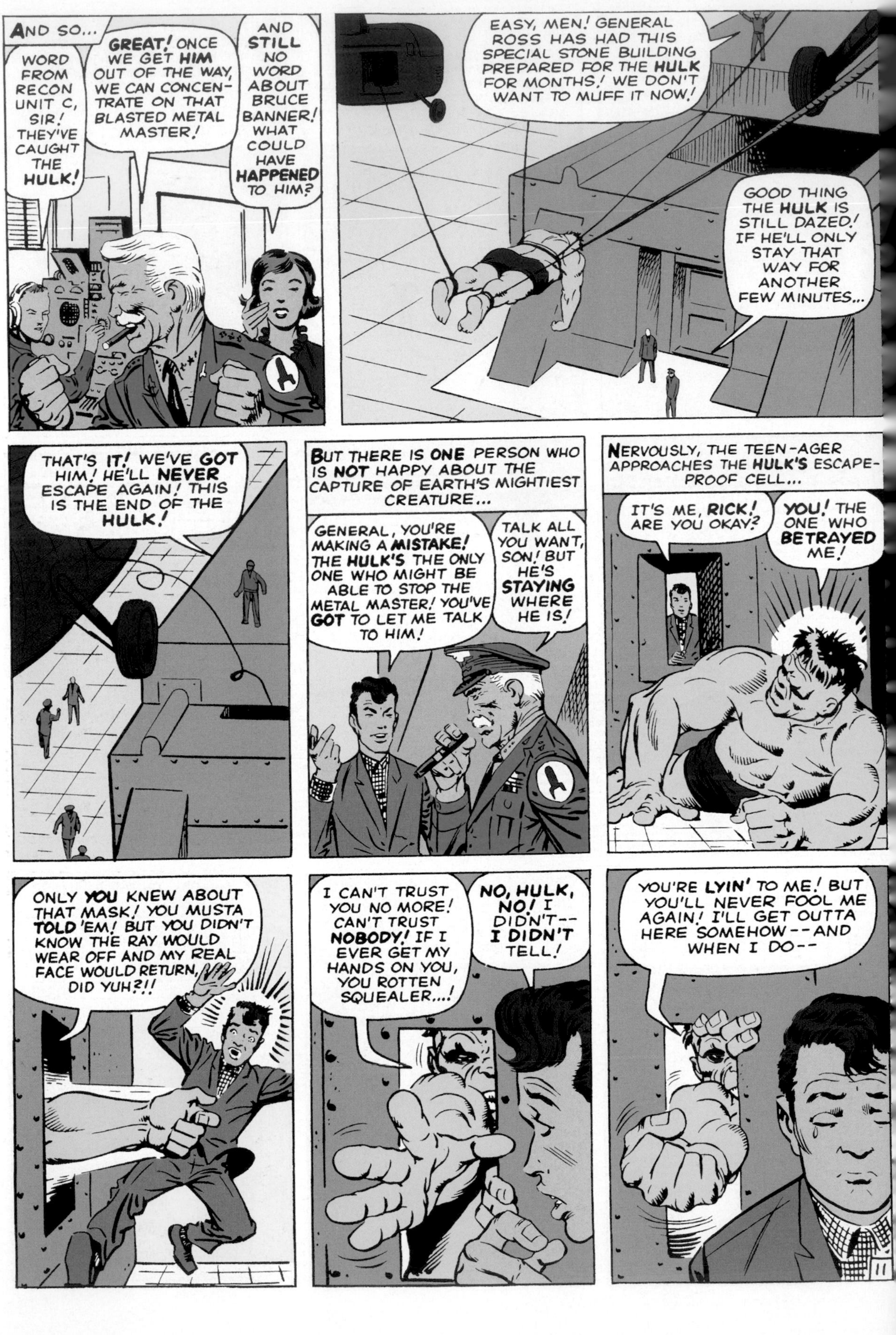

AND SO...
WORD FROM RECON UNIT C, SIR! THEY'VE CAUGHT THE HULK!
GREAT! ONCE WE GET HIM OUT OF THE WAY, WE CAN CONCENTRATE ON THAT BLASTED METAL MASTER!
AND STILL NO WORD ABOUT BRUCE BANNER! WHAT COULD HAVE HAPPENED TO HIM?
EASY, MEN! GENERAL ROSS HAS HAD THIS SPECIAL STONE BUILDING PREPARED FOR THE HULK FOR MONTHS! WE DON'T WANT TO MUFF IT NOW!
GOOD THING THE HULK IS STILL DAZED! IF HE'LL ONLY STAY THAT WAY FOR ANOTHER FEW MINUTES...
THAT'S IT! WE'VE GOT HIM! HE'LL NEVER ESCAPE AGAIN! THIS IS THE END OF THE HULK!
BUT THERE IS ONE PERSON WHO IS NOT HAPPY ABOUT THE CAPTURE OF EARTH'S MIGHTIEST CREATURE...
GENERAL, YOU'RE MAKING A MISTAKE! THE HULK'S THE ONLY ONE WHO MIGHT BE ABLE TO STOP THE METAL MASTER! YOU'VE GOT TO LET ME TALK TO HIM!
TALK ALL YOU WANT, SON! BUT HE'S STAYING WHERE HE IS!
NERVOUSLY, THE TEEN-AGER APPROACHES THE HULK'S ESCAPE-PROOF CELL...
IT'S ME, RICK! ARE YOU OKAY?
YOU! THE ONE WHO BETRAYED ME!
ONLY YOU KNEW ABOUT THAT MASK! YOU MUSTA TOLD 'EM! BUT YOU DIDN'T KNOW THE RAY WOULD WEAR OFF AND MY REAL FACE WOULD RETURN, DID YUH?!!
I CAN'T TRUST YOU NO MORE! CAN'T TRUST NOBODY! IF I EVER GET MY HANDS ON YOU, YOU ROTTEN SQUEALER...!
NO, HULK, NO! I DIDN'T-- I DIDN'T TELL!
YOU'RE LYIN' TO ME! BUT YOU'LL NEVER FOOL ME AGAIN! I'LL GET OUTTA HERE SOMEHOW--AND WHEN I DO--
11

AND WHEN I DO--WHEN I BREAK OUTTA HERE-- I'LL HAVE MY REVENGE! ON **EVERYBODY!** DO YA **HEAR**-- ON **EVERYBODY!!**

AND I **WILL** GET OUT! I **WILL!**

NO MATTER **HOW** LONG IT TAKES--I'LL GET OUT!

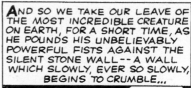

AND SO WE TAKE OUR LEAVE OF THE MOST INCREDIBLE CREATURE ON EARTH, FOR A SHORT TIME, AS HE POUNDS HIS UNBELIEVABLY POWERFUL FISTS AGAINST THE SILENT STONE WALL-- A WALL WHICH SLOWLY, EVER SO SLOWLY, BEGINS TO CRUMBLE...

I'LL GET OUT!

BUT WHAT OF RICK JONES? HURT, BEWILDERED, HE TURNS TO THUNDERBOLT ROSS...

GENERAL, WHERE DO I GO TO ENLIST IN THE ARMY?

NOWHERE YET, SON! YOU'RE ONLY SIXTEEN! YOU'RE TOO YOUNG!

BUT I'M TIRED OF BEIN' JUST A **NOTHIN'!** I WANNA BE WHERE THE **ACTION** IS!

I KNOW HOW YOU FEEL, MY BOY, BUT IF YOU REALLY WANT TO SERVE YOUR COUNTRY...

...THE BEST THING TO DO IS STAY IN SCHOOL! AMERICA NEEDS TRAINED MEN, IN EVERY FIELD-- EVEN IN THE ARMY! AND **THEN,** WHEN YOU'RE OLD ENOUGH...

COOL IT, GENERAL! I GET THE MESSAGE!

AND SLOWLY, INEXORABLY, FATE DRAWS HER LITTLE WEB CLOSER AND CLOSER... FOR, AT THAT MOMENT, THE METAL MASTER DESTROYS OIL WELLS IN THE HEART OF THE NEAR EAST...

BEHOLD! IT IS THE **METAL MASTER!**

THEN SPEEDS ON TO TOPPLE CONSTRUCTION IN AFRICA, AFFECT SHIPPING IN THE MEDITERRANEAN, AND UPROOT BRIDGES IN THE HEART OF EUROPE!

ONLY THE **METAL MASTER** COULD DO ALL THIS!

AND, BEFORE LONG, THE ENTIRE EARTH HAS SEEN AWESOME DEMONSTRATIONS OF THE SEEMINGLY ENDLESS POWER OF THE MENACE FROM AN- OTHER GALAXY! NOT A HUMAN BREATHES ON EARTH WHO DOES NOT TREMBLE AT THE NAME...

THE METAL MASTER!

12

AND, AT THIS POINT, WE RETURN TO A DISHEARTENED RICK JONES...

HECK! THE WHOLE WORLD'S IN TROUBLE, AND THERE'S NOTHIN' A CAT MY AGE CAN **DO** ABOUT IT!

WHY NOT TAKE THE GENERAL'S ADVICE, RICK, AND JUST STICK TO YOUR EDUCATION! THAT'S WHAT THE **REST** OF US ARE DOING!

SURE, IT'S OKAY FOR **HIM** TO TALK! HE WAS NEVER THE **HULK'S** PARTNER! HOW CAN I GO BACK TO BEIN' AN ORDINARY KID AFTER SOMETHIN' LIKE **THAT!**

LOOK, THERE'S RICK JONES!

HEY, RICK-O! COME HERE-- WE'VE GOT SOMETHIN' TO **SHOW** YOU!

WAIT'LL YA SEE WHAT THE GANG'S BEEN DOIN'! YOU'LL **FLIP**, SON!

SORRY, DADDY-O! I AIN'T IN A FLIPPIN' MOOD!

COME ON, SOURPUSS, WHAT HAVE YA GOT TO LOSE?

AND SO, RICK ACCOMPANIES HIS FRIENDS AND FINDS...

WE ALL CHIPPED IN TO BUY THIS HAM RADIO! ISN'T IT **COOL?**

WE CAN TALK TO **OTHER** HAMS ALL OVER THE COUNTRY!

HEY! WADDAYA **KNOW?!!**

THAT'S **IT!** THE IDEA I'VE BEEN LOOKIN' FOR! IT'S PERFECT! THEY CAN'T STOP US ON ACCOUNT OF OUR AGE! AND WE CAN HELP THE ARMY, THE POLICE, **EVERYBODY!**

WHAT DO YOU **MEAN**, RICK?

WITH A BUNCH OF CATS LIKE US, ALL OVER THE COUNTRY, KEEPIN' IN TOUCH BY RADIO, WE CAN HAVE THE GREATEST SET-UP IN THE WORLD! WE'LL FORM A CLUB-- CALL IT SOMETHIN' LIKE -- THE **TEEN BRIGADE** -- AND BE READY TO HELP OUT WHEREVER WE'RE NEEDED!

HEY, THE **TEEN BRIGADE!** IT SOUNDS NEAT!

REET! I'LL BUY IT!

MINUTE AFTER MINUTE, HOUR AFTER HOUR, HIS MIGHTY, SEEMINGLY TIRELESS FISTS POUND AGAINST THE STONE WALL, CHIPPING IT AWAY BIT BY BIT, UNTIL--AT LAST--

AND SO, THE **TEEN BRIGADE** IS BORN! A BAND OF LOYAL TEEN-AGERS OF WHOM WE WILL SHORTLY HEAR MORE! BUT NOW, BACK TO THE **HULK**--

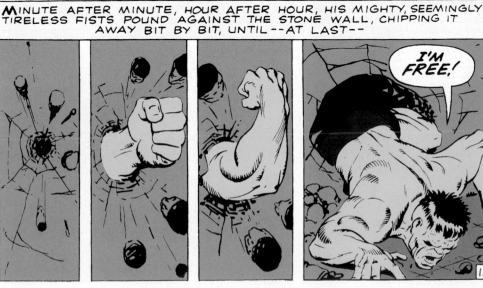

I'M **FREE!**

13

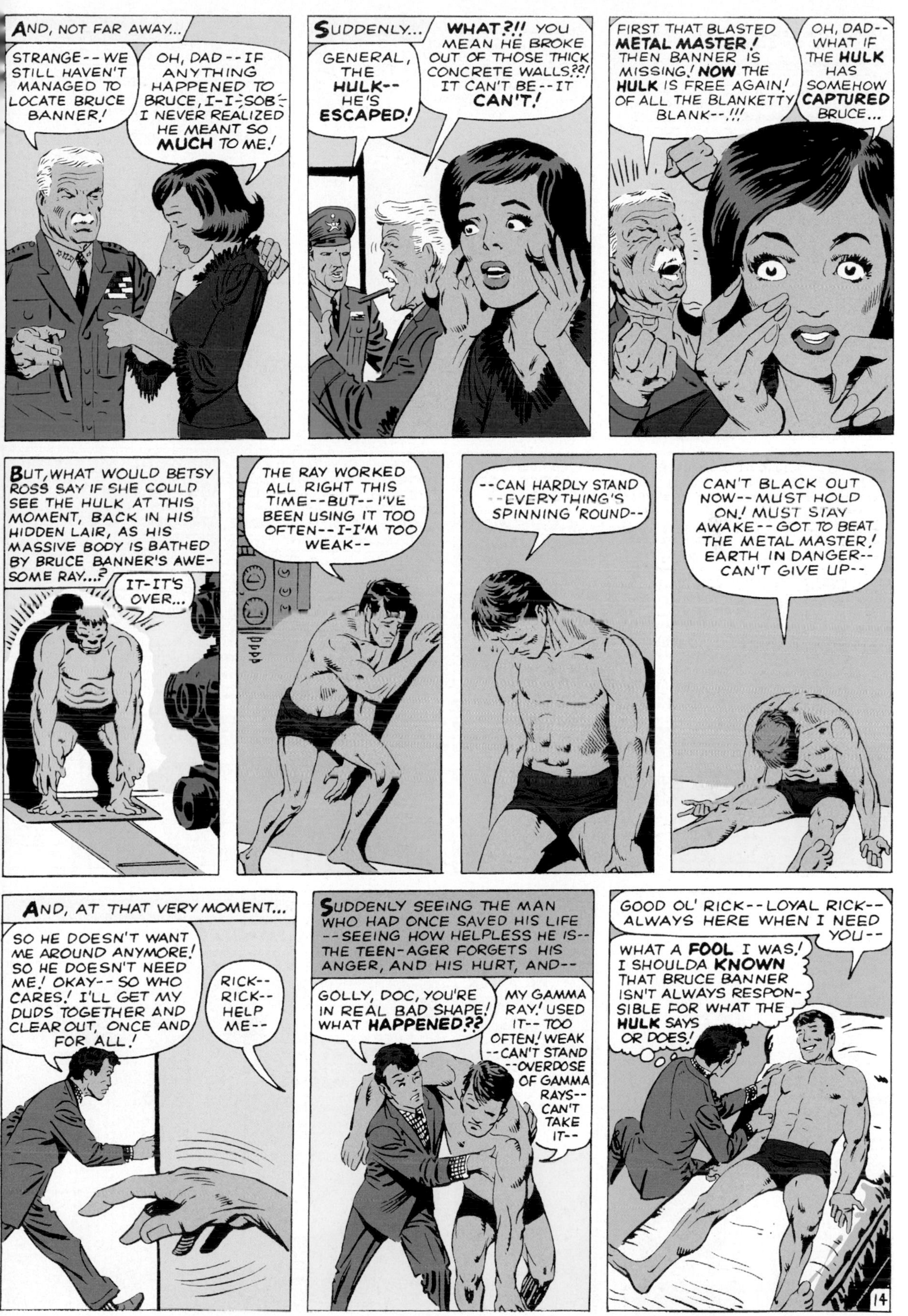
AND, NOT FAR AWAY...
STRANGE--WE STILL HAVEN'T MANAGED TO LOCATE BRUCE BANNER!
OH, DAD--IF ANYTHING HAPPENED TO BRUCE, I-I--SOB--I NEVER REALIZED HE MEANT SO MUCH TO ME!
SUDDENLY...
GENERAL, THE HULK--HE'S ESCAPED!
WHAT?!! YOU MEAN HE BROKE OUT OF THOSE THICK CONCRETE WALLS??! IT CAN'T BE--IT CAN'T!
FIRST THAT BLASTED METAL MASTER! THEN BANNER IS MISSING! NOW THE HULK IS FREE AGAIN! OF ALL THE BLANKETTY BLANK--!!!
OH, DAD--WHAT IF THE HULK HAS SOMEHOW CAPTURED BRUCE...
BUT, WHAT WOULD BETSY ROSS SAY IF SHE COULD SEE THE HULK AT THIS MOMENT, BACK IN HIS HIDDEN LAIR, AS HIS MASSIVE BODY IS BATHED BY BRUCE BANNER'S AWESOME RAY...?
IT-IT'S OVER...
THE RAY WORKED ALL RIGHT THIS TIME--BUT--I'VE BEEN USING IT TOO OFTEN--I-I'M TOO WEAK--
--CAN HARDLY STAND --EVERYTHING'S SPINNING 'ROUND--
CAN'T BLACK OUT NOW--MUST HOLD ON! MUST STAY AWAKE--GOT TO BEAT THE METAL MASTER! EARTH IN DANGER--CAN'T GIVE UP--
AND, AT THAT VERY MOMENT...
SO HE DOESN'T WANT ME AROUND ANYMORE! SO HE DOESN'T NEED ME! OKAY--SO WHO CARES! I'LL GET MY DUDS TOGETHER AND CLEAR OUT, ONCE AND FOR ALL!
RICK--RICK--HELP ME--
SUDDENLY SEEING THE MAN WHO HAD ONCE SAVED HIS LIFE--SEEING HOW HELPLESS HE IS--THE TEEN-AGER FORGETS HIS ANGER, AND HIS HURT, AND--
GOLLY, DOC, YOU'RE IN REAL BAD SHAPE! WHAT HAPPENED??
MY GAMMA RAY! USED IT--TOO OFTEN! WEAK--CAN'T STAND--OVERDOSE OF GAMMA RAYS--CAN'T TAKE IT--
GOOD OL' RICK--LOYAL RICK--ALWAYS HERE WHEN I NEED YOU--
WHAT A FOOL I WAS! I SHOULDA KNOWN THAT BRUCE BANNER ISN'T ALWAYS RESPONSIBLE FOR WHAT THE HULK SAYS OR DOES!
14

DOC, I'VE GOT TO GET YOU TO A HOSPITAL!

NO! NO TIME! I'VE THOUGHT OF A WAY TO BEAT THE **METAL MASTER!** BUT, NEED HELP! CAN'T DO IT ALONE!

WELL, GEE, WHAT CAN--? **WAIT A SEC!** I KNOW! YOU JUST TELL ME WHAT YOU NEED, DOC, AND MY **TEEN BRIGADE** WILL GO INTO ACTION!

TEEN BRIGADE--?

A SHORT TIME LATER, AFTER BEING SURE THAT BRUCE BANNER IS RESTING COMFORTABLY...

HERE'S THE PITCH, GANG! YOU'VE ALL HEARD OF DOCTOR BRUCE BANNER! WELL, HE'S GOT AN ANGLE ON HOW TO BEAT THE **METAL MASTER**, BUT IT'S UP TO **US** TO GET HIM THE EQUIPMENT HE NEEDS! NOW HERE'S WHAT WE WANT--

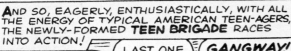

AND SO, EAGERLY, ENTHUSIASTICALLY, WITH ALL THE ENERGY OF TYPICAL AMERICAN TEEN-AGERS, THE NEWLY-FORMED **TEEN BRIGADE** RACES INTO ACTION!

WHAT ARE WE **WAITIN'** FOR?

LAST ONE BACK IS A ROTTEN EGG!

GANGWAY!

NORTH, SOUTH, EAST, AND WEST-- INTO EVERY CORNER OF THE UNITED STATES, THE TEEN BRIGADE RADIO THEIR MESSAGES! AND PARTS AND SUPPLIES START POURING IN FROM ALL OVER, IN A DESPERATE STRUGGLE TO STOP THE METAL MASTER!

JUST REACHED PITTSBURGH! OUR CONDENSERS ARE ON THE WAY!

HERE'S THE TUBES AND CIRCUITS RICK ASKED FOR--FROM SEATTLE!

BLUE-PRINTS ON THE WAY! OVER AND OUT!

AND, ONCE MORE, ALONE AND UNSUSPECTED, A SLENDER FIGURE STANDS IN FRONT OF THE GAMMA RAY MACHINE...

CAN'T AFFORD TO REST ANY LONGER! IT'S NOW OR NEVER!

IT'S WORKING!

AHHH-- I CAN FEEL THE POWER SURGING THRU MY BODY! I'M **STRONG** AGAIN! I'M THE **HULK** AGAIN!

AND SO OUR GRIPPING TALE GATHERS MOMENTUM AS IT RACES TOWARDS ITS INEVITABLE CLIMAX! FOR THE **METAL MASTER** IS STILL AT LARGE, AND EARTH HAS STILL FOUND NO WAY TO COPE WITH HIS DIRE MENACE!

WE'VE TRIED EVERY WEAPON-- EVERY SCHEME-- **NOTHING** CAN STOP THE METAL MASTER!

THE PEOPLE ARE GROWING PANICKY! SOMETHING MUST BE DONE SOON! BUT **WHAT??**

15

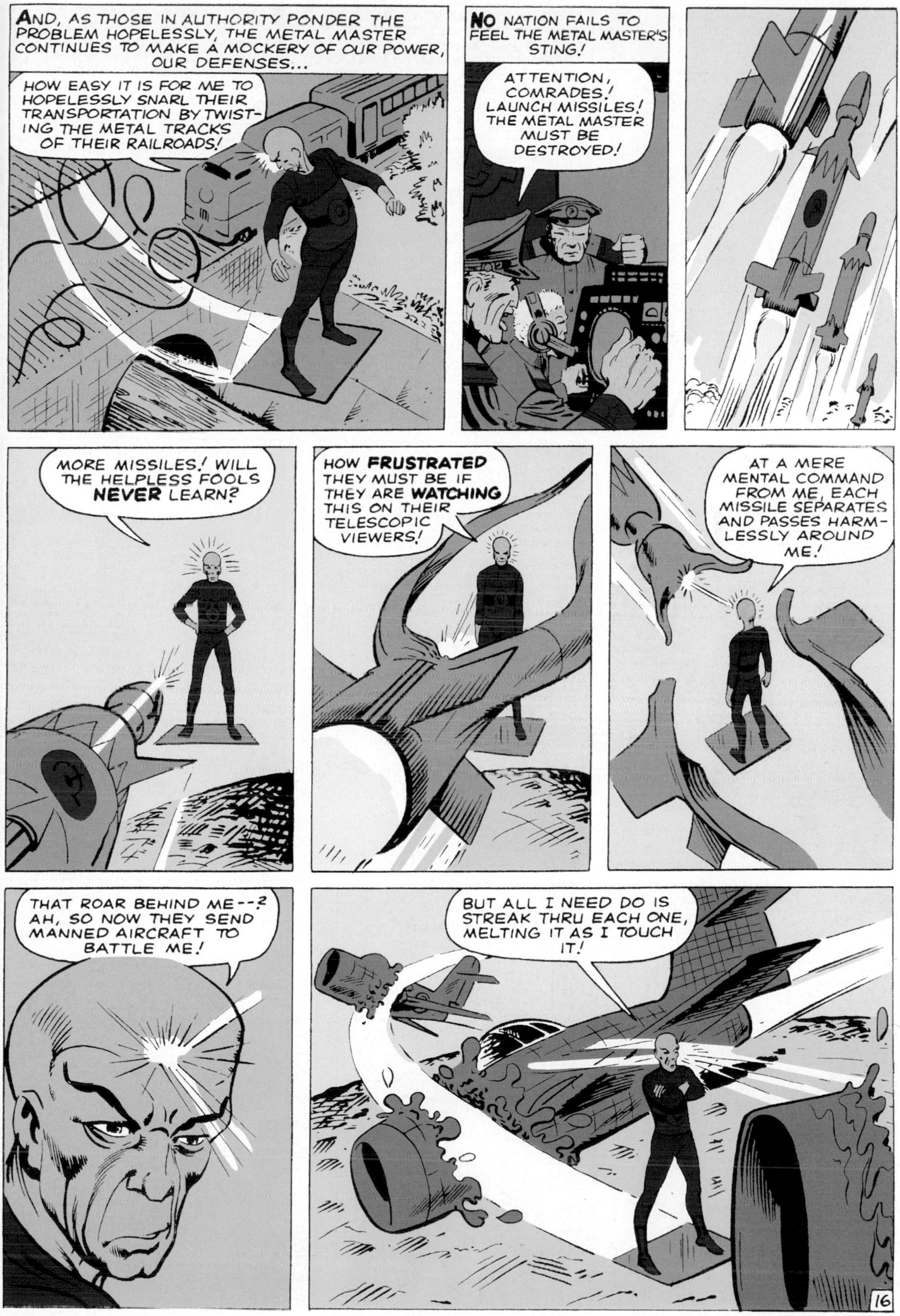
AND, AS THOSE IN AUTHORITY PONDER THE PROBLEM HOPELESSLY, THE METAL MASTER CONTINUES TO MAKE A MOCKERY OF OUR POWER, OUR DEFENSES...
HOW EASY IT IS FOR ME TO HOPELESSLY SNARL THEIR TRANSPORTATION BY TWISTING THE METAL TRACKS OF THEIR RAILROADS!
NO NATION FAILS TO FEEL THE METAL MASTER'S STING!
ATTENTION, COMRADES! LAUNCH MISSILES! THE METAL MASTER MUST BE DESTROYED!
MORE MISSILES! WILL THE HELPLESS FOOLS NEVER LEARN?
HOW FRUSTRATED THEY MUST BE IF THEY ARE WATCHING THIS ON THEIR TELESCOPIC VIEWERS!
AT A MERE MENTAL COMMAND FROM ME, EACH MISSILE SEPARATES AND PASSES HARMLESSLY AROUND ME!
THAT ROAR BEHIND ME--? AH, SO NOW THEY SEND MANNED AIRCRAFT TO BATTLE ME!
BUT ALL I NEED DO IS STREAK THRU EACH ONE, MELTING IT AS I TOUCH IT!
16

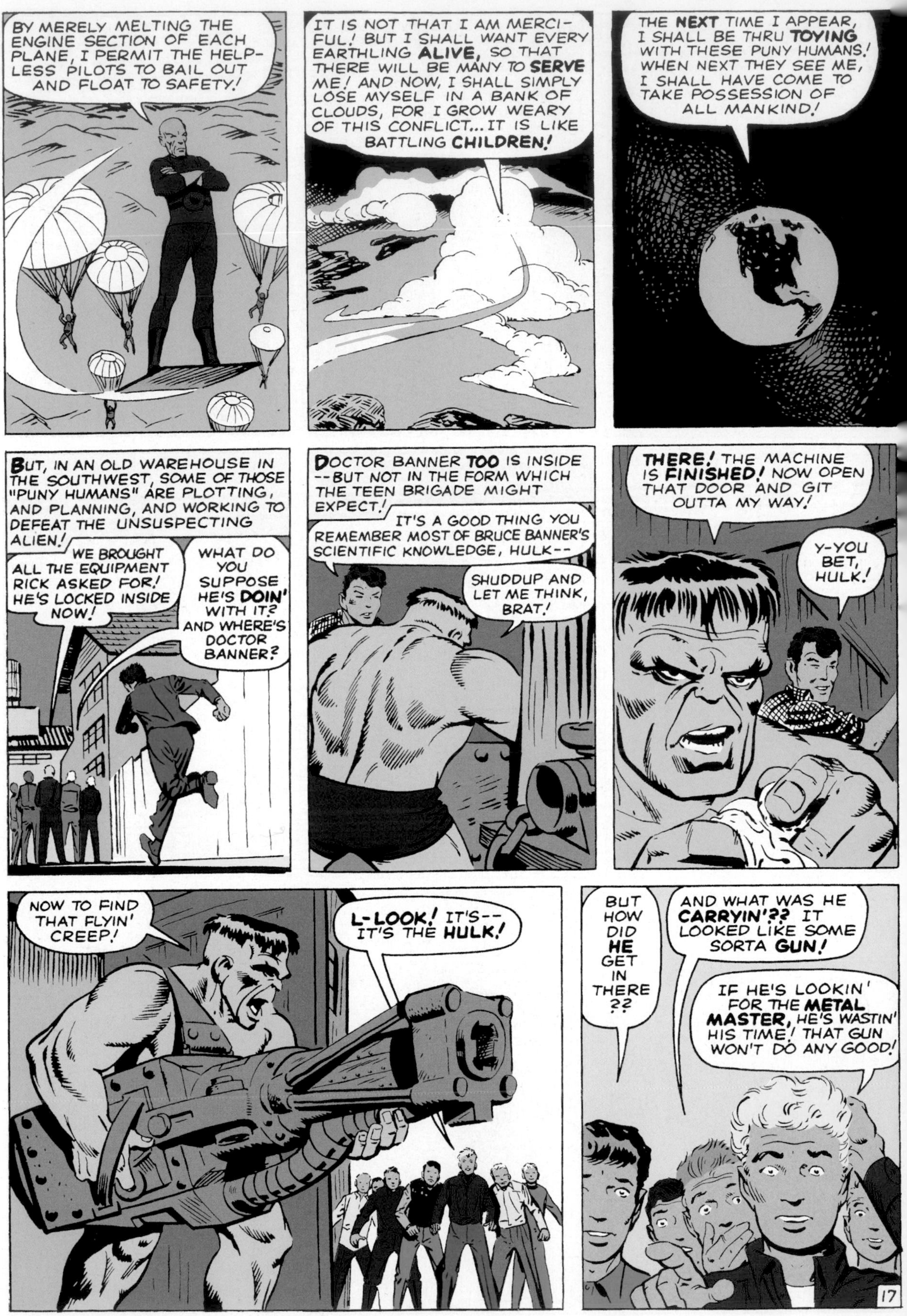
BY MERELY MELTING THE ENGINE SECTION OF EACH PLANE, I PERMIT THE HELPLESS PILOTS TO BAIL OUT AND FLOAT TO SAFETY!
IT IS NOT THAT I AM MERCIFUL! BUT I SHALL WANT EVERY EARTHLING ALIVE, SO THAT THERE WILL BE MANY TO SERVE ME! AND NOW, I SHALL SIMPLY LOSE MYSELF IN A BANK OF CLOUDS, FOR I GROW WEARY OF THIS CONFLICT... IT IS LIKE BATTLING CHILDREN!
THE NEXT TIME I APPEAR, I SHALL BE THRU TOYING WITH THESE PUNY HUMANS! WHEN NEXT THEY SEE ME, I SHALL HAVE COME TO TAKE POSSESSION OF ALL MANKIND!
BUT, IN AN OLD WAREHOUSE IN THE SOUTHWEST, SOME OF THOSE "PUNY HUMANS" ARE PLOTTING, AND PLANNING, AND WORKING TO DEFEAT THE UNSUSPECTING ALIEN!
WE BROUGHT ALL THE EQUIPMENT RICK ASKED FOR! HE'S LOCKED INSIDE NOW!
WHAT DO YOU SUPPOSE HE'S DOIN' WITH IT? AND WHERE'S DOCTOR BANNER?
DOCTOR BANNER TOO IS INSIDE --BUT NOT IN THE FORM WHICH THE TEEN BRIGADE MIGHT EXPECT!
IT'S A GOOD THING YOU REMEMBER MOST OF BRUCE BANNER'S SCIENTIFIC KNOWLEDGE, HULK--
SHUDDUP AND LET ME THINK, BRAT!
THERE! THE MACHINE IS FINISHED! NOW OPEN THAT DOOR AND GIT OUTTA MY WAY!
Y-YOU BET, HULK!
NOW TO FIND THAT FLYIN' CREEP!
L-LOOK! IT'S-- IT'S THE HULK!
BUT HOW DID HE GET IN THERE ??
AND WHAT WAS HE CARRYIN'?? IT LOOKED LIKE SOME SORTA GUN!
IF HE'S LOOKIN' FOR THE METAL MASTER, HE'S WASTIN' HIS TIME! THAT GUN WON'T DO ANY GOOD!
17

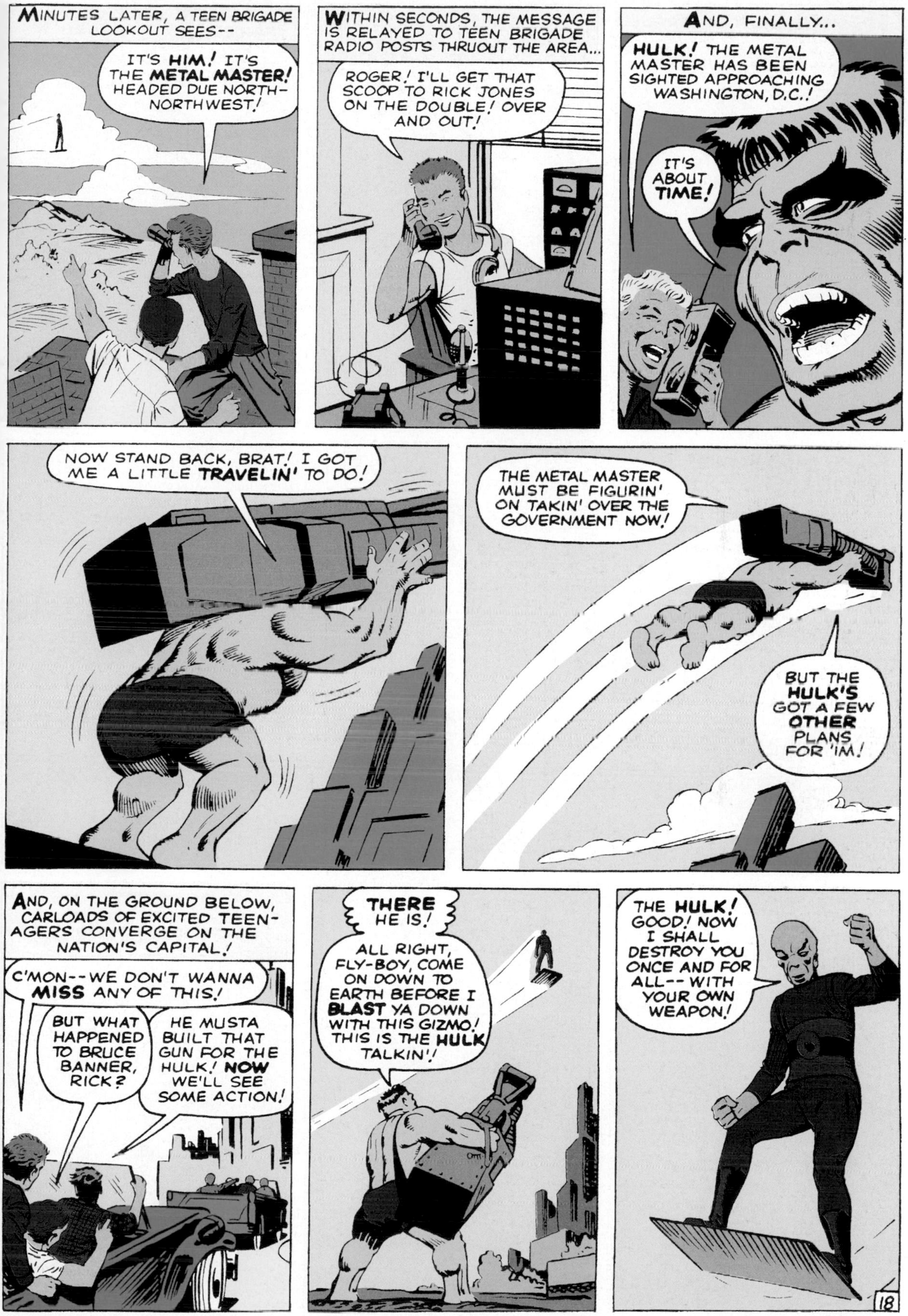
MINUTES LATER, A TEEN BRIGADE LOOKOUT SEES--
IT'S HIM! IT'S THE METAL MASTER! HEADED DUE NORTH-NORTHWEST!
WITHIN SECONDS, THE MESSAGE IS RELAYED TO TEEN BRIGADE RADIO POSTS THRUOUT THE AREA...
ROGER! I'LL GET THAT SCOOP TO RICK JONES ON THE DOUBLE! OVER AND OUT!
AND, FINALLY...
HULK! THE METAL MASTER HAS BEEN SIGHTED APPROACHING WASHINGTON, D.C.!
IT'S ABOUT TIME!
NOW STAND BACK, BRAT! I GOT ME A LITTLE TRAVELIN' TO DO!
THE METAL MASTER MUST BE FIGURIN' ON TAKIN' OVER THE GOVERNMENT NOW!
BUT THE HULK'S GOT A FEW OTHER PLANS FOR 'IM!
AND, ON THE GROUND BELOW, CARLOADS OF EXCITED TEEN-AGERS CONVERGE ON THE NATION'S CAPITAL!
C'MON--WE DON'T WANNA MISS ANY OF THIS!
BUT WHAT HAPPENED TO BRUCE BANNER, RICK?
HE MUSTA BUILT THAT GUN FOR THE HULK! NOW WE'LL SEE SOME ACTION!
THERE HE IS!
ALL RIGHT, FLY-BOY, COME ON DOWN TO EARTH BEFORE I BLAST YA DOWN WITH THIS GIZMO! THIS IS THE HULK TALKIN'!
THE HULK! GOOD! NOW I SHALL DESTROY YOU ONCE AND FOR ALL--WITH YOUR OWN WEAPON!
18

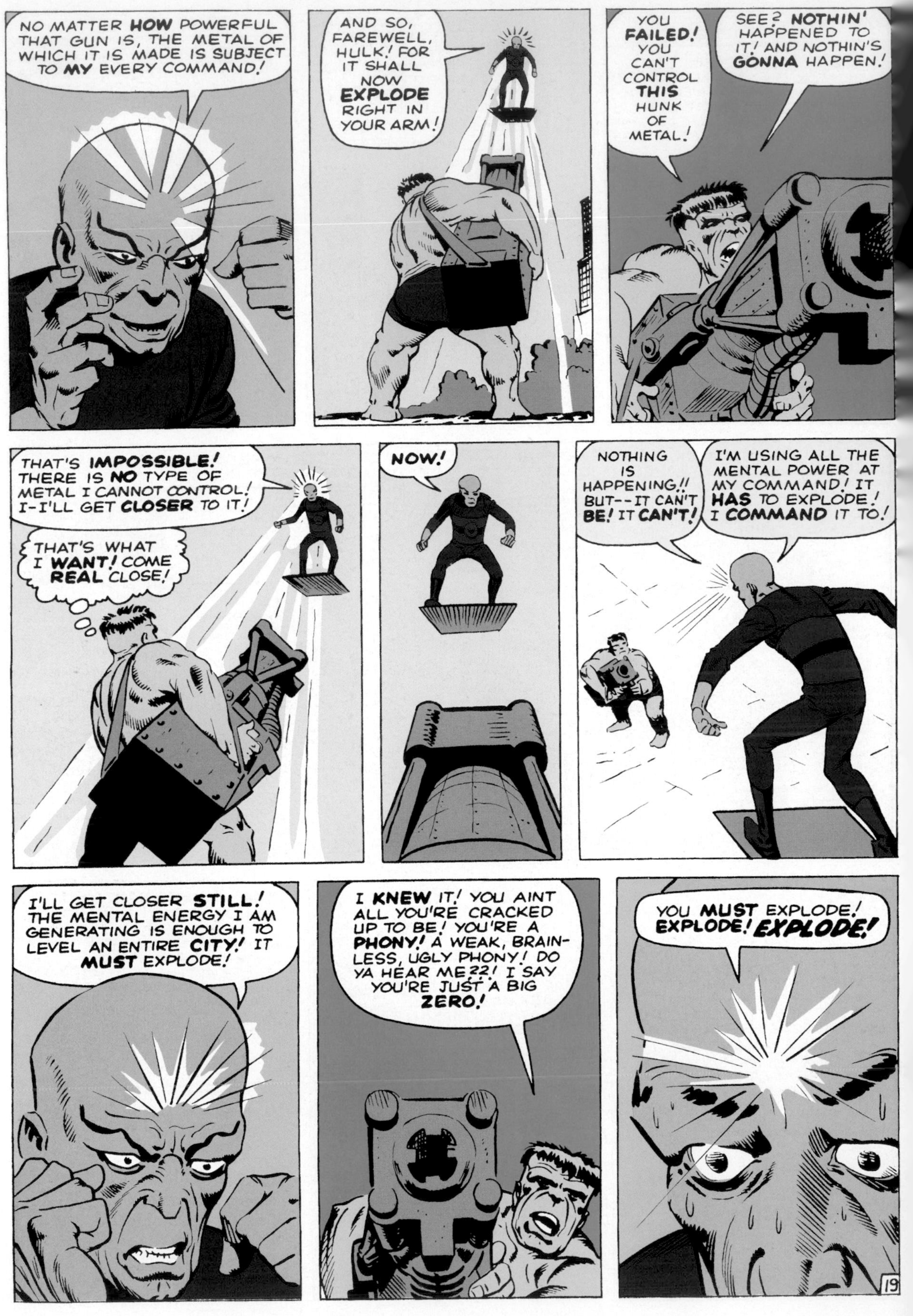
NO MATTER HOW POWERFUL THAT GUN IS, THE METAL OF WHICH IT IS MADE IS SUBJECT TO MY EVERY COMMAND!
AND SO, FAREWELL, HULK! FOR IT SHALL NOW EXPLODE RIGHT IN YOUR ARM!
YOU FAILED! YOU CAN'T CONTROL THIS HUNK OF METAL!
SEE? NOTHIN' HAPPENED TO IT! AND NOTHIN'S GONNA HAPPEN!
THAT'S IMPOSSIBLE! THERE IS NO TYPE OF METAL I CANNOT CONTROL! I-I'LL GET CLOSER TO IT!
THAT'S WHAT I WANT! COME REAL CLOSE!
NOW!
NOTHING IS HAPPENING!! BUT--IT CAN'T BE! IT CAN'T!
I'M USING ALL THE MENTAL POWER AT MY COMMAND! IT HAS TO EXPLODE! I COMMAND IT TO!
I'LL GET CLOSER STILL! THE MENTAL ENERGY I AM GENERATING IS ENOUGH TO LEVEL AN ENTIRE CITY! IT MUST EXPLODE!
I KNEW IT! YOU AINT ALL YOU'RE CRACKED UP TO BE! YOU'RE A PHONY! A WEAK, BRAIN-LESS, UGLY PHONY! DO YA HEAR ME??! I SAY YOU'RE JUST A BIG ZERO!
YOU MUST EXPLODE! EXPLODE! EXPLODE!
19

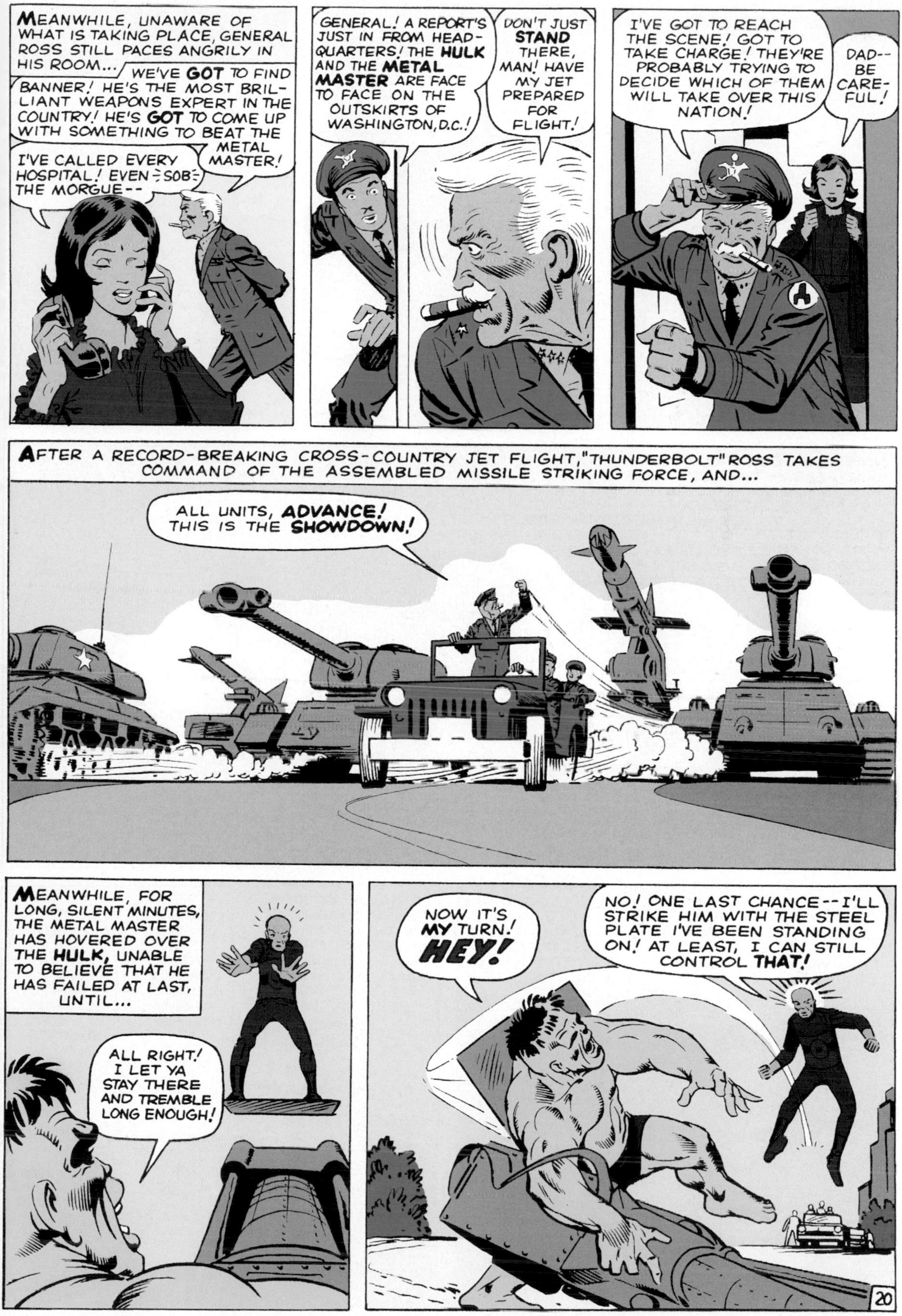
MEANWHILE, UNAWARE OF WHAT IS TAKING PLACE, GENERAL ROSS STILL PACES ANGRILY IN HIS ROOM...
WE'VE GOT TO FIND BANNER! HE'S THE MOST BRILLIANT WEAPONS EXPERT IN THE COUNTRY! HE'S GOT TO COME UP WITH SOMETHING TO BEAT THE METAL MASTER!
I'VE CALLED EVERY HOSPITAL! EVEN -SOB- THE MORGUE--
GENERAL! A REPORT'S JUST IN FROM HEADQUARTERS! THE HULK AND THE METAL MASTER ARE FACE TO FACE ON THE OUTSKIRTS OF WASHINGTON, D.C.!
DON'T JUST STAND THERE, MAN! HAVE MY JET PREPARED FOR FLIGHT!
I'VE GOT TO REACH THE SCENE! GOT TO TAKE CHARGE! THEY'RE PROBABLY TRYING TO DECIDE WHICH OF THEM WILL TAKE OVER THIS NATION!
DAD-- BE CAREFUL!
AFTER A RECORD-BREAKING CROSS-COUNTRY JET FLIGHT, "THUNDERBOLT" ROSS TAKES COMMAND OF THE ASSEMBLED MISSILE STRIKING FORCE, AND...
ALL UNITS, ADVANCE! THIS IS THE SHOWDOWN!
MEANWHILE, FOR LONG, SILENT MINUTES, THE METAL MASTER HAS HOVERED OVER THE HULK, UNABLE TO BELIEVE THAT HE HAS FAILED AT LAST, UNTIL...
ALL RIGHT! I LET YA STAY THERE AND TREMBLE LONG ENOUGH!
NOW IT'S MY TURN! HEY!
NO! ONE LAST CHANCE--I'LL STRIKE HIM WITH THE STEEL PLATE I'VE BEEN STANDING ON! AT LEAST, I CAN STILL CONTROL THAT!
20

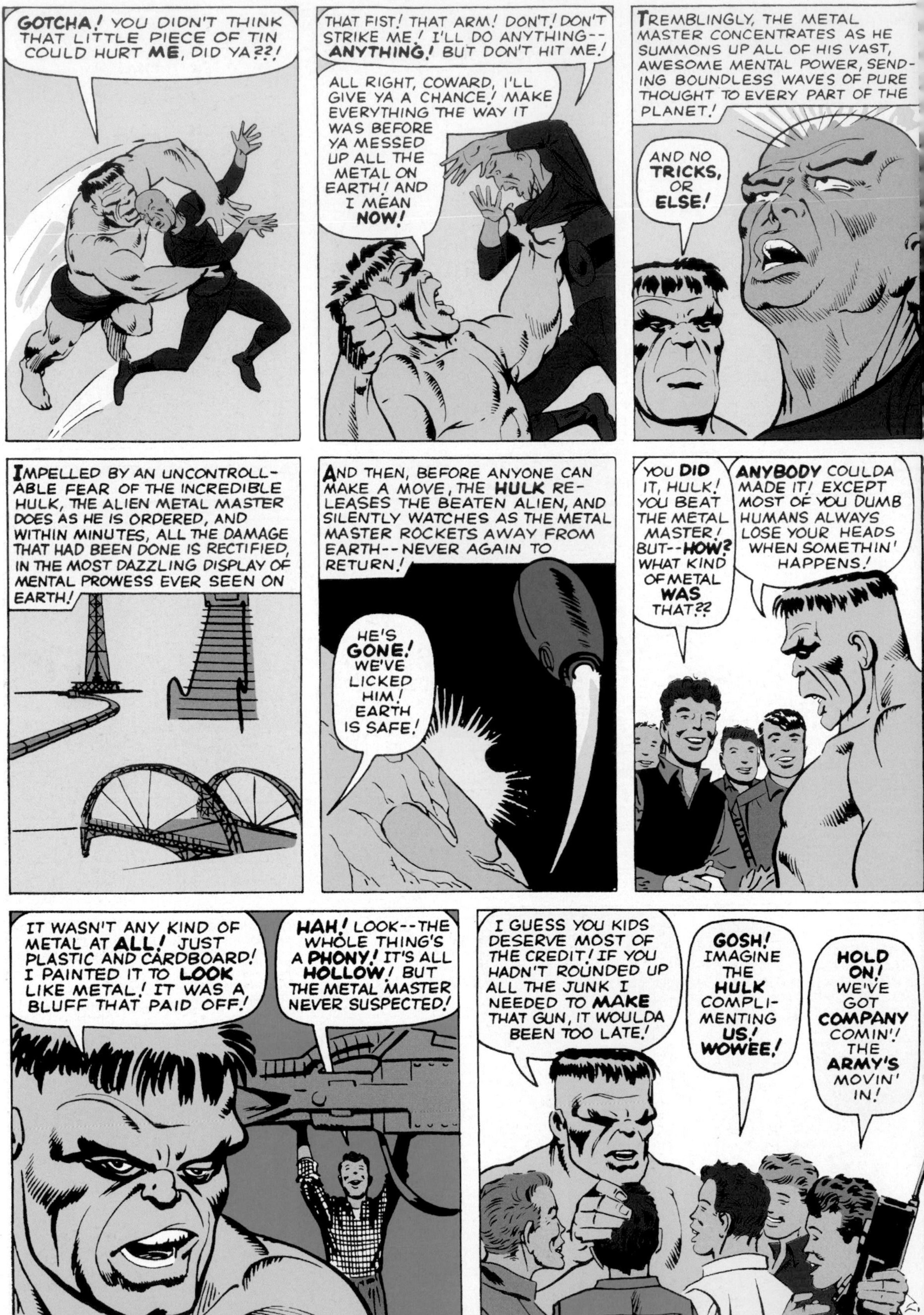
GOTCHA! YOU DIDN'T THINK THAT LITTLE PIECE OF TIN COULD HURT ME, DID YA??!
THAT FIST! THAT ARM! DON'T! DON'T STRIKE ME! I'LL DO ANYTHING--ANYTHING! BUT DON'T HIT ME!
ALL RIGHT, COWARD, I'LL GIVE YA A CHANCE! MAKE EVERYTHING THE WAY IT WAS BEFORE YA MESSED UP ALL THE METAL ON EARTH! AND I MEAN NOW!
TREMBLINGLY, THE METAL MASTER CONCENTRATES AS HE SUMMONS UP ALL OF HIS VAST, AWESOME MENTAL POWER, SENDING BOUNDLESS WAVES OF PURE THOUGHT TO EVERY PART OF THE PLANET!
AND NO TRICKS, OR ELSE!
IMPELLED BY AN UNCONTROLLABLE FEAR OF THE INCREDIBLE HULK, THE ALIEN METAL MASTER DOES AS HE IS ORDERED, AND WITHIN MINUTES, ALL THE DAMAGE THAT HAD BEEN DONE IS RECTIFIED, IN THE MOST DAZZLING DISPLAY OF MENTAL PROWESS EVER SEEN ON EARTH!
AND THEN, BEFORE ANYONE CAN MAKE A MOVE, THE HULK RELEASES THE BEATEN ALIEN, AND SILENTLY WATCHES AS THE METAL MASTER ROCKETS AWAY FROM EARTH--NEVER AGAIN TO RETURN!
HE'S GONE! WE'VE LICKED HIM! EARTH IS SAFE!
YOU DID IT, HULK! YOU BEAT THE METAL MASTER! BUT--HOW? WHAT KIND OF METAL WAS THAT??
ANYBODY COULDA MADE IT! EXCEPT MOST OF YOU DUMB HUMANS ALWAYS LOSE YOUR HEADS WHEN SOMETHIN' HAPPENS!
IT WASN'T ANY KIND OF METAL AT ALL! JUST PLASTIC AND CARDBOARD! I PAINTED IT TO LOOK LIKE METAL! IT WAS A BLUFF THAT PAID OFF!
HAH! LOOK--THE WHOLE THING'S A PHONY! IT'S ALL HOLLOW! BUT THE METAL MASTER NEVER SUSPECTED!
I GUESS YOU KIDS DESERVE MOST OF THE CREDIT! IF YOU HADN'T ROUNDED UP ALL THE JUNK I NEEDED TO MAKE THAT GUN, IT WOULDA BEEN TOO LATE!
GOSH! IMAGINE THE HULK COMPLIMENTING US! WOWEE!
HOLD ON! WE'VE GOT COMPANY COMIN'! THE ARMY'S MOVIN' IN!
21

THERE HE IS -- UP AHEAD! STEADY NOW, MEN! PROCEED WITH CAUTION!

HANG ON, BRAT -- WE'RE HEADIN' HOME! I GOT NO TIME FOR ANY EXPLAININ' NOW!

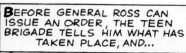

BEFORE GENERAL ROSS CAN ISSUE AN ORDER, THE TEEN BRIGADE TELLS HIM WHAT HAS TAKEN PLACE, AND...

--AND THAT'S HOW IT HAPPENED, SIR! THE **HULK** BEAT THE METAL MASTER -- HE SAVED THE WHOLE EARTH!

WELL, I'LL BE--!!!

AND SO, MANY MANY MILES AND MANY HOURS LATER...

WELL, HERE GOES **NUTHIN'** AGAIN...

WHA-WHAT **HAPPENED??** I DIDN'T CHANGE!

I'M STILL THE **HULK!**

WHAT DID I DO WRONG? EVERYTHING'S SET RIGHT -- EVERYTHING'S CONNECTED--

BANNER ALWAYS **FELT** THAT THE BLASTED MACHINE SHOULDN'T BE USED TOO MUCH! THE GAMMA RAYS ARE TOO STRONG -- TOO HARD TO CONTROL!

I ALWAYS **HATED** BANNER'S WEAK BODY -- ALWAYS WISHED I COULD **STAY** AS THE **HULK!** BUT NOW -- TO BE THE **HULK** FOREVER -- TO ALWAYS BE HUNTED -- FEARED--

22

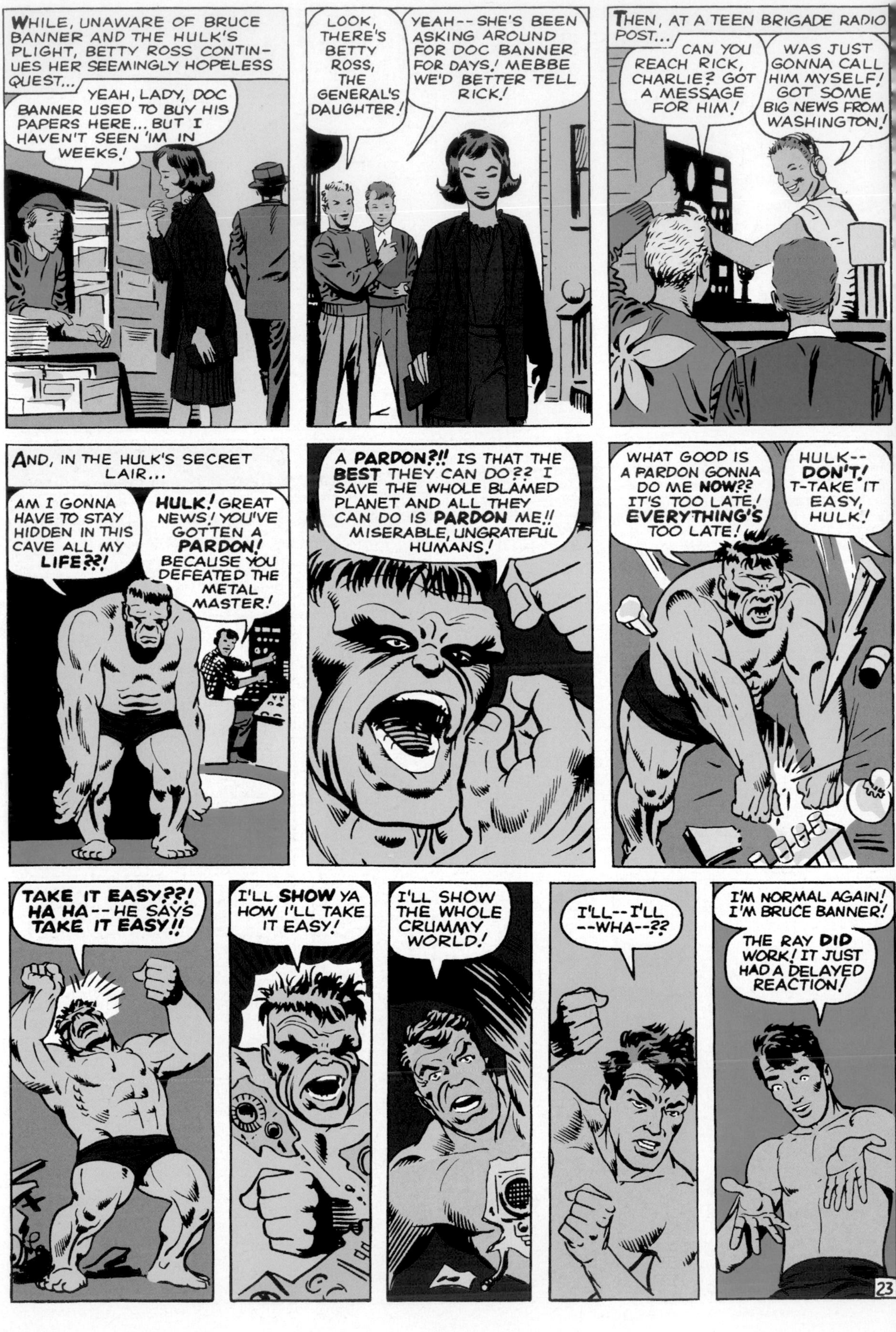
WHILE, UNAWARE OF BRUCE BANNER AND THE HULK'S PLIGHT, BETTY ROSS CONTINUES HER SEEMINGLY HOPELESS QUEST...
YEAH, LADY, DOC BANNER USED TO BUY HIS PAPERS HERE... BUT I HAVEN'T SEEN 'IM IN WEEKS!
LOOK, THERE'S BETTY ROSS, THE GENERAL'S DAUGHTER!
YEAH-- SHE'S BEEN ASKING AROUND FOR DOC BANNER FOR DAYS! MEBBE WE'D BETTER TELL RICK!
THEN, AT A TEEN BRIGADE RADIO POST...
CAN YOU REACH RICK, CHARLIE? GOT A MESSAGE FOR HIM!
WAS JUST GONNA CALL HIM MYSELF! GOT SOME BIG NEWS FROM WASHINGTON!
AND, IN THE HULK'S SECRET LAIR...
AM I GONNA HAVE TO STAY HIDDEN IN THIS CAVE ALL MY LIFE??!
HULK! GREAT NEWS! YOU'VE GOTTEN A PARDON! BECAUSE YOU DEFEATED THE METAL MASTER!
A PARDON?!! IS THAT THE BEST THEY CAN DO?? I SAVE THE WHOLE BLAMED PLANET AND ALL THEY CAN DO IS PARDON ME!! MISERABLE, UNGRATEFUL HUMANS!
WHAT GOOD IS A PARDON GONNA DO ME NOW?? IT'S TOO LATE! EVERYTHING'S TOO LATE!
HULK-- DON'T! T-TAKE IT EASY, HULK!
TAKE IT EASY??! HA HA-- HE SAYS TAKE IT EASY!!
I'LL SHOW YA HOW I'LL TAKE IT EASY!
I'LL SHOW THE WHOLE CRUMMY WORLD!
I'LL-- I'LL --WHA--??
I'M NORMAL AGAIN! I'M BRUCE BANNER!
THE RAY DID WORK! IT JUST HAD A DELAYED REACTION!

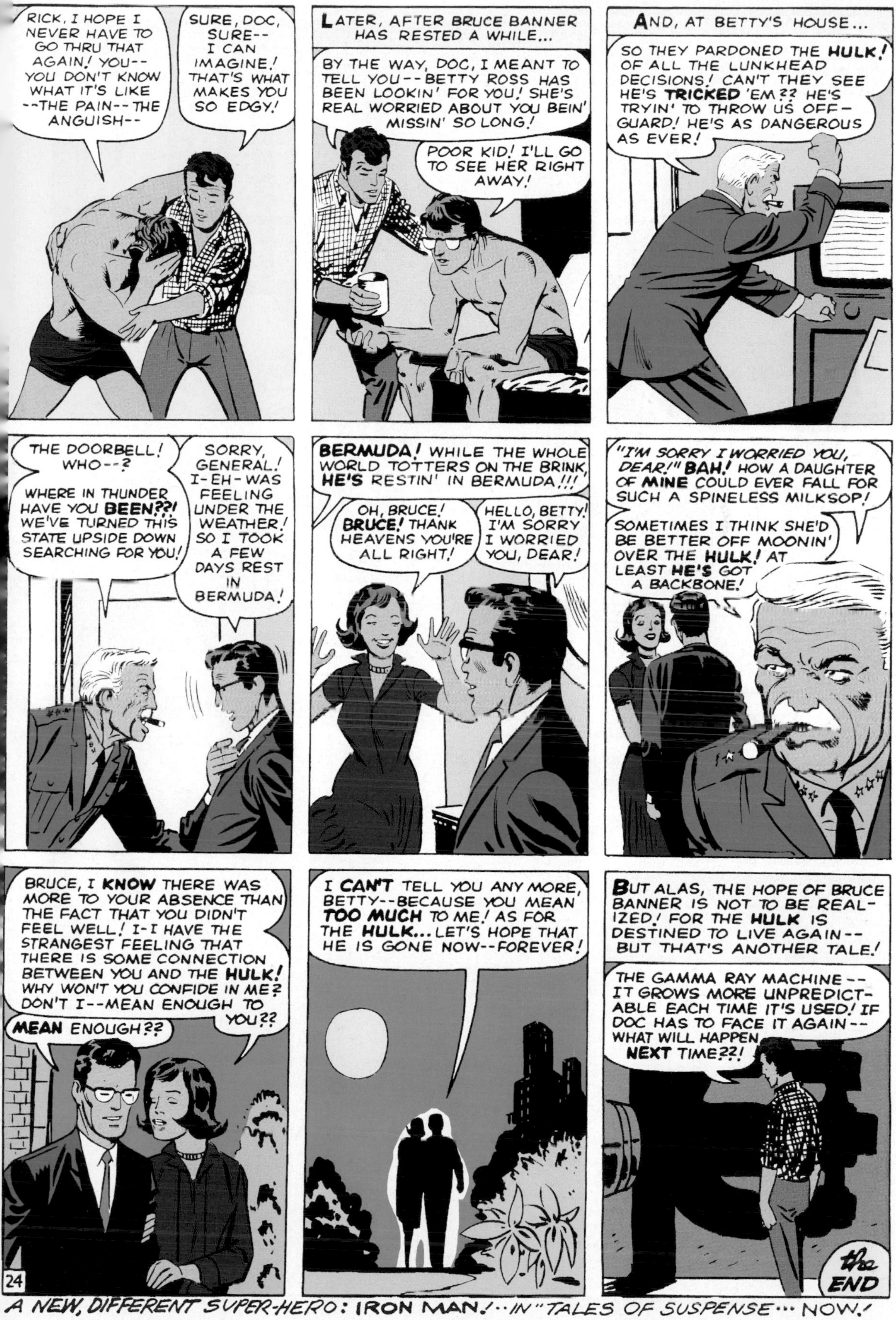

RICK, I HOPE I NEVER HAVE TO GO THRU THAT AGAIN! YOU-- YOU DON'T KNOW WHAT IT'S LIKE --THE PAIN--THE ANGUISH--
SURE, DOC, SURE-- I CAN IMAGINE! THAT'S WHAT MAKES YOU SO EDGY!
LATER, AFTER BRUCE BANNER HAS RESTED A WHILE...
BY THE WAY, DOC, I MEANT TO TELL YOU--BETTY ROSS HAS BEEN LOOKIN' FOR YOU! SHE'S REAL WORRIED ABOUT YOU BEIN' MISSIN' SO LONG!
POOR KID! I'LL GO TO SEE HER RIGHT AWAY!
AND, AT BETTY'S HOUSE...
SO THEY PARDONED THE HULK! OF ALL THE LUNKHEAD DECISIONS! CAN'T THEY SEE HE'S TRICKED 'EM?? HE'S TRYIN' TO THROW US OFF-GUARD! HE'S AS DANGEROUS AS EVER!
THE DOORBELL! WHO--?
WHERE IN THUNDER HAVE YOU BEEN??! WE'VE TURNED THIS STATE UPSIDE DOWN SEARCHING FOR YOU!
SORRY, GENERAL! I-EH-WAS FEELING UNDER THE WEATHER! SO I TOOK A FEW DAYS REST IN BERMUDA!
BERMUDA! WHILE THE WHOLE WORLD TOTTERS ON THE BRINK, HE'S RESTIN' IN BERMUDA!!!
OH, BRUCE! BRUCE! THANK HEAVENS YOU'RE ALL RIGHT!
HELLO, BETTY! I'M SORRY I WORRIED YOU, DEAR!
"I'M SORRY I WORRIED YOU, DEAR!" BAH! HOW A DAUGHTER OF MINE COULD EVER FALL FOR SUCH A SPINELESS MILKSOP!
SOMETIMES I THINK SHE'D BE BETTER OFF MOONIN' OVER THE HULK! AT LEAST HE'S GOT A BACKBONE!
BRUCE, I KNOW THERE WAS MORE TO YOUR ABSENCE THAN THE FACT THAT YOU DIDN'T FEEL WELL! I-I HAVE THE STRANGEST FEELING THAT THERE IS SOME CONNECTION BETWEEN YOU AND THE HULK! WHY WON'T YOU CONFIDE IN ME? DON'T I--MEAN ENOUGH TO YOU??
MEAN ENOUGH??
I CAN'T TELL YOU ANY MORE, BETTY--BECAUSE YOU MEAN TOO MUCH TO ME! AS FOR THE HULK... LET'S HOPE THAT HE IS GONE NOW--FOREVER!
BUT ALAS, THE HOPE OF BRUCE BANNER IS NOT TO BE REALIZED! FOR THE HULK IS DESTINED TO LIVE AGAIN-- BUT THAT'S ANOTHER TALE!
THE GAMMA RAY MACHINE-- IT GROWS MORE UNPREDICTABLE EACH TIME IT'S USED! IF DOC HAS TO FACE IT AGAIN-- WHAT WILL HAPPEN NEXT TIME??!
24
THE END

A NEW, DIFFERENT SUPER-HERO: IRON MAN!--IN "TALES OF SUSPENSE"... NOW!

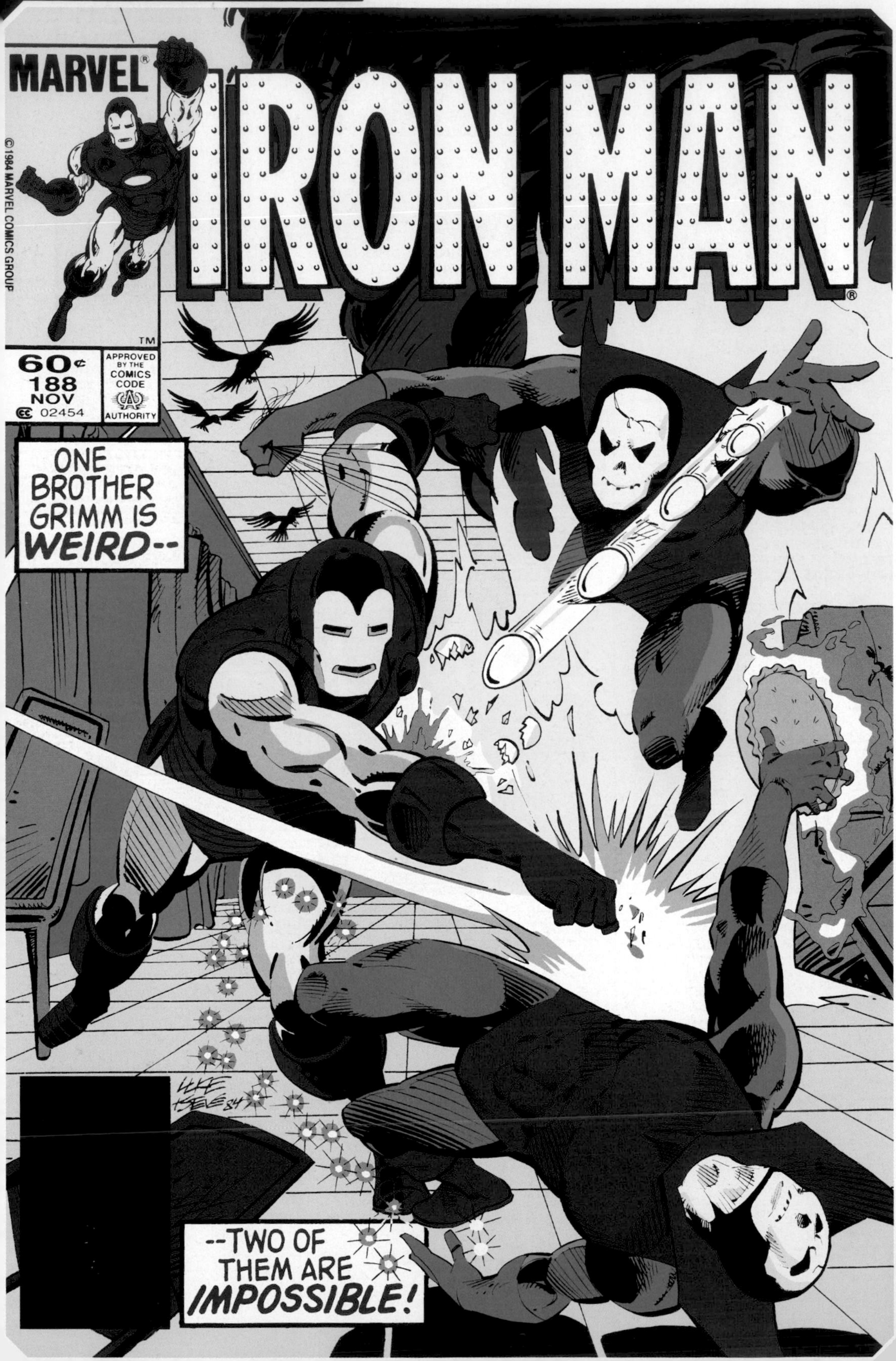
MARVEL
IRON MAN
©1984 MARVEL COMICS GROUP
60¢
188
NOV
02454
APPROVED BY THE COMICS CODE AUTHORITY
ONE BROTHER GRIMM IS *WEIRD*--
--TWO OF THEM ARE *IMPOSSIBLE!*

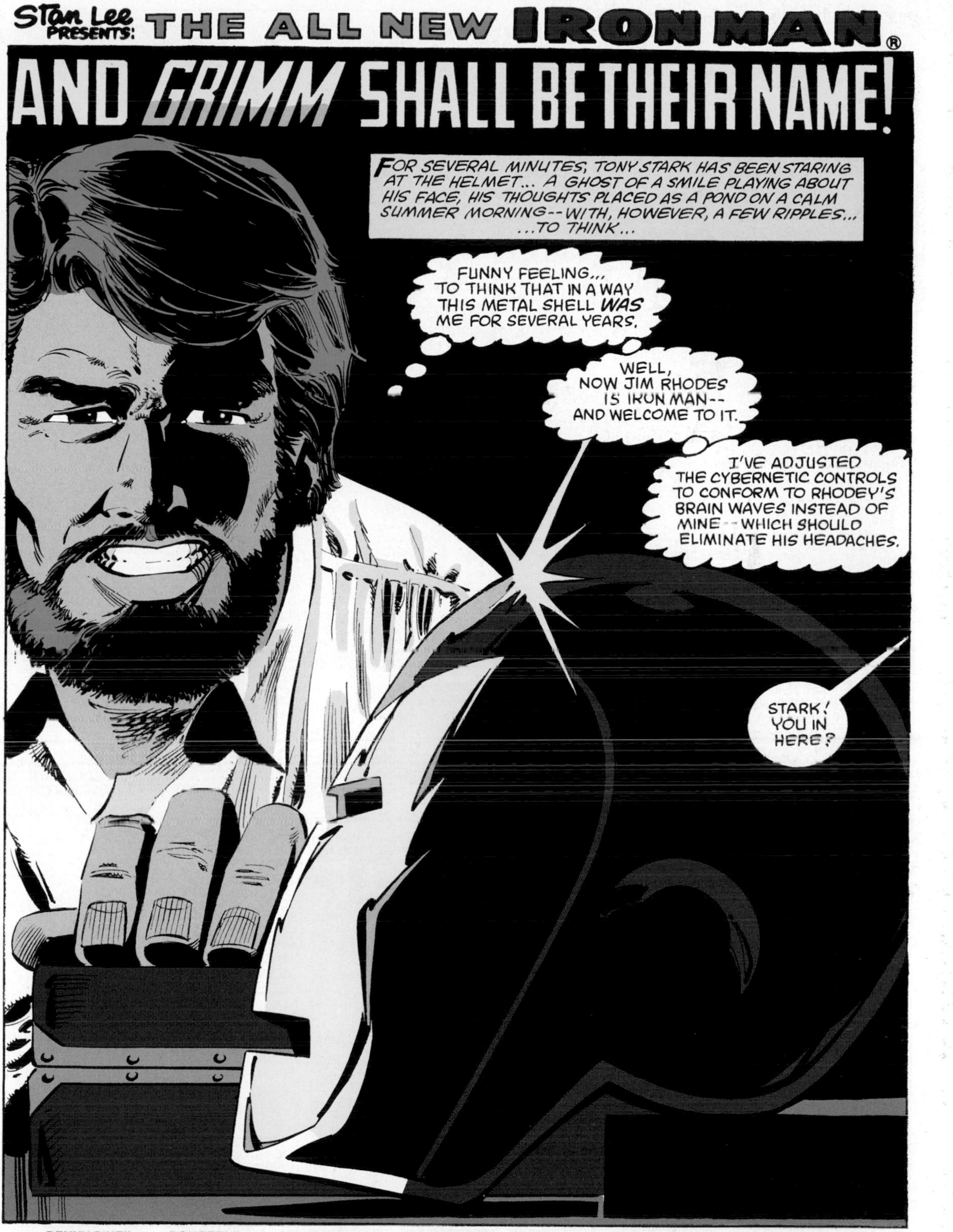
Stan Lee PRESENTS: THE ALL NEW IRON MAN®
AND GRIMM SHALL BE THEIR NAME!
FOR SEVERAL MINUTES, TONY STARK HAS BEEN STARING AT THE HELMET... A GHOST OF A SMILE PLAYING ABOUT HIS FACE, HIS THOUGHTS PLACED AS A POND ON A CALM SUMMER MORNING--WITH, HOWEVER, A FEW RIPPLES... ...TO THINK...
FUNNY FEELING... TO THINK THAT IN A WAY THIS METAL SHELL WAS ME FOR SEVERAL YEARS.
WELL, NOW JIM RHODES IS IRON MAN-- AND WELCOME TO IT.
I'VE ADJUSTED THE CYBERNETIC CONTROLS TO CONFORM TO RHODEY'S BRAIN WAVES INSTEAD OF MINE--WHICH SHOULD ELIMINATE HIS HEADACHES.
STARK! YOU IN HERE?

DENNY O'NEIL WRITER · **DON PERLIN** GUEST PENCILER · **STEVE MITCHELL** INKER · **RICK PARKER** LETTERER · **BOB SHAREN** COLORIST · **MARK GRUENWALD** EDITOR · **JIM SHOOTER** EDITOR IN CHIEF

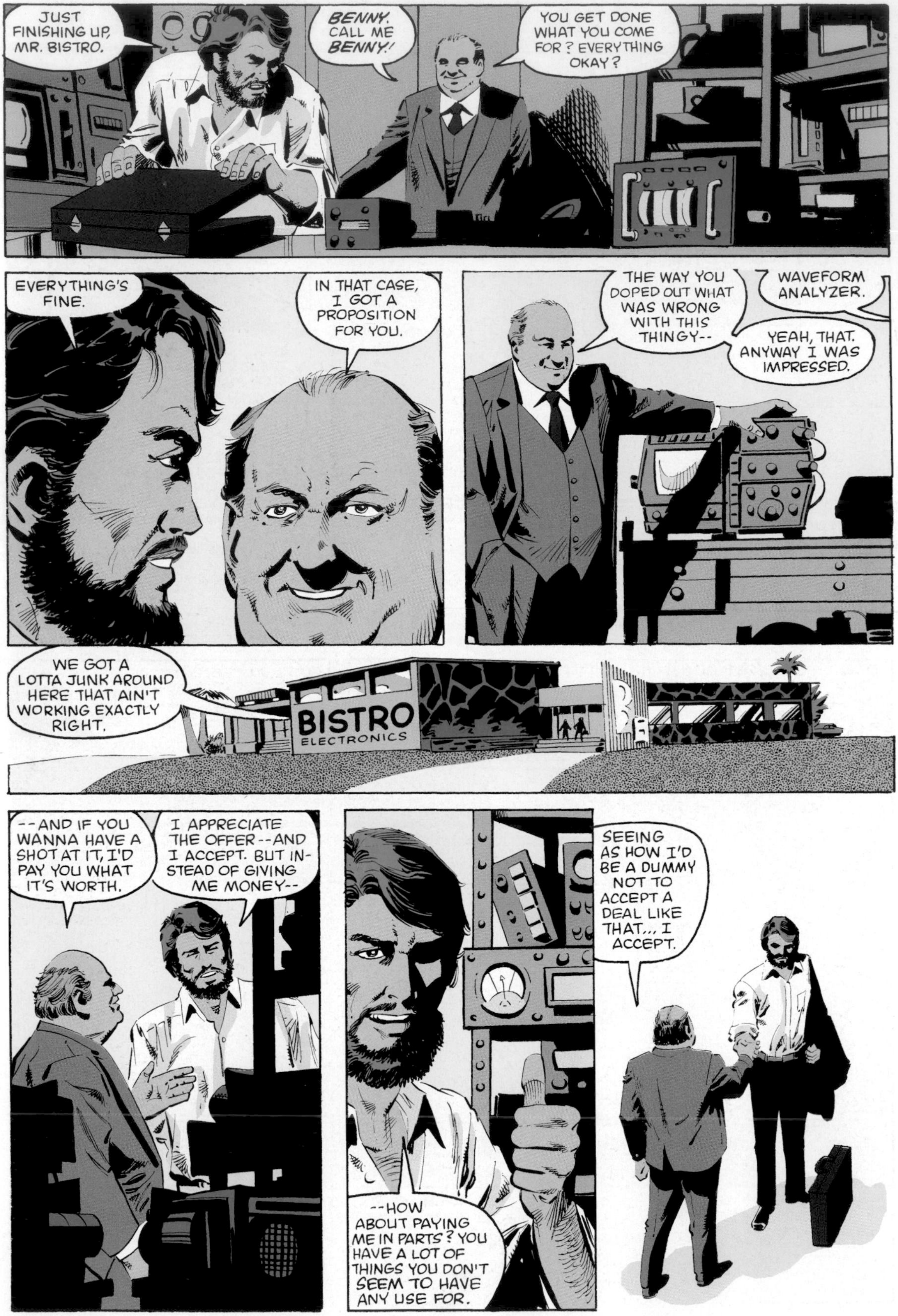
JUST FINISHING UP, MR. BISTRO.
BENNY. CALL ME BENNY!
YOU GET DONE WHAT YOU COME FOR? EVERYTHING OKAY?
EVERYTHING'S FINE.
IN THAT CASE, I GOT A PROPOSITION FOR YOU.
THE WAY YOU DOPED OUT WHAT WAS WRONG WITH THIS THINGY--
WAVEFORM ANALYZER.
YEAH, THAT. ANYWAY I WAS IMPRESSED.
WE GOT A LOTTA JUNK AROUND HERE THAT AIN'T WORKING EXACTLY RIGHT.
BISTRO ELECTRONICS
--AND IF YOU WANNA HAVE A SHOT AT IT, I'D PAY YOU WHAT IT'S WORTH.
I APPRECIATE THE OFFER--AND I ACCEPT. BUT INSTEAD OF GIVING ME MONEY--
--HOW ABOUT PAYING ME IN PARTS? YOU HAVE A LOT OF THINGS YOU DON'T SEEM TO HAVE ANY USE FOR.
SEEING AS HOW I'D BE A DUMMY NOT TO ACCEPT A DEAL LIKE THAT... I ACCEPT.

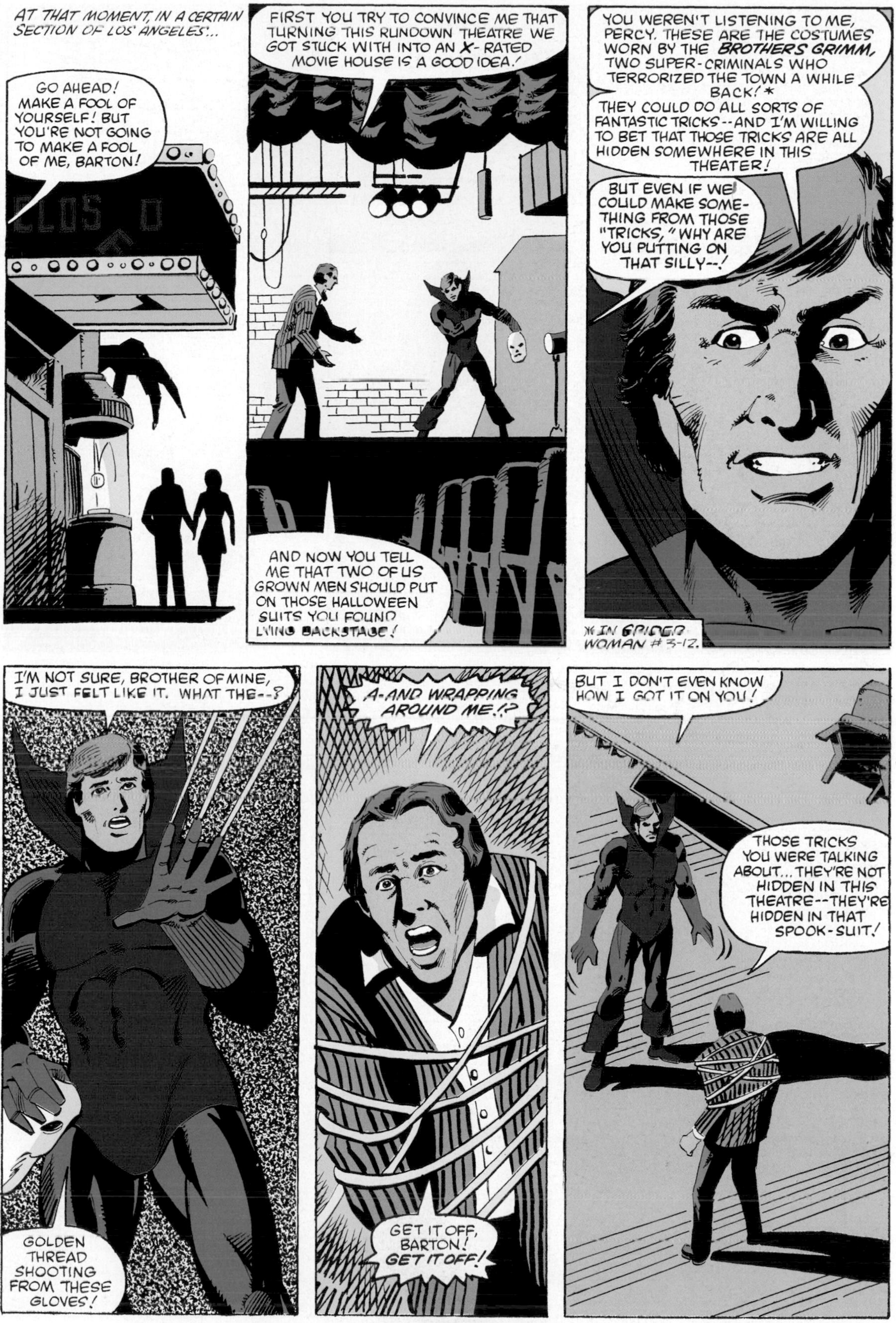

AT THAT MOMENT, IN A CERTAIN SECTION OF LOS ANGELES...
GO AHEAD! MAKE A FOOL OF YOURSELF! BUT YOU'RE NOT GOING TO MAKE A FOOL OF ME, BARTON!
FIRST YOU TRY TO CONVINCE ME THAT TURNING THIS RUNDOWN THEATRE WE GOT STUCK WITH INTO AN X-RATED MOVIE HOUSE IS A GOOD IDEA!
AND NOW YOU TELL ME THAT TWO OF US GROWN MEN SHOULD PUT ON THOSE HALLOWEEN SUITS YOU FOUND LYING BACKSTAGE!
YOU WEREN'T LISTENING TO ME, PERCY. THESE ARE THE COSTUMES WORN BY THE BROTHERS GRIMM, TWO SUPER-CRIMINALS WHO TERRORIZED THE TOWN A WHILE BACK!*
THEY COULD DO ALL SORTS OF FANTASTIC TRICKS--AND I'M WILLING TO BET THAT THOSE TRICKS ARE ALL HIDDEN SOMEWHERE IN THIS THEATER!
BUT EVEN IF WE COULD MAKE SOMETHING FROM THOSE "TRICKS," WHY ARE YOU PUTTING ON THAT SILLY--!
*IN SPIDER-WOMAN #3-12.
I'M NOT SURE, BROTHER OF MINE, I JUST FELT LIKE IT. WHAT THE--?
GOLDEN THREAD SHOOTING FROM THESE GLOVES!
A-AND WRAPPING AROUND ME!?
GET IT OFF, BARTON! GET IT OFF!
BUT I DON'T EVEN KNOW HOW I GOT IT ON YOU!
THOSE TRICKS YOU WERE TALKING ABOUT... THEY'RE NOT HIDDEN IN THIS THEATRE--THEY'RE HIDDEN IN THAT SPOOK-SUIT!

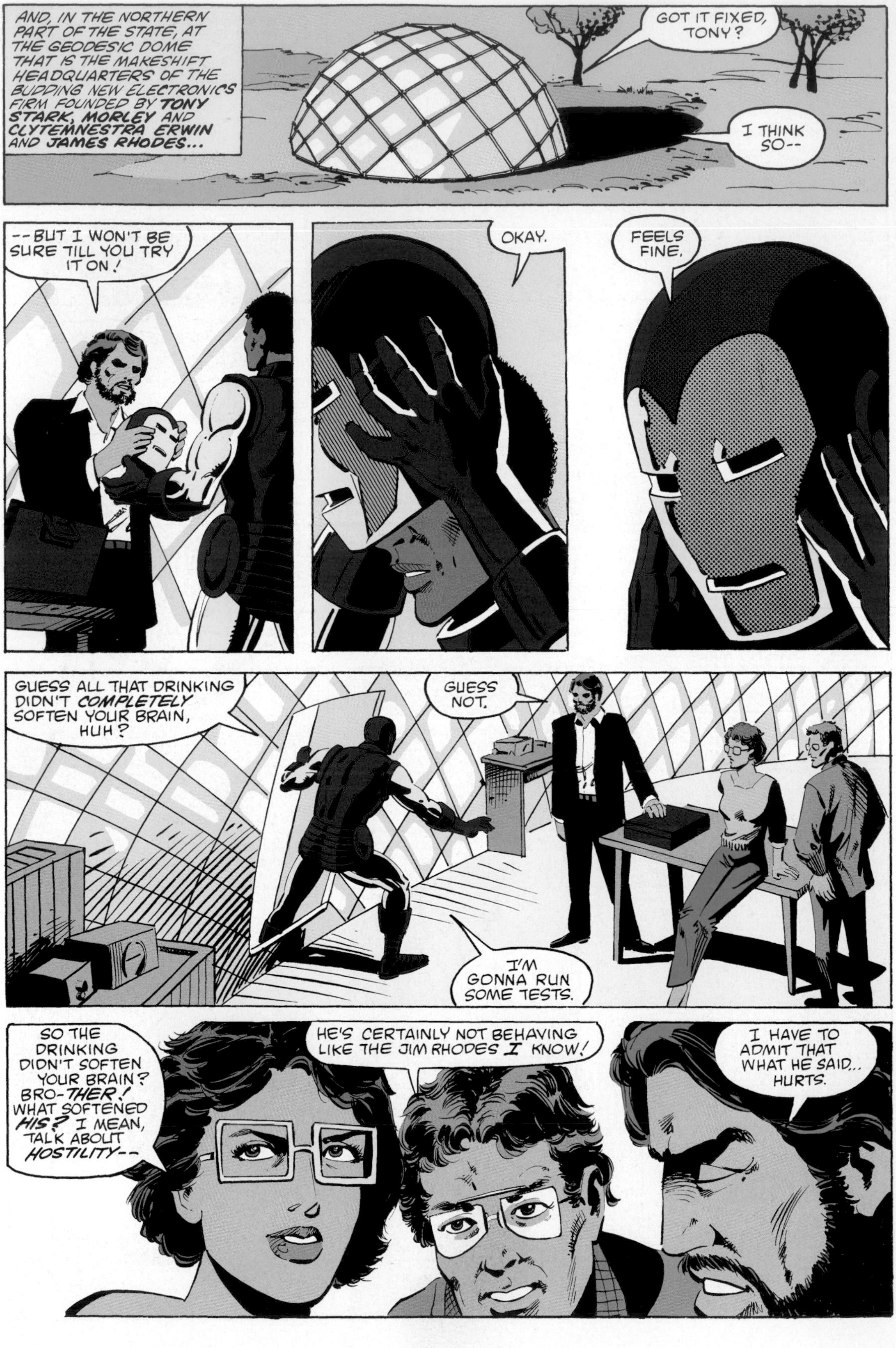

AND, IN THE NORTHERN PART OF THE STATE, AT THE GEODESIC DOME THAT IS THE MAKESHIFT HEADQUARTERS OF THE BUDDING NEW ELECTRONICS FIRM FOUNDED BY TONY STARK, MORLEY AND CLYTEMNESTRA ERWIN AND JAMES RHODES...
GOT IT FIXED, TONY?
I THINK SO--
--BUT I WON'T BE SURE TILL YOU TRY IT ON!
OKAY.
FEELS FINE.
GUESS ALL THAT DRINKING DIDN'T COMPLETELY SOFTEN YOUR BRAIN, HUH?
GUESS NOT.
I'M GONNA RUN SOME TESTS.
SO THE DRINKING DIDN'T SOFTEN YOUR BRAIN? BRO-THER! WHAT SOFTENED HIS? I MEAN, TALK ABOUT HOSTILITY--
HE'S CERTAINLY NOT BEHAVING LIKE THE JIM RHODES I KNOW!
I HAVE TO ADMIT THAT WHAT HE SAID... HURTS.

WHY?

WHY DID I *SAY* THAT?

THE WORDS JUST... *BLURTED!* AND THE WORST OF IT IS--

-- I CAN'T REALLY SAY I REGRET THEM!

AND *THAT* DOESN'T MAKE SENSE, EITHER!

I OWE TONY STARK *EVERYTHING.* WITHOUT HIM, I WOULDN'T BE ZOOMING THROUGH THE AIR--

-- OR BLASTING *USELESS* MOUNTAINS INTO ITTY BITS--

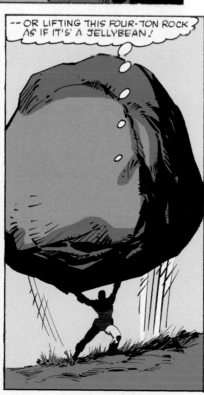

-- OR LIFTING THIS FOUR-TON ROCK AS IF IT'S A JELLYBEAN!

I'D BE JUST ANOTHER HOTSHOT JET-JOCKEY CHASING WOMEN AND SCRATCHING FOR THE RENT.

HE INVENTED THE TIN SUIT, ME-- I ONLY WEAR...

AAGGH!

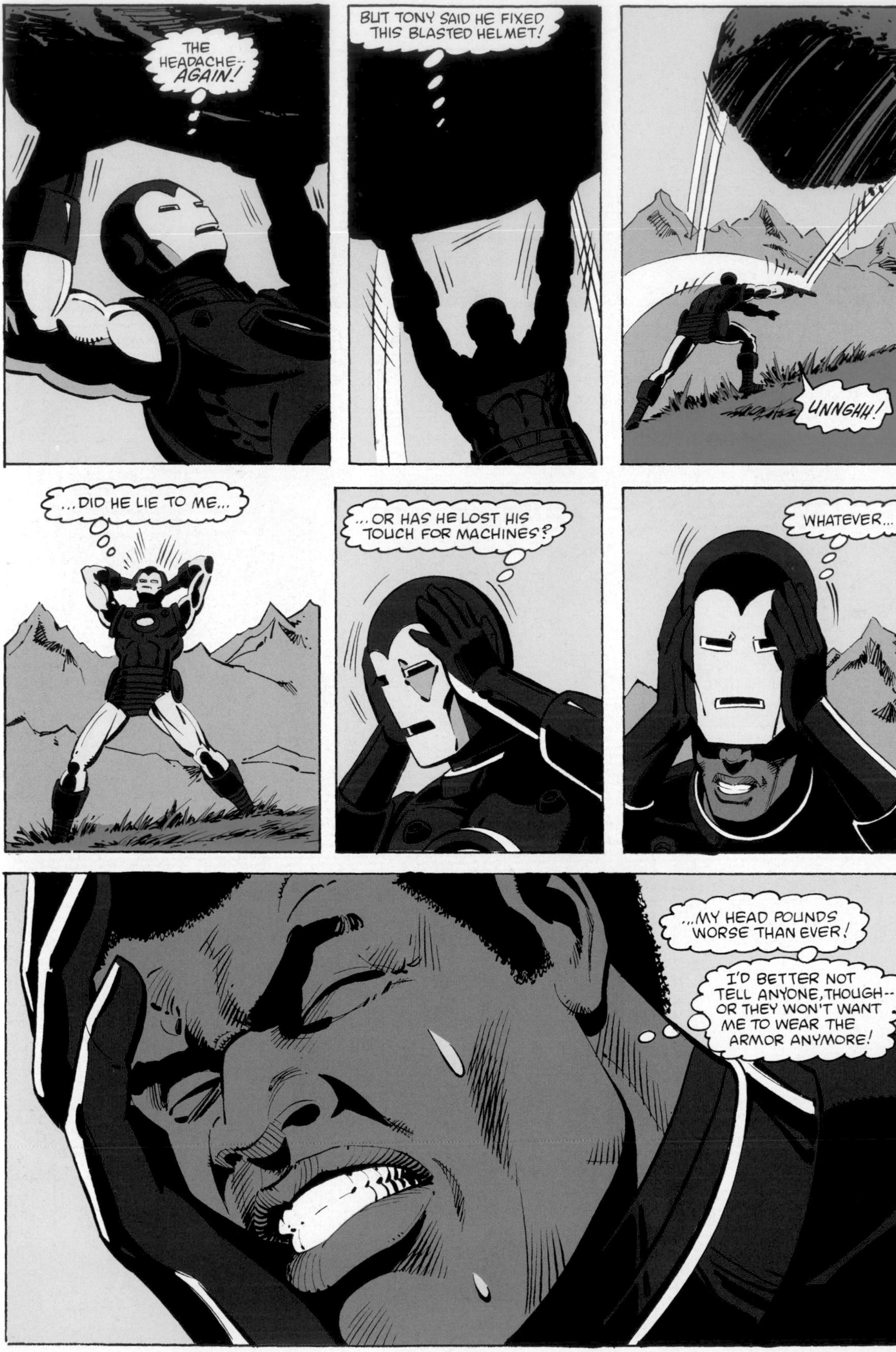
THE HEADACHE-- AGAIN!
BUT TONY SAID HE FIXED THIS BLASTED HELMET!
UNNGHH!
...DID HE LIE TO ME...
...OR HAS HE LOST HIS TOUCH FOR MACHINES?
WHATEVER...
...MY HEAD POUNDS WORSE THAN EVER!
I'D BETTER NOT TELL ANYONE, THOUGH-- OR THEY WON'T WANT ME TO WEAR THE ARMOR ANYMORE!

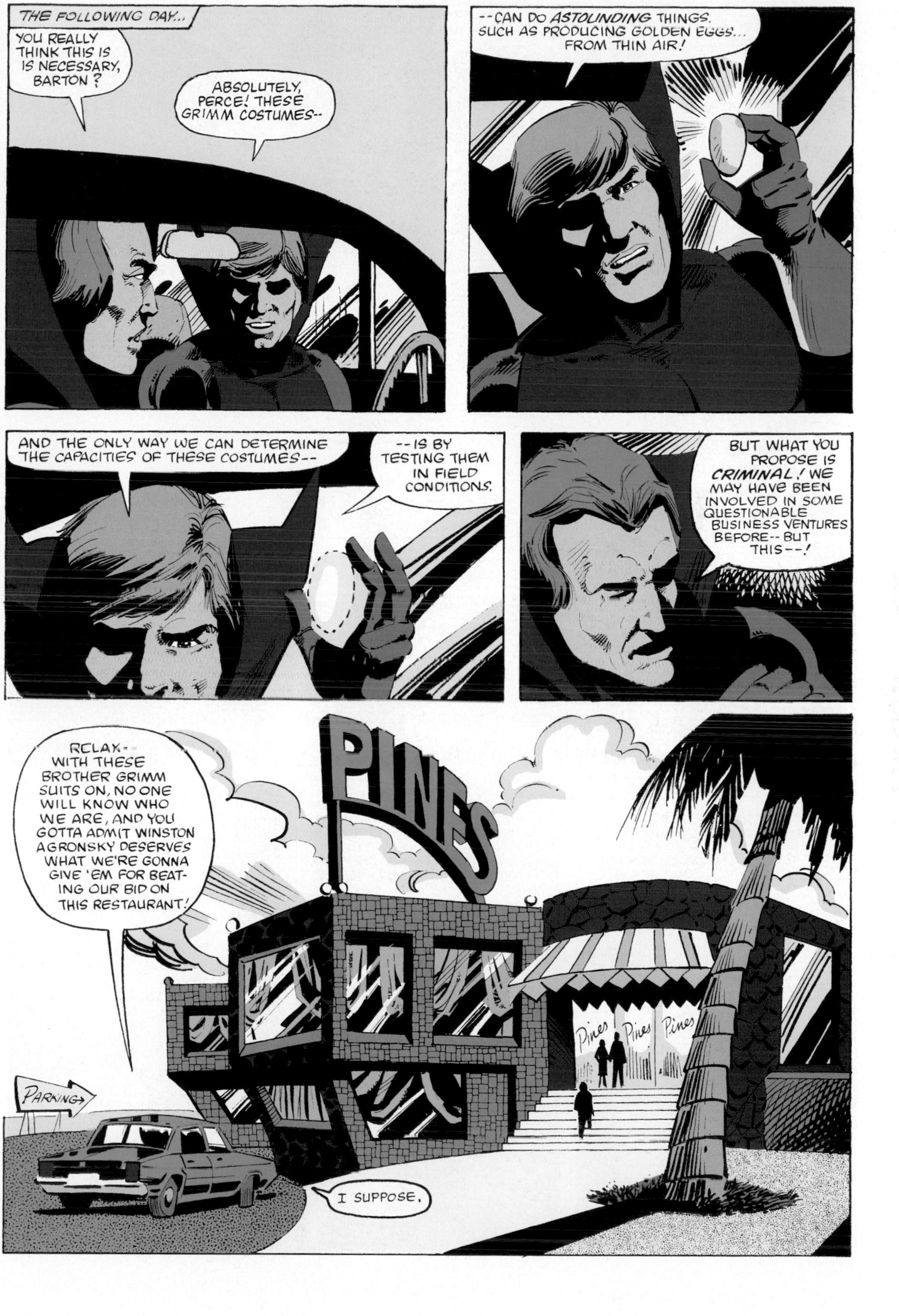
THE FOLLOWING DAY...
YOU REALLY THINK THIS IS IS NECESSARY, BARTON?
ABSOLUTELY, PERCE! THESE GRIMM COSTUMES--
--CAN DO ASTOUNDING THINGS. SUCH AS PRODUCING GOLDEN EGGS... FROM THIN AIR!
AND THE ONLY WAY WE CAN DETERMINE THE CAPACITIES OF THESE COSTUMES--
--IS BY TESTING THEM IN FIELD CONDITIONS.
BUT WHAT YOU PROPOSE IS CRIMINAL! WE MAY HAVE BEEN INVOLVED IN SOME QUESTIONABLE BUSINESS VENTURES BEFORE-- BUT THIS--!
PINES
RELAX-- WITH THESE BROTHER GRIMM SUITS ON, NO ONE WILL KNOW WHO WE ARE, AND YOU GOTTA ADMIT WINSTON AGRONSKY DESERVES WHAT WE'RE GONNA GIVE 'EM FOR BEATING OUR BID ON THIS RESTAURANT!
Pines Pines Pines
PARKING
I SUPPOSE.

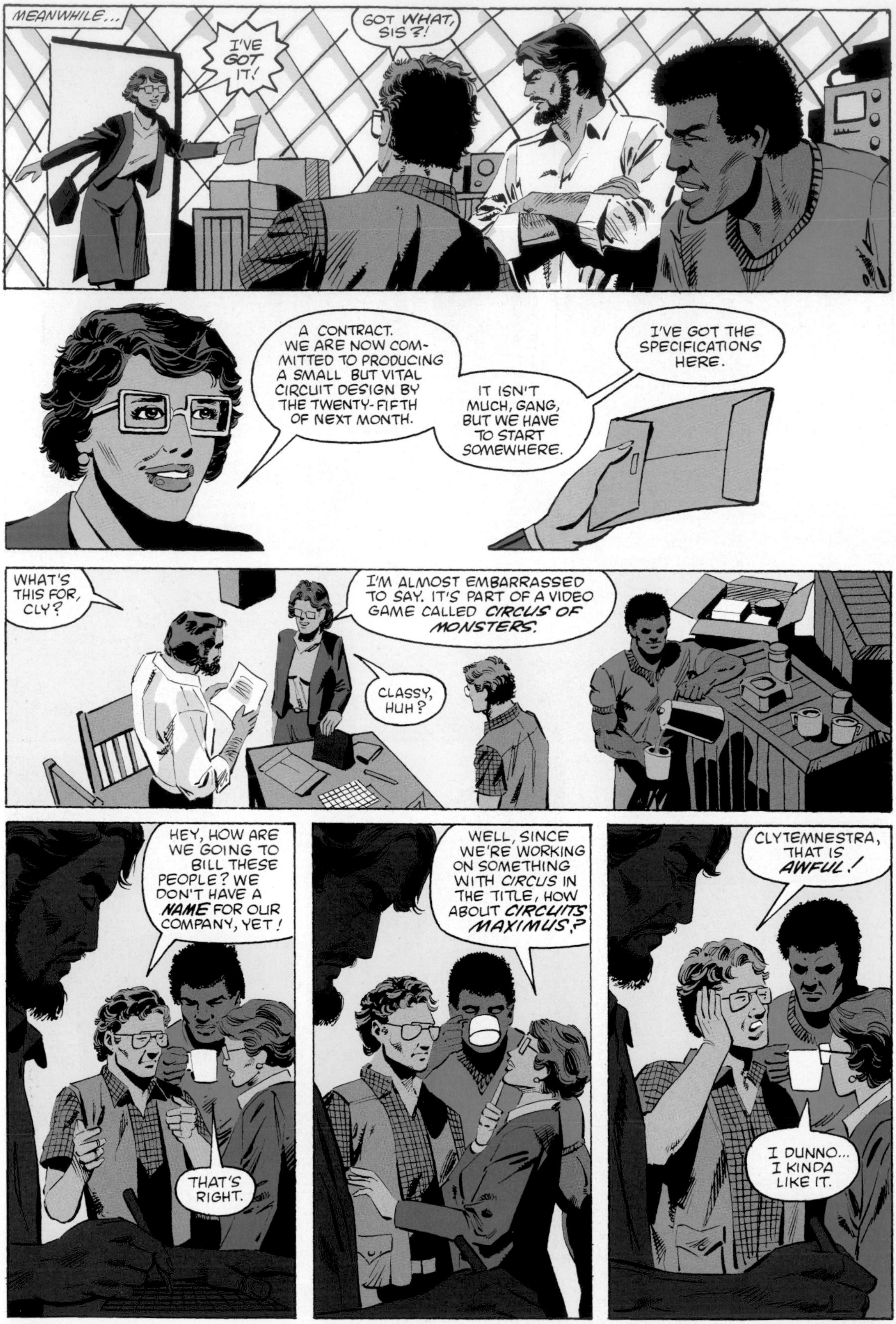
MEANWHILE...
I'VE GOT IT!
GOT WHAT, SIS?!
A CONTRACT. WE ARE NOW COMMITTED TO PRODUCING A SMALL BUT VITAL CIRCUIT DESIGN BY THE TWENTY-FIFTH OF NEXT MONTH.
IT ISN'T MUCH, GANG, BUT WE HAVE TO START SOMEWHERE.
I'VE GOT THE SPECIFICATIONS HERE.
WHAT'S THIS FOR, CLY?
I'M ALMOST EMBARRASSED TO SAY. IT'S PART OF A VIDEO GAME CALLED CIRCUS OF MONSTERS.
CLASSY, HUH?
HEY, HOW ARE WE GOING TO BILL THESE PEOPLE? WE DON'T HAVE A NAME FOR OUR COMPANY, YET!
THAT'S RIGHT.
WELL, SINCE WE'RE WORKING ON SOMETHING WITH CIRCUS IN THE TITLE, HOW ABOUT CIRCUITS MAXIMUS?
CLYTEMNESTRA, THAT IS AWFUL!
I DUNNO... I KINDA LIKE IT.

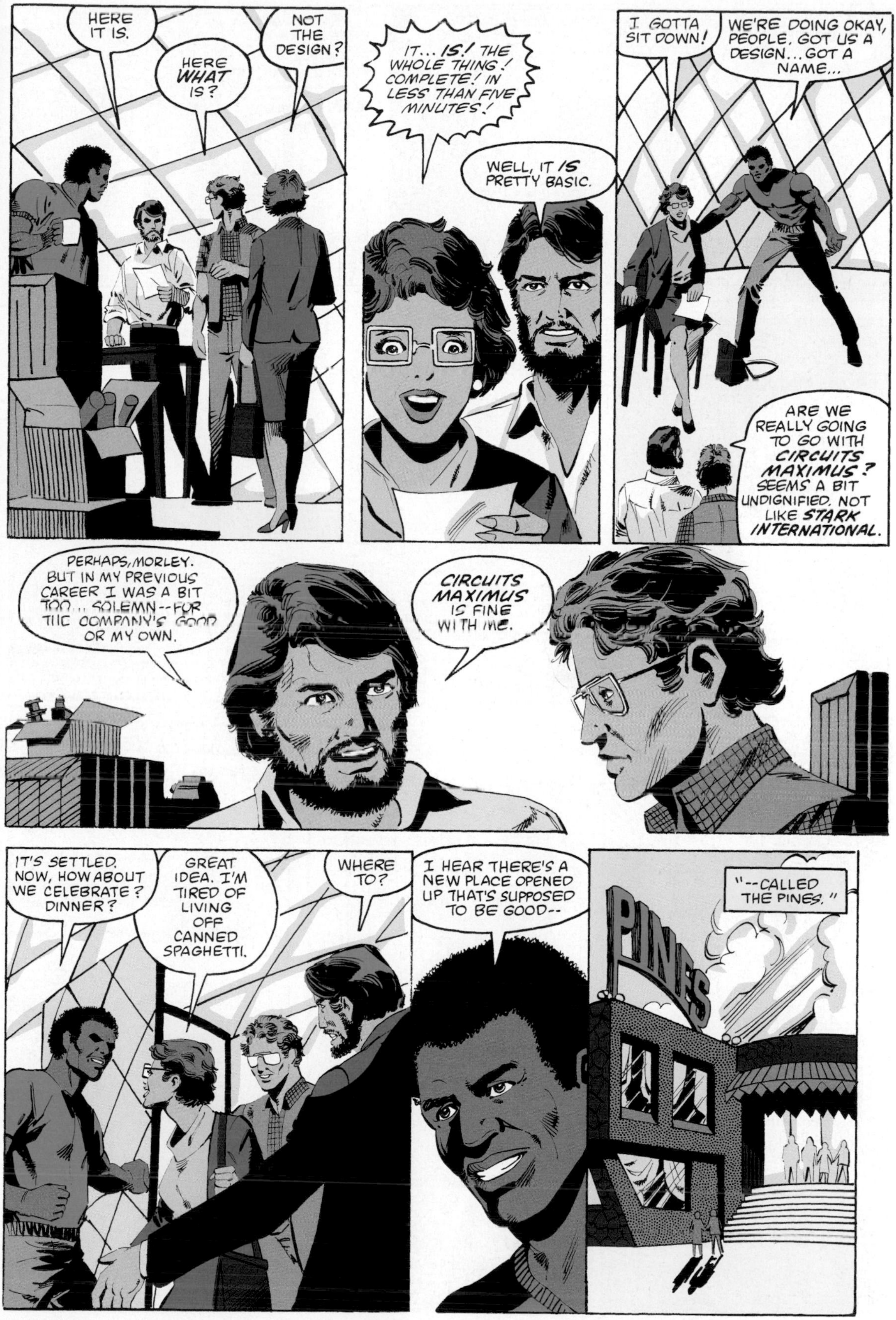
HERE IT IS.
HERE WHAT IS?
NOT THE DESIGN?
IT... IS! THE WHOLE THING! COMPLETE! IN LESS THAN FIVE MINUTES!
WELL, IT IS PRETTY BASIC.
I GOTTA SIT DOWN!
WE'RE DOING OKAY, PEOPLE. GOT US A DESIGN... GOT A NAME...
ARE WE REALLY GOING TO GO WITH CIRCUITS MAXIMUS? SEEMS A BIT UNDIGNIFIED. NOT LIKE STARK INTERNATIONAL.
PERHAPS, MORLEY. BUT IN MY PREVIOUS CAREER I WAS A BIT TOO... SOLEMN--FOR THE COMPANY'S GOOD OR MY OWN.
CIRCUITS MAXIMUS IS FINE WITH ME.
IT'S SETTLED. NOW, HOW ABOUT WE CELEBRATE? DINNER?
GREAT IDEA. I'M TIRED OF LIVING OFF CANNED SPAGHETTI.
WHERE TO?
I HEAR THERE'S A NEW PLACE OPENED UP THAT'S SUPPOSED TO BE GOOD--
"--CALLED THE PINES."
PINES

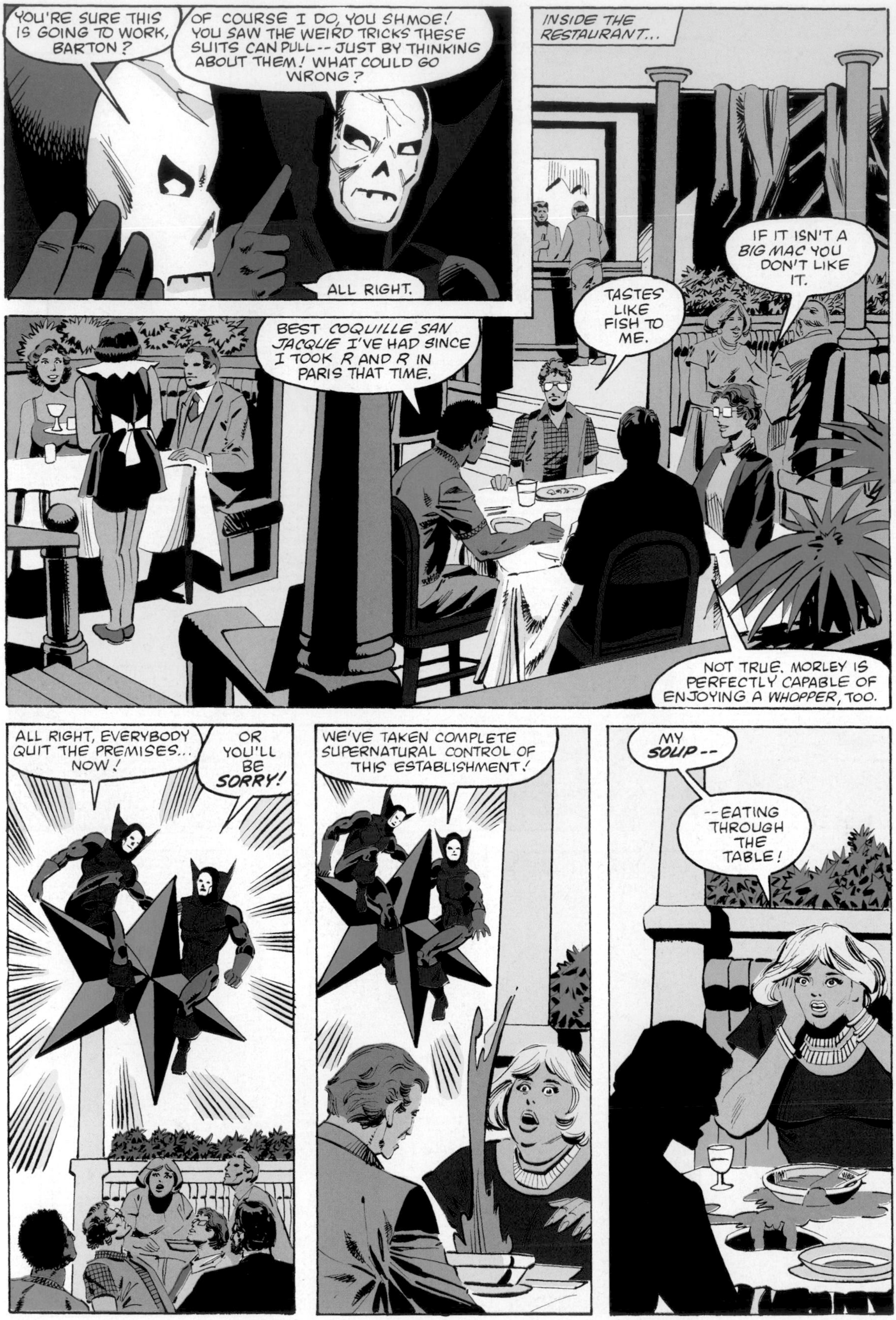
YOU'RE SURE THIS IS GOING TO WORK, BARTON?
OF COURSE I DO, YOU SHMOE! YOU SAW THE WEIRD TRICKS THESE SUITS CAN PULL-- JUST BY THINKING ABOUT THEM! WHAT COULD GO WRONG?
ALL RIGHT.
INSIDE THE RESTAURANT...
IF IT ISN'T A BIG MAC YOU DON'T LIKE IT.
TASTES LIKE FISH TO ME.
BEST COQUILLE SAN JACQUE I'VE HAD SINCE I TOOK R AND R IN PARIS THAT TIME.
NOT TRUE. MORLEY IS PERFECTLY CAPABLE OF ENJOYING A WHOPPER, TOO.
ALL RIGHT, EVERYBODY QUIT THE PREMISES... NOW!
OR YOU'LL BE SORRY!
WE'VE TAKEN COMPLETE SUPERNATURAL CONTROL OF THIS ESTABLISHMENT!
MY SOUP--
--EATING THROUGH THE TABLE!

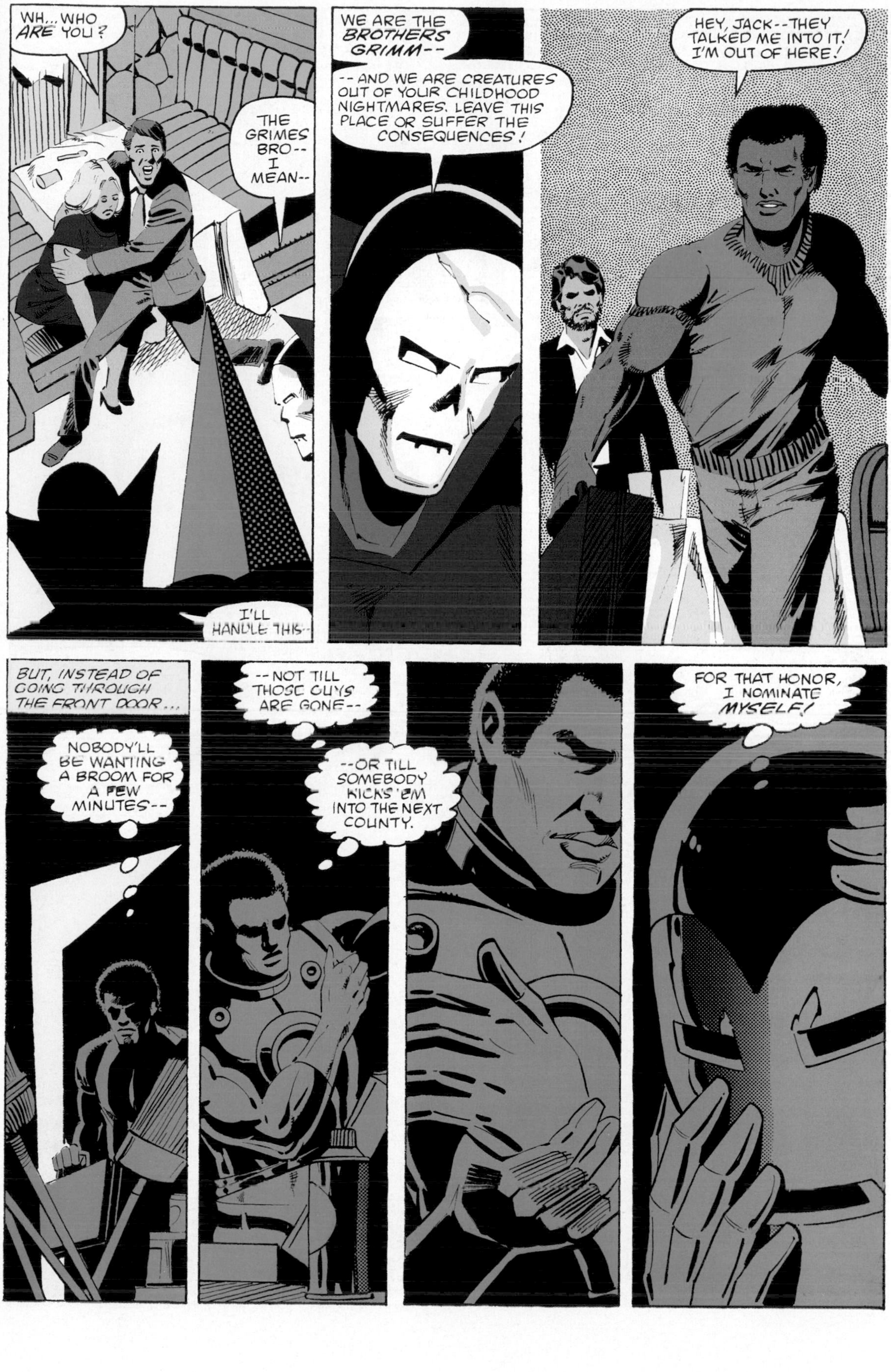

WH... WHO ARE YOU?
THE GRIMES BRO-- I MEAN--
I'LL HANDLE THIS--
WE ARE THE BROTHERS GRIMM--
--AND WE ARE CREATURES OUT OF YOUR CHILDHOOD NIGHTMARES. LEAVE THIS PLACE OR SUFFER THE CONSEQUENCES!
HEY, JACK--THEY TALKED ME INTO IT! I'M OUT OF HERE!
BUT, INSTEAD OF GOING THROUGH THE FRONT DOOR...
NOBODY'LL BE WANTING A BROOM FOR A FEW MINUTES--
--NOT TILL THOSE GUYS ARE GONE--
--OR TILL SOMEBODY KICKS 'EM INTO THE NEXT COUNTY.
FOR THAT HONOR, I NOMINATE MYSELF!

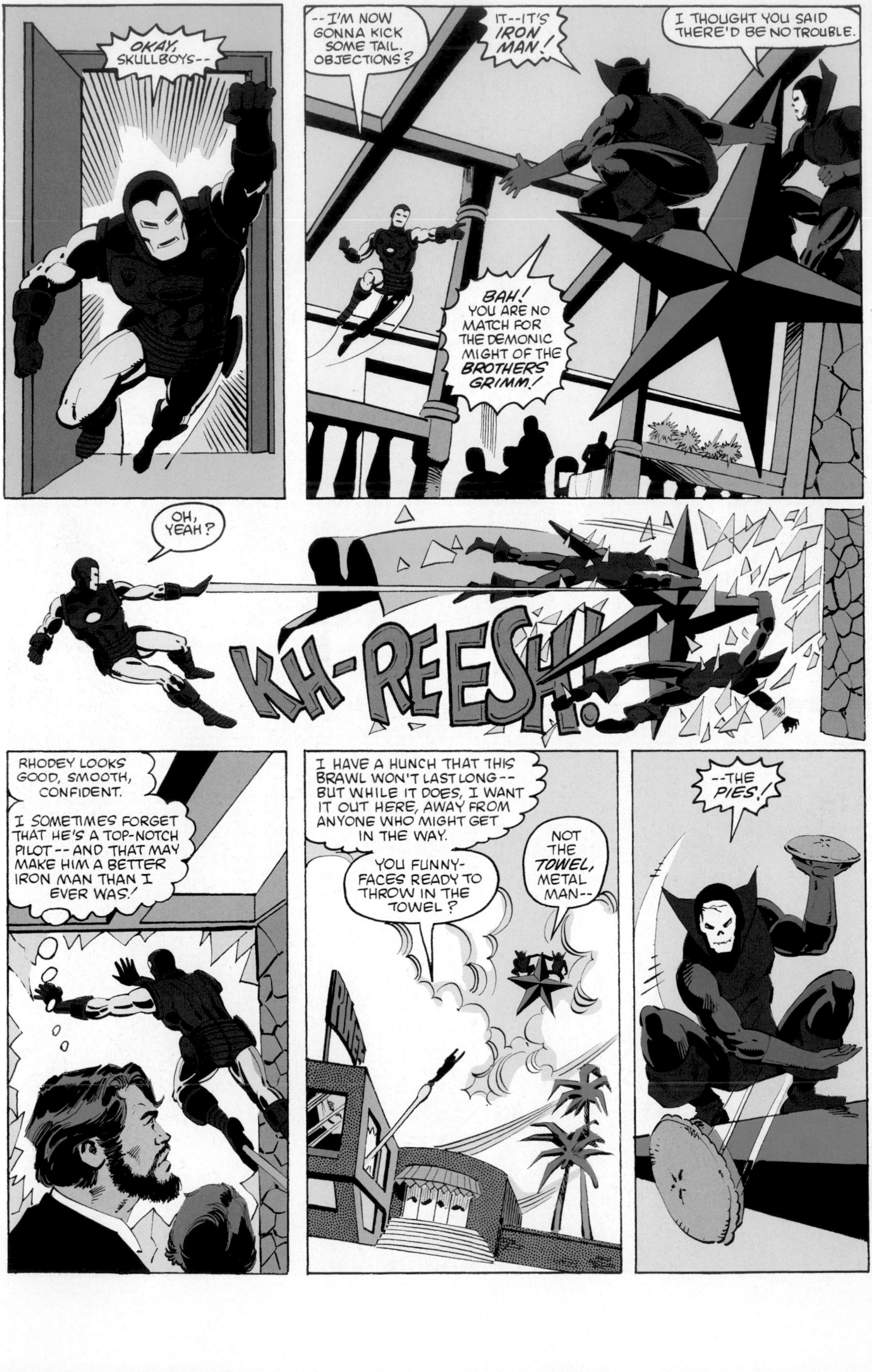
OKAY, SKULLBOYS--
--I'M NOW GONNA KICK SOME TAIL. OBJECTIONS?
IT--IT'S IRON MAN!
I THOUGHT YOU SAID THERE'D BE NO TROUBLE.
BAH! YOU ARE NO MATCH FOR THE DEMONIC MIGHT OF THE BROTHERS GRIMM!
OH, YEAH?
KH-REESH!
RHODEY LOOKS GOOD, SMOOTH, CONFIDENT.
I SOMETIMES FORGET THAT HE'S A TOP-NOTCH PILOT--AND THAT MAY MAKE HIM A BETTER IRON MAN THAN I EVER WAS!
I HAVE A HUNCH THAT THIS BRAWL WON'T LAST LONG--BUT WHILE IT DOES, I WANT IT OUT HERE, AWAY FROM ANYONE WHO MIGHT GET IN THE WAY.
YOU FUNNY-FACES READY TO THROW IN THE TOWEL?
NOT THE TOWEL, METAL MAN--
--THE PIES!

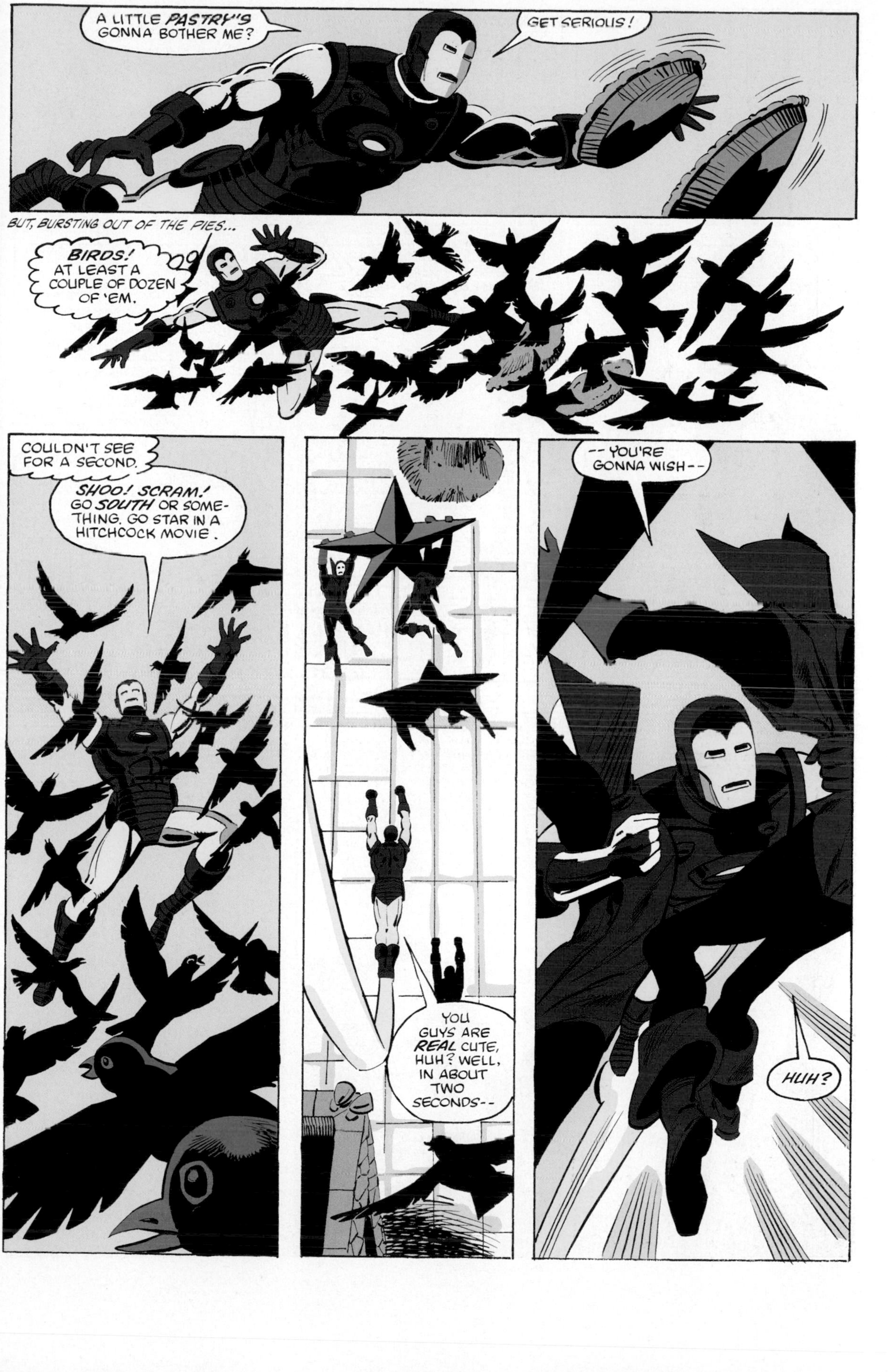
A LITTLE PASTRY'S GONNA BOTHER ME?
GET SERIOUS!
BUT, BURSTING OUT OF THE PIES...
BIRDS! AT LEAST A COUPLE OF DOZEN OF 'EM.
COULDN'T SEE FOR A SECOND.
SHOO! SCRAM! GO SOUTH OR SOMETHING. GO STAR IN A HITCHCOCK MOVIE.
YOU GUYS ARE REAL CUTE, HUH? WELL, IN ABOUT TWO SECONDS--
--YOU'RE GONNA WISH--
HUH?

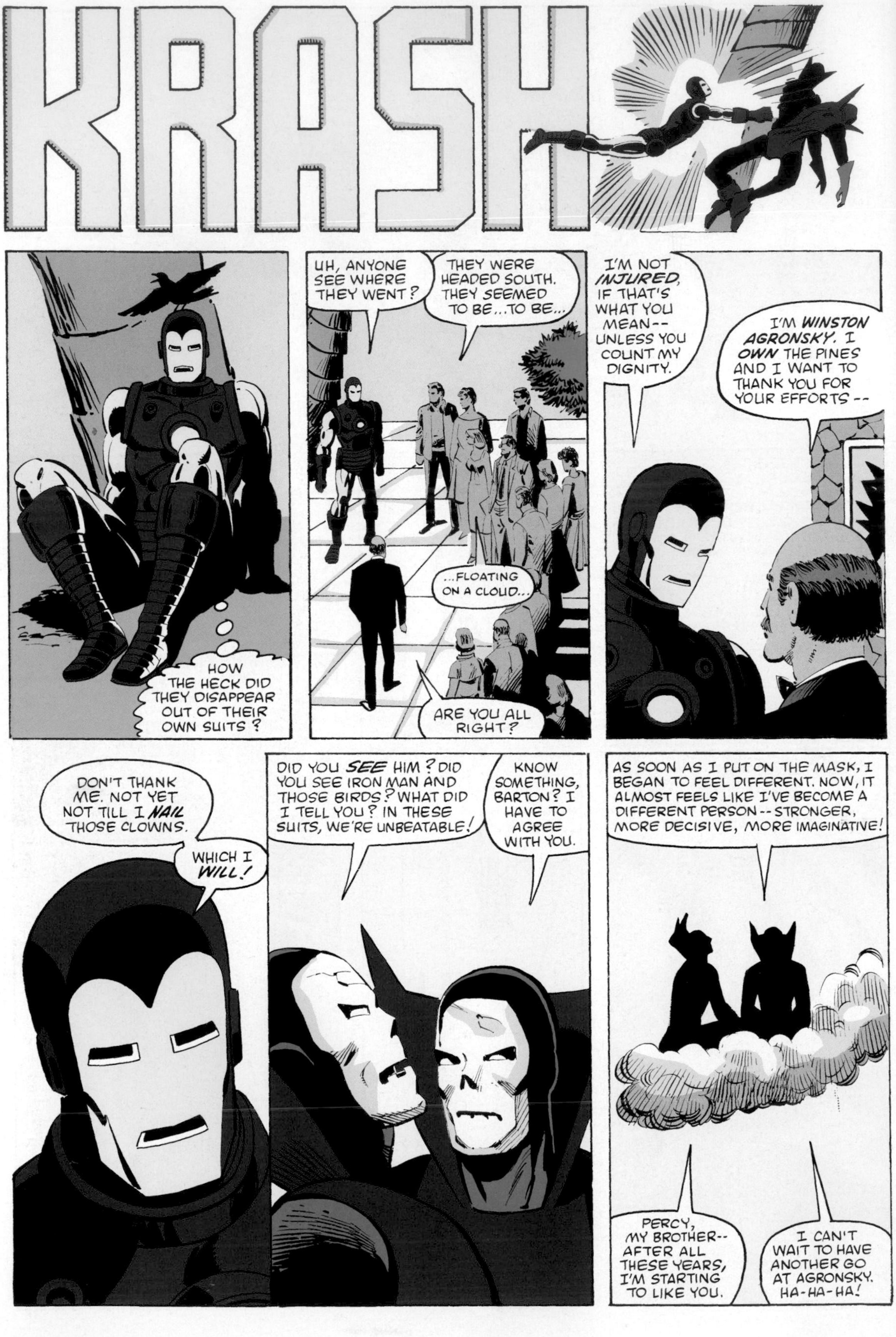
KRASH
HOW THE HECK DID THEY DISAPPEAR OUT OF THEIR OWN SUITS?
UH, ANYONE SEE WHERE THEY WENT?
THEY WERE HEADED SOUTH. THEY SEEMED TO BE... TO BE...
...FLOATING ON A CLOUD...
ARE YOU ALL RIGHT?
I'M NOT INJURED, IF THAT'S WHAT YOU MEAN-- UNLESS YOU COUNT MY DIGNITY.
I'M WINSTON AGRONSKY. I OWN THE PINES AND I WANT TO THANK YOU FOR YOUR EFFORTS--
DON'T THANK ME. NOT YET NOT TILL I NAIL THOSE CLOWNS.
WHICH I WILL!
DID YOU SEE HIM? DID YOU SEE IRON MAN AND THOSE BIRDS? WHAT DID I TELL YOU? IN THESE SUITS, WE'RE UNBEATABLE!
KNOW SOMETHING, BARTON? I HAVE TO AGREE WITH YOU.
AS SOON AS I PUT ON THE MASK, I BEGAN TO FEEL DIFFERENT. NOW, IT ALMOST FEELS LIKE I'VE BECOME A DIFFERENT PERSON -- STRONGER, MORE DECISIVE, MORE IMAGINATIVE!
PERCY, MY BROTHER-- AFTER ALL THESE YEARS, I'M STARTING TO LIKE YOU.
I CAN'T WAIT TO HAVE ANOTHER GO AT AGRONSKY. HA-HA-HA!

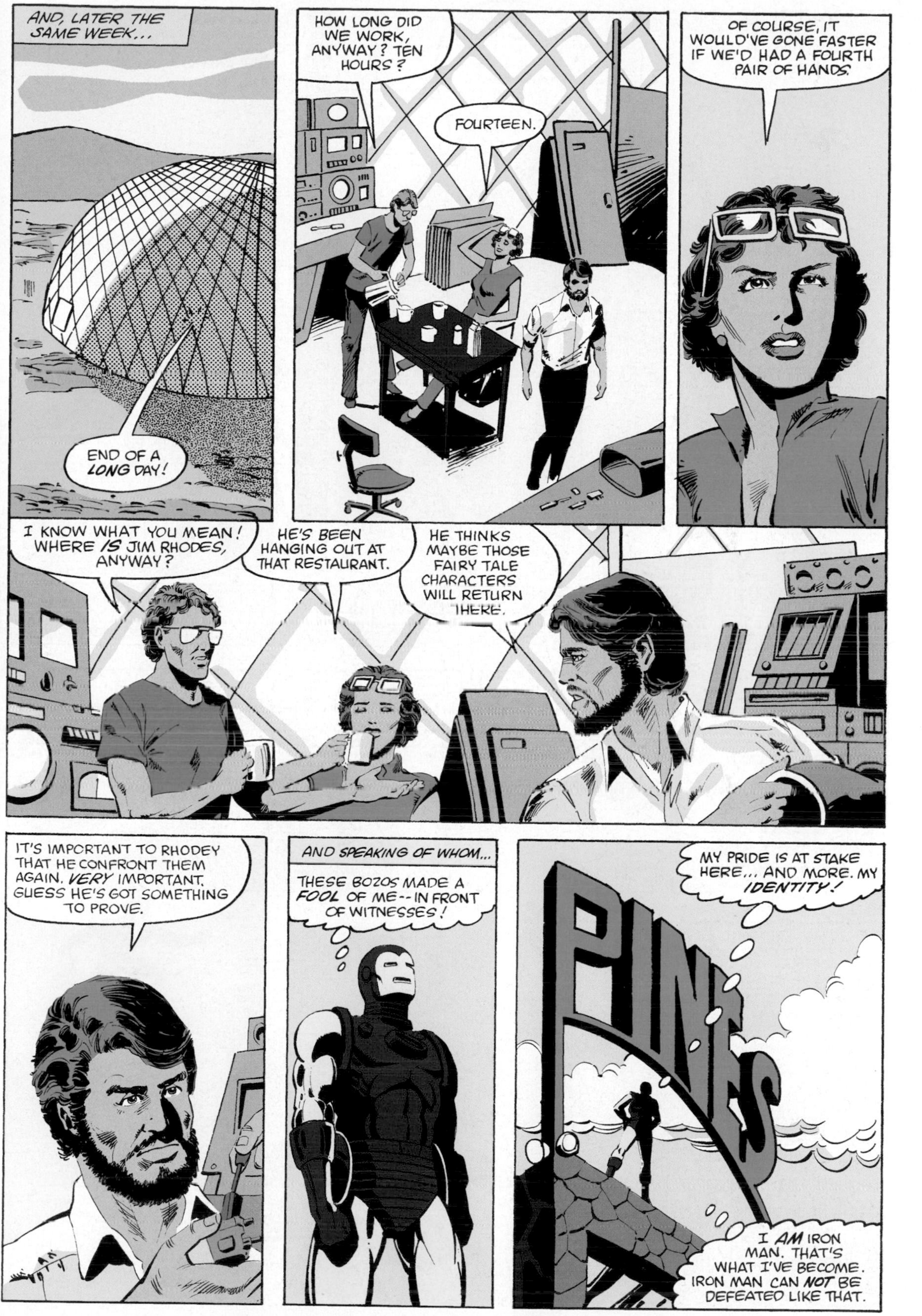
AND, LATER THE SAME WEEK...
END OF A LONG DAY!
HOW LONG DID WE WORK, ANYWAY? TEN HOURS?
FOURTEEN.
OF COURSE, IT WOULD'VE GONE FASTER IF WE'D HAD A FOURTH PAIR OF HANDS.
I KNOW WHAT YOU MEAN! WHERE IS JIM RHODES, ANYWAY?
HE'S BEEN HANGING OUT AT THAT RESTAURANT.
HE THINKS MAYBE THOSE FAIRY TALE CHARACTERS WILL RETURN THERE.
IT'S IMPORTANT TO RHODEY THAT HE CONFRONT THEM AGAIN. VERY IMPORTANT. GUESS HE'S GOT SOMETHING TO PROVE.
AND SPEAKING OF WHOM...
THESE BOZOS MADE A FOOL OF ME--IN FRONT OF WITNESSES!
MY PRIDE IS AT STAKE HERE... AND MORE. MY IDENTITY!
PINES
I AM IRON MAN. THAT'S WHAT I'VE BECOME. IRON MAN CAN NOT BE DEFEATED LIKE THAT.

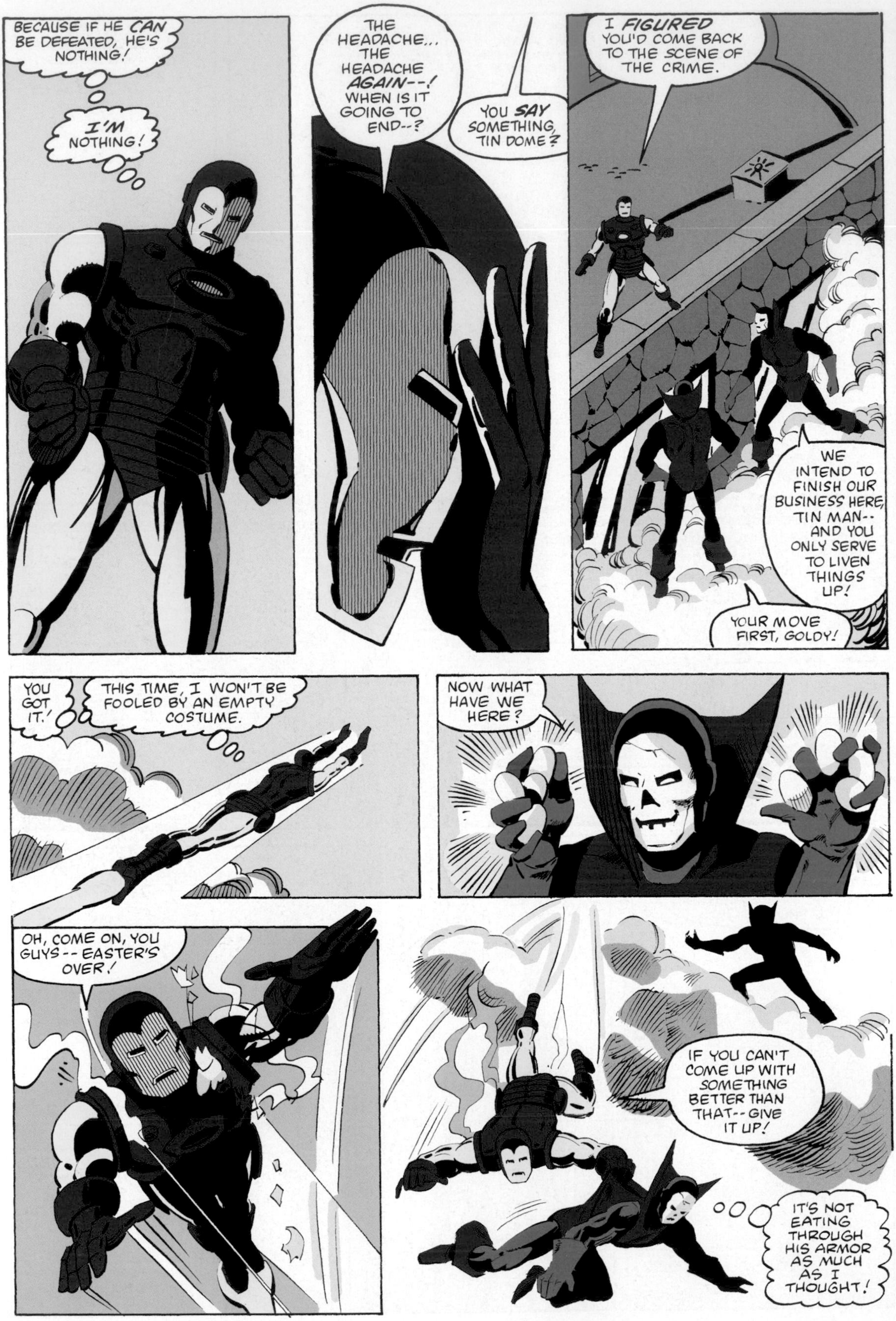

BECAUSE IF HE CAN BE DEFEATED, HE'S NOTHING!
I'M NOTHING!
THE HEADACHE... THE HEADACHE AGAIN--! WHEN IS IT GOING TO END--?
YOU SAY SOMETHING, TIN DOME?
I FIGURED YOU'D COME BACK TO THE SCENE OF THE CRIME.
WE INTEND TO FINISH OUR BUSINESS HERE, TIN MAN-- AND YOU ONLY SERVE TO LIVEN THINGS UP!
YOUR MOVE FIRST, GOLDY!
YOU GOT IT.
THIS TIME, I WON'T BE FOOLED BY AN EMPTY COSTUME.
NOW WHAT HAVE WE HERE?
OH, COME ON, YOU GUYS -- EASTER'S OVER!
IF YOU CAN'T COME UP WITH SOMETHING BETTER THAN THAT-- GIVE IT UP!
IT'S NOT EATING THROUGH HIS ARMOR AS MUCH AS I THOUGHT!

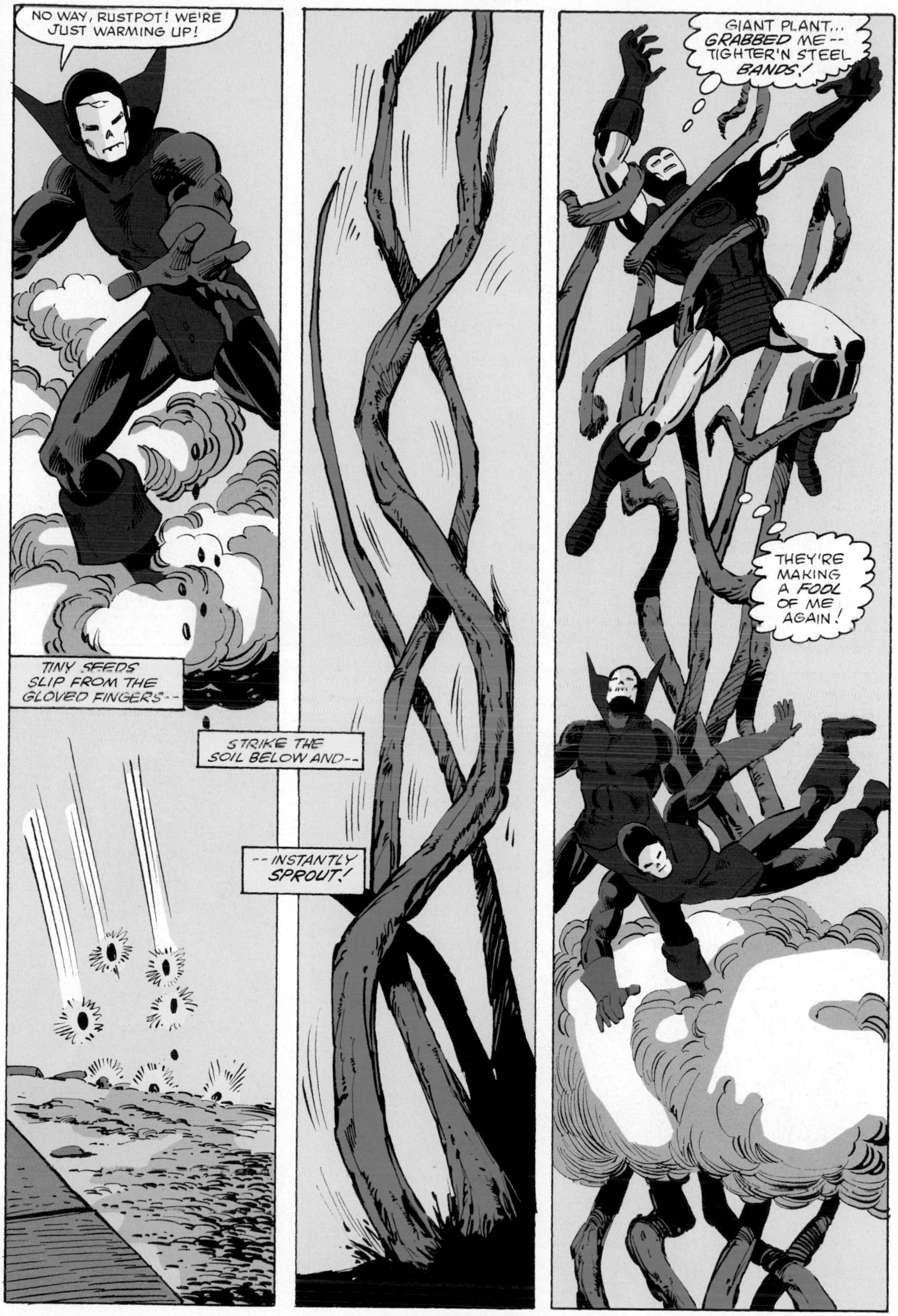
NO WAY, RUSTPOT! WE'RE JUST WARMING UP!
TINY SEEDS SLIP FROM THE GLOVED FINGERS--
--STRIKE THE SOIL BELOW AND--
--INSTANTLY SPROUT!
GIANT PLANT... GRABBED ME-- TIGHTER'N STEEL BANDS!
THEY'RE MAKING A FOOL OF ME AGAIN!

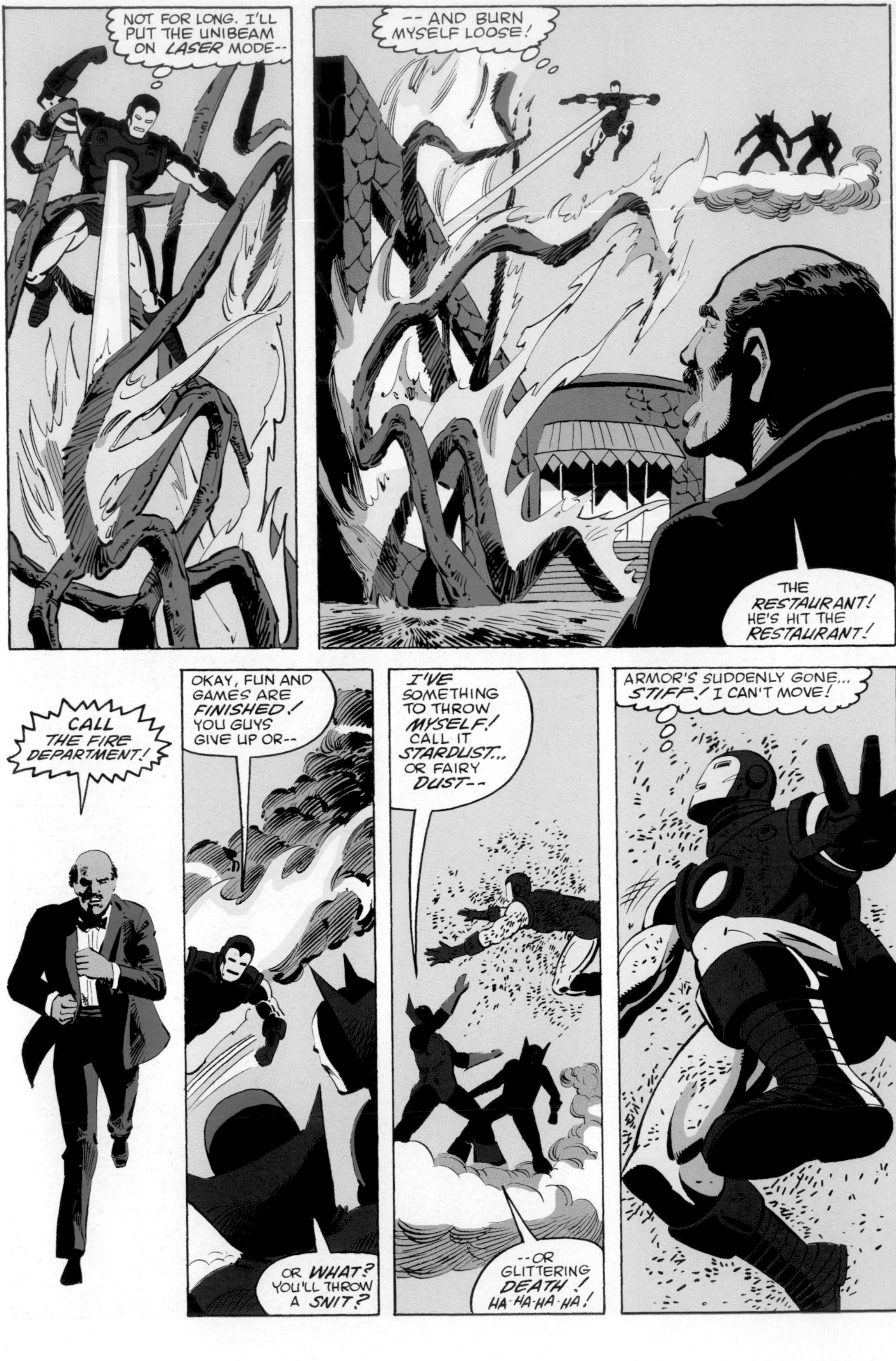
NOT FOR LONG. I'LL PUT THE UNIBEAM ON LASER MODE--
--AND BURN MYSELF LOOSE!
THE RESTAURANT! HE'S HIT THE RESTAURANT!
CALL THE FIRE DEPARTMENT!
OKAY, FUN AND GAMES ARE FINISHED! YOU GUYS GIVE UP OR--
OR WHAT? YOU'LL THROW A SNIT?
I'VE SOMETHING TO THROW MYSELF! CALL IT STARDUST... OR FAIRY DUST--
--OR GLITTERING DEATH! HA-HA-HA-HA!
ARMOR'S SUDDENLY GONE... STIFF! I CAN'T MOVE!

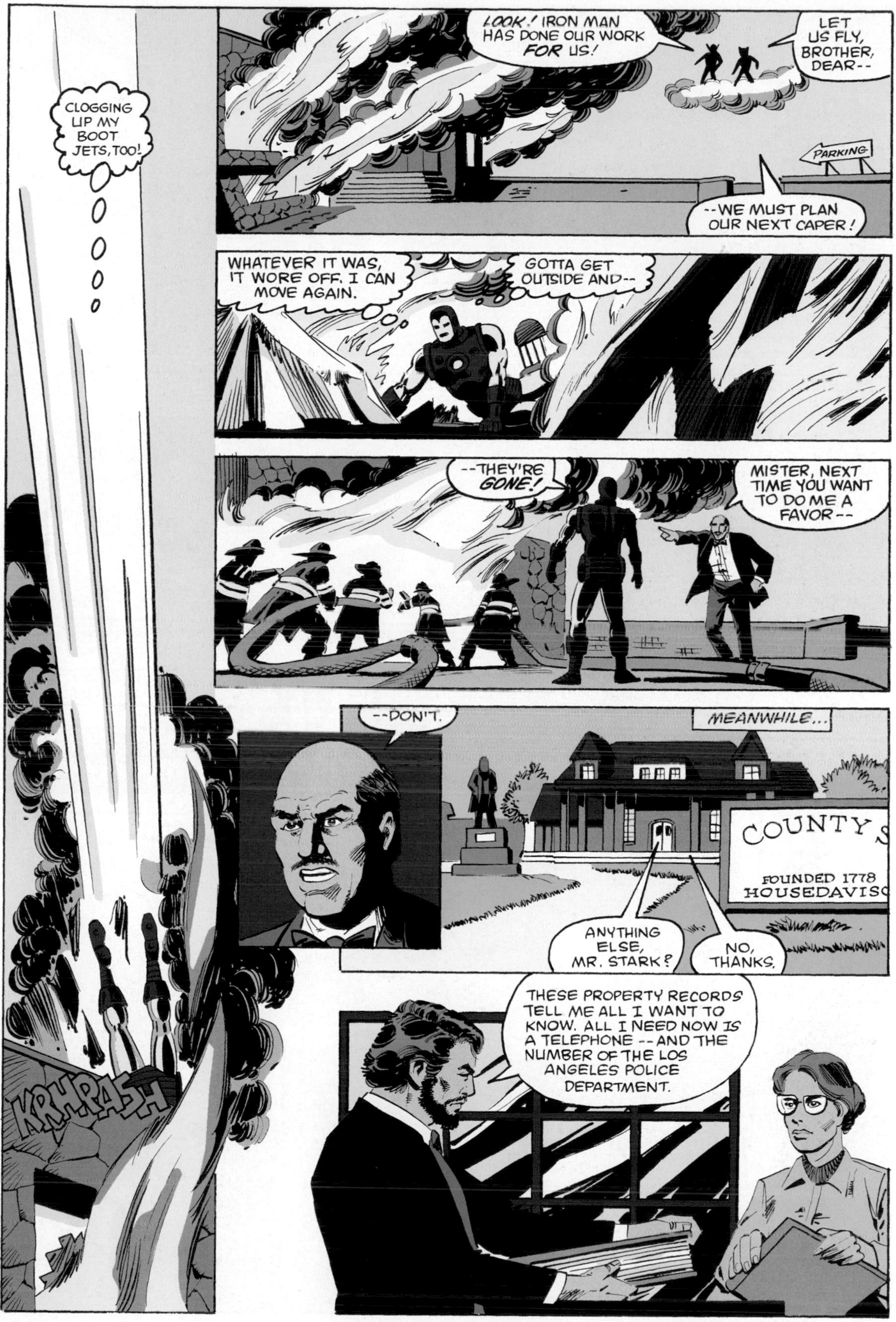
CLOGGING UP MY BOOT JETS, TOO!
LOOK! IRON MAN HAS DONE OUR WORK FOR US!
LET US FLY, BROTHER, DEAR--
PARKING
--WE MUST PLAN OUR NEXT CAPER!
WHATEVER IT WAS, IT WORE OFF. I CAN MOVE AGAIN.
GOTTA GET OUTSIDE AND--
--THEY'RE GONE!
MISTER, NEXT TIME YOU WANT TO DO ME A FAVOR--
--DON'T.
KRHRASH
MEANWHILE...
COUNTY S
FOUNDED 1778
HOUSEDAVISC
ANYTHING ELSE, MR. STARK?
NO, THANKS.
THESE PROPERTY RECORDS TELL ME ALL I WANT TO KNOW. ALL I NEED NOW IS A TELEPHONE -- AND THE NUMBER OF THE LOS ANGELES POLICE DEPARTMENT.

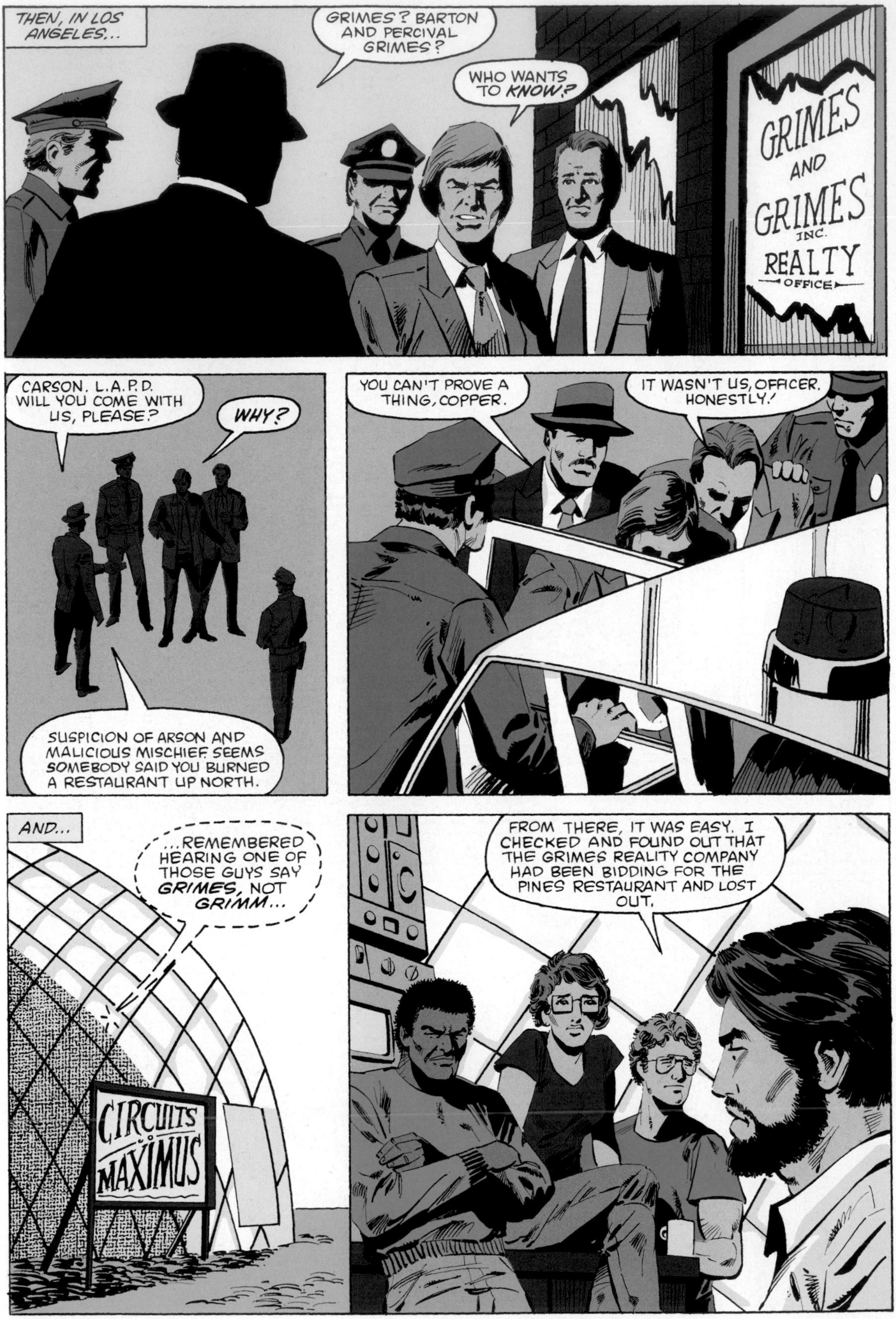
THEN, IN LOS ANGELES...
GRIMES? BARTON AND PERCIVAL GRIMES?
WHO WANTS TO KNOW?
GRIMES AND GRIMES INC. REALTY OFFICE
CARSON. L.A.P.D. WILL YOU COME WITH US, PLEASE?
WHY?
SUSPICION OF ARSON AND MALICIOUS MISCHIEF. SEEMS SOMEBODY SAID YOU BURNED A RESTAURANT UP NORTH.
YOU CAN'T PROVE A THING, COPPER.
IT WASN'T US, OFFICER, HONESTLY!
AND...
...REMEMBERED HEARING ONE OF THOSE GUYS SAY GRIMES, NOT GRIMM...
CIRCUITS MAXIMUS
FROM THERE, IT WAS EASY. I CHECKED AND FOUND OUT THAT THE GRIMES REALITY COMPANY HAD BEEN BIDDING FOR THE PINES RESTAURANT AND LOST OUT.

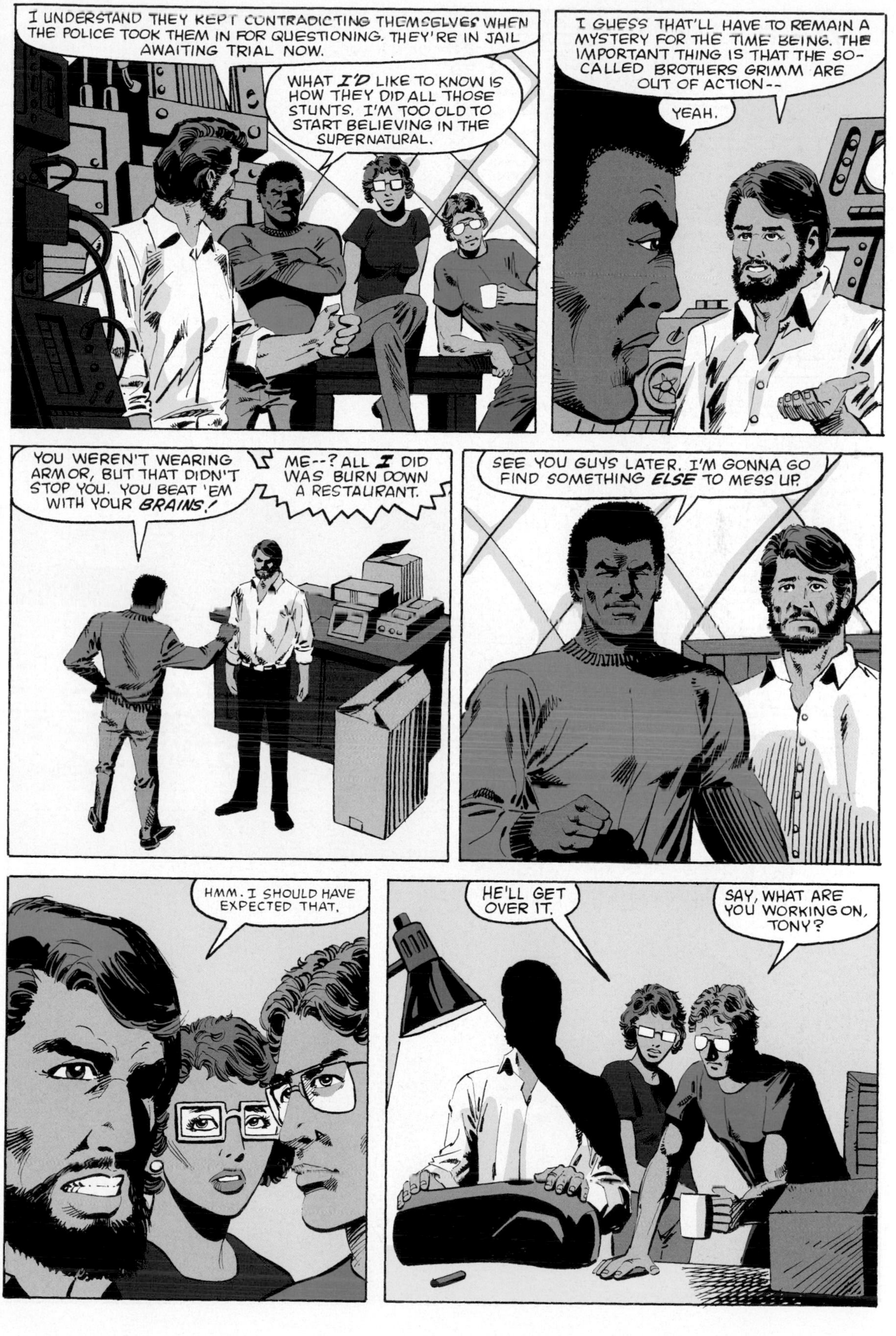

I UNDERSTAND THEY KEPT CONTRADICTING THEMSELVES WHEN THE POLICE TOOK THEM IN FOR QUESTIONING. THEY'RE IN JAIL AWAITING TRIAL NOW.
WHAT I'D LIKE TO KNOW IS HOW THEY DID ALL THOSE STUNTS. I'M TOO OLD TO START BELIEVING IN THE SUPERNATURAL.
I GUESS THAT'LL HAVE TO REMAIN A MYSTERY FOR THE TIME BEING. THE IMPORTANT THING IS THAT THE SO-CALLED BROTHERS GRIMM ARE OUT OF ACTION--
YEAH.
YOU WEREN'T WEARING ARMOR, BUT THAT DIDN'T STOP YOU. YOU BEAT 'EM WITH YOUR BRAINS!
ME--? ALL I DID WAS BURN DOWN A RESTAURANT.
SEE YOU GUYS LATER. I'M GONNA GO FIND SOMETHING ELSE TO MESS UP.
HMM. I SHOULD HAVE EXPECTED THAT.
HE'LL GET OVER IT.
SAY, WHAT ARE YOU WORKING ON, TONY?

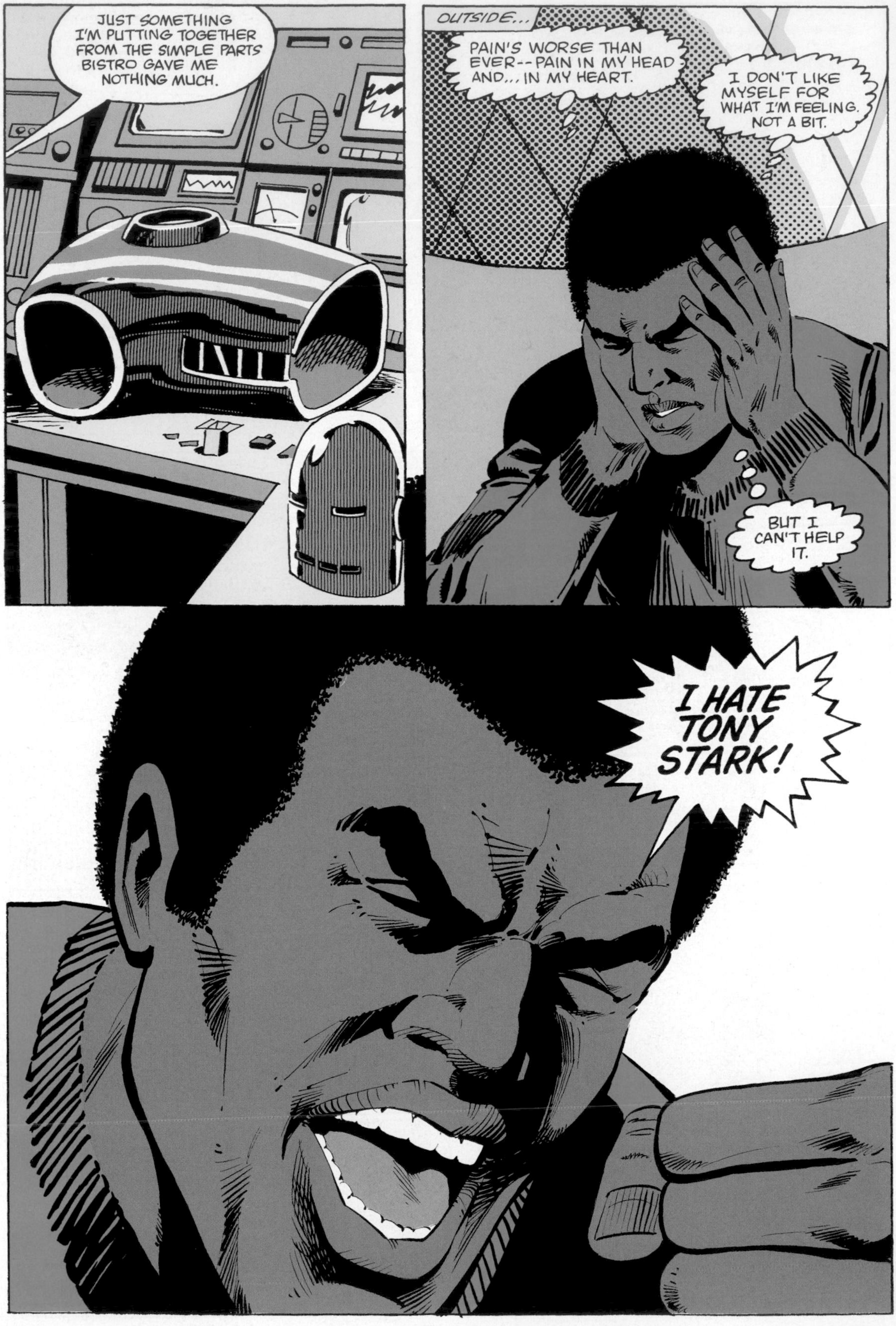
JUST SOMETHING I'M PUTTING TOGETHER FROM THE SIMPLE PARTS BISTRO GAVE ME NOTHING MUCH.
OUTSIDE...
PAIN'S WORSE THAN EVER--PAIN IN MY HEAD AND... IN MY HEART.
I DON'T LIKE MYSELF FOR WHAT I'M FEELING. NOT A BIT.
BUT I CAN'T HELP IT.
I HATE TONY STARK!

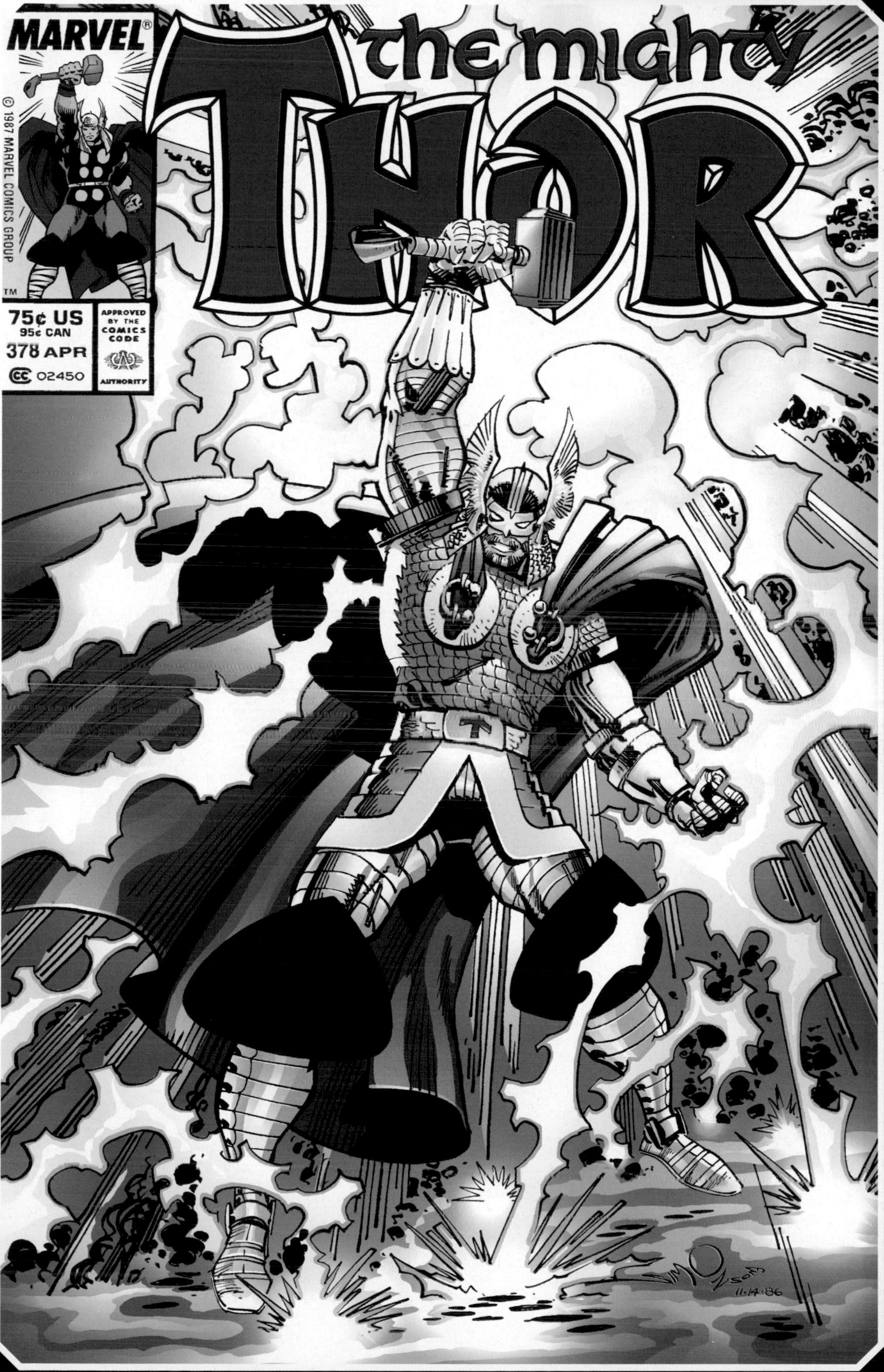
MARVEL
the mighty
THOR
© 1987 MARVEL COMICS GROUP
TM
75¢ US
95¢ CAN
378 APR
02450
APPROVED BY THE COMICS CODE AUTHORITY
11·14·86

STAN LEE PRESENTS: the MIGHTY THOR®

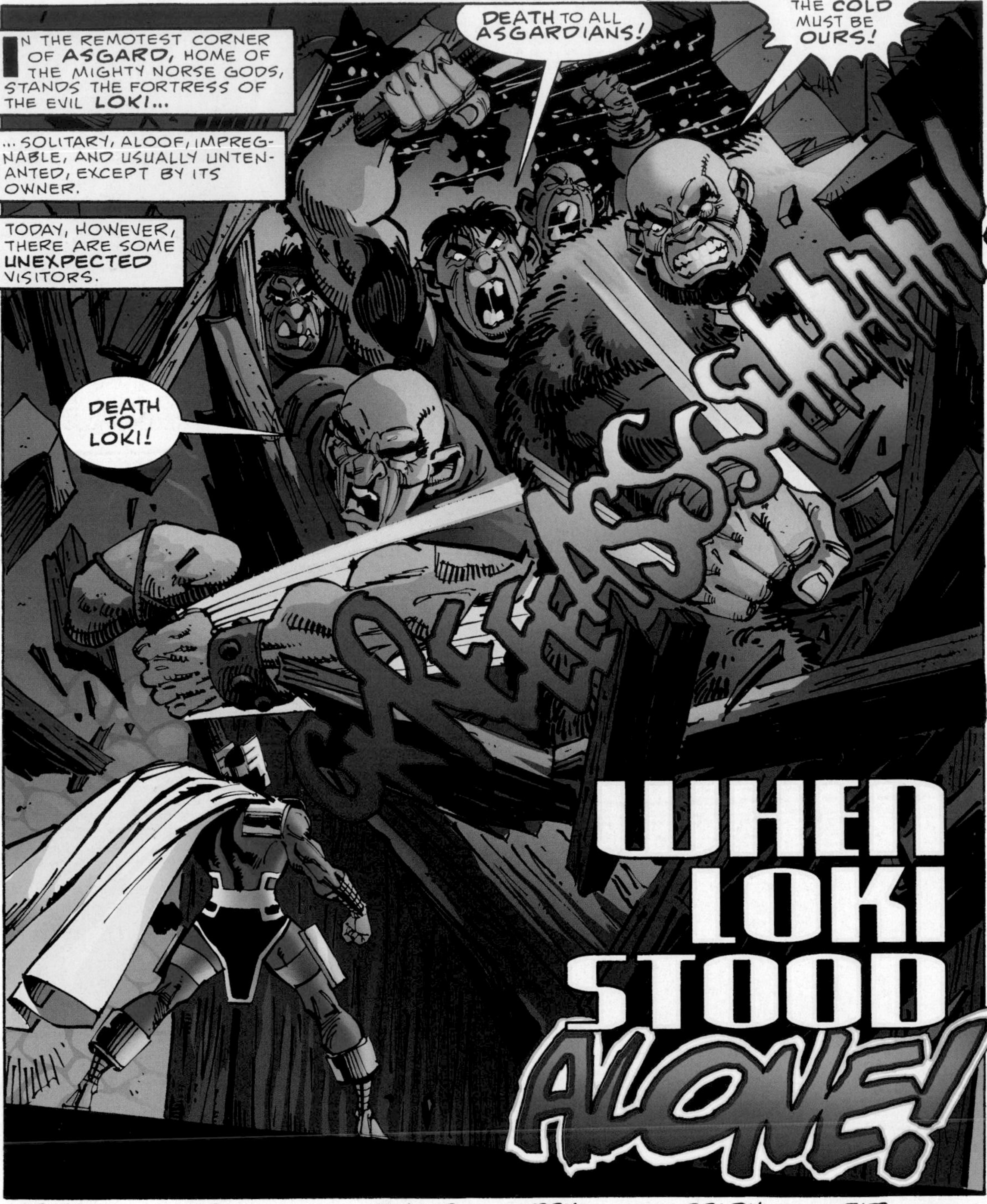
IN THE REMOTEST CORNER OF ASGARD, HOME OF THE MIGHTY NORSE GODS, STANDS THE FORTRESS OF THE EVIL LOKI...
...SOLITARY, ALOOF, IMPREGNABLE, AND USUALLY UNTENANTED, EXCEPT BY ITS OWNER.
TODAY, HOWEVER, THERE ARE SOME UNEXPECTED VISITORS.
DEATH TO ALL ASGARDIANS!
THE COLD MUST BE OURS!
DEATH TO LOKI!
WHEN LOKI STOOD ALONE!

WALTER SIMONSON WRITING | SAL BUSCEMA DRAWING | JOHN E. WORKMAN LETTERING | MAX SCHEELE COLORING | RALPH MACCHIO EDITING | JIM SHOOTER EDITING IN CHIEF

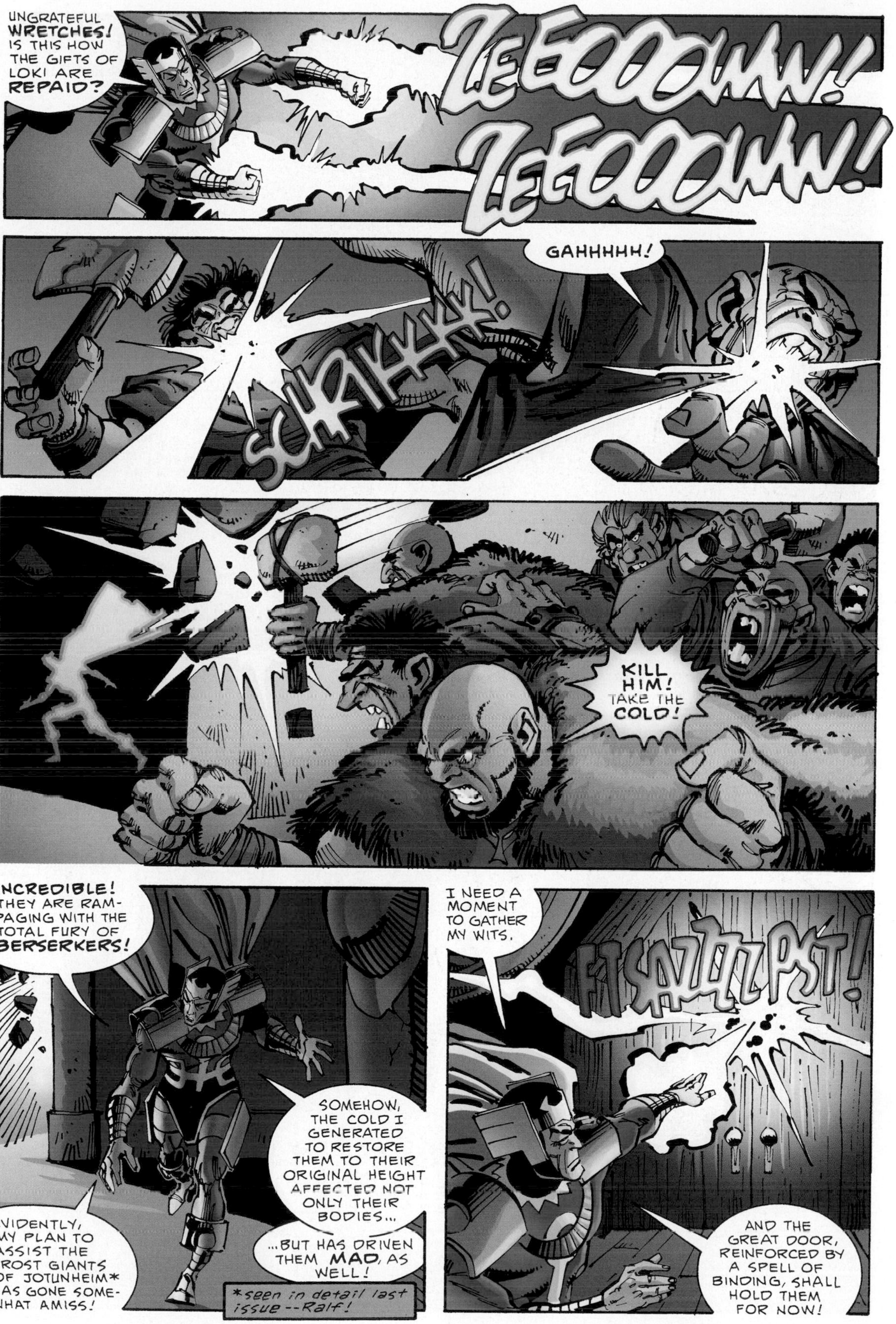
UNGRATEFUL WRETCHES! IS THIS HOW THE GIFTS OF LOKI ARE REPAID?
ZEEOOOWW! ZEEOOOWW!
GAHHHHH!
SCHRAKKK!
KILL HIM! TAKE THE COLD!
INCREDIBLE! THEY ARE RAMPAGING WITH THE TOTAL FURY OF BERSERKERS!
SOMEHOW, THE COLD I GENERATED TO RESTORE THEM TO THEIR ORIGINAL HEIGHT AFFECTED NOT ONLY THEIR BODIES...
...BUT HAS DRIVEN THEM MAD, AS WELL!
EVIDENTLY, MY PLAN TO ASSIST THE FROST GIANTS OF JOTUNHEIM* HAS GONE SOMEWHAT AMISS!
*seen in detail last issue --Ralf!
I NEED A MOMENT TO GATHER MY WITS.
FTSAZZZZPST!
AND THE GREAT DOOR, REINFORCED BY A SPELL OF BINDING, SHALL HOLD THEM FOR NOW!

A MOMENT! 'TIS MY HATED STEP-BROTHER, **THOR**, STILL UNCONSCIOUS SINCE I BROUGHT HIM HERE!

"HIS BATTLE WITH THE DARK ELVES AND THEIR DEADLY WARRIOR, GRENDELL, HATH LEFT HIM WITH ALL MANNER OF INJURIES, INCLUDING A BROKEN HAND AND LEG."

AND THE CURSE OF HELA PREVENTS HIM FROM DYING FROM SUCH WOUNDS *.

*details all over the last few issues, Thorophiles! -- R.

HOW DELIGHTFULLY IRONIC!

LET THE GIANTS PLAY WITH A **NEW** TOY WHILE LOKI ARRANGES THEIR TOTAL DEFEAT FOR THIS BETRAYAL!

THOR WILL PROVE USEFUL TO ME AT **LAST**!

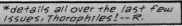

THPAPPP!

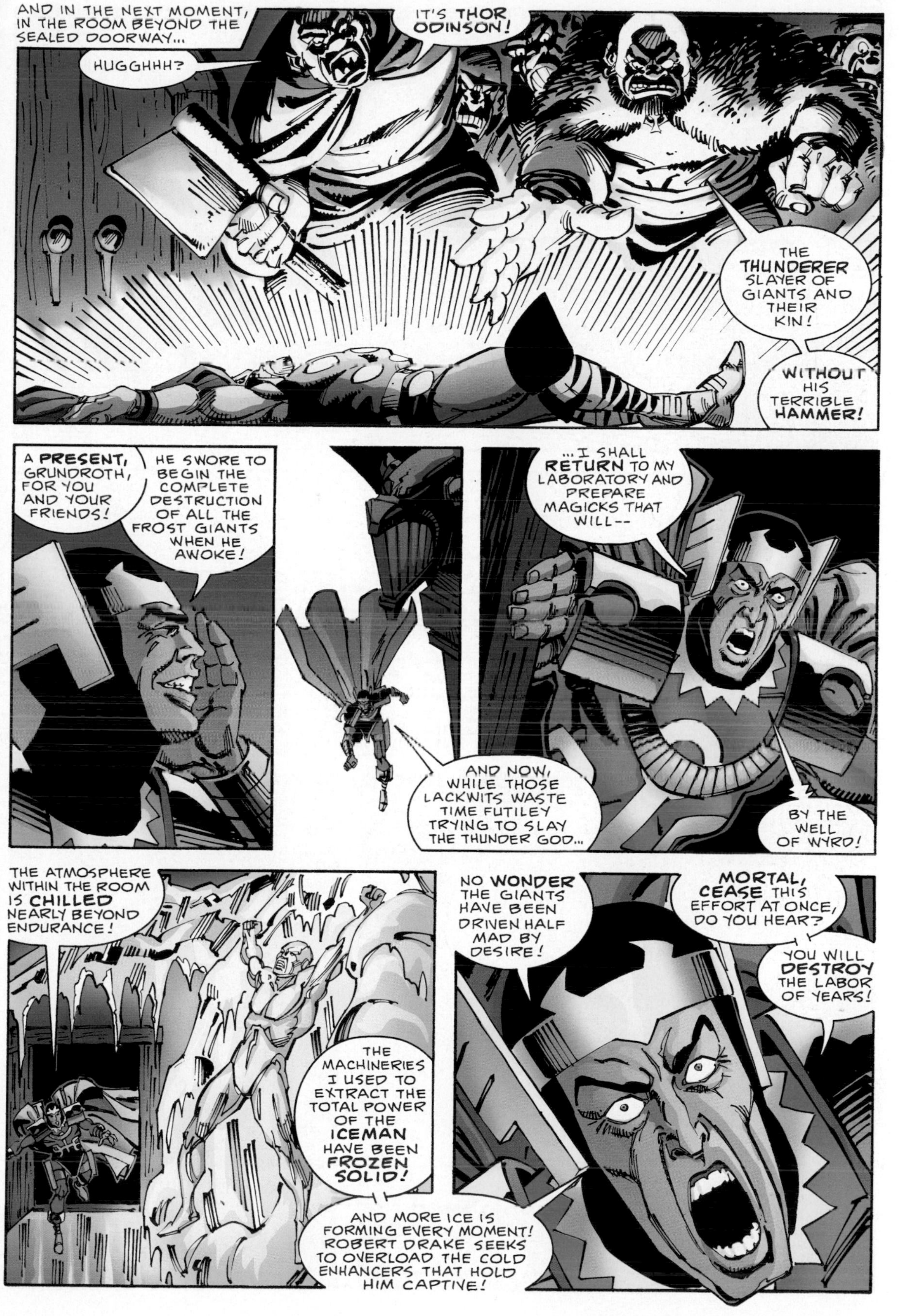
AND IN THE NEXT MOMENT, IN THE ROOM BEYOND THE SEALED DOORWAY...
IT'S THOR ODINSON!
HUGGHHH?
THE THUNDERER SLAYER OF GIANTS AND THEIR KIN!
WITHOUT HIS TERRIBLE HAMMER!
A PRESENT, GRUNDROTH, FOR YOU AND YOUR FRIENDS!
HE SWORE TO BEGIN THE COMPLETE DESTRUCTION OF ALL THE FROST GIANTS WHEN HE AWOKE!
AND NOW, WHILE THOSE LACKWITS WASTE TIME FUTILEY TRYING TO SLAY THE THUNDER GOD...
...I SHALL RETURN TO MY LABORATORY AND PREPARE MAGICKS THAT WILL--
BY THE WELL OF WYRD!
THE ATMOSPHERE WITHIN THE ROOM IS CHILLED NEARLY BEYOND ENDURANCE!
THE MACHINERIES I USED TO EXTRACT THE TOTAL POWER OF THE ICEMAN HAVE BEEN FROZEN SOLID!
AND MORE ICE IS FORMING EVERY MOMENT! ROBERT DRAKE SEEKS TO OVERLOAD THE COLD ENHANCERS THAT HOLD HIM CAPTIVE!
NO WONDER THE GIANTS HAVE BEEN DRIVEN HALF MAD BY DESIRE!
MORTAL, CEASE THIS EFFORT AT ONCE, DO YOU HEAR?
YOU WILL DESTROY THE LABOR OF YEARS!

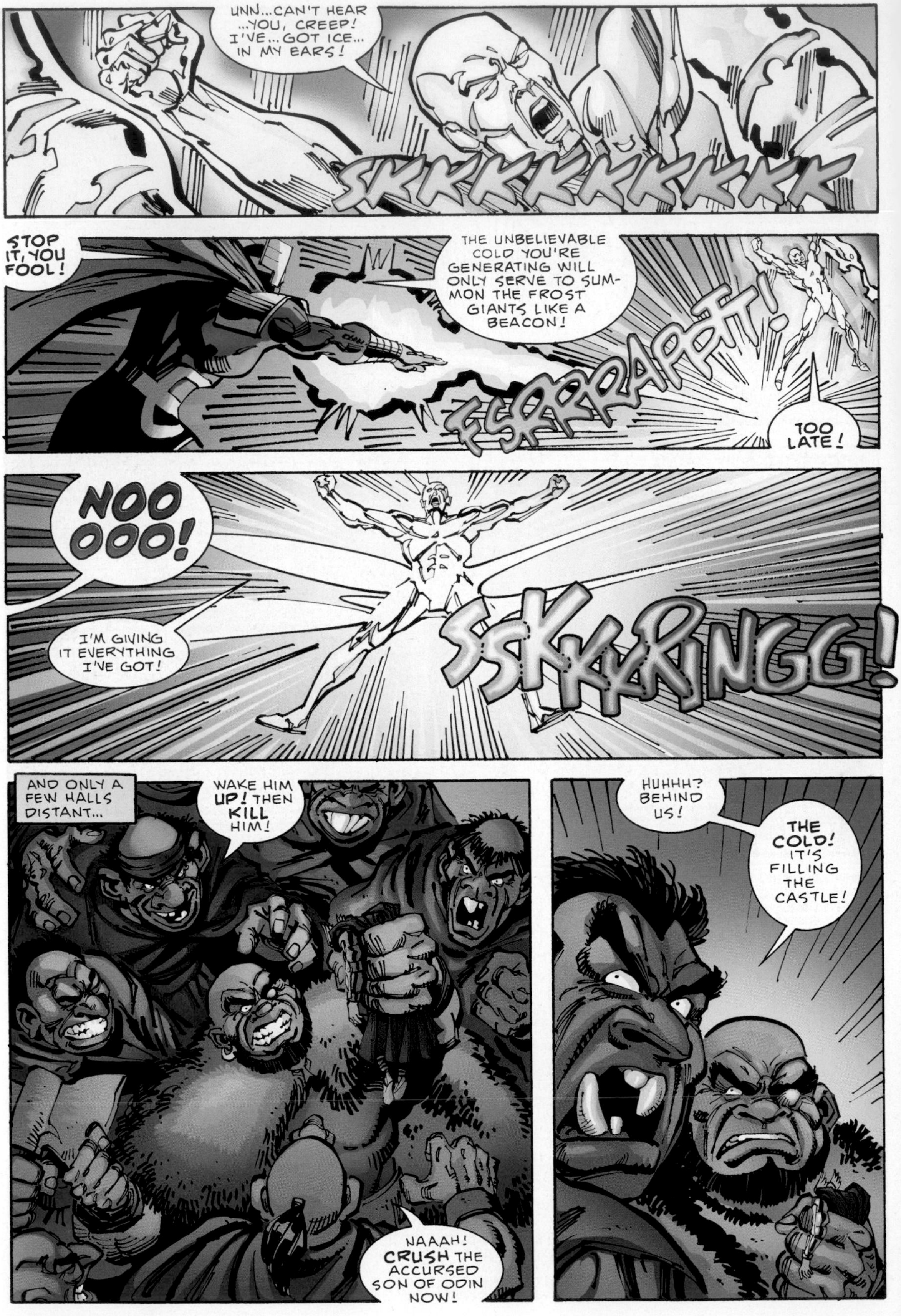
UNN...CAN'T HEAR ...YOU, CREEP! I'VE...GOT ICE... IN MY EARS!
SKKKKKKKKKK
STOP IT, YOU FOOL!
THE UNBELIEVABLE COLD YOU'RE GENERATING WILL ONLY SERVE TO SUMMON THE FROST GIANTS LIKE A BEACON!
FSRRRAPPTT!
TOO LATE!
NOOOOO!
I'M GIVING IT EVERYTHING I'VE GOT!
SSKKRINGG!
AND ONLY A FEW HALLS DISTANT...
WAKE HIM UP! THEN KILL HIM!
NAAAH! CRUSH THE ACCURSED SON OF ODIN NOW!
HUHHH? BEHIND US!
THE COLD! IT'S FILLING THE CASTLE!

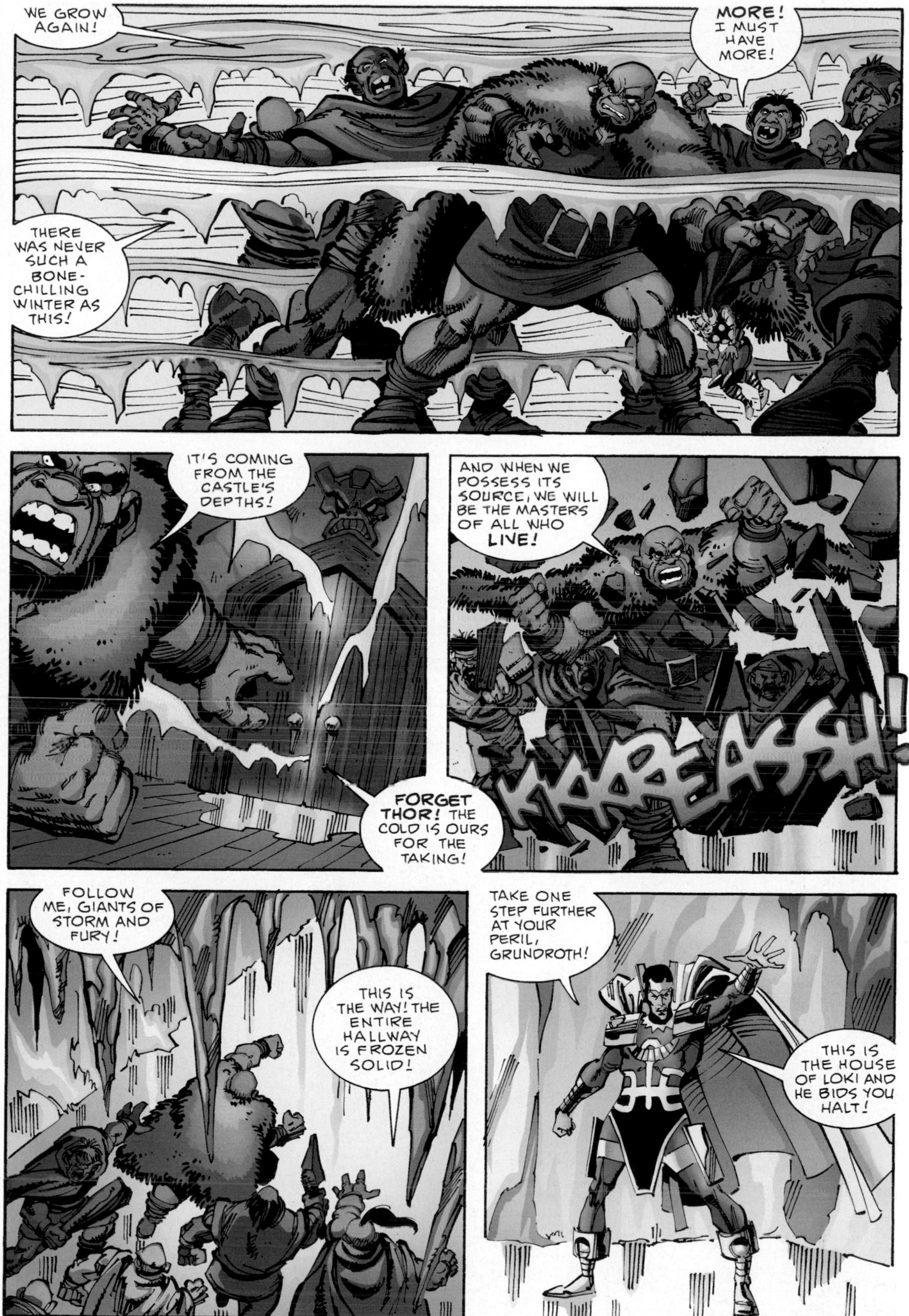
WE GROW AGAIN!
MORE! I MUST HAVE MORE!
THERE WAS NEVER SUCH A BONE-CHILLING WINTER AS THIS!
IT'S COMING FROM THE CASTLE'S DEPTHS!
FORGET THOR! THE COLD IS OURS FOR THE TAKING!
AND WHEN WE POSSESS ITS SOURCE, WE WILL BE THE MASTERS OF ALL WHO LIVE!
KKAREASH!
FOLLOW ME, GIANTS OF STORM AND FURY!
THIS IS THE WAY! THE ENTIRE HALLWAY IS FROZEN SOLID!
TAKE ONE STEP FURTHER AT YOUR PERIL, GRUNDROTH!
THIS IS THE HOUSE OF LOKI AND HE BIDS YOU HALT!

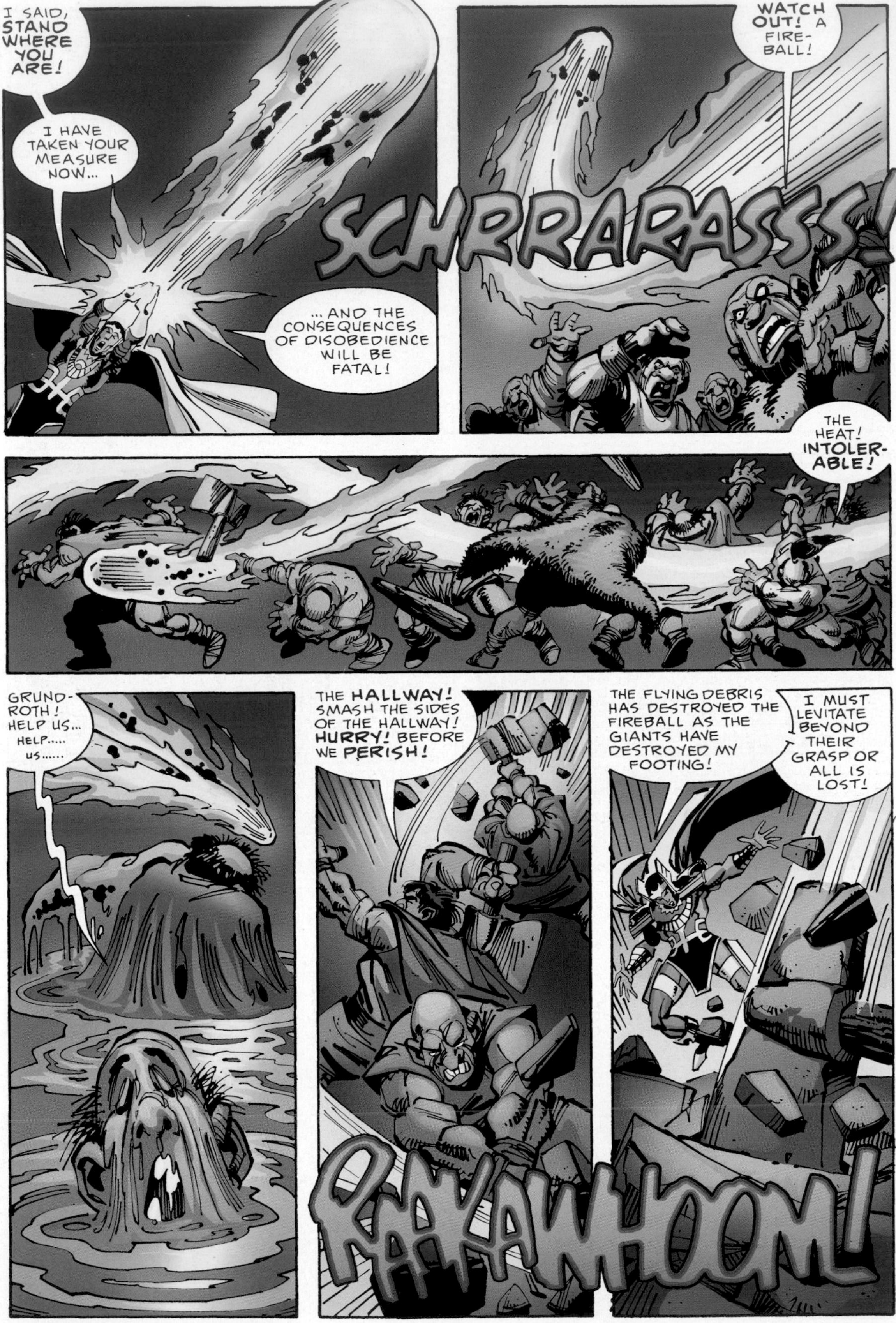

I SAID, STAND WHERE YOU ARE!
I HAVE TAKEN YOUR MEASURE NOW...
...AND THE CONSEQUENCES OF DISOBEDIENCE WILL BE FATAL!
WATCH OUT! A FIRE-BALL!
SCHRRARASSS!
THE HEAT! INTOLER-ABLE!
GRUND-ROTH! HELP US... HELP..... US......
THE HALLWAY! SMASH THE SIDES OF THE HALLWAY! HURRY! BEFORE WE PERISH!
THE FLYING DEBRIS HAS DESTROYED THE FIREBALL AS THE GIANTS HAVE DESTROYED MY FOOTING!
I MUST LEVITATE BEYOND THEIR GRASP OR ALL IS LOST!
RAKAWHOOM!

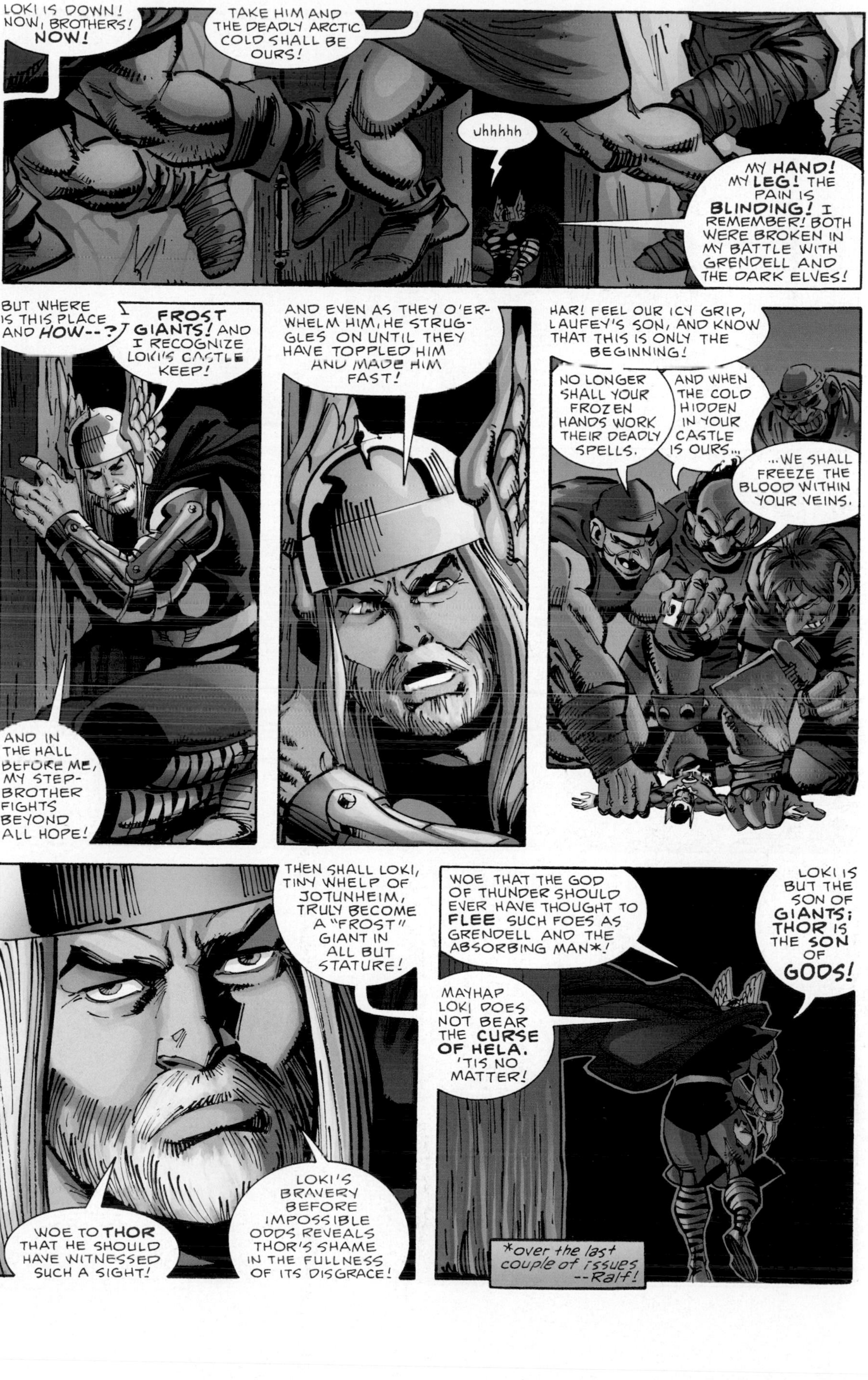
LOKI IS DOWN! NOW, BROTHERS! NOW!
TAKE HIM AND THE DEADLY ARCTIC COLD SHALL BE OURS!
uhhhhh
MY HAND! MY LEG! THE PAIN IS BLINDING! I REMEMBER! BOTH WERE BROKEN IN MY BATTLE WITH GRENDELL AND THE DARK ELVES!
BUT WHERE IS THIS PLACE AND HOW--?
FROST GIANTS! AND I RECOGNIZE LOKI'S CASTLE KEEP!
AND IN THE HALL BEFORE ME, MY STEP-BROTHER FIGHTS BEYOND ALL HOPE!
AND EVEN AS THEY O'ER-WHELM HIM, HE STRUG-GLES ON UNTIL THEY HAVE TOPPLED HIM AND MADE HIM FAST!
HAR! FEEL OUR ICY GRIP, LAUFEY'S SON, AND KNOW THAT THIS IS ONLY THE BEGINNING!
NO LONGER SHALL YOUR FROZEN HANDS WORK THEIR DEADLY SPELLS.
AND WHEN THE COLD HIDDEN IN YOUR CASTLE IS OURS...
...WE SHALL FREEZE THE BLOOD WITHIN YOUR VEINS.
THEN SHALL LOKI, TINY WHELP OF JOTUNHEIM, TRULY BECOME A "FROST" GIANT IN ALL BUT STATURE!
WOE TO THOR THAT HE SHOULD HAVE WITNESSED SUCH A SIGHT!
LOKI'S BRAVERY BEFORE IMPOSSIBLE ODDS REVEALS THOR'S SHAME IN THE FULLNESS OF ITS DISGRACE!
WOE THAT THE GOD OF THUNDER SHOULD EVER HAVE THOUGHT TO FLEE SUCH FOES AS GRENDELL AND THE ABSORBING MAN*!
MAYHAP LOKI DOES NOT BEAR THE CURSE OF HELA. 'TIS NO MATTER!
LOKI IS BUT THE SON OF GIANTS; THOR IS THE SON OF GODS!
*over the last couple of issues --Ralf!

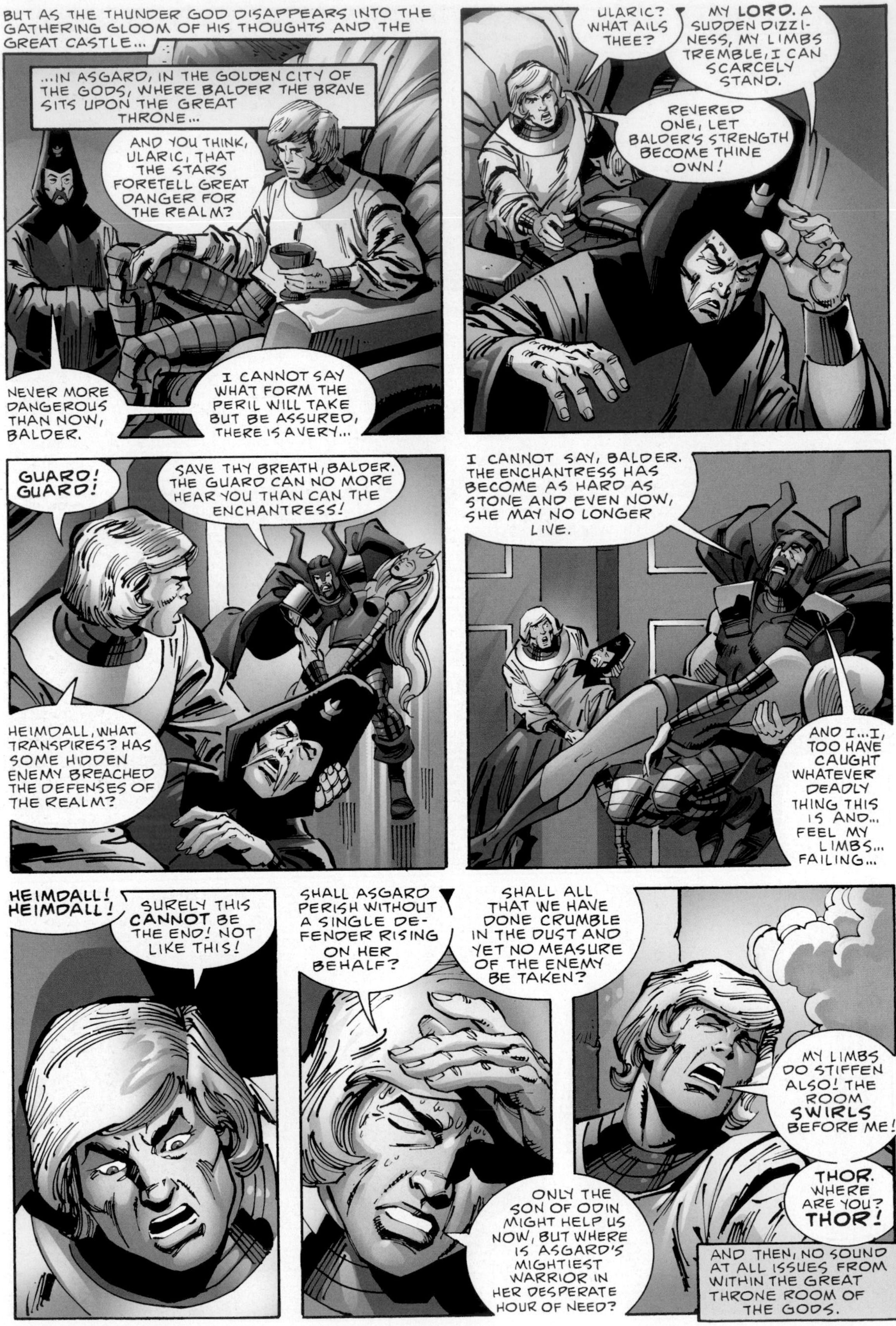

BUT AS THE THUNDER GOD DISAPPEARS INTO THE GATHERING GLOOM OF HIS THOUGHTS AND THE GREAT CASTLE...
...IN ASGARD, IN THE GOLDEN CITY OF THE GODS, WHERE BALDER THE BRAVE SITS UPON THE GREAT THRONE...
AND YOU THINK, ULARIC, THAT THE STARS FORETELL GREAT DANGER FOR THE REALM?
NEVER MORE DANGEROUS THAN NOW, BALDER.
I CANNOT SAY WHAT FORM THE PERIL WILL TAKE BUT BE ASSURED, THERE IS A VERY...
ULARIC? WHAT AILS THEE?
MY LORD. A SUDDEN DIZZINESS, MY LIMBS TREMBLE, I CAN SCARCELY STAND.
REVERED ONE, LET BALDER'S STRENGTH BECOME THINE OWN!
GUARD! GUARD!
SAVE THY BREATH, BALDER. THE GUARD CAN NO MORE HEAR YOU THAN CAN THE ENCHANTRESS!
HEIMDALL, WHAT TRANSPIRES? HAS SOME HIDDEN ENEMY BREACHED THE DEFENSES OF THE REALM?
I CANNOT SAY, BALDER. THE ENCHANTRESS HAS BECOME AS HARD AS STONE AND EVEN NOW, SHE MAY NO LONGER LIVE.
AND I...I, TOO HAVE CAUGHT WHATEVER DEADLY THING THIS IS AND... FEEL MY LIMBS... FAILING...
HEIMDALL! HEIMDALL!
SURELY THIS CANNOT BE THE END! NOT LIKE THIS!
SHALL ASGARD PERISH WITHOUT A SINGLE DEFENDER RISING ON HER BEHALF?
SHALL ALL THAT WE HAVE DONE CRUMBLE IN THE DUST AND YET NO MEASURE OF THE ENEMY BE TAKEN?
ONLY THE SON OF ODIN MIGHT HELP US NOW, BUT WHERE IS ASGARD'S MIGHTIEST WARRIOR IN HER DESPERATE HOUR OF NEED?
MY LIMBS DO STIFFEN ALSO! THE ROOM SWIRLS BEFORE ME!
THOR. WHERE ARE YOU? THOR!
AND THEN, NO SOUND AT ALL ISSUES FROM WITHIN THE GREAT THRONE ROOM OF THE GODS.

BUT IN LOKI'S CASTLE, THE SOUNDS ARE HOWLS OF VICTORY.

UNCONSCIOUS.

WELL, WE'LL WAKE HIM UP SOON ENOUGH WHEN WE HAVE THE SECRET OF HIS COLD.

BUT SUDDENLY, WITHOUT WARNING...

NOOOO-- ARRRGH GGHGH!

KCREEEAKSH' CROALIMM!

THE WALL!

AND FOR A MOMENT, SILENCE REIGNS WITHIN THE WALLS OF LOKI'S CASTLE AS WELL.

THE GIANTS HAVE FLED IN FEAR OF THE COLLAPSING HALL.

THOUGH SOON ENOUGH, THEY SHALL RETURN, DRAWN BY THE BITTER COLD IN THE HALLS BEYOND.

BUT I HAVE TIME ENOUGH.

THUS DOES THOR REGAIN HIS HAMMER ...AND HIS BROTHER.

THIS ONE'S BODY DID PROTECT LOKI FROM THE FALL- ING DEBRIS.

COME, TRICKSTER. THOUGH YOU AND I HAVE EVER FOUGHT AND HATED IN THE PAST, YOU SHALL NOT DIE ALONE, UNMOURNED, THIS DAY.

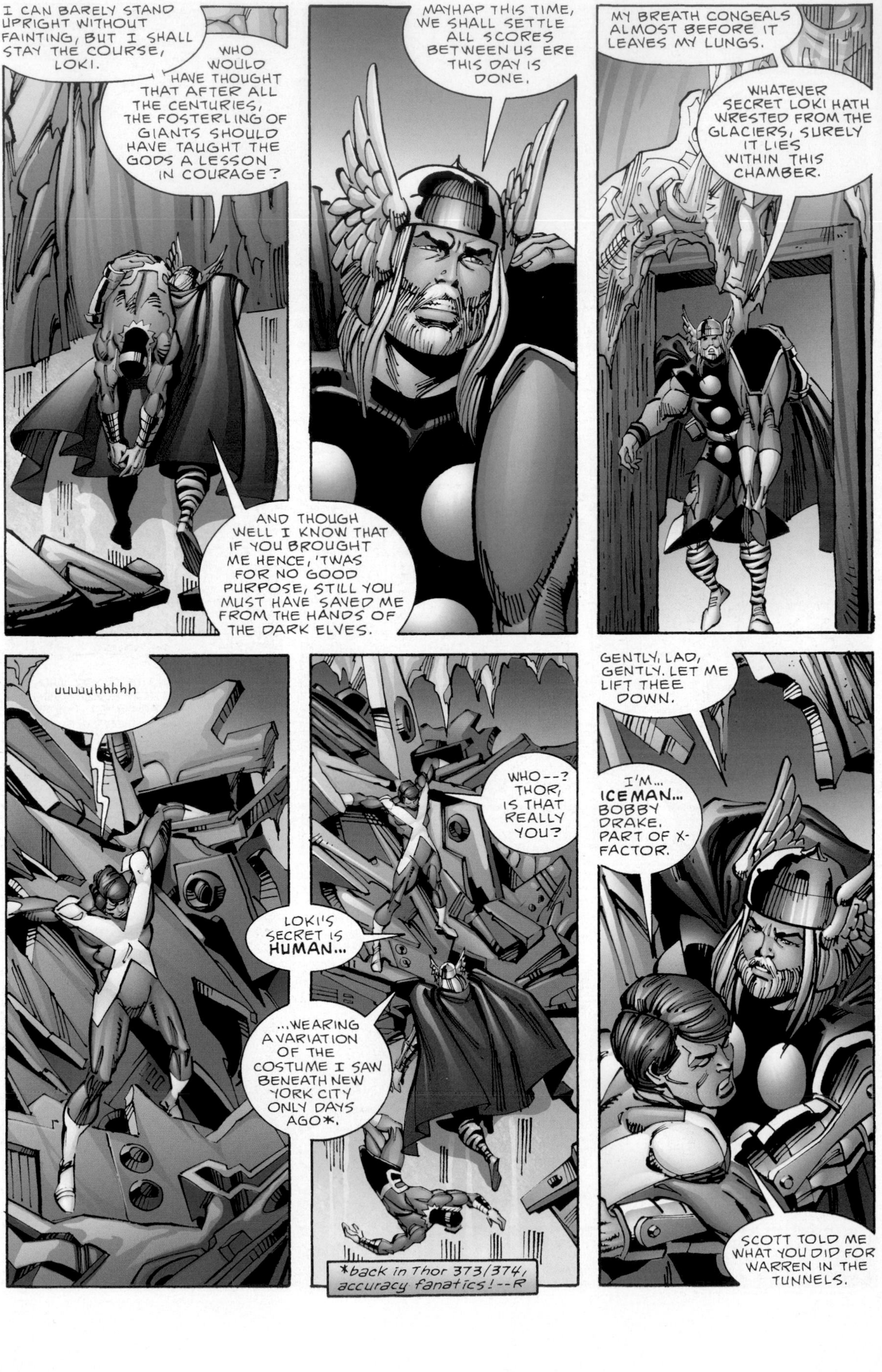
I CAN BARELY STAND UPRIGHT WITHOUT FAINTING, BUT I SHALL STAY THE COURSE, LOKI.
WHO WOULD HAVE THOUGHT THAT AFTER ALL THE CENTURIES, THE FOSTERLING OF GIANTS SHOULD HAVE TAUGHT THE GODS A LESSON IN COURAGE?
AND THOUGH WELL I KNOW THAT IF YOU BROUGHT ME HENCE, 'TWAS FOR NO GOOD PURPOSE, STILL YOU MUST HAVE SAVED ME FROM THE HANDS OF THE DARK ELVES.
MAYHAP THIS TIME, WE SHALL SETTLE ALL SCORES BETWEEN US ERE THIS DAY IS DONE.
MY BREATH CONGEALS ALMOST BEFORE IT LEAVES MY LUNGS.
WHATEVER SECRET LOKI HATH WRESTED FROM THE GLACIERS, SURELY IT LIES WITHIN THIS CHAMBER.
uuuuuhhhhh
WHO--? THOR, IS THAT REALLY YOU?
LOKI'S SECRET IS **HUMAN...**
...WEARING A VARIATION OF THE COSTUME I SAW BENEATH NEW YORK CITY ONLY DAYS AGO*.
*back in Thor 373/374, accuracy fanatics! --R
GENTLY, LAD, GENTLY. LET ME LIFT THEE DOWN.
I'M... **ICEMAN...** BOBBY DRAKE. PART OF X-FACTOR.
SCOTT TOLD ME WHAT YOU DID FOR WARREN IN THE TUNNELS.

YOU... MAKING A HABIT OUT OF SAVING US?

I FEAR NOT, BOBBY. THIS TIME, I DOUBT IF I COULD EVEN SAVE MYSELF.

HOW CAME YOU HERE?

LOKI TOLD ME, BRAGGED ...ABOUT IT.

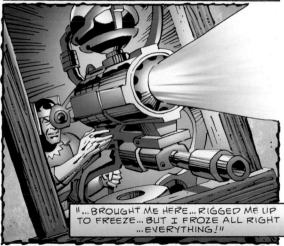

"SAID HE HAD SOME KIND OF DEVICE THAT CREATED SPHERES OF ENERGY...THEY COULD TRANSPORT STUFF INSTANTANEOUSLY...

"...BROUGHT ME HERE...RIGGED ME UP TO FREEZE...BUT I FROZE ALL RIGHT ...EVERYTHING!"

I'VE NEVER BEEN ABLE TO GENERATE SUCH COLD IN MY LIFE.

DON'T THINK...HE LIKED IT...

UNCONSCIOUS. HE HAS GIVEN UP TOO MUCH ENERGY. AND THE GIANTS HAVE RECOVERED FROM THEIR SURPRISE!

BROOAMM! BROOAMM!

THE DOOR WILL NOT HOLD LONG AGAINST THEIR FURIOUS ONSLAUGHT.

A PITY, LOKI, THAT YOU ARE NOT AWAKE TO GREET YOUR GUESTS.

NO MATTER. THE BOY HAS TOLD ME ENOUGH. I RECOGNIZE FROM HIS DESCRIPTION THE GREAT MACHINE THAT ONCE BROUGHT THE ABSORBING MAN TO EARTH* SO LONG AGO.

AND I SEE IT HERE.

*about a zillion issues ago, actually--Ralf.

THOR HAS NOT FORGOTTEN THAT WERE IT NOT FOR YOU, THERE SHOULD HAVE BEEN NO VICTORY OVER SURTUR IN THE FINAL ENCOUNTER *.

AND TODAY, WIN OR LOSE, THAT DEBT SHALL BE PAID.

YOU HAVE TAUGHT THE THUNDER GOD A LESSON IN COURAGE...

...MAYHAP HE CAN TEACH YOU ONE OF HONOR.

*Thor 353 --Ralf.

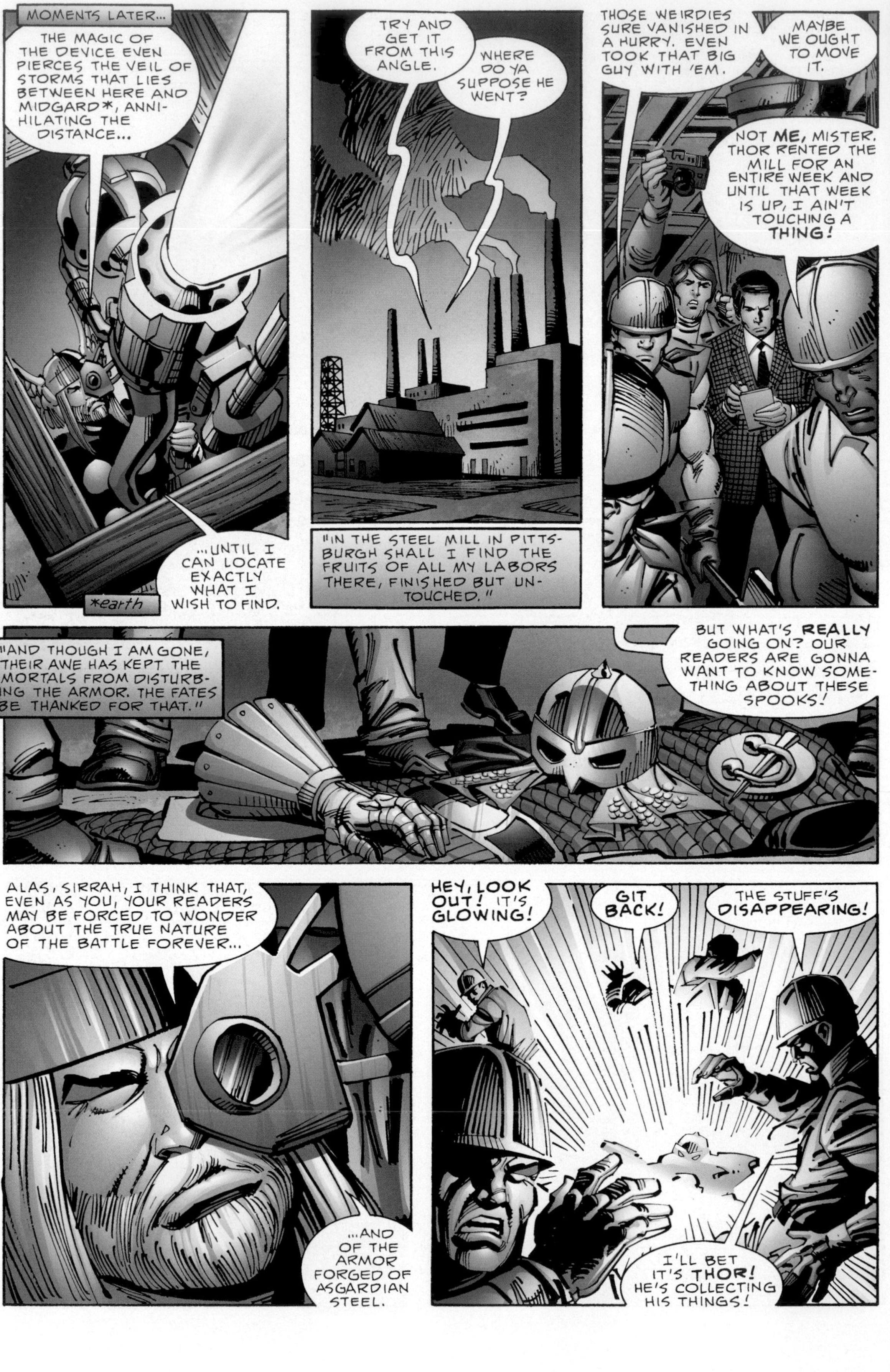
MOMENTS LATER...
THE MAGIC OF THE DEVICE EVEN PIERCES THE VEIL OF STORMS THAT LIES BETWEEN HERE AND MIDGARD*, ANNIHILATING THE DISTANCE...
...UNTIL I CAN LOCATE EXACTLY WHAT I WISH TO FIND.
*earth
TRY AND GET IT FROM THIS ANGLE.
WHERE DO YA SUPPOSE HE WENT?
"IN THE STEEL MILL IN PITTSBURGH SHALL I FIND THE FRUITS OF ALL MY LABORS THERE, FINISHED BUT UNTOUCHED."
THOSE WEIRDIES SURE VANISHED IN A HURRY. EVEN TOOK THAT BIG GUY WITH 'EM.
MAYBE WE OUGHT TO MOVE IT.
NOT ME, MISTER. THOR RENTED THE MILL FOR AN ENTIRE WEEK AND UNTIL THAT WEEK IS UP, I AIN'T TOUCHING A THING!
"AND THOUGH I AM GONE, THEIR AWE HAS KEPT THE MORTALS FROM DISTURBING THE ARMOR. THE FATES BE THANKED FOR THAT."
BUT WHAT'S REALLY GOING ON? OUR READERS ARE GONNA WANT TO KNOW SOMETHING ABOUT THESE SPOOKS!
ALAS, SIRRAH, I THINK THAT, EVEN AS YOU, YOUR READERS MAY BE FORCED TO WONDER ABOUT THE TRUE NATURE OF THE BATTLE FOREVER...
...AND OF THE ARMOR FORGED OF ASGARDIAN STEEL.
HEY, LOOK OUT! IT'S GLOWING!
GIT BACK!
THE STUFF'S DISAPPEARING!
I'LL BET IT'S THOR! HE'S COLLECTING HIS THINGS!

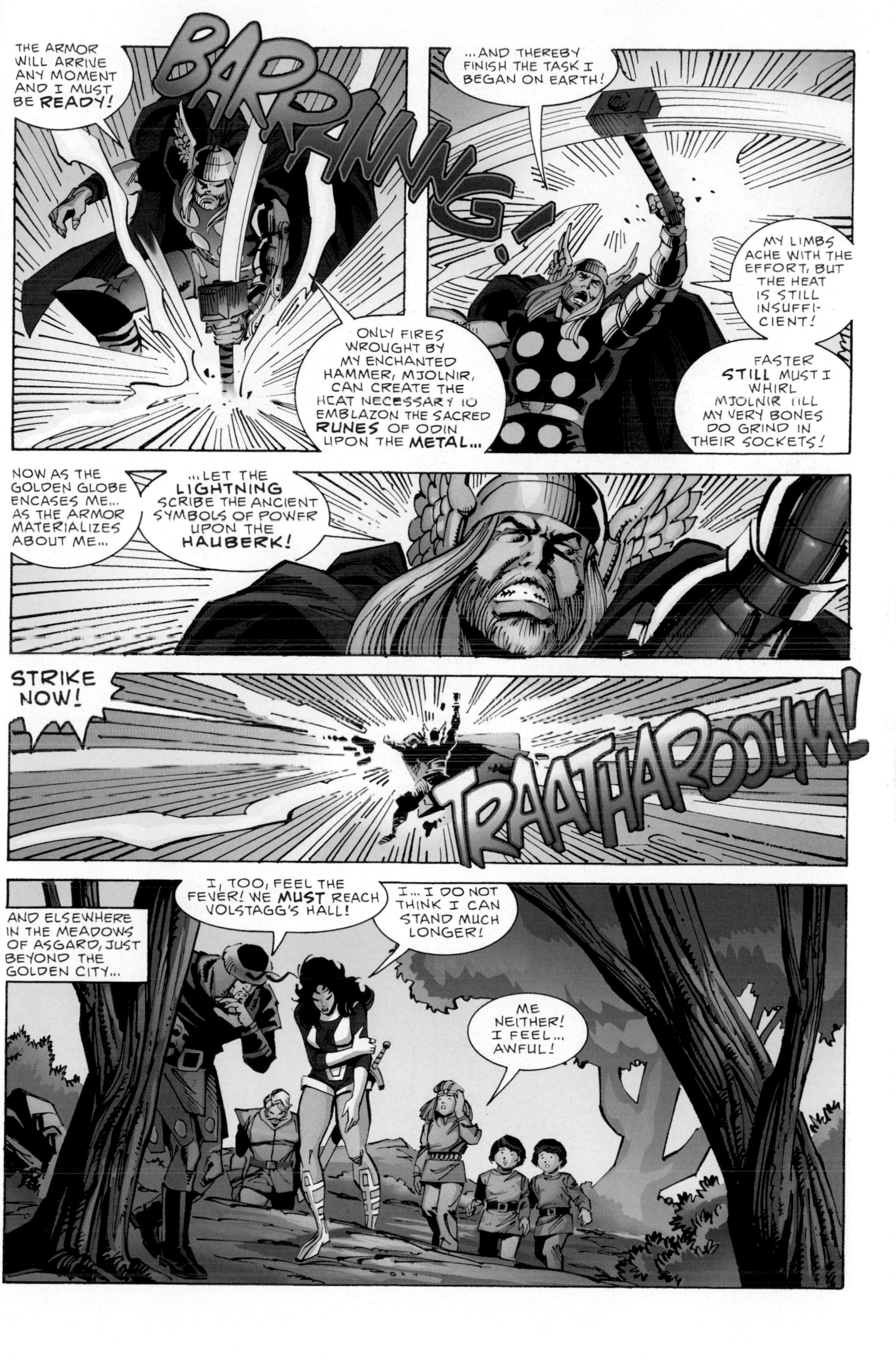
THE ARMOR WILL ARRIVE ANY MOMENT AND I MUST BE READY!
BARRANNG!
...AND THEREBY FINISH THE TASK I BEGAN ON EARTH!
ONLY FIRES WROUGHT BY MY ENCHANTED HAMMER, MJOLNIR, CAN CREATE THE HEAT NECESSARY TO EMBLAZON THE SACRED RUNES OF ODIN UPON THE METAL...
MY LIMBS ACHE WITH THE EFFORT, BUT THE HEAT IS STILL INSUFFICIENT!
FASTER STILL MUST I WHIRL MJOLNIR TILL MY VERY BONES DO GRIND IN THEIR SOCKETS!
NOW AS THE GOLDEN GLOBE ENCASES ME... AS THE ARMOR MATERIALIZES ABOUT ME...
...LET THE LIGHTNING SCRIBE THE ANCIENT SYMBOLS OF POWER UPON THE HAUBERK!
STRIKE NOW!
TRAATHAROOUM!
AND ELSEWHERE IN THE MEADOWS OF ASGARD, JUST BEYOND THE GOLDEN CITY...
I, TOO, FEEL THE FEVER! WE MUST REACH VOLSTAGG'S HALL!
I... I DO NOT THINK I CAN STAND MUCH LONGER!
ME NEITHER! I FEEL... AWFUL!

SIF!

Ohhhhh...

UNCONSCIOUS! AND ALREADY HER LIMBS ARE AS FRIGID AS THE MOUNTAINS OF JOTUNHEIM!

HILDY!

WAHH HHHH!

I... I CAN'T LIFT MY FEET ANYMORE!

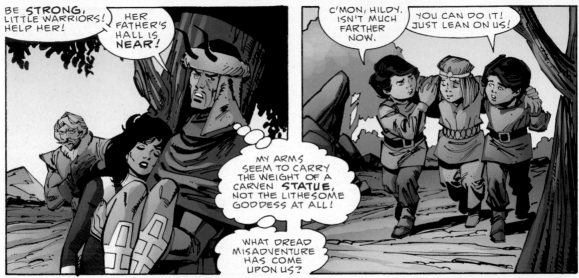

BE STRONG, LITTLE WARRIORS! HELP HER!

HER FATHER'S HALL IS NEAR!

MY ARMS SEEM TO CARRY THE WEIGHT OF A CARVEN STATUE, NOT THE LITHESOME GODDESS AT ALL!

WHAT DREAD MISADVENTURE HAS COME UPON US?

C'MON, HILDY, ISN'T MUCH FARTHER NOW.

YOU CAN DO IT! JUST LEAN ON US!

THE GREAT HALL IS SILENT!

WHERE ARE THE SOUNDS OF ETERNAL PLAY THAT SHOULD SURROUND THE ENORMOUS ONE'S DWELLING?

oh no!

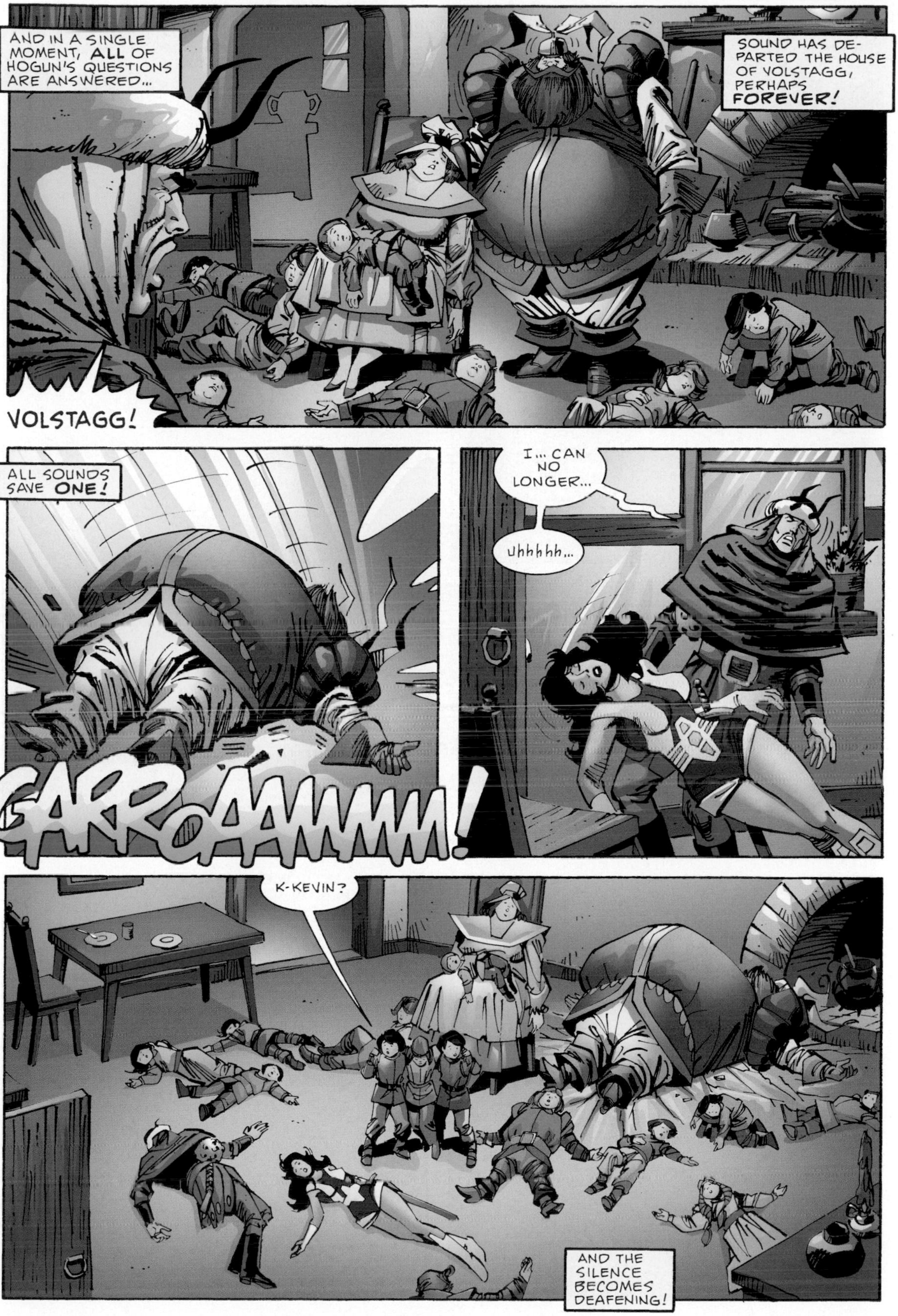
AND IN A SINGLE MOMENT, ALL OF HOGUN'S QUESTIONS ARE ANSWERED...
SOUND HAS DEPARTED THE HOUSE OF VOLSTAGG, PERHAPS FOREVER!
VOLSTAGG!
ALL SOUNDS SAVE ONE!
GARROAAMMM!
I... CAN NO LONGER...
uhhhhh...
K-KEVIN?
AND THE SILENCE BECOMES DEAFENING!

MEANWHILE, IN THE CASTLE OF LOKI...

THE WAY IS CLEAR!

BBRRATHAAM!

THERE LIES LOKI, BUT HOW CAME HE **HERE** FROM BENEATH THE FALLEN WALL?

AND THOUGH THE ROOM FAIRLY **VIBRATES** WITH COLD, WHERE ARE HIS SECRET **MAGICKS?**

WHERE IS THE HIDDEN SOURCE OF COLD?

GRUNDROTH! **FEEL!**

THE **YOUTH!** COLD RADIATES FROM HIM UNCEASINGLY! ENOUGH TO STING EVEN **MY FINGERS!**

AND BY THE LOOK OF HIM, A **MORTAL!**

SO HE IS! AND THAT PLACES HIM UNDER **MY** PRO-TECTION, GRUNDROTH!

WHO--? IN YON CORNER, A BLINDING LIGHT?!?

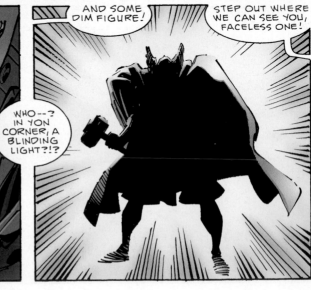

AND SOME DIM FIGURE!

STEP OUT WHERE WE CAN SEE YOU, FACELESS ONE!

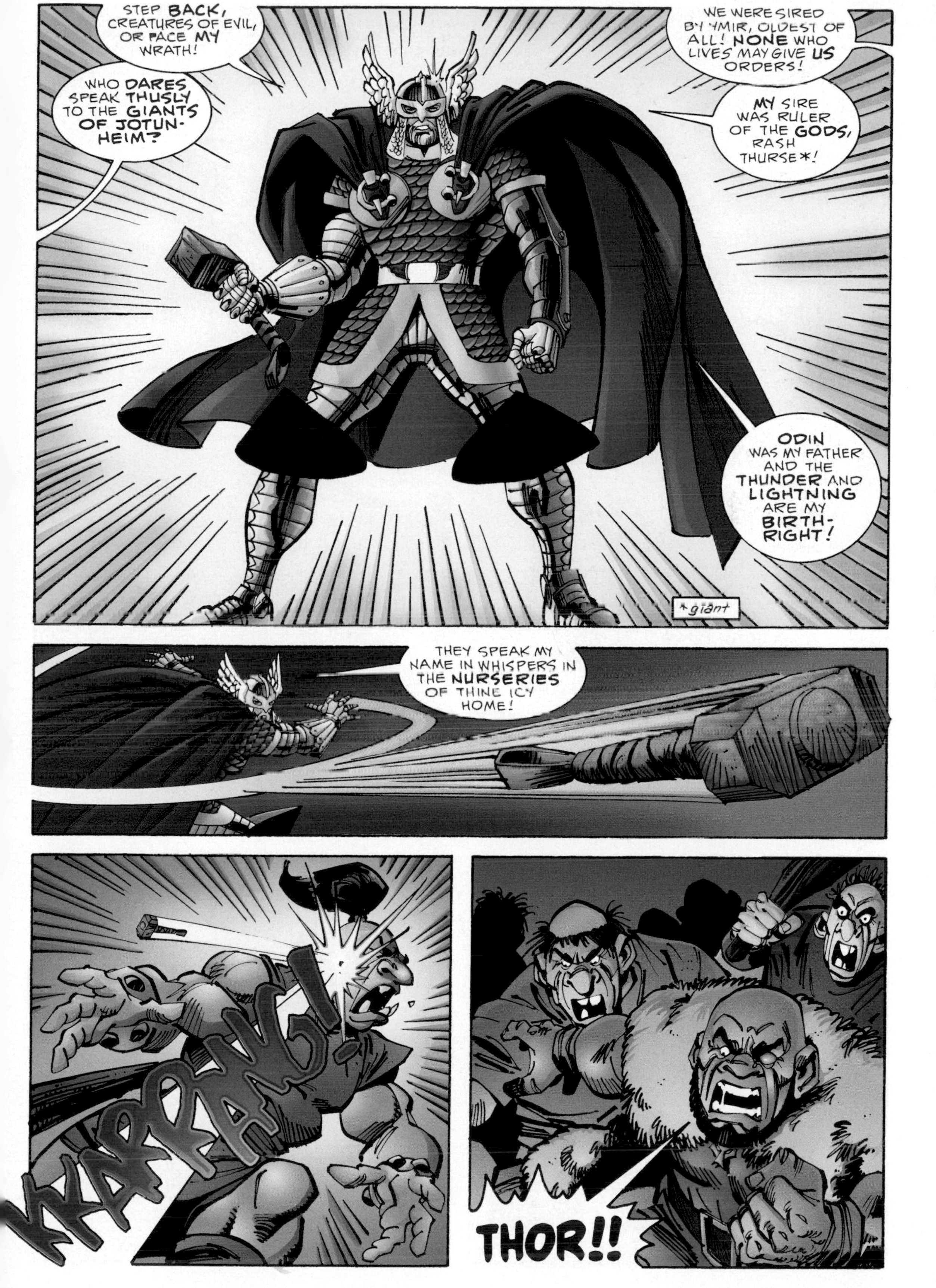
STEP BACK, CREATURES OF EVIL, OR FACE MY WRATH!
WHO DARES SPEAK THUSLY TO THE GIANTS OF JOTUNHEIM?
WE WERE SIRED BY YMIR, OLDEST OF ALL! NONE WHO LIVES MAY GIVE US ORDERS!
MY SIRE WAS RULER OF THE GODS, RASH THURSE*!
ODIN WAS MY FATHER AND THE THUNDER AND LIGHTNING ARE MY BIRTHRIGHT!
*giant
THEY SPEAK MY NAME IN WHISPERS IN THE NURSERIES OF THINE ICY HOME!
KKRAKK!
THOR!!

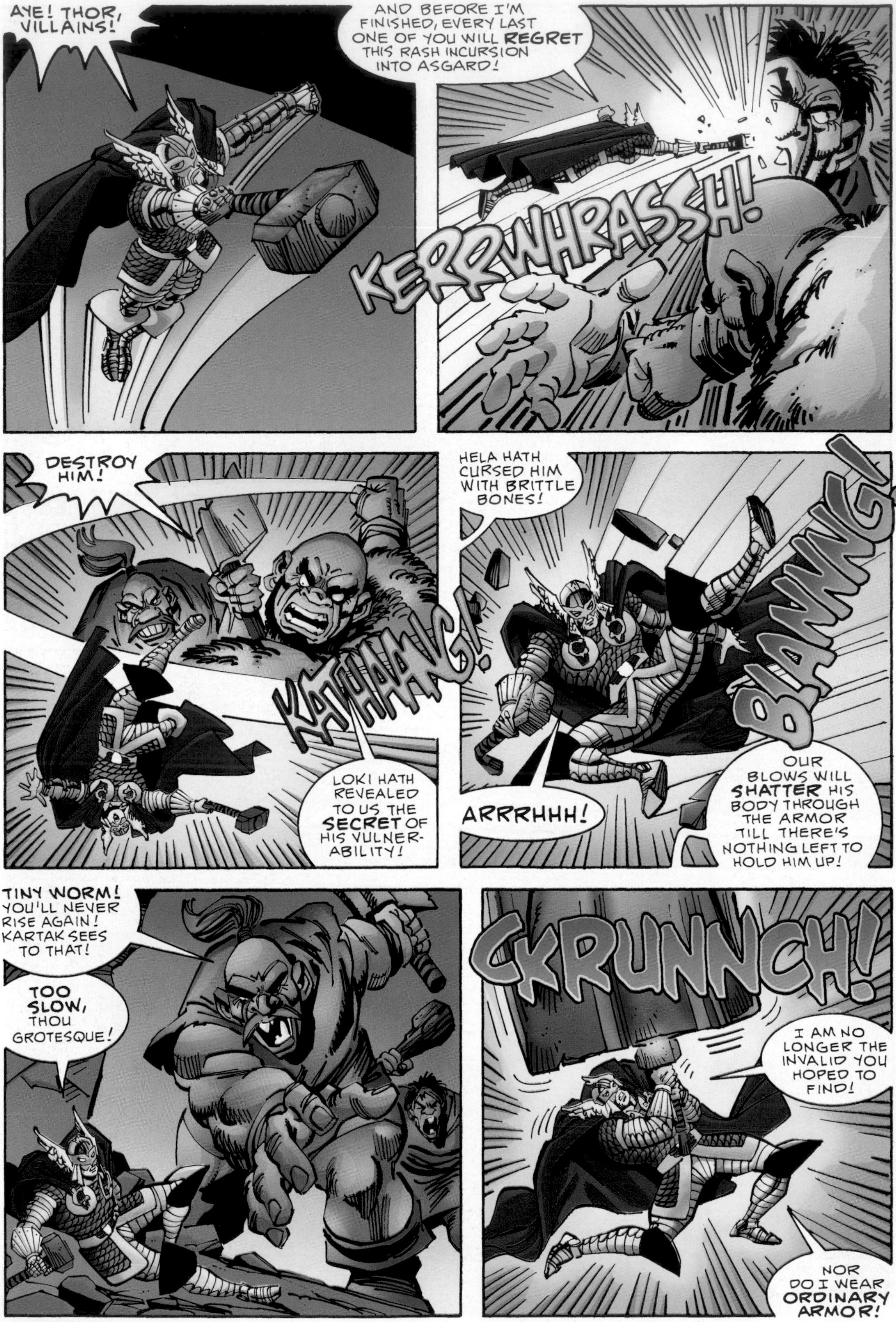
AYE! THOR, VILLAINS!
AND BEFORE I'M FINISHED, EVERY LAST ONE OF YOU WILL REGRET THIS RASH INCURSION INTO ASGARD!
KERRWHRASSH!
DESTROY HIM!
KATHAAG!
LOKI HATH REVEALED TO US THE SECRET OF HIS VULNER-ABILITY!
HELA HATH CURSED HIM WITH BRITTLE BONES!
BLANNG!
ARRRHHH!
OUR BLOWS WILL SHATTER HIS BODY THROUGH THE ARMOR TILL THERE'S NOTHING LEFT TO HOLD HIM UP!
TINY WORM! YOU'LL NEVER RISE AGAIN! KARTAK SEES TO THAT!
TOO SLOW, THOU GROTESQUE!
CKRUNNCH!
I AM NO LONGER THE INVALID YOU HOPED TO FIND!
NOR DO I WEAR ORDINARY ARMOR!

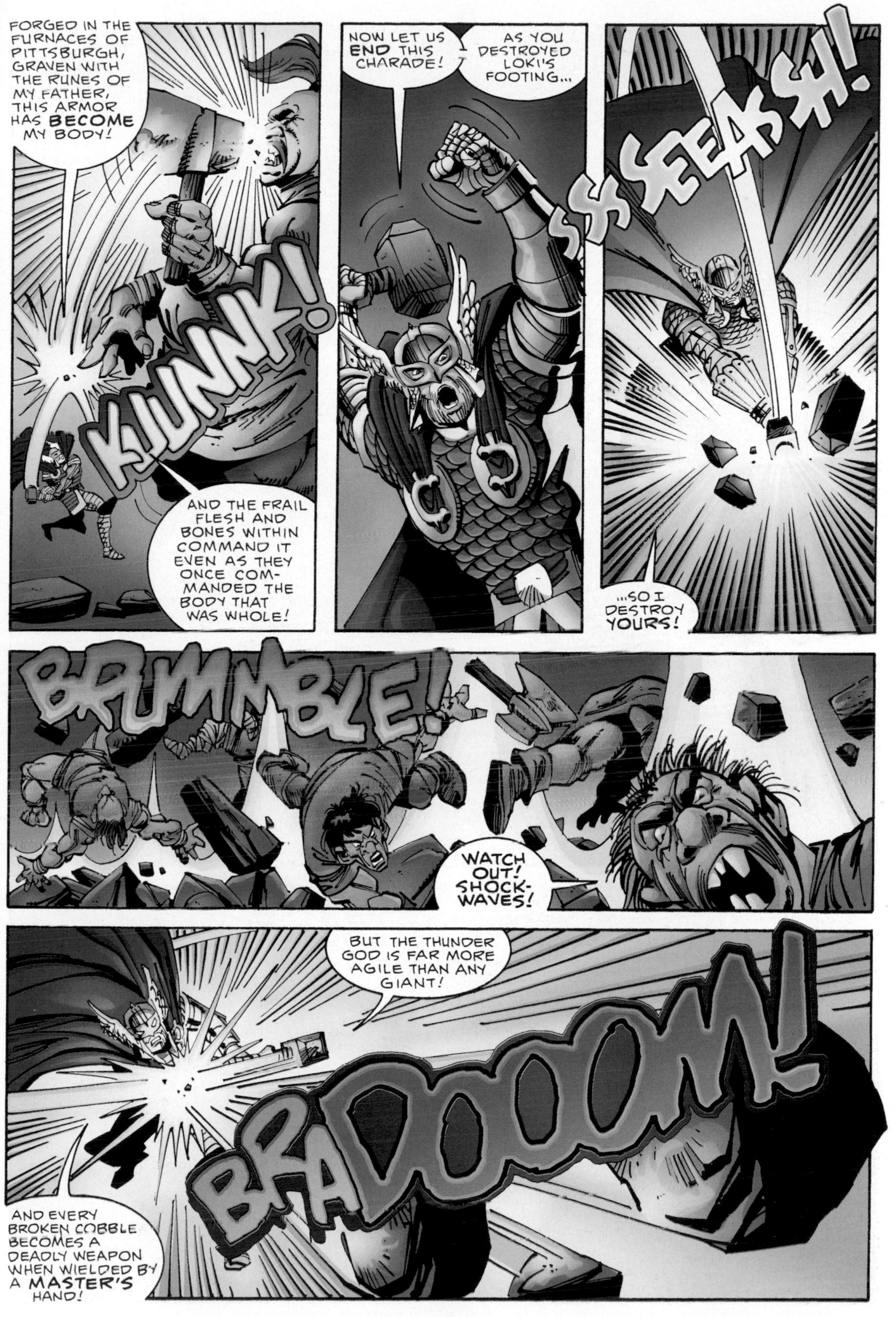
FORGED IN THE FURNACES OF PITTSBURGH, GRAVEN WITH THE RUNES OF MY FATHER, THIS ARMOR HAS **BECOME** MY BODY!
KLUNNK!
AND THE FRAIL FLESH AND BONES WITHIN COMMAND IT EVEN AS THEY ONCE COMMANDED THE BODY THAT WAS WHOLE!
NOW LET US **END** THIS CHARADE!
AS YOU DESTROYED LOKI'S FOOTING...
SSSFEASH!
...SO I DESTROY **YOURS!**
BRUMMBLE!
WATCH OUT! SHOCK-WAVES!
BUT THE THUNDER GOD IS FAR MORE AGILE THAN ANY GIANT!
BRADOOOM!
AND EVERY BROKEN COBBLE BECOMES A DEADLY WEAPON WHEN WIELDED BY A **MASTER'S** HAND!

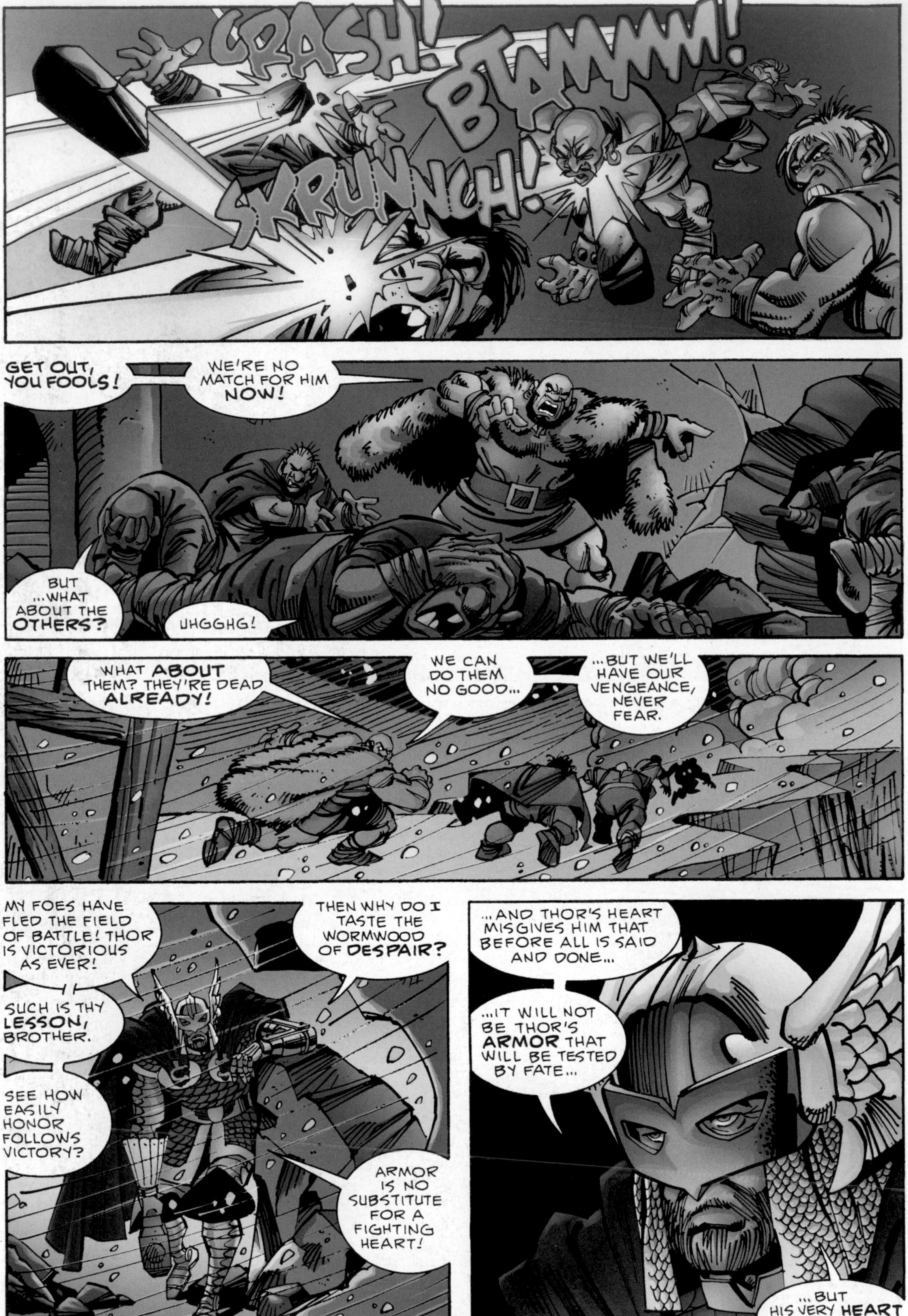
CRASH!
BTAMMM!
SKRUNNCH!
GET OUT, YOU FOOLS!
WE'RE NO MATCH FOR HIM NOW!
BUT ...WHAT ABOUT THE OTHERS?
UHGGHG!
WHAT ABOUT THEM? THEY'RE DEAD ALREADY!
WE CAN DO THEM NO GOOD...
...BUT WE'LL HAVE OUR VENGEANCE, NEVER FEAR.
MY FOES HAVE FLED THE FIELD OF BATTLE! THOR IS VICTORIOUS AS EVER!
SUCH IS THY LESSON, BROTHER.
SEE HOW EASILY HONOR FOLLOWS VICTORY?
THEN WHY DO I TASTE THE WORMWOOD OF DESPAIR?
ARMOR IS NO SUBSTITUTE FOR A FIGHTING HEART!
...AND THOR'S HEART MISGIVES HIM THAT BEFORE ALL IS SAID AND DONE...
...IT WILL NOT BE THOR'S ARMOR THAT WILL BE TESTED BY FATE...
...BUT HIS VERY HEART AND SOUL!

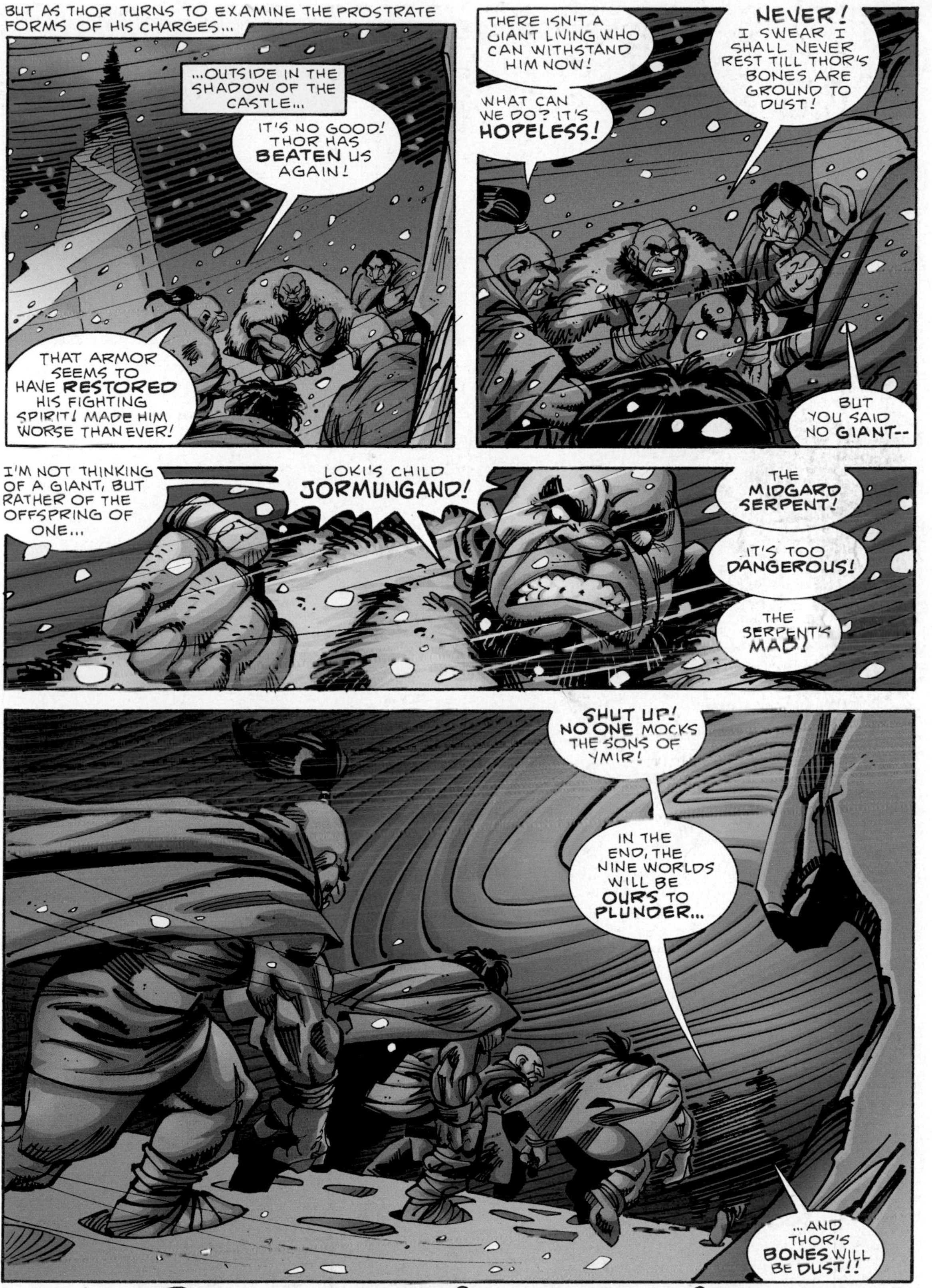
BUT AS THOR TURNS TO EXAMINE THE PROSTRATE FORMS OF HIS CHARGES...
...OUTSIDE IN THE SHADOW OF THE CASTLE...
IT'S NO GOOD! THOR HAS BEATEN US AGAIN!
THAT ARMOR SEEMS TO HAVE RESTORED HIS FIGHTING SPIRIT! MADE HIM WORSE THAN EVER!
THERE ISN'T A GIANT LIVING WHO CAN WITHSTAND HIM NOW!
WHAT CAN WE DO? IT'S HOPELESS!
NEVER! I SWEAR I SHALL NEVER REST TILL THOR'S BONES ARE GROUND TO DUST!
BUT YOU SAID NO GIANT--
I'M NOT THINKING OF A GIANT, BUT RATHER OF THE OFFSPRING OF ONE...
LOKI'S CHILD JORMUNGAND!
THE MIDGARD SERPENT!
IT'S TOO DANGEROUS!
THE SERPENT'S MAD!
SHUT UP! NO ONE MOCKS THE SONS OF YMIR!
IN THE END, THE NINE WORLDS WILL BE OURS TO PLUNDER...
...AND THOR'S BONES WILL BE DUST!!

next: **A Discourse of Heroes and Villains!**

FEATURING THE GLORIOUS RETURN OF... FIN FANG FOOM! (SAY WHAT?) DON'T MISS IT!

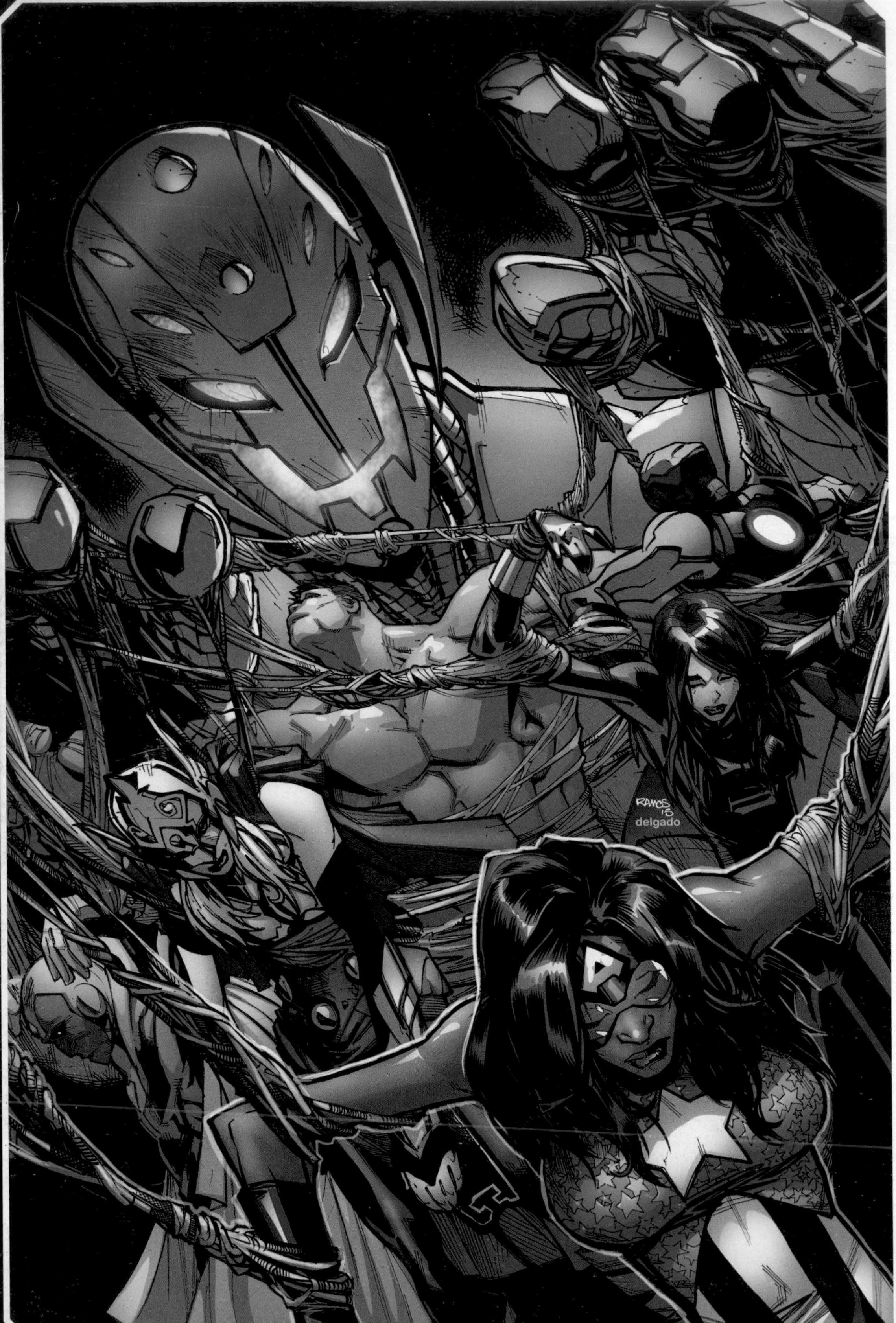
RAMOS '15
delgado

NEW AVENGERS: ULTRON FOREVER #1 VARIANT

by HUMBERTO RAMOS & EDGAR DELGADO